McNae's

ESSENTIAL LAW FOR JOURNALISTS

Twenty-fourth edition

Mike Dodd   Mark Hanna

OXFORD
UNIVERSITY PRESS

Great Clarendon Street, Oxford, OX2 6DP,
United Kingdom

Oxford University Press is a department of the University of Oxford.
It furthers the University's objective of excellence in research, scholarship,
and education by publishing worldwide. Oxford is a registered trade mark of
Oxford University Press in the UK and in certain other countries

Twenty-first edition 2012
Twenty-second edition 2014
Twenty-third edition 2016

Impression: 1

Published in the United States of America by Oxford University Press
198 Madison Avenue, New York, NY 10016, United States of America

British Library Cataloguing in Publication Data
Data available

Library of Congress Control Number: 2017964275

ISBN 978-0-19-880957-9

Printed in Italy by L.E.G.O. S.p.A.

For my wife Sarah, whose ceaseless support and encouragement are the only things which keep me from retirement.

Mike Dodd

To my wife Linda, son Rory, mother Mary, father Michael and sister Lynn.

Mark Hanna

Preface

Democracies claim to espouse free speech. But in the UK continuing and growing threats are eroding the media's freedom to report information so it can be subjected to in-depth analysis. This means the public's right to read, hear and view important information is undermined.

Politicians, public and private institutions strive to spin and shape the news in their own self-interest by releasing only that information which suits their purposes, and by shutting doors against probing journalists.

Individuals involved or mentioned in court cases argue that privacy or other laws should protect them from publicity. For example, police officers increasingly claim that media reports identifying them when they appear in open court will put their lives at risk. Some courts have been swayed into granting officers anonymity when there is nothing to show that such risk is real in those particular cases. Such rulings weaken the open justice principle, explained in ch. 15, that publishing names may lead to fresh evidence coming to light.

Technological advances have enabled legislatures to give state agencies ever wider powers of surveillance, and to gather and retain communications data. The professed objectives of these laws are to counter the real threats of terrorism and serious crime. But these powers—including those detailed in the UK's Investigatory Powers Act 2016—make it much harder for journalists to protect the identities of their confidential sources, the whistleblowers who leak the facts about inefficiency or wrongdoing in Government departments, public bodies such as councils and quangos, and private companies (bearing in mind that many public services are now contracted out to such companies). Without that protection, these sources could face the sack or prosecution, as ch. 34 warns.

The Law Commission's proposals for tougher law on official secrets—mentioned in ch. 33—and Parliament's approval of the 2016 Act were among developments which led the Reporters Without Borders organisation to announce in 2017 that the UK had slipped another two places—to 40th out of 180 countries—in the World Press Freedom Index.

In the two years since publication of the previous edition of *McNae's* there have been further examples of the UK news media having to spend time and money fighting incursions into the freedoms which enable it to keep society informed.

Notable examples featured in this new edition include:

- A High Court hearing to ensure that journalists could attend and report on a meeting of the Royal Borough of Kensington and Chelsea's Cabinet which was due to discuss the horrific fire in its Grenfell Tower block in which 71 tenants died—see ch. 31, Other information rights and access to meetings, 31.3.1.
- Media organisations having to argue in the Court of Appeal for the right to identify two teenagers convicted of murdering the mother

and younger sister of one of them, so that these tragic crimes could be explained to the public who would otherwise have little idea of what led to the victims being brutally killed in their home—see ch. 16, Challenging the courts, 16.7.1.1.

- The financial news service Bloomberg having to fight a High Court bid to make it take down an online story about a law enforcement agency's investigation into a businessman's company and its activities—an article the judge described as a serious piece of journalism about a serious topic—see ch. 5, Crime—media coverage prior to any court case, 5.11.

- News groups which own *The Times* and the *Oxford Mail* having to defend in the Supreme Court the principle of open justice, so their reports could identify a businessman named in evidence during open proceedings against other men for serious sexual offences—see ch. 16, Challenging the courts, 16.5.2.

We have no doubt that many more similar battles will have to be fought in the future.

All this is taking place against the worrying backdrop of economic pressures on mainstream media which continue to reduce the number of trained journalists available to be vigilant on the public's behalf, from the grassroots to the corridors of power in Whitehall, Parliament, the courts and the City of London.

On the positive side, the national, regional and local press and the UK broadcasters still break important news each day, while the internet is a vibrant platform enabling trained reporters, bloggers and 'citizen journalists' operating at hyperlocal level to publish disclosures and opinions for relatively little cost. We hope this book informs all journalists of their rights, gives them confidence about what they can publish, and helps them avert legal problems.

As well as avoiding legal pitfalls, anyone publishing material should meet ethical standards, including those ensuring accuracy and guarding against unwarranted intrusion into people's privacy. In that respect, this edition gives us opportunity to highlight adjudications on ethical matters made by the Independent Press Standards Organisation (Ipso) in its first three years of operation, using the Editors' Code of Practice; to explain that Impress is now a 'recognised' regulator of the press, with its own code; and to point to recent rulings by Ofcom based on its Broadcasting Code.

Other parts of this book cover the helpful guidance given by the Chief Coroner to coroners on matters relating to the media, which journalists can cite at inquests if they need to. New case studies in the book and in its Additional Material on www.mcnaes.com help explain other developments, including in defamation, privacy and copyright law.

This edition follows the practice in previous editions of using the term 'media organisations' to encompass the publishers of newspapers, magazines and websites, and broadcasters. As we have acknowledged previously, the term is not wholly satisfactory, especially where the point being made also applies to freelance journalists or to any individual 'blogger' or 'tweeter', but we felt it remains the most practical option to reflect the technological convergence in how journalism is published. The law covered is that of England and Wales, unless specified otherwise.

Acknowledgements

As authors we are grateful to the NCTJ's chief executive Joanne Butcher and NCTJ staff for support as we wrote this edition. We also owe much thanks to the NCTJ's principal examiner Mandy Ball, a principal lecturer at Nottingham Trent University, and to our other colleagues on the NCTJ's media law examinations board. These include Brian Pillans, lecturer at Glasgow Caledonian University, to whom we owe a particular debt for his contributions about Scottish law. We again owe a similar debt of gratitude to Colm Murphy, subject leader in media, film and journalism at Ulster University, for helping us update the chapter on Northern Ireland law.

Special thanks are due to Felicity Boughton, senior publishing editor for higher education (law) at Oxford University Press for all her guidance.

We also thank the Judicial College for permitting use of diagram material, the Regulatory Funding Company for permitting reproduction of the Editors' Code of Practice, Ofcom for allowing us to cite extracts from its Broadcasting Code, Impress for permission to use extracts from its Standards Code and the *Western Telegraph* for allowing us to quote from its notes of a judge's comments.

The following have helped us greatly by answering queries or with advice: Ed Owen, head of communications at Her Majesty's Courts and Tribunals Service; Bianca Strohmann, Ipso's head of complaints; Heather Rogers QC of One Brick Court, Robin Hopkins of 11 KBW, Gervase de Wilde of 5RB, Gavin Millar QC, and Guy Vassall-Adams QC of Matrix Chambers, Adam Wolanski of 5RB. We also thank all the other solicitors and barristers, too numerous to count, who have been so generous in sharing their time and expertise with us. If despite their assistance, we have made any errors, they are our own and nobody else's.

We continue to be grateful to our employers—in Mike's case the Press Association and in Mark's the Department of Journalism Studies, Sheffield University—for their support and encouragement.

The main body of the text of this edition was completed in early December 2017 but it was possible to add to the Late News section until late March 2018. The book's website carries updates.

Readers should feel free to send us their comments about this edition and its website.

Mike Dodd, Legal Editor, Press Association
Email: m_dodd@msn.com

Mark Hanna, Chair of the NCTJ Media Law Examinations Board
Email: M.Hanna@sheffield.ac.uk

This book bears the name of its first author, the late Leonard McNae, who was Editor of the Press Association's Special Reporting Service.

Summary Contents

Contents

Part 2   Crime, courts and tribunals   **59**

Late News

Channel 5 eviction footage unjustifiably breached privacy

In February 2018 a High Court judge ruled that the broadcasting of footage shot inside a couple's home while they were being legally evicted had intruded too far into their privacy. Shakir Ali and his wife Shahida Aslam owed rent arrears said to total, including court and legal fees, more than £11,000. High Court enforcement agents (HCEAs) carrying out the eviction, employed by Direct Collection Bailiffs Ltd, wore body cameras provided by TV production company Brinkworth Films Ltd. It was making a programme for the Channel 5 *Can't Pay? We'll Take It Away* series. Brinkworth also used a film crew. It followed the two HCEAs into the house in Fanshawe Avenue, Barking, after the landlord's son unlocked its front door for the eviction to begin. The programme and its repeats were viewed by 9.65 million people in total. The evicted tenants Mr Ali and Mrs Aslam sued the channel. They said that the broadcasting of the footage of their home's interior, including a bedroom, in the state it was in when the eviction and film crew took them by surprise, and showing them in shock and distress was a misuse of private information. They said the programme led to their daughter (who was not there during the filming) being ridiculed and bullied at school. Channel 5 argued that any 'reasonable expectation of privacy' the couple had was undermined by the fact that the court order authorising the eviction meant they were trespassing in the landlord's property. Mr Justice Arnold ruled for the couple, saying they did have that 'reasonable expectation' in the circumstances (see this book's 27.6 about that criterion). He awarded each £10,000 damages. He said that the programme contributed to a debate of general interest about the consequences of increasing levels of personal debt, but that inclusion of 'private information' in the footage went beyond what was justified for that purpose. The judge said that Mr Ali had been too drowsy, when awoken by the eviction, to give informed consent to what was filmed at that stage. The judge said too that footage 'rushes' showed that HCEA Paul Bohill encouraged the landlord's son Omar Ahmed to taunt the couple because it would make 'good television', that such taunting was broadcast, that at no stage during the eviction were the couple told the film crew was filming for Channel 5, and that the couple had objected during the eviction to the filming (*Ali and Aslam v Channel 5 Broadcast Limited* [2018] EWHC 298 (Ch)].

Data protection law and past events

As this 24th edition of McNae's passed its deadline, there were examples of people citing data protection law to argue that aspects of their past lives should be hidden from public view.

www.mcnaes.com

McNae's Essential Law for Journalists is accompanied by a free-to-use website—www.mcnaes.com—that features extra resources for both students and journalists.

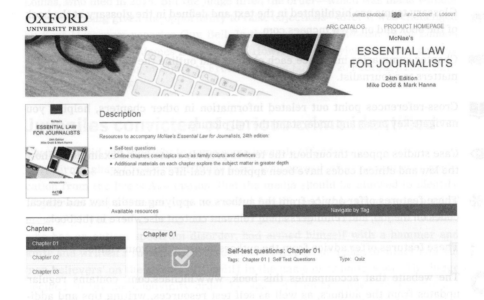

Updates

Whether you are studying or a working journalist, keep your knowledge up-to-date at www.mcnaes.com with regular updates from the authors on key changes affecting media law and ethics.

Self-test questions

Test your media law know-how and get instant feedback with chapter-related questions—ideal preparation for exams or to refresh your knowledge.

Online-only chapters

Access additional online chapters on

> The incitement of hate
>
> Scottish media law
>
> Terrorism and the effect of counter-terrorism law

as well as extended versions of ch. 14 (family law), ch. 31 (information rights) and ch. 33 (official secrets).

Glossary

Need to check a key term at court or on the way to class? Download the *McNae's* glossary for on-the-go access to essential legal terms. The glossary is also available to download as flashcards for ready-made exam preparation.

Additional material

Find additional detail and resources on a range of topics, including media coverage before trial, reporting on juveniles, challenging the courts and privacy.

Extra resources

Writing tips—including how to avoid clichés and advice on commonly confused words—from the experts at Oxford University Press.

www.mcnaes.com also features regular discussion pieces and information on the history of *McNae's*, as well as key news from OUP and the authors.

Part 1

The landscape of law, ethics and regulation

Introduction

Chapter summary

The UK media enjoy freedoms which are the envy of journalists in oppressed societies. Nevertheless, the UK has more laws affecting journalism than some other democracies, so a sound, thorough knowledge of legal matters is especially important for UK journalists, particularly in their role as 'watchdogs' acting on the public's behalf. This chapter explains how the UK's laws are made and how the European Convention on Human Rights helps safeguard freedom of expression. It also outlines the distinction between criminal and civil law, and between solicitors and barristers.

1.1 Free but with restrictions

Although the UK has a free press in comparison to the censorship which stifles liberty in many other nations, the description must be qualified because of the many and growing restrictions on what can be published. This book covers the increasing number of laws affecting journalism.

The importance of freedom of expression, and of the journalist's position as a watchdog ensuring a properly informed public in a democratic society, have been stressed by both the UK courts and the European Court of Human Rights in Strasbourg.

In 2000 senior law lord Lord Bingham said in a case in the House of Lords, predecessor of the Supreme Court:

see 22.7.2.3
The nature
of press
conferences

> In a modern, developed society it is only a small minority of citizens who can participate directly in the discussions and decisions which shape the public life of that society. The majority can participate only indirectly, by exercising their rights as citizens to vote, express their opinions, make representations to the authorities, form pressure groups and so on. But the majority cannot participate in the public life of their society in these ways if they are not alerted to and

informed about matters which call or may call for consideration and action. It is very largely through the media, including of course the press, that they will be so alerted and informed. The proper functioning of a modern participatory democracy requires that the media be free, active, professional and enquiring. (*McCartan Turkington Breen v Times Newspapers Ltd* [2001] 2 AC 277) **"**

It is the journalist's job to help safeguard freedom of expression and a free media, by reporting accurately and ensuring that people are properly informed about what is being done in their name by those who claim to govern them. It is also the job of journalists to safeguard the principle of an independent judiciary by reporting what is going on in the courts which apply laws intended to safeguard the interests of all.

To do all this, journalists must know the law: where it comes from, what it says and what it lets them do—or stops them doing.

The UK has a vibrant and wide-ranging media—newspapers, magazines, radio and television stations, and the ever-growing internet, with the myriad text and audio-visual sites it offers—and the law applies to all of them. Many are also subject to regulatory systems. This book explains how reporting restrictions, libel and privacy laws limit what may be published—and the financial consequences of mistakes or recklessness in journalism. But it also emphasises the freedoms to publish and investigate. Only by knowing what is and is not possible, and what may or may not be done, can journalists, broadcasters, website operators and those who work with them keep the freedoms and variety of platforms they have now, campaign for greater freedom, and ensure that their work is not discredited or curtailed by some foolish but expensive error.

chs. 2 and 3 focus on codes of ethics

Observing ethical codes should be an integral part of how journalists operate, to produce respected, fair journalism and preserve freedoms. Failure to respect these codes risks the creation of punitive laws aimed at curbing malpractices and limiting everyone's freedoms.

1.2 Sources of law

→ glossary   The main sources of the law have traditionally been custom, precedent and **statute**.

1.2.1 Custom

When the English legal system began to take shape in the Middle Ages, royal judges were appointed to administer the 'law and custom of the realm'. This devel-

→ glossary   oped into the **common law**.

1.2.2 Precedent

As judges applied the common law to the cases before them, lawyers recorded their decisions. This process continues. Records of leading cases give the facts considered by a court and the reasons for its decision. The UK has a hierarchy of courts, so a decision made by a lower court can be challenged by appeal to a higher court. The decisions made by the higher courts—precedents—are binding on all lower courts, thus shaping their future rulings. Precedents evolve and develop the common law.

Figure 1.1 is a diagram of the hierarchy of the courts in England and Wales. The nature and role of these courts is explained further in later chapters.

A **Supreme Court** judgment binds all other UK courts, apart from—in most respects—Scottish criminal courts. But the Supreme Court can overrule its own previous decisions, which otherwise can only be overturned or reversed by legislation.

Below the Supreme Court, the Court of Appeal's decisions bind the High Court and the lower courts, and High Court decisions bind all lower courts.

 → glossary

 ch. 9 and ch. 13 explain the roles of the Court of Appeal and High Court

 Ch. 37 explains Northern Ireland's courts, and the www.mcnaes.com chapter on Scotland outlines that nation's courts system.

1.2.3 Statutes and statutory instruments

Common law can be modified or replaced by statutes—Acts of Parliament, which are primary legislation. But British governments have made increasing use of secondary legislation known as **statutory instruments**. Parliament frequently

→ glossary

Figure 1.1 Hierarchy of the courts

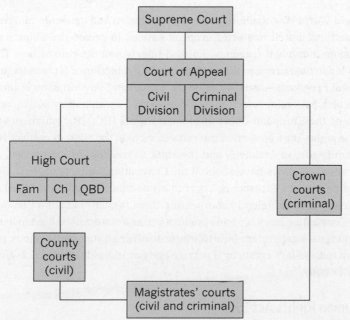

Fam = Family (civil); Ch = Chancery (civil); QBD = Queen's Bench Division (civil and criminal)—see chs. 9, 13 and 14 for these High Court roles

uses Acts to enshrine broad principles in legislation, but delegates the detailed framing of the new law to the departmental Minister concerned, who sets its detail out in statutory instruments in the form of regulations or rules. Statutory instruments must be approved by Parliament.

1.2.4 European regulations and directives

The UK is at present part of the European Union, so EU treaties and other EU law are currently part of UK law. The EU's Council and its Parliament agree regulations and directives which are binding on member states as part of the EU's raison d'être of encouraging trade between member states by harmonising their laws. EU regulations apply in the form in which they are drawn up, but member states decide how directives should be implemented through their own legislation.

The European Court of Justice (ECJ), based in Luxembourg, clarifies—for the national courts of EU member states—interpretation of EU legislation. It can, for example, rule on allegations that a member state has infringed EU law to gain advantage in trade and penalise a state for such infringement. The UK's decision in a referendum to leave the EU means that after a transitional period the UK will adopt as national laws those EU laws it wishes to keep. This ECJ is not to be confused with the European Court of Human Rights.

1.3 The European Convention on Human Rights

After the Second World War the horrors of the repression and genocide inflicted by the Nazi Party prompted western European nations to create the Council of Europe to promote individual freedom, political liberty and the rule of law. The Council's work led to the European Convention for the Protection of Human Rights and Fundamental Freedoms—usually called the European Convention on Human Rights—which sets out rights which must be protected by signatory states, and the foundation of the European Court of Human Rights (ECtHR), which sits in Strasbourg. The rights the Convention guarantees include the right to respect for privacy and family life, in Article 8, and the right to freedom of expression, in Article 10. Forty-seven states have adopted the Convention, and any of their citizens can take a case to the Strasbourg court to argue that the state has failed to protect them from, or to sufficiently compensate them for, a breach of a Convention right. The Convention has very wide application, as a state will be held to have breached a right if its legal system fails to stop or to offer an adequate remedy for a violation of an individual's rights by a private body or individual as well as by a state authority or body.

1.3.1 The Human Rights Act 1998

The Human Rights Act 1998 came into force on 2 October 2000, putting the Convention into UK law and greatly increasing its influence on UK courts. Individuals can require any UK court to consider their rights under the Convention in the context of any case.

The Act requires any UK court determining a question in connection with a Convention right to take account of the ECtHR's decisions, says new UK legislation must be compatible with Convention rights, and says old and new legislation must be construed so far as possible to conform with them.

It is unlawful for UK public authorities to act in a manner incompatible with the Convention.

1.3.2 Convention rights

Adopting the Convention directly into UK law has required judges systematically to consider Convention rights, which conflict in many cases.

For journalists, the most important part of the Convention is Article 10, which says in part: 'Everyone has the right to freedom of expression. This right shall include freedom to hold opinions and to receive and impart information and ideas without interference by public authority.'

Article 10 makes clear that restrictions on this right must be justified, necessary in a democratic society, **proportionate**, and 'prescribed by law'.   → glossary

Journalists wanting to exercise their Article 10 rights sometimes find themselves facing a claim under Article 8—the right to respect for privacy and family life—such as someone seeking an injunction to stop publication of a story about his/her personal life, or seeking damages if the material has been published.

Extracts from European Convention on Human Rights

Article 8: Right to respect for private and family life

" 1) Everyone has the right to respect for his private and family life, his home and his correspondence.

2) There shall be no interference by a public authority with the exercise of this right except such as is in accordance with the law and is necessary in a democratic society in the interests of national security, public safety or the economic well-being of the country, for the prevention of disorder or crime, for the protection of health or morals, or for the protection of the rights and freedoms of others.

Article 10: Freedom of expression

1) Everyone has the right to freedom of expression. This right shall include freedom to hold opinions and to receive and impart information and ideas without interference by public authority and regardless of frontiers.

   This Article shall not prevent States from requiring the licensing of broadcasting, television or cinema enterprises.

2) The exercise of these freedoms, since it carries with it duties and responsibilities, may be subject to such formalities, conditions, restrictions or penalties as are prescribed by law and are necessary in a democratic society, in the interests of national security, territorial integrity or public safety, for the prevention of disorder or crime, for the protection of health or morals, for the protection of the reputation or rights of others, for preventing the disclosure of information received in confidence, or for maintaining the authority and impartiality of the judiciary. **" "**

privacy rights are explained in ch. 27

1.3.3 Weighing competing rights

The methodology a court should use to decide in any particular case whether one Convention right should prevail over another was detailed in *Re S (A Child) (Identification: Restrictions on Publication)* [2004] UKHL 47. In that House of Lords judgment, Lord Steyn said:

" First, neither article has as such precedence over the other. Secondly, where the values under the two articles are in conflict, an intense focus on the comparative importance of the specific rights being claimed in the individual case is necessary. Thirdly, the justifications for interfering with or restricting each right must be   taken into account. Finally, the **proportionality** test must be applied to each. For convenience I will call this the ultimate balancing test. **" "**

> See 16.5.1, Open justice requires that reports should identify the defendant.

Lord Steyn was emphasising that the particular circumstances of each case must be intensely considered to decide which Convention right—and therefore which party to the argument—prevails in each matter to be decided.

In some judgments relevant to the media, Article 2 (the right to life) and Article 3 (the prohibition of torture and inhuman or degrading treatment or punishment) are cited and, by their very nature, can have great weight—for example, if it is argued with justification that someone's name or address should not be published to protect him/her from violent criminals or vigilantes.

1.4 Divisions of the law

There are two main divisions of law—criminal and civil.

> See chs. 5–10 for more detail about the criminal justice system, a huge source of news for journalists.

Criminal law deals with offences which harm the whole community and thus are considered to be offences against the sovereign. A Crown court case in which John Smith is accused of an offence is listed as *R v Smith*. 'R' stands for Regina (the Queen) or Rex (the King), depending on the monarch at the time, and 'v' for 'versus'.

A lawyer talking about this case would generally refer to it as 'The Queen (or the King) *and* Smith' (italics added).

Civil law concerns disputes between individuals and organisations, and includes the redress of torts—that is, wrongs suffered. Medical negligence, defamation and breach of copyright are all torts. A case in which Mary Brown sues John Smith will be known in writing as *Brown v Smith*. Lawyers will speak of the case as 'Brown *and* Smith'. → glossary

In practice, the two divisions overlap: many acts or omissions are criminal offences for which an individual may be prosecuted and punished as well as civil 'wrongs' for which the injured party may recover compensation—for example, a motorist in a road accident may be prosecuted for dangerous driving and sued by someone who was injured in the crash.

Civil and criminal law cases have different terminologies. In criminal courts a defendant is prosecuted, pleads guilty or not guilty, is acquitted or convicted and, if convicted, is sentenced—for example, fined or jailed. In civil courts a **claimant** sues a defendant or respondent, who admits or denies liability, is found either to be liable or not liable and, if liable, is ordered to pay damages. → glossary

Civil courts also resolve disputes between couples such as divorce actions.

 Chs. 13 and 14 explain the civil courts, which have newsworthy cases. Other chapters cover civil laws, such as privacy and copyright, which journalists can be accused of infringing.

1.5 The legal profession

Lawyers are either solicitors or barristers.

By tradition and practice, solicitors deal directly with the client—a defendant in a criminal case or someone seeking advice or representation in a civil case. Solicitors advise, prepare the client's case and take advice, when necessary, from a barrister specialising in a particular area of the law. Solicitors may represent their clients in court, and solicitor-advocates may appear in the higher courts.

Barristers are known, singly or collectively, as 'counsel'. A barrister wears a wig and gown in the higher courts, the Crown courts and county courts, but not in magistrates' courts. Barristers who have been practising for at least 10 years may apply to the Lord Chancellor for appointment as a Queen's Counsel and, if successful, use the letters QC after their names.

1.6 High offices in law

The constitutional position in the UK and other democracies is that the nation's 'executive' (the government) is separate from the judiciary (the judges), to help ensure that the judiciary is independent of political influence and that the government is subject to the rule of law, just as other organisations and citizens are.

The head of the judiciary is the Lord Chief Justice.

The UK government is advised on law by the Attorney General, which is a political role with holders attending Cabinet meetings. The Attorney General also has a prosecution role—he/she approves the instigation of, and may personally conduct, prosecutions in certain important cases. These include, as ch. 19 explains, proceedings against media organisations for contempt of court.

➡ Recap of major points

- The media are the eyes and ears of the general public, and free media are an essential element in maintaining parliamentary democracy.

- The European Convention on Human Rights has codified fundamental freedoms, including that of freedom of expression.

- Sources of UK law include custom, precedent, statutes and statutory instruments, and European Union regulations.

- The two main divisions of the law are criminal law and civil law, and journalists need to use correctly the legal terms appropriate for the type of court case they are reporting.

((•)) Useful Websites

www.parliament.uk/about/how/laws/
   UK Parliament—'Making laws'

www.echr.coe.int
   European Court of Human Rights—the 'Official Texts' link leads to the Convention

www.judiciary.gov.uk/
   Judiciary of England and Wales—information on judges and the courts system

www.lawsociety.org.uk/law-careers/becoming-a-solicitor/
   Law Society information on solicitors

www.barcouncil.org.uk/about-the-bar/about-barristers/
   Bar Council site—'About barristers'

www.attorneygeneral.gov.uk
   Attorney General's Office

2

Press regulation

Chapter summary

People aggrieved by what has been published about them, or by how journalists have treated them, may want a watchdog body to intervene in or adjudicate on their complaint. For most of the UK's newspapers or magazines, and their websites, this watchdog is the Independent Press Standards Organisation. Ipso uses the Editors' Code of Practice to adjudicate on complaints. This chapter introduces and outlines that Code, and refers to Impress, the regulator recognised by the Press Recognition Panel, and its Code.

2.1 Introduction

There are no state controls in the UK on who can own or run newspapers, magazines, their online versions or any kind of news website—publications defined by the term 'the press'. Anyone with the resources can launch a new publication. These liberties help keep the UK's media relatively free from state influence. Newspapers, magazines and websites are free to be partisan about social and political issues. Editors may use leader columns, news stories and features to campaign on any issue, from environmental law to local hospital closures. They and their journalists may also publish, subject to the restraints of libel and other laws, their own fierce criticisms of those in the news, or anyone else. The lack of any requirement for these media sectors to be impartial contrasts with the position of the broadcasting industry, as the next chapter explains.

But newspaper and magazine owners recognise that irresponsible journalism could lead Parliament to introduce a statutory system of regulation involving financial penalties, or even forcing editors to publish corrections or replies.

The UK broadcasting sector has such a statutory system, as explained in the next chapter. But broadcast journalism in its routine form may be tamer than the daily output of the press, which can be raucous and more likely to probe.

2.1.1 Fragmentation of press regulation

The press industry created the Press Complaints Commission in 1991 to keep the threat of statutory regulation at bay. But the PCC was discredited in 2011 because it failed to realise or investigate the extent of phone-hacking by journalists at the *News of the World*. As a result, Lord Justice Leveson was appointed to chair a public inquiry into 'the culture, practices and ethics' of the UK press. The Leveson Report, published in 2012, called for a new regulator which should be more independent of the industry than the PCC was, with better investigatory powers and the ability to fine the newspapers, magazines and websites it regulated if they seriously or systemically breached its code of ethics. This led most of the UK's major newspaper and magazine groups, including high-circulation national newspapers and most of the regional and local press, to establish and fund—and be bound by the decisions of—a new regulator, the Independent Press Standards Organisation (Ipso). It replaced the PCC in 2014. Ipso is, in effect, the hub of a revamped, self-regulatory system created by these press groups to adjudicate on complaints against their journalism or journalistic activity.

ch. 35 outlines the phone-hacking scandal

The Ipso system has been criticised for failing to embody all the Leveson Report's recommendations. Ipso's critics say it is not fully independent of the press groups which fund it, and that they should have made Ipso comply with the model of press regulation set out in a Royal Charter—law created by Government Ministers— which was approved by Parliament in 2012 as a response to the Leveson Report. The Charter system established a 'Recognition Panel' to initially recognise (approve), and periodically review the work of, any regulator which chose to join that system. One regulator, Impress, joined it, as this chapter explains.

Ipso has no connection to the Charter system, because the press groups which founded it and are its members view the 'recognition' requirement of the Charter as a step towards statutory regulation of the press and political interference in UK press freedoms.

 For more background about the Charter model of regulation, and the legislation passed to encourage—critics say compel—the press to conform to it, see the Additional Material for ch. 2 on www.mcnaes.com.

The PCC's demise means that UK press regulation is now fragmented. Three national newspapers—the *Financial Times, The Guardian, The Observer*—as well as the website-only *Independent* and *Independent on Sunday,* and the *Evening Standard* in London are owned by groups which have so far decided against joining either the Ipso system or founding or joining a regulator 'recognised' under the Charter. Each of these groups has its own system to consider complaints against their newspapers and websites. Despite being outside the Ipso system, they expect their editors and journalists to comply with the Editors' Code of Practice, which was inherited from the PCC system and is also used by Ipso and its members. Thus, the vast majority of UK press journalists are expected to know and comply with the Code's ethics. For many this is a contractual requirement.

see the Appendix for the full Code

The Code is discussed in detail in this and in other chapters. Its clauses are reviewed by the Editors' Code of Practice Committee—the Code Committee—which is part of the Ipso system. The Committee consists mainly of editors but, following the Leveson Report, now includes people independent of the press.

((•))
see Useful
Websites
at the end
of this
chapter for
the Code's
history

A 27-year continuity in the Code's use means that the PCC's jurisprudence—that is, its adjudication decisions, based on the Code—will continue to be valuable guidance for journalists. This book draws on it as well on Ipso's adjudications. But Ipso is not bound by how the PCC interpreted the Code and each year builds its own jurisprudence. Ipso's complaints committee makes its adjudications, but for brevity is usually referred to as Ipso. This book cites adjudications by case name and date of their issue or conclusion.

2.2 The Independent Press Standards Organisation

Under the Ipso system a person or organisation aggrieved by what has been published or how journalists have behaved should complain first to the relevant editor. A complainant who remains dissatisfied should then contact Ipso. He/she will be asked to state which part or parts of the Editors' Code have been breached. Ipso offers a free process involving guidance, mediation and, if the complaint remains unresolved, an adjudication. Ipso's complaints committee decides to what extent it needs to make such an adjudication. Ipso says a complaint must be made within four months of the publication of the complained-of material or of the date of the alleged misconduct by journalists, but that it may be able to take a complaint about an article which remains accessible on a newspaper's website within 12 months of publication.

This chapter concentrates on Ipso's complaints process, which is free of charge for complainants but which does not offer financial redress to those whose complaints it upholds.

Ipso runs a scheme to enable its members to offer arbitration to complainants seeking financial redress (damages) because of what was published or other journalistic activity. Arbitration is a system under which complainants can bring claims for defamation, harassment, intrusion into privacy and, in some cases, breach of data protection, without having to go to court. Such complainants (who will be referred to as claimants) pay a maximum of £100, split into a £50 fee at the start and a further £50 if the case goes to final ruling, while publishers fund the rest of the administration cost and all of the arbitrators' fees.

The scheme also offers:

- protections to ensure that members of the public representing themselves do not have to pay large legal costs to publishers, even if they lose a case;
- the ability for claimants to recover their own legal costs from publishers, with safeguards to ensure that neither side incurs unreasonable costs;
- a power for arbitrators to require publishers to pay aggravated damages to a successful claimant, within the overall cap of £50,000;
- and limits on the circumstances in which a publisher can recover fees and costs from a claimant.

But at the time this book went to press, no complainant had opted for arbitration under the Ipso scheme, and some Ipso members—including regional and local newspapers—did not offer arbitration. Ipso cannot compel them to offer it.

 The Additional Material for ch. 2 on www.mcnaes.com has more on this arbitration scheme.

As Ipso's complaints process is free to use, and all media organisations signed up with Ipso are contractually required to cooperate with it, this—rather than arbitration—will continue to be the route used by most complainants.

✳ Remember

Ipso has the contractual power to fine any member publication—newspaper, magazine or website—up to £1 million for a serious or systemic breach of the Code. The PCC did not have this power. But this is a financial penalty on the publisher, not compensation for any complainant.

 The Additional Material for ch. 2 on www.mcnaes.com provides detail on Ipso's governing board and about how Ipso is funded by its member publishers.

2.2.1 Compliance procedures

ch. 3 explains the regulation of broadcasters by Ofcom

The Ipso system emphasises that member publications must have formal compliance procedures, so that they can demonstrate—for example, in annual reports—what ethical training they give their journalists and how complaints are handled, as ideally these should be resolved without the need for Ipso involvement. Thus Ipso members have adopted formal internal procedures, including 'audit trails', which major broadcast organisations already had for making and recording decisions on ethical issues.

2.3 The Ipso complaints process

Ipso may rule that a complaint was not justified or that, even if it was, an editor's response, such as a private or published apology or an offer to publish a correction, was enough to resolve the issue. It might negotiate a resolution to a problem. It might also intervene before anything is published, as the PCC did—for example, in cases in which people want the press to leave them alone. But if Ipso proceeds to a formal adjudication, it will require an editor to publish any adverse adjudication, which it can also publish on its website. This public acknowledgement that the Code was breached is the redress for those whose complaints are upheld, as it was under the PCC.

Ipso, because of its contractual powers to impose financial penalties, can also specify where—for example, which page in a newspaper—a member organisation should publish an adverse adjudication, to ensure suitable prominence.

Ipso also publishes adjudications which do not uphold a complaint, because adjudications illustrate how it interprets the Code.

In 2016—its second full year of operation—Ipso received 14,445 complaints and inquiries. Most did not raise any potential breach of the Code or were not followed up by those complainants or were not dealt with by Ipso for other reasons (for example, 3,310 of these were 'third party' complaints, which in most instances Ipso does not accept, because what was published or done journalistically did not directly affect the complainant). Of the rest, 226 were resolved between the complainant and publisher, and 108 resolved with Ipso mediation—some resolutions being the agreed publication of clarification or corrections, or 'taking down' of online material; while 218 which could not otherwise be resolved were referred to Ipso's complaints committee. The committee upheld 47 of these by deciding that one or more of the Code's clauses had been breached. Ipso reports of cases resolved without being referred to the committee show that some involved possible or admitted breaches of the Code.

see Useful Websites at the end of this chapter for Ipso's Annual report and 'third party' policy

2.4 The scope of the Editors' Code

The Editors' Code—as explained earlier, also used by some UK press organisations not in the Ipso system—has 16 clauses. These set out ethical standards on a range of issues including accuracy, protecting people's privacy and children's welfare, preventing harassment and intrusion into grief or shock, and banning the use of excessive detail in coverage of suicides, as well as governing how journalists make inquiries at hospitals and their use of undercover tactics involving secret filming, subterfuge or misrepresentation.

see the Appendix for the full Code

In this book most of the Code's clauses are featured with case studies in relevant chapters—for example, ch. 4 has a focus on avoiding intrusion in newsgathering, and so features clause 2 on privacy, clause 3 on harassment, clause 4 on intrusion into grief or shock, clause 6 on children's welfare, clause 8 on hospitals and institutions and part of clause 9 on relatives of crime suspects and defendants. This book's index entry for the Editors' Code lists pages featuring each clause. This chapter deals with the other clauses of wide application and clauses governing comparatively rare practices or specialist work in journalism.

The Editors' Codebook, produced by the Code Committee, is online and offers guidance on the Code and adjudications. It is also useful to browse Ipso's website for adjudications.

The Code does not deal with issues of taste and decency, for example if an article causes offence—the industry's position has been that, as these are subjective matters, rulings on them could compromise freedom of expression, and Ipso's position reflects this (for example, *Elgy v The Sun*, 26 October 2017).

see Useful Websites at the end of this chapter for the Codebook and Ipso site

- Note that, for convenience, all references to the Code in this book adopt the clause numbering used in the latest version, which took effect from 1 January 2018 although some earlier versions had different numbering.

✳ Remember

→ glossary

Breaching the Editors' Code is not a criminal offence or a civil **tort**. But observing its requirements is ethical conduct and can help journalists avoid legal problems. Judges ruling on claims of media intrusion into privacy must take relevant codes into account—see 27.12, Relevance of ethical codes.

 See the Additional Material for ch. 28 on www.mcnaes.com.

2.4.1 Public interest exceptions in the Editors' Code

Some clauses or sub-clauses in the Code are marked with an asterisk, which indicates that breaches of these parts can be justified if an editor can demonstrate that what was done was 'in the public interest'.

The Code says the public interest includes, but is not confined to:

- detecting or exposing crime, or the threat of crime, or serious impropriety;
- protecting public health or safety;
- protecting the public from being misled by an action or statement of an individual or organisation;
- disclosing a person or organisation's failure or likely failure to comply with any obligation to which he/she/it is subject;
- disclosing a miscarriage of justice;
- raising or contributing to a matter of public debate, including serious cases of impropriety, unethical conduct or incompetence concerning the public;
- disclosing concealment, or likely concealment, of any of the above.

→ glossary

The Code says editors seeking to rely on public interest exceptions 'will need to demonstrate that they reasonably believed publication—or journalistic activity taken with a view to publication—would both serve, and be **proportionate** to, the public interest and explain how they reached that decision at the time'. This wording means there is a requirement for there to be an audit trail—documents recording why a decision was taken to publish in the public interest material which would otherwise breach the Code. The audit trial should record too, during an early stage

→ glossary

of an investigation, what **prima facie** evidence about a particular matter gave rise to the editor's 'reasonable belief' that it was in the public interest, for example, for his or her journalists to probe deeper by using deception or intruding into privacy. This could be a reasonable belief that the investigation's target was or could be committing a crime or guilty of serious impropriety, or was or could be misleading the public or putting people's health or safety at risk.

An editor will also need to be able to demonstrate to Ipso that there was careful consideration, based on the prima facie evidence and as the investigation continued, that the methods to be used would be proportionate and necessary—for example, that steps were taken to limit any breach of privacy to what was necessary for the particular investigative aim. So there should be records of what led to the editor's reasonable belief and to show that a careful approach was adopted at each stage of the investigation to ensure that Ipso will not rule that any undercover tactics used—for example, deception (subterfuge)—breached the Code. For example, in 2017 Ipso cleared *The Sun* of a complaint that using subterfuge and a hidden camera to show that a police officer was involved in selling 'threesome' sexual services breached the Code. The newspaper provided Ipso with a summary of internal correspondence between a reporter and its newsdesk, originating prior to the undercover work, and told Ipso that before publication the managing editor and legal department had given further careful consideration to the public interest justification (*Moss v The Sun*, 19 May 2017).

 See 2.4.4, Deception (subterfuge and misrepresentation), for the Code's clause on subterfuge.

It may be that the investigative journalism finds that there is nothing which needs exposure and so nothing is published. But if there is a complaint about the methods used, the audit trail helps prove to Ipso why the 'reasonable belief' existed that such activity was necessary in the public interest to discover what was true. Being able to prove there was such reasonable belief could also be important in data protection law, explained in ch. 28, and—as ch. 23 explains—would help the media organisation use the public interest defence successfully against a defamation lawsuit, if material was published.

Use of the term 'in the public interest' in the Code denotes that the journalism has a particularly high potential to be beneficial to society. But the Code also says: 'There is a public interest in freedom of expression itself.'

It stresses the need to protect young people, adding: 'An exceptional public interest would need to be demonstrated to over-ride the normally paramount interests of children under 16.'

 The Code's clause 6, covering the welfare of children, is explained in 4.13, Protecting children's privacy and welfare and clause 7, covering children in sexual offence cases, is explained in 11.9, Ethical considerations.

2.4.2 Accuracy and opportunity to reply

Clause 1 of the Code says: 'The Press must take care not to publish inaccurate, misleading or distorted information or images, including headlines not supported by the text.'

Clause 1 also says that the press 'while free to editorialise and campaign, must distinguish clearly between comment, conjecture and fact'.

Most complaints to Ipso allege inaccuracy. Clause 1 is not subject to the public interest exception—there is no public interest in inaccuracy. This is the only clause for which Ipso will routinely accept 'third party' complaints, because it accepts that if a significant inaccuracy is published on a general point of fact, this could affect many people in that media organisation's readership/audience.

Publications which led to Ipso adjudicating that clause 1 was breached have included:

- a report which suggested that hypnotist and author Paul McKenna had apologised for being drunk on a transatlantic flight, when—as the newspaper later accepted—he had not been drunk and had not made such an apology (*McKenna v The Sun*, 2 June 2016);

- a headline which said that a fatal attack on a woman might have been an 'Islamic honour killing', when there was no basis for saying that religion played a role in the killing (*Versi v Mail Online*, 18 July 2016);

- a report of a crime victim's testimony in court which presented what were merely her 'yes' or 'no' replies as if they were fuller, direct (verbatim) quotes by attributing to her words paraphrased from questions put to her, so giving 'a significantly misleading impression of the manner' in which she gave evidence (*Goring v Press and Journal*, 16 May 2017).

Ipso does not require that press coverage of controversies or disputes between people or organisations should meet a legal standard of proof about who is right or wrong. The emphasis in clause 1 is that 'care' must be taken to avoid publication of inaccurate or misleading information. For example, if 'speculation' is presented as fact, that breaches the clause (*Ahmed and Begum v The Sun*, 21 June 2017).

 In the Additional Material for this chapter on www.mcnaes.com there is a guide to what Ipso regards as sufficient 'care' in accuracy, based on its adjudications.

✱ Remember

Publishing unproven allegations could lead to the publisher being sued for defamation. A person defamed may not complain to Ipso, or may not be satisfied with its adjudication, and decide to sue. Chapters 20–23 cover defamation law.

2.4.2.1 Corrections and apologies

Clause 1 says that 'a significant inaccuracy, misleading statement or distortion' must be corrected 'promptly and with due prominence', and, where appropriate, with a published apology, and that in cases involving Ipso due prominence should be as it stipulates.

see Useful Websites at the end of this chapter for the Codebook

The Editors' Codebook says that if a correction is offered promptly, a significant inaccuracy will not be a breach of the Code. It gives advice on what 'due prominence' is. Ipso has no power to compel publication of apologies. But a failure to offer one when appropriate can lead to a complaint being upheld. Ipso has said that when an error has been 'personal to' and has the potential to be 'seriously damaging to' the complainant, an apology is 'required' (*McIntosh v The Herald (Glasgow)*, 8 June 2015).

 For the danger in defamation law of the wording and publishing of apologies, see 22.8.2, Care needed in apologies and corrections.

2.4.3 Coverage of suicides

Research has found that news of suicides may prompt others to take their own lives in the same way. To minimise this risk, clause 5 of the Code says reports of suicides should avoid giving 'excessive detail' about the method used.

 See 17.11, Ethical considerations when covering deaths, on coverage of inquest cases of suicide. But the clause applies to any report of a suicide.

2.4.4 Deception (subterfuge and misrepresentation)

Clause 10 of the Code says:

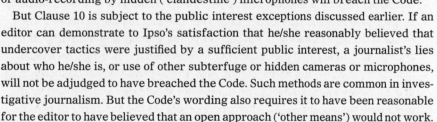

> i) The press must not seek to obtain or publish material acquired by using hidden cameras or clandestine listening devices; or by intercepting private or mobile telephone calls, messages or emails; or by the unauthorised removal of documents or photographs; or by accessing digitally-held information without consent.
>
> ii) Engaging in misrepresentation or subterfuge, including by agents or intermediaries, can generally be justified only in the public interest and then only when the material cannot be obtained by other means.

see also 2.4.4.2 Recording interviews and phone calls

This clause makes clear that journalists should normally be open when seeking information or comment by declaring from the outset to anyone unfamiliar with them that they are journalists and the purpose of the inquiries. It also means that normally covert photography or covert filming, or eavesdropping by using 'bugs', or audio-recording by hidden ('clandestine') microphones will breach the Code.

But Clause 10 is subject to the public interest exceptions discussed earlier. If an editor can demonstrate to Ipso's satisfaction that he/she reasonably believed that undercover tactics were justified by a sufficient public interest, a journalist's lies about who he/she is, or use of other subterfuge or hidden cameras or microphones, will not be adjudged to have breached the Code. Such methods are common in investigative journalism. But the Code's wording also requires it to have been reasonable for the editor to have believed that an open approach ('other means') would not work.

Irrespective of the Code, using hidden cameras or microphones could breach the civil law of privacy or data protection law, as chs. 27 and 28 explain, and 'hacking' into phone or email systems secretly to gain information (interception) or into other people's computers will normally be a crime—see ch. 35. But 'public interest' justifications may exist too for journalistic activity which would otherwise breach these laws.

2.4.4.1 'Fishing expeditions'

The Code does not permit subterfuge or misrepresentation—including using hidden cameras or recording devices—or infringement of privacy in 'fishing

expeditions'. A 'fishing expedition' is an investigation launched without sufficient prima facie grounds to justify it. For example, investigating an institution
or business chosen at random, with no ground to suspect it of wrongdoing, would
be a 'fishing expedition'.

👁 Case study

In 2016 Ipso cleared *The Sun on Sunday* of a complaint about its undercover investigation into private cosmetic surgery clinics. A slender, female
reporter, aged 20, posing as a 'hard up student', had visited four clinics, telling each she wanted cosmetic surgery to increase her confidence following
the break-up of a relationship, but that her mother did not want her to have it
because of her age. The paper reported that one clinic had told her it would
be 'morally wrong' to offer her surgery, but that the other three had told
her she could undergo what it reported as 'thousands of pounds worth of
arguably unnecessary ops'. Barbara Foy was sales team leader for The Hospital Group, one of these three clinics. The paper reported she had quoted
the reporter £6,495 for breast enlargement and liposuction, telling her 'you
want to get out there and look the best you can'. Ms Foy complained to Ipso
that the reporter's failure to identify herself as a journalist and her use of
a clandestine recording device breached clause 10. The newspaper said it
launched the investigation after being contacted by a reliable source who
had worked in healthcare for many years and had 'extensive knowledge' of
the cosmetic surgery industry. The source had said colleagues had told her
they were concerned that 'vulnerable' young women were being encouraged
to have procedures as an 'ego boost', putting their health at risk. This account
was supported by a second source who had also worked in the cosmetic
surgery industry, the newspaper said. The first source had mentioned The
Hospital Group as offering to liposuction young women who did not 'fit the
criteria' for surgery, and the newspaper had decided the investigation should
include three other 'big name' clinics. Also, the General Medical Council was
at the time reviewing guidelines on how clinics should deal with patients, and
there were figures showing a 'dramatic increase' in the popularity of plastic
surgery. The newspaper said an open approach to the clinics would have
provided the clinics' polished versions of events, not the specific case studies
required. Ipso said that the undercover recording did not demonstrate that
Barbara Foy had acted improperly but that there was still a public interest in
reporting on the reporter's experience at the clinic, and the ease with which a
person in her position had been offered cosmetic surgical procedures costing
almost £6,500. Ipso ruled that the newspaper's use of subterfuge, including the reporter misrepresenting herself, was justified in the public interest
and that the level of subterfuge was proportionate, in that the reporter when
undercover had limited the discussion with Barbara Foy to the matters under

investigation. The newspaper could not have tested the clinic's practices by open means, and contrasting those findings with the reporter's undercover experience at other clinics informed a debate about whether the practices taking place nationwide were acceptable, which was in the public interest, Ipso said (*Foy v The Sun on Sunday*, 19 April 2016).

see Useful Websites at the end of this chapter for the full adjudication

2.4.4.2 Recording interviews and phone calls

Journalists, particularly those involved in investigations, may decide to record their own telephone calls—for example, when they are interviewing the target of their inquiries—or record a face-to-face encounter. The recording may be needed as proof if the subject sues for defamation over what is published, claiming to have been misquoted or not approached. In the UK it is not a crime for a person making or receiving a phone call to record it, even if the other person is unaware this is being done. This is not 'interception', see, Recording phone calls.

Ipso has ruled that a journalist recording a face-to-face interview conducted openly is not deploying subterfuge or misrepresentation, or using a clandestine listening device, even if the other person is not aware that he/she is being recorded. So such recording does not engage clause 10 and so does not require a public interest justification. Ipso regards recording by a journalist who has made clear he/she is a journalist, and the purpose of the contact, as merely note-taking (*Cameron v Scottish Daily Mail*, 16 September 2016, not upheld). So it can be safely construed that Ipso would rule, as the PCC did, that recording a phone interview does not breach clause 10 if the interviewee knows that the caller is a journalist seeking comment.

But a journalist who fails to declare in a phone call or visit that he/she is a journalist may breach the Code's ban on subterfuge and misrepresentation, unless one of the Code's public interest exception applies and it was reasonable to conclude that there was no other way to obtain the information. The editor would also have to consider if publishing material from the recording would breach the Code's clause 2 on privacy. That clause is covered in ch. 4.

2.4.5 Discriminatory material

Clause 12 of the Code says the press must avoid prejudicial or pejorative reference to an individual's race, colour, religion, sex, gender identity or sexual orientation, or to any physical or mental illness or disability, and that details of an individual's race, colour, religion, gender identity, sexual orientation, physical or mental illness or disability must be avoided unless genuinely relevant to the story.

see Useful Websites at the end of this chapter for guidance on reporting mental illness

Ipso accepts that the inclusion in an article of a person's biographical details, including nationality, would not generally breach the terms of this clause (*Yates v Mail Online*, 15 June 2015, clause 12 complaint not upheld) but has said that a prejudicial or pejorative reference to an individual's race or colour could be

for scope of
clause 12,
see Useful
Websites
below

made by reference to nationality (*Miller v Mail Online*, 25 April 2017, not upheld). Clause 12 only applies to material which identifies an individual, so does not cover general reference to groups or categories of people, such as migrants or ethnic groups, even if pejorative—a limitation which has proved controversial, although Ipso can consider under clause 1 (accuracy) some complaints about references to religious groups (for example, *Versi v Mail Online*, 18 July 2016).

> The Additional Material for this chapter in www.mcnaes.com has a case study of Ipso upholding a clause 12 complaint.

2.4.6 Financial journalism

Clause 13 of the Code seeks to prevent journalists making personal profit by anticipating movements in share prices on the basis of information leaked to them by business contacts. It says journalists 'must not use for their own profit financial information they receive in advance of its general publication, nor should they pass such information to others'. It also bans journalists from dealing in shares or securities about which they have recently written, or intend to write, as what they publish might affect market prices and it would be unethical for them to take financial advantage of this power. It says journalists must not write about shares or securities in which they or close relatives have a significant financial interest without disclosing it to their editor or financial editor.

((•))
see Useful
Websites at
the end of this
chapter for the
Note

This clause, as well as Ipso's existence as regulator to police the Code, and the Financial Journalism Best Practice Note issued by the Editors' Code of Practice Committee, some of which specifies mandatory practice, led in 2016 to UK journalists being legally exempted from the similar provisions of the European Union's Regulatory Technical Standards of the Market Abuse Regulation.

2.4.7 Payments to witnesses

Media organisations covering high-profile stories may pay people, including the victims of notorious crimes, for the exclusive right to publish their accounts of events. In the case of crime victims, those accounts would be more than the evidence they could give in court, which would not have exclusive value, and could, for example, include descriptions not limited by the rules of evidence. Clause 15 of the Code aims to prevent these chequebook journalism deals from interfering with the process of justice. The risk of contempt of court which can arise from these deals, or from a reporter interviewing anyone due to testify in a trial, is explained in ch. 19.

The first part of clause 15 says: 'No payment or offer of payment to a witness— or any person who may reasonably be expected to be called as a witness—should be made in any case once proceedings are active as defined by the Contempt of Court Act 1981.' The ban applies until a case ceases to be active or the suspect pleads guilty or there is a verdict.

The second part says that:

> " Where proceedings are not yet active but are likely and foreseeable, editors must not make or offer payment to any person who may reasonably be expected to be called as a witness, unless the information concerned ought demonstrably to be published in the public interest and there is an over-riding need to make or promise payment for this to be done; and all reasonable steps have been taken to ensure that no financial dealings influence the evidence those witnesses give. In no circumstances should such payment be conditional on the outcome of a trial. "

It says a payment or an offer of payment made to a person later cited to testify in proceedings must be disclosed to the prosecution and defence.

2.4.8 Payments to criminals

Clause 16 of the Code says: 'Payment or offers of payment for stories, pictures or information, which seek to exploit a particular crime or to glorify or glamorise crime in general, must not be made directly or via agents to convicted or confessed criminals or to their associates—who may include family, friends and colleagues.' This recognises that people, particularly crime victims, are likely to condemn a deal under which criminals or those close to them profit from tales of wrongdoing. But the clause also recognises that press payment to a criminal may be justified by the Code's public interest exceptions.

2.5 Impress and its Code

In October 2016 the Press Recognition Panel, formed in 2014 under the Royal Charter model of press regulation, 'recognised' as a regulator The Independent Monitor for the Press, known as Impress. This was founded to be 'Leveson-compliant' by people who see Ipso as lacking full independence from the press groups which it regulates. Initially Impress used the Editors' Code of Practice, but in July 2017 adopted its own 'standards code'. Its scope is wider in terms of specified detail of ethical provision than the Editors' Code. For example, Impress's Code requires general disclosure of journalists' conflicts of interest. But much of the content of both codes is based on broadly accepted ethical principles, and both have 'public interest' exceptions. Impress issued guidance on how its Code should be interpreted.

When this book went to press, Impress had published four adjudications on complaints and was regulating more than 40 publishers, responsible for 86 titles, which pay it membership fees. Many of these publishers were hyperlocal or small local publishers. No major press group has joined Impress. Another complaint, dealt with under its arbitration system, resulted in the investigative website Byline being required to pay £2,500 damages for a tweet ruled to be defamatory.

see 2.1.1, Fragmentation of press regulation, on 'recognition'

see Useful Websites at the end of this chapter for Impress's Code and guidance

 For more detail of the Charter system, why most UK newspaper and magazine groups oppose it, and the failed legal attempt by the News Media Association to oppose the Panel's 'recognition' of Impress, see the Additional Material for this chapter on www.mcnaes.com.

➡ **Recap of major points**

- The Editors' Code sets standards for journalists working for the UK's largest publishers of newspapers, magazines and websites.

- It has clauses to uphold accuracy and to protect people's privacy.

- It permits undercover reporting, but only if justified by special 'public interest' factors.

- The Independent Press Standards Organisation, which adjudicates on complaints against editors and journalists in its member press groups, requires editors to publish adverse adjudications.

- In 2017 the Impress regulator adopted its own Code.

((•)) **Useful Websites**

www.ipso.co.uk
 Ipso

www.ipso.co.uk/about-ipso/annual-reports/
 Ipso's Annual Reports

www.ipso.co.uk/editors-code-of-practice/
 Editors' Code of Practice

www.editorscode.org.uk/history_of_the_code.php
 History of Editors' Code

www.editorscode.org.uk/
 Editors' Codebook

www.ipso.co.uk/news-press-releases/ipso-blog/ipso-blog-legsit-and-third-party-complaints/
 Ipso on third party complaints

www.ipso.co.uk/rulings-and-resolution-statements/ruling/?id=00026-16
 Ipso ruling in *Foy v The Sun on Sunday*

https://www.ipso.co.uk/news-press-releases/blog/ipso-blog-how-clause-12-discrimination-works/
 Ipso blog on scope of clause 12

www.editorscode.org.uk/guidance_notes_9.php
 Financial Journalism Best Practice Note

www.editorscode.org.uk/guidance_notes_2.php
 PCC guidance on the reporting of mental health issues

http://impressproject.org/
 Impress Project

https://impress.press/standards/impress-standards-code.html
 Impress Standards Code and guidance

Broadcast regulation

Chapter summary

Television and radio journalism in the UK is regulated by **statute**, through an independent regulator, the Office of Communications (Ofcom). Ofcom's Broadcasting
Code says commercial broadcast organisations must be impartial when covering
politics and social issues, and must be accurate, treat people fairly, respect privacy and avoid causing harm and offence. Ofcom can impose substantial fines for
breaches of the Code. The BBC is also required to be impartial and ethical, and is
subject to the Code.

→ glossary

3.1 Introduction

In the UK commercial broadcasters—those funded by subscription or advertising revenue—are regulated to ensure their owners are law-abiding, and all broadcasters are regulated about programmes, including journalism. While newspaper,
magazine and online-only publishers are free to be politically partisan, broadcasters and their journalists must, when reporting news, be impartial about politics
and social issues, although they are free to cover them in depth. The regulatory
system also requires broadcasters to observe 'due accuracy' in news, and other
ethical norms. The regulator, Ofcom—the Office of Communications—can levy
substantial fines, or revoke the licence of a commercial broadcaster which seriously
breaches the Broadcasting Code.

3.2 Why regulate broadcasters?

Historically, broadcast media have been seen as having particular potential to
influence, offend or harm their audiences. The emotional impact of moving images and sound, particularly on children in the audience, can be greater than that of
printed text and still pictures—for example, if a programme has sexual content, or
shows death or violence. As television and radio can air material instantaneously

they have great potential to provoke immediate public disorder or violence. Television is also seen as having great potential—because moving images and sound can often portray intimate or harrowing experiences more vividly than photographs or text—to intrude into the privacy of those being filmed.

Politicians also decided that broadcasting must be regulated because, for decades, transmission was only possible on analogue wavelengths. These are relatively scarce, so the consensus was that a regulator was needed to vet broadcasters and specify requirements for quality in programmes and diversity in output.

These justifications for regulating broadcast media have lost much force as technological advances mean that newspapers, magazines and other publishers can 'webcast' audio-visual material on websites, so the power of moving images and sound is no longer exclusive to TV and radio. Digital transmission also allows many more channels, giving the public greater freedom of choice, while social media have become the favoured means of communicating for many.

There is also an argument that regulating broadcast journalism is a societally beneficial counterbalance to the unregulated, partisan journalism of newspaper, magazine and website-only publishers, although it could also be said that regulation means broadcast journalism tends, in its routine forms, to have less impact than newspapers.

3.3 Ofcom—its role and sanctions

Commercial broadcasters must be licensed by Ofcom, which began operating in 2003 and replaced previous regulators. It is structurally independent of the Government, although the Secretary of State for Culture, Media and Sport appoints its chair and non-executive main board members. Its budget for 2017/18 was £121.7 million, provided mainly by licence fees paid by broadcasters and through other charges it imposes, but also with some Government funding. Its range of duties includes regulating phone services.

The Communications Act 2003 makes Ofcom responsible for ensuring the existence of a wide range of TV and radio services of high quality and wide appeal, and for maintaining plurality in broadcasting. When considering applications for national, regional or local broadcast licences, it examines the proposed programming and whether the applicant is 'fit and proper'. Ofcom monitors whether broadcasters comply with the conditions of their licences—for instance, by meeting a public service obligation to provide news. Licences are granted for set durations—for example, 12 years—and can be renewed.

for more detail, see 3.5, The BBC

The 2003 Act and the Broadcasting Act 1996 require Ofcom to draw up standards for programme content. These are detailed in the Ofcom Broadcasting Code. Anyone aggrieved by a programme's content or by how they were treated when it was made can—as long as the programme has been broadcast—complain to Ofcom, which assesses complaints against the standards set in the Code. Ofcom does not regulate all aspects of the BBC's output. Web content, even on sites run by broadcasters, is not subject to Ofcom regulation, as it is not defined in UK law as 'broadcast' material (although a recent change in the law means Ofcom does regulate the BBC's UK 'on demand' programme services, including BBC iPlayer).

If Ofcom upholds a complaint, it can direct that a programme should not be repeated, or order the broadcaster to air a correction or a statement of Ofcom's findings. It can impose a fine if it considers a breach of the Code to be serious or reckless.

If broadcasters consistently breach the Code, Ofcom can shorten or suspend their licences, or, in the worst cases, revoke them. Ofcom used this power in 2012 to close Press TV, the controversial news channel funded by the Iranian Government but broadcasting in English from the UK. Press TV failed to respond to concerns that it breached its licence because it did not control its own editorial content, which, it had indicated, was controlled from Tehran.

Ofcom cannot shorten, suspend or revoke the licences of the BBC, S4C or Channel 4—they are public service broadcasters. But it can fine the BBC or S4C up to £250,000 for a Code breach. For other broadcasters, the maximum fine is £250,000 or 5 per cent of the broadcaster's qualifying revenue.

◉ Case study

The highest regulatory fine imposed for unethical broadcast journalism is £2 million, paid by Central Independent Television, part of the ITV network, after a 1998 Independent Television Commission ruling that scenes in *The Connection*—a documentary which claimed to show a new heroin-smuggling route from Columbia to the UK—were fabricated. The ITC said this was 'a wholesale breach' of the trust viewers placed in programme-makers. *The Connection* had won awards before its authenticity was questioned in an investigation published by *The Guardian* newspaper, which led to the ITC's findings (ITC press release and *The Guardian*, 18 December 1998).

3.4 The scope of the Broadcasting Code

The Broadcasting Code's most recent version took effect in April 2017. It has rules on: protecting under-18s (section 1); avoiding harm and offence (section 2); covering crime, disorder, hatred and abuse (section 3); covering religion (section 4); due impartiality and due accuracy, and undue prominence of views and opinions (section 5); covering elections and referendums (section 6); fairness (section 7); protecting privacy (section 8); commercial references in television programming (section 9); and commercial communications in radio programming (section 10).

see Useful Websites at the end of this chapter for the Code's full text

The Code covers all broadcast output, not just journalism.

3.4.1 Protecting under-18s

Section 1 of the Code says: 'Material that might seriously impair the physical, mental or moral development of people under 18 must not be broadcast' (rule 1.1).

see also
3.4.6,
Imitation
of harmful
behaviour

Broadcasters must take all reasonable steps to protect those under 18 (rule 1.2), it says, adding: 'Children must also be protected by appropriate scheduling from material that is unsuitable for them' (rule 1.3). 'Children' here is those under 15.

3.4.2 The TV watershed

Rule 1.4 says television broadcasters must observe the 9pm 'watershed' marking the transition for free-to-air TV channels between the times of day—from 5.30am to 9pm—when children are most likely to be watching and later slots for which the audience is assumed to be more adult. Material unsuitable for children must not, in general, be broadcast pre-watershed, and the transition to post-watershed material must not be unduly abrupt (rule 1.6).

For pre-watershed broadcasts clear information should, if appropriate, be given about content which might distress children (rule 1.7)—for example, news anchors can warn if footage about to be shown portrays violence. Violence or its after-effects must be 'appropriately limited' in pre-watershed broadcasts and be justified by context (rule 1.11).

Rules also limit the pre-watershed televising of offensive language (rules 1.14–1.16) and portrayal or discussion of sexual behaviour (rule 1.20).

3.4.3 Times when children are likely to be listening to radio

The term 'watershed' is not used for radio. But the Code says radio broadcasters must have particular regard to what is aired 'when children are particularly likely to be listening' (rules 1.5–1.6). Rules on content involving violence, offensive language, sexual material and so on apply to radio at such times—for example, breakfast time.

3.4.4 Protecting children involved in programmes

((•))
see Useful
Websites at
the end of
this chapter
for Ofcom
guidance

The Broadcasting Code's rule 1.28 says broadcasters must take 'due care' over 'the physical and emotional welfare and the dignity' of children under 18 who take part or are involved in programmes, irrespective of any consent they, their parents or guardians give. Ofcom guidance says that 'due' means 'appropriate to the particular circumstances'. Rule 1.29 says that such children must not be caused unnecessary distress or anxiety by involvement in programmes or by broadcast of them.

Other elements of the Code's protection of children are dealt with elsewhere in this chapter or book.

 See too: 3.4.13.1, Informed consent, about children; 4.13, Protecting children's welfare and privacy; 5.15, Juveniles under investigation, on children involved in 'pre-trial investigations' into crime; 11.9.1, 'Children in sex cases', on children in sexual offence cases.

3.4.5 Harm and offence

Section 2 of the Broadcasting Code says in rule 2.1 that 'generally accepted standards' must be applied to the content of television and radio broadcasts, so as to provide adequate protection for the public from the inclusion of harmful and/or offensive material. Material which may cause offence includes: pictures or sounds of distress, humiliation or violation of human dignity; offensive language; violence; sex; and discriminatory treatment or language. Material which may cause offence must be justified by context, and appropriate information should be broadcast where it would help avoid or minimise offence (rule 2.3)—for example, a warning that news footage shows people distressed and badly injured after a terrorist attack.

Section 2 says context includes the programme's editorial content, the time of the broadcast, and the likely size and composition of the potential audience.

◉ Case study

In 2017 Ofcom ruled that entertainment channel Talking Pictures TV breached rule 2.3 by broadcasting in 2016 an anecdote told by comedian and singer Joan Turner, who is white, during a chat show first broadcast in 1978. She referred to applying to her legs a 'tan' substance used by dancing girls. She said her booking agent had told her in 1937 to take it off and that he said: 'You look like a bloody chocolate covered coon'. Ofcom said the word 'coon' was racist and capable of being highly offensive, that use of the phrase was not justified by context, and that its broadcast before the 'watershed' also breached rule 1.14, because children viewing would not necessarily have been aware of 'historical differences in attitudes to offensive language' (*Ofcom Broadcast Bulletin*, No. 320, 9 January 2017).

The Code says demonstrations of exorcism, the occult, the paranormal, divination or related practices which purport to be real (as opposed to entertainment) must be treated with due objectivity, and if they are for entertainment, this must be made clear (rules 2.6 and 2.7). There is also a general rule (2.2) that factual programmes or items, or portrayals of factual matters, must not materially mislead the audience, as this could cause harm or offence (though accuracy in news output is regulated under the Code's section 5: see 3.4.11, Due impartiality and due accuracy).

3.4.6 Imitation of harmful behaviour

Programmes should not include material which, taking the context into account, condones or glamorises violent, dangerous or seriously anti-social behaviour and is likely to encourage others—particularly children—to copy it (rule 2.4, and see rules 1.12 and 1.13).

Methods of suicide and self-harm must not be included in programmes except when justified editorially and by context, to avoid people imitating them (rule 2.5).

 For the rationale of rule 2.5, see 2.4.3, Coverage of suicides, about the Editors' Code content, and see 17.11, Ethical considerations when covering deaths.

3.4.6.1 Photosensitive epilepsy

Broadcasters must take precautions to maintain a low level of risk to viewers who have photosensitive epilepsy (rule 2.12), who can be affected by broadcasts of flashing lights, including news footage of photographers using flash equipment.

3.4.7 Crime, disorder, hatred and abuse

Section 3 of the code says material likely to encourage or incite the commission of crime or lead to disorder must not be included in television, radio or BBC 'on demand' services (rule 3.1). In 2016 Ofcom amended the section to make clearer that the rule bans material 'promoting or encouraging engagement in terrorism' or which is 'hate speech which is likely to encourage criminal activity or lead to disorder'. It added new rules 3.2 and 3.3 to say that material containing 'hate speech' (even if not likely to encourage crime or disorder) or abusive or derogatory treatment of individuals, groups, religions or communities, must not be included in programmes except where justified by the context. The code defines 'hate speech' as 'all forms of expression which spread, incite, promote or justify hatred based on intolerance on the grounds of disability, ethnicity, gender, gender reassignment, nationality, race, religion, or sexual orientation'. The section makes clear it does not ban broadcasters interviewing people with extreme or challenging views in news and current affairs coverage, 'which is clearly in the public interest', but warns against giving 'an uncritical platform for an authoritative figure to advocate criminal activity or disorder'.

◉ Case study

In 2017 Ofcom fined the Ariana International satellite channel, which originates from Afghanistan but broadcasts in the UK, £200,000 for breaching rules 2.3, 3.1 and 3.2 of the code. It had broadcast a news item which included a video lasting more than two minutes made by 17-year-old Muhammad Riyad before he carried out a terrorist attack in which he stabbed five people on a train in Southern Germany. In it he made clear his allegiance to the Islamic State terrorist organisation, spoke of his intention to kill non-Muslims, brandished a knife and boasted about the forthcoming attack. Ofcom said it was 'a prolonged example of hate speech' with clear potential to influence impressionable viewers by encouraging serious crime including murder, and that there were no statements in the programme which challenged the video's inflammatory effect or 'the considerable level of potential offence'. Ariana said it was 'gravely regretful' that 'breakdown' of editorial controls led to the full video being aired (*Ofcom Broadcast Bulletin*, No. 333, 17 July 2017).

 The Broadcasting Code uses the UK law's definition of terrorism, explained on www.mcnaes.com in the chapter, 'Terrorism and the effect of counter-terrorism law'.

Section 3 also says that descriptions of criminal techniques with detail which could enable the commission of crime must not be broadcast unless editorially justified (rule 3.4).

Rule 3.8 says broadcasters must use their best endeavours not to broadcast material which could endanger lives or prejudice the success of attempts to deal with a hijack or kidnapping.

✳ Remember

Police dealing with kidnaps may ask news media to observe a news 'blackout' to help preserve the victim's life. Also, coverage of an anti-terrorist or hostage recovery operation should not include broadcasts of live material which might alert the terrorists to armed police or special forces launching a rescue operation.

3.4.8 Payments to criminals

Section 3 forbids making any payment or promise of payment, directly or indirectly, to 'convicted or confessed criminals' for a programme contribution by the criminal relating to his/her crime, unless doing so is in the public interest (rule 3.5).

As with similar provision in the Editor's Code—see, Payments to criminals—this is to avoid distressing victims of crime and outraging the public.

 see 4.3, Public interest exceptions in the Broadcasting Code

3.4.9 Payments to witnesses

Section 3 also prohibits broadcasters making or offering payments to witnesses in 'active' criminal cases, or to anyone who might reasonably be expected to be called as a witness, though they can be paid expenses (rule 3.6). If a criminal case is not 'active', but is likely and foreseeable, payment should not be made to anyone who might reasonably be expected to be a witness unless there is a clear public interest. Any payment should be disclosed to the defence and prosecution if the person becomes a witness (rule 3.7).

These rules are to ensure broadcasters do not jeopardise the administration of justice or commit contempt of court.

 ch. 19 explains contempt law and 'active'

3.4.10 Religion

Section 4 of the Broadcasting Code says the views and beliefs of those belonging to a particular religion or religious denomination must not be subject to abusive treatment. Rule 4.7 says religious programmes containing claims that a living person (or group) has special powers or abilities must treat such claims with due objectivity. They must not be broadcast when significant numbers of children may be expected to be watching or listening or likely to access them from the BBC 'on demand' services.

3.4.11 Due impartiality and due accuracy

Section 5 of the Code sets out impartiality and accuracy requirements for broadcasters.

Rule 5.1 says: 'News, in whatever form, must be reported with due accuracy and presented with due impartiality.'

The Code says impartiality means not favouring one side over another, and the qualification 'due' means adequate or appropriate to the programme's subject and nature. It adds: 'So "due impartiality" does not mean an equal division of time has to be given to every view, or that every argument and every facet of every argument has to be represented. The approach to due impartiality may vary according to the nature of the subject, the type of programme and channel, the likely expectation of the audience as to content, and the extent to which the content and approach is signalled to the audience.'

Politicians may not be used as newsreaders, interviewers or reporters in any news programme unless, exceptionally, this is editorially justified and the individual's political allegiance is made clear (rule 5.3).

Owners of broadcast organisations may not use them to project their own views on 'matters of political or industrial controversy and matters relating to current public policy'. The Code offers a general definition of such matters in this section.

Rules 5.5–5.12 require the providers of television programme services, teletext services, national radio and national digital sound programme services to preserve due impartiality on such matters in their output. This may be achieved over a series of programmes 'taken as a whole' rather than in a single programme.

The Code seeks to ensure the presentation of a diversity of opinion in respect of major political and industrial controversy and major matters of current public policy, saying 'an appropriately wide range of significant views must be included and given due weight in each programme or in clearly linked and timely programmes. Views and facts must not be misrepresented' (rule 5.12).

👁 Case study

In 2016 Ofcom ruled that in coverage of the US Presidential election the Fox News channel breached the Code's impartiality rules 5.11 and 5.12 in three, one-hour programmes in the *Hannity* current affairs strand broadcast in the

UK. The programmes presented 'an over-whelmingly one-sided view' in support of Republican Party candidate Donald Trump 'on a matter of major political controversy and major matter relating to current public policy'—in this case, 'the policies and actions of the two principal candidates' in that election, Trump and Democratic Party candidate Hillary Clinton, it said. It also ruled that these *Hannity* programmes breached rule 6.1 which requires due impartiality in coverage of elections, including those abroad (*Ofcom Broadcast Bulletin*, No. 317, 21 November 2016).

ch. 32 deals with UK election coverage

Any personal interest of a reporter or presenter which would call the due impartiality of the programme into question must be made clear (rule 5.8).

3.4.11.1 'Personal view' and 'authored' programmes

Rule 5.9 says: 'Presenters and reporters (with the exception of news presenters and reporters in news programmes), presenters of "personal view" or "authored" programmes or items, and chairs of discussion programmes may express their own views on matters of political or industrial controversy or matters relating to current public policy. However, alternative viewpoints must be adequately represented either in the programme, or in a series of programmes taken as a whole. Additionally, presenters must not use the advantage of regular appearances to promote their views in a way which compromises the requirement for due impartiality. Presenter phone-ins must encourage and must not exclude alternative views.'

'Personal view' programmes are defined as those presenting a particular view or perspective. These could involve a person who is a member of a lobby group and is campaigning on a subject expressing highly partial views, or 'the considered 'authored' opinion of a journalist, commentator or academic, with expertise or a specialism in an area which enables her or him to express opinions which are not necessarily mainstream'. The Code says a personal view or authored programme or item must be clearly signalled as such at the outset.

3.4.12 Accuracy considerations

Ofcom guidance says that the clarification of the term 'due' in respect of impartiality (see earlier in the chapter) also applies to the accuracy requirement.

((•))

see Useful Websites at the end of this chapter for this guidance

---

👁 Case study

Ofcom ruled that Channel 4 News breached accuracy rule 5.1 on 22 March 2017 by naming Abu Izzadeen, formerly Trevor Brooks, as the terrorist shot dead earlier that day by police after he drove a 4 x 4 vehicle at people on Westminster Bridge, killing three and injuring dozens, and fatally stabbed a policeman guarding Parliament. But Abu Izzadeen—whose name was supplied as being the terrorist's to the programme by a 'single source' it regarded as reliable—was in jail, and so played no part in the attack, as Channel 4 indicated to viewers later in the programme. The terrorist, it emerged, was Khalid Masood. Ofcom expressed particular concern that this breach of the rule was the fourth by Channel 4 in three years (*Ofcom Broadcast Bulletin*, No. 336, 11 September 2017).

The Code says significant mistakes in news should normally be acknowledged and corrected on air quickly. Corrections should be appropriately scheduled (rule 5.2). Views and facts must not be misrepresented (rule 5.7).

✳ Remember

A journalist who, to produce a dramatic effect, edits footage or an audio recording in a way which, when it is broadcast, misrepresents a sequence of events will breach the Code, as will a broadcaster which stages and airs a reconstruction of a news event and fails to make clear to the audience that it is not the real event.

3.4.12.1 Undue prominence of views and opinions

Rule 5.13, which applies to local radio services and local digital sound programme services, including those at community level, says their broadcasters 'should not give undue prominence to the views and opinions of particular persons or bodies on matters of political or industrial controversy and matters relating to current public policy' in programming when 'taken as a whole', by which it means programming 'dealing with the same or related issues within an appropriate period'.

It defines 'undue prominence of views and opinions' as a significant imbalance of views.

 Section 6 of the Code sets out specific requirements for broadcasters to maintain impartiality during election and referendum periods—see ch. 32.

3.4.13 Fairness

Section 7 of the Code sets out general principles on how programme-makers should treat people or organisations participating or featured in programmes.

Rule 7.1 says: 'Broadcasters must avoid unjust or unfair treatment of individuals or organisations in programmes.'

The section details 'Practices to be followed'. A failure to follow these which leads to unfair treatment will be a breach of the Code.

Practice 7.2 says broadcasters and programme-makers should be fair in dealings with potential contributors to programmes unless, exceptionally, doing otherwise is justified.

3.4.13.1 Informed consent

Practice 7.3 says people or organisations who agree to take part in programmes should do so on the basis of 'informed consent', which requires that a person invited to contribute to a programme should—unless the subject matter is trivial or their participation minor—normally be told:

- its nature and purpose, and what it is about, and be given a clear explanation of why he/she has been asked to contribute and when and where it is likely to be broadcast;
- the kind of contribution he/she is expected to make—live, pre-recorded, interview, discussion, edited, unedited, etc;
- the areas of questioning and, wherever possible, the nature of other likely contributions.

It lists other information the person should be told and says the public interest or other provisions might justify withholding all or some of this information.

If a contributor is under 16, a parent's or guardian's consent should normally be obtained. Those under 16 should not be asked for views on matters likely to be beyond their capacity to answer properly without such consent (practice 7.4).

 See the Additional Material for ch. 4 on www.mcnaes.com for a case study on 'informed consent'.

The Code says: 'Guarantees given to contributors, for example relating to the content of a programme, confidentiality or anonymity, should normally be honoured' (practice 7.7).

 see ch. 34 for cases in which journalists ethically kept secret the identities of their sources

3.4.13.2 Getting facts right and airing the other side of the story

Practice 7.9 says that before broadcasting a factual programme, including programmes examining past events, broadcasters should take reasonable care to satisfy themselves that material facts have not been presented, disregarded or omitted in a way that is unfair to an individual or organisation; and that anyone whose omission could be unfair to an individual or organisation has been offered an opportunity to contribute. Practice 7.11 says that if a programme alleges wrongdoing or incompetence or makes other significant allegations, those concerned should normally be given an appropriate and timely opportunity to respond. Where a person approached to contribute to a programme chooses to make no comment or refuses to appear, the broadcast should make this clear—and give that person's explanation if it would be unfair not to do so (practice 7.12).

3.4.14 Public interest exceptions in the Broadcasting Code

Ofcom accepts that programme-makers may be justified in breaching some of the Code's provisions in the public interest. It uses the term **warranted** to indicate

 → glossary

when there must be a public interest or some other exceptional justification to merit breaching the usual rules.

- Section 8 says that examples of public interest include:
  - revealing or detecting crime;
  - protecting public health or safety;
  - exposing misleading claims made by individuals or organisations; or
  - disclosing incompetence that affects the public.

 There are similar public interest exceptions in the Editors' Code—see 2.4.1, Public interest exceptions in the Editors' Code.

3.4.15 Deception and misrepresentation

The Broadcasting Code says in practice 7.14 that:

" Broadcasters or programme makers should not normally obtain or seek information, audio, pictures or an agreement to contribute through misrepresentation or deception. . . . "

But it adds that it may be warranted to use material gained by such tactics if it is in the public interest *and* the material cannot reasonably be obtained by other means.

Thus, a journalist who lies about the nature of a programme in order to trick a criminal into taking part will not breach the Code if the programme's purpose is to expose sufficiently serious offences. Similarly, giving a false reason to a public institution when seeking consent to film its activities will not be a breach if the public interest is sufficient, such as exposing incompetence affecting the public. The public interest can justify journalists misrepresenting themselves—for example, by posing as members of another profession or an uninformed citizen. But in all such instances, if a complaint is made, Ofcom will consider whether what was done was **proportionate** (not excessive) and whether there was any other way the material could reasonably have been obtained.

3.4.16 Secret filming and recording—deception and privacy

The Code says in practice 7.14 that 'surreptitious'—secret or undercover—filming or recording is a type of deception. Under the Code material gained in this way should not normally be broadcast unless the person filmed or recorded consents.

Surreptitious filming or recording includes using long lenses or recording devices, or leaving an unattended camera or recording device on private property without the full and informed consent of the occupiers, or deliberately continuing a recording when the other party thinks it has ended (section 8).

- But practice 7.14 says it may be warranted to use, without consent, film or audio gained surreptitiously if it is in the public interest and the material cannot reasonably be obtained by other means.

Practice 7.14 adds that if an individual or organisation filmed or recorded surreptitiously is not identifiable in the programme as broadcast, their consent to be included in it is not required (though their right to privacy would need to be taken into account).

Surreptitious filming or recording can violate privacy—for example, by recording private conversations without consent—even if the person is not identified, or the conversations included, in what is broadcast.

Section 8 of the Code, on privacy, says any infringement of privacy in programmes, or in connection with obtaining material included in programmes, must be with the consent of the person and/or organisation or be otherwise warranted (rule 8.1 and practice 8.5), and the means of obtaining material must be 'proportionate in all the circumstances' (practice 8.9). Practices 8.13 and 8.14 say surreptitious filming or recording should only be done when warranted and that normally it will only be warranted if:

- there is **prima facie** evidence of a story in the public interest; and   → glossary
- reasonable grounds to suspect that further material evidence could be obtained; and
- it is necessary to the programme's credibility and authenticity.

The requirement for prima facie evidence is to prevent arbitrary 'fishing expeditions'.

Ofcom will deem a failure by programme-makers to observe the 'practices to be followed' in section 8 as breaching the Code if it leads to an unwarranted infringement of privacy.

 for explanation of 'fishing expeditions' see 2.4.4.1

Ofcom guidance says broadcasters should take care not to infringe the privacy of bystanders who might inadvertently be caught in a covert recording—for example, it might be necessary to obscure the identities of those recorded incidentally.

> See the Additional Material for ch. 3 on www.mcnaes.com for a case study of how in 2017 Ofcom cleared the BBC's *Watchdog* programme of a complaint by the RAC Group Ltd about the programme's undercover investigation into sales of car batteries to motorists.

3.4.16.1 Recording phone calls

Practice 8.12 of the Code says broadcasters can record telephone calls if they have, from the outset of the call, identified themselves, and explained to the other person the call's purpose and that it is being recorded for possible broadcast (if that is the case) unless it is warranted not to identify themselves or give such explanation. This means that failing to tell the person that the call is being recorded for broadcast, failing to explain its purpose or broadcasting a recording of it without the person's consent can be justified if the journalism is 'in the public interest'.

Ofcom might class recording a phone call without the other person's knowledge as a surreptitious recording, and therefore—if the intention is to broadcast it—practices 7.14 and 8.13 apply. But Ofcom guidance says it is acceptable for journalists to record their own calls for note-taking purposes.

> See Useful Websites at the end of this chapter for Ofcom guidance, and see 2.4.4.2, Recording interviews and phone calls, on how it is not a crime to record one's own calls.

3.4.17 Privacy in general

Section 8 of the Code includes general provisions for protecting people's privacy in relation to journalists openly filming or audio-recording. These are explained in ch. 4, which also explains the Code's use of the term 'legitimate expectation of privacy' and its restrictions on 'doorstepping'.

3.4.18 Financial journalism

Appendix 4 of the Code sets out 'binding guidance' on how journalists working for commercial broadcasters must operate to comply with legislation on investment recommendations.

3.4.19 Other parts of the Broadcasting Code

Section 9 regulates commercial references in television programming and section 10 regulates commercial communications in radio programming. These rules seek to ensure there is a distinction between editorial and advertising content, and set out specific principles of editorial independence as regards television—for example, news and current affairs programmes on television must not be sponsored (rule 9.15).

3.5 The BBC

((•))
see Useful
Websites at
the end of
this chapter
for the BBC's
complaints
process

The BBC, the biggest broadcasting organisation in the world, has nine national TV channels plus regional programming, 10 national radio stations and more than 40 regional and local radio stations, plus its website.

The legal basis for the BBC's independent existence is its Royal Charter, which is renewed every 10 years, and the accompanying Agreement. The Government amended these to make the BBC's programmes, including its UK 'on demand' services funded by the licence fee (e.g. BBC iPlayer), subject from April 2017 to Ofcom regulation under all sections of the Broadcasting Code. Previously the

BBC Trust, now abolished, had regulated the BBC's impartiality and accuracy obligations. Anyone dissatisfied with the BBC's response to a complaint can complain to Ofcom. But Ofcom does not regulate the BBC's World Service.

'On demand' services can be accessed by people at times they choose, so the Broadcasting Code requires the BBC to put in place in them measures which provide a safeguard for children in their audiences 'equivalent' to that achieved by scheduling of transmission times—see 3.4.2, The TV watershed and 3.4.3, Times when children are likely to be listening to the radio.

((•))
see Useful Websites at the end of this chapter for the Guidelines

The BBC's Editorial Guidelines set out standards for its journalism.

Ofcom does not regulate the BBC's online content, which include its news web-pages. So, if an online item is justifiably complained about, Ofcom cannot sanction the BBC. But if such a complainant is unhappy with the BBC's response, Ofcom can investigate and publish its 'independent opinion'.

➡ Recap of major points

- Broadcast journalism is regulated by the Office of Communications (Ofcom).

- Broadcast organisations must comply with the Broadcasting Code, which requires them to avoid causing harm and offence, to be fair and to protect people's privacy.

- Ofcom can fine broadcasters for the worst transgressions of the Code and can close a commercial broadcaster which persistently or recklessly flouts it.

- There must be 'due accuracy' and 'due impartiality' in all broadcast news.

((•)) Useful Websites

www.ofcom.org.uk/about/what-is-ofcom/
What is Ofcom?

https://www.ofcom.org.uk/tv-radio-and-on-demand/broadcast-codes/broadcast-code
Ofcom Broadcasting Code

www.ofcom.org.uk/tv-radio-and-on-demand/information-for-industry/guidance/programme-guidance
Ofcom's guidance on the Code

www.ofcom.org.uk/__data/assets/pdf_file/0022/101893/bbc-online-procedures.pdf
Procedures for Ofcom to handle complaints about BBC website material

www.bbc.co.uk/aboutthebbc/insidethebbc/whatwedo
About the BBC

www.bbc.co.uk/editorialguidelines/
BBC Editorial Guidelines and Guidance

www.bbc.co.uk/editorialguidelines/guidance/secret-recording
  BBC guidance on secret recording

www.bbc.co.uk/complaints/
  BBC complaints system

www.bbc.co.uk/academy/journalism
  BBC Academy—provides training content for broadcast journalists, including on impartiality and ethics

4

News-gathering avoiding unjustified intrusion

Chapter summary

Journalists should avoid unnecessary intrusion into people's lives, but know when it can be justified. They should combine knowledge of the legal basics with a good grasp of the codes used by media regulators. This chapter shows how regulators' adjudications on complaints about intrusion provide guidance covering a far wider range of situations than is dealt with in privacy case law. Ch. 27 covers privacy law, but few people can afford to go to court if they feel their privacy is breached. Many complain to regulators about journalists taking photos, filming and audio-recording, and about what is published. A journalist could be accused of harassment, which is unethical and could be a crime. Publishing 'user-generated' photographs, or footage supplied by the public, or material from social media sites can be unethical. This chapter shows too how the codes seek to minimise intrusion into grief and have particular rules for when children are interviewed, filmed or photographed by journalists.

4.1 The codes and intrusion

People may suffer intrusion if they are being photographed, filmed or audio-recorded without their consent by the media (references to 'filming' include videoing). Or the intrusion may be from publication of such material, or of other intrinsically private information—for example, someone's medical records, or what an ex-partner betrays of an individual's confidential conversations or sex life.

Judges in privacy lawsuits arising from such media activity or publication weigh the **claimant's** rights to respect for privacy under Article 8 of the European Convention on Human Rights against the Article 10 rights of the media and public to impart and receive information. Such cases, which might include claims for breach of confidence or of data protection law, could lead to the claimant winning damages. Those laws are explained in detail in chs. 26, 27 and 28.

→ glossary

ch. 1
explains the
Convention

The legal test for assessing whether an individual's privacy rights are engaged is: Did the person have 'a reasonable expectation of privacy' in circumstances in which the alleged intrusion occurred?

The UK media regulators—the Independent Press Standards Organisation (Ipso), Impress and Ofcom, introduced in chapters 2 and 3—each has its own code of ethics to adjudicate on complaints against media organisations. These codes are not law, but each contains the criterion of 'reasonable expectation of privacy' for the regulator to assess complaints that intrusion occurred. Ofcom's Broadcasting Code also uses the term 'legitimate expectation', but this means the same. If the regulator decides the complainant, in the relevant circumstances, did have that expectation, intrusion caused by what a media organisation has → glossary   done will breach the relevant code, unless there is a sufficiently strong **public interest** justification. That may be expressed in terms of Article 10 rights but the concept of public interest and protection of freedom of expression have, anyway, a long history in UK law and media ethics. As outlined in this chapter, the term 'public interest' in the context of journalism signifies that the story being pursued is of a particularly high value to society, including when a media organisation intends to publish material to contribute to a general debate about an important issue.

4.1.1 Proportionality

Even when a media organisation can successfully argue that a public interest factor existed, a judge or media regulator will consider the degree of harm or distress which publication of the intrusive images or recordings might cause or have caused to the person depicted or recorded. For example, publishing a close-up of a face can be more intrusive than a long shot, and broadcasting lengthy footage more intrusive than a brief clip being shown. Regulators and the courts say that → glossary   the media must adopt a **'proportionate'** approach to what is published. There may be a strong public interest in showing something of the situation, or revealing part of what was said, but not everything. A face in the image captured may need to be pixelated before publication, to prevent violation of privacy.

Breach of privacy is not the only kind of intrusion covered by the codes, as this chapter explains.

4.1.2 Adjudications cited in this chapter and its Additional Material

As regards use of cameras and microphones, this chapter mainly considers what the regulators' codes and adjudications say about journalists working openly. What codes say about covert (undercover) photography, filming or recording is covered in chs. 2 and 3. But even when journalists work openly, it is possible that people—for example, in crowds or in the chaos after an accident—might be unaware that their images or voices are being captured.

When this book went to press, Impress—the youngest of the regulators—had not adjudicated on a complaint about intrusion, so this chapter refers only to Ipso and Ofcom's adjudications. Ipso adjudications (rulings) can be read on its website. Ofcom's Broadcast Bulletins can be read on its website. The Additional Material for this chapter on www.mcnaes.com has relevant case studies, including of adjudications alluded to in this chapter. The Additional Material includes a 'Checklist on Intrusion'.

for how Ipso's adjudications are cited, see 2.1.1

((•)) For the full text of the Editors' Code, see this book's Appendix. See Useful Websites at the end of this chapter for the full text of the other codes, and the regulators' home webpages.

4.2 The codes' general protection of privacy

Breaching the codes is not necessarily to breach privacy law, but complying with the codes is ethical and helps reduce the likelihood of a privacy claim, or of such a claim succeeding.

Clause 2 (Privacy) of the Editors' Code, used by Ipso, states:

see 27.12, on how judges consider relevant codes

" i)   Everyone is entitled to respect for his or her private and family life, home, health and correspondence, including digital communications.

ii)   Editors will be expected to justify intrusions into any individual's private life without consent. In considering an individual's reasonable expectation of privacy, account will be taken of the complainant's own public disclosures of information and the extent to which the material complained about is already in the public domain or will become so.

iii) It is unacceptable to photograph individuals, without their consent, in public or private places where there is a reasonable expectation of privacy. "

Note that sub-clause i) draws on the wording of Article 8, see 4.1, The codes and intrusion. References to photography in the Editors' Code include filming.

The Impress Code's clause 7.1 says: 'Except where justified by the public interest, publishers must respect people's reasonable expectation of privacy'.

Rule 8.1 of the Broadcasting Code says: 'Any infringement of privacy in programmes, or in connection with obtaining material included in programmes, must be warranted'. Practice 8.3 says: 'When people are caught up in events which are covered by the news they still have a right to privacy in both the making and the broadcast of a programme, unless it is warranted to infringe it'.

 For the term 'practice', see 3.4.16, Secret filming and recording—deception and privacy.

Most principles in the Broadcasting Code's rules for TV and radio output are similar to those in the Editors' Code for newspapers, magazines and websites, and in the Impress Code. The term **'warranted'** in the Broadcasting Code includes reference to public interest exceptions.

→ glossary

✳ Remember

All three codes make clear that, if people complain that a media organisation has unjustifiably published private information about them, the regulator will take into account the extent to which it was already in the public domain. For example, a celebrity may have previously chosen to publicise information about his or her private life, to gain publicity, which will reduce or nullify the likelihood of a complaint being upheld.

4.3　Public interest exceptions in the codes

The codes allow that breaching some of their rules, including those protecting privacy, may be justifiable if the media activity is covered by public interest exceptions, which cover types of particularly valuable journalistic activity. These—and the necessary 'audit trail' procedure—are outlined in chs. 2 and 3, and include exposing crime or negligence imperilling people's safety, and how the public have been misled by an organisation or individual, such as a politician. There are differences in how each code defines the exceptions. But there is no code requirement for the media to rely on a public interest exception if someone does not have a reasonable expectation of privacy in a place or situation, or consents to being photographed, filmed or recorded, or to publication of details of his or her private life.

 See 2.4.1, Public Interest Exceptions in the Editors' Code, and 2.5, Impress and its Code; and 3.4.14, Public Interest Exceptions in the Broadcasting Code.

4.4　Public and private places

Ipso has repeatedly ruled that photographing a person in a public space, such as a public highway, does not breach clause 2 of the Editors' Code, because there is no reasonable expectation of privacy there and that publication of such photos does not breach the clause when it does not reveal anything private about the individual (for example, *Sword v The Times*, 13 June 2017, involving a man photographed walking a dog).

Ipso's predecessor the Press Complaints Commission (PCC) ruled that a man had a reasonable expectation of privacy when he was dining in a 'quiet' café where he was not easily visible from the street. Members of the public had a right of free entry into the café, but the PCC upheld his complaint about being included in a photo published in a review of the café (*Tunbridge v Dorking Advertiser*, 23 May 2002).

 see also 4.13, Protecting children's welfare and privacy, on families in public places

The Impress Code's guidance says: 'People may also have a reasonable expectation of privacy in a public place, when they are engaging in an activity that is part of their private or family life'.

Ofcom says that normally filming and recording someone in a public place does not breach the Broadcasting Code. But section 8 of this code says: 'Legitimate expectations of privacy will vary according to the place, and nature of the information, activity or condition in question, the extent to which it is in the public domain (if at all) and whether the individual concerned is already in the public eye. There may be circumstances where people can reasonably expect privacy even in a public place. Some activities and conditions may be of such a private nature that filming or recording, even in a public place, could involve an infringement of privacy.'

The Broadcasting Code adds in practice 8.4: 'Broadcasters should ensure that words, images or actions filmed or recorded in, or broadcast from, a public place, are not so private that prior consent is required before broadcast from the individual or organisation concerned, unless broadcasting without their consent is warranted.'

◉ Case study:

Ofcom ruled that a woman filmed by a CCTV system in Chester when vomiting and being arrested for being drunk and disorderly had a 'legitimate expectation of privacy' because of her vulnerable state. But it said this expectation was limited because she was in a public street, and that Channel 5's broadcast of the footage in the *Criminals: Caught on Camera* series, which identified her by showing her face but not in close-up, did not breach the Broadcasting Code because of the channel's right to freedom of expression, and the public interest in showing how CCTV operators helped police deal with criminal and anti-social behaviour. Ofcom took into account that by the time the footage was broadcast the woman had been fined by a court for the offence, and was not shown doing 'anything particularly confidential' (*Ofcom Broadcast Bulletin*, No. 252, 14 April 2014).

Ofcom guidance says property which is privately owned but readily accessible to the public, such as a railway station or shop, can be a public place.

But in 2016 Ofcom upheld a complaint by a woman that the inclusion without her consent in TLC channel programme *Say Yes To The Dress* of three seconds of footage shot in a bridal boutique, in which she was identifiable in the background, wearing her wedding dress, was an unwarranted infringement of her privacy (*Ofcom Broadcast Bulletin*, No. 330, 5 June 2017).

((•))
see Useful Websites at the end of this chapter for Ofcom guidance

 See the Additional Material for ch. 4 on www.mcnaes.com for more details of this case.

Ofcom guidance says: 'Some activities and conditions may be of such a private nature that filming, even in a public place where there was normally no reasonable expectation of privacy, could involve an infringement of privacy. For example, a child in state of undress, someone with disfiguring medical condition or CCTV footage of suicide attempt.'

 No law bans the act of photographing, filming or recording what is happening in a public street. But publication might infringe an individual's rights. Ch. 36 covers the legal right to photograph and film in public places. For context, see too ch. 27 including 27.6 on the *Peck* case, which involved broadcast of CCTV footage of an attempted suicide, and ch. 28 about data protection law.

4.4.1 'Long lens' photos

Unless the camera is hidden, use of a 'long' (telephoto) lens does not fall under clause 10 of the Editors' Code, a clause explained in 2.4.4. But a long lens can mean people are unaware of being photographed. In 2016 Princess Beatrice complained about long lens photos published by *Mail Online* showing her in a bikini on a luxury yacht at Monaco. Ipso ruled they breached clause 2 of the Editors' Code. The yacht was moored 200 metres from the shore, where the photographer was. *Mail Online* argued that the Princess did not have a reasonable expectation of privacy while on the yacht's deck. Ipso ruled she had. It was not satisfied that she would have been identifiable to anyone looking from the shore. Ipso said she was unaware of the photographer and that the 'gratuitous and invasive focus' on parts of her body 'which would not ordinarily be subject to public scrutiny' represented a serious intrusion into her privacy (*HRH Princess Beatrice of York v Mail Online*, 1 November 2016).

 See too the Prince Harry case study in the Additional Material for ch. 4 on www.mcnaes.com.

see also
4.13.1,
Children in
crowds and
at public
occasions

4.4.2 Crowds

Ipso and Ofcom will not adjudicate against images of people in crowds being published if what is shown is innocuous or in the public interest. But a regulator may make an adverse adjudication if there was an intrusive focus on an individual—for example, if he or she was identifiably shown as having fallen ill in the crowd.

4.4.3 Addresses

Ipso says that in general disclosing the address of someone's home does not usually breach clause 2 of the Editors' Code, but may in special circumstances—for example if a person with a 'high public profile' may face security problems if their home address is published and is not already in the public domain (*Beckham v Mail Online*, issued 6 June 2017, not upheld).

Practice 8.2 of the Broadcasting Code says information which discloses the location of a person's home or family should not be revealed without permission, unless this is warranted. Ofcom adjudications show this does not mean that shots of a person's home cannot be broadcast, because that image alone does not reveal to many people where it is, but that the property's street number should be blurred if in shot, and other distinguishing characteristics of the property should not be shown.

4.4.4 People at home

In 2007 Ipso's predecessor the Press Complaints Commission ruled that a newspaper's publication of a long lens picture showing a politician's wife in her back garden did not breach her privacy—she was visible from a public road and so had no reasonable expectation of privacy, and the picture was 'innocuous' because it did not show her doing anything private (*Sheridan v the Scottish Sun*, 3 May 2007).

✳ Remember

Ipso has said that a journalist venturing on to private property could be an intrusive breach of clause 2 (*Beckham v Mail Online,* cited earlier). Journalists also need to know the law on trespass, dealt with in 36.3, Trespass and bye-laws.

 For adjudications on people being filmed or photographed after opening their home's door, see this chapter's Additional Material on www.mcnaes.com. Legal and ethical issues arising from journalists accompanying police on 'raids' to arrest people or search their properties are covered in the Additional Material there for ch. 5.

4.5 Doorstepping

Section 8 of the Broadcasting Code defines 'doorstepping' as 'the filming or recording of an interview or attempted interview with someone, or announcing that a call is being filmed or recorded for broadcast purposes, without any prior warning'.

Doorstepping is an ambush technique which can be used against someone unlikely to agree to an interview—for example, a crook being investigated or a politician in a scandal, when they open the door at their home or workplace.

Practice 8.11 of the Code says: 'Doorstepping for factual programmes should not take place unless a request for an interview has been refused or it has not been possible to request an interview, or there is good reason to believe that an investigation will be frustrated if the subject is approached openly, and it is warranted to doorstep.' In 2017 Ofcom ruled that the BBC consumer affairs programme *X Ray* did not breach the Code by 'doorstepping' a car dealer on his showroom's forecourt about complaints by car purchasers (*Ofcom Broadcast Bulletin*, No. 330, 5 June 2017).

Practice 8.11 adds that broadcasters may normally, without prior warning, interview, film or record people in the news when they are in public places.

It also makes clear that vox-pops (short surveys sampling the views of random members of the public) are not considered 'doorstepping'.

4.6 The codes' protection against harassment

Clause 3 (Harassment) of the Editors' Code says:

" i)   Journalists must not engage in intimidation, harassment or persistent pursuit.

ii)   They must not persist in questioning, telephoning, pursuing or photographing individuals once asked to desist; nor remain on property when asked to leave and must not follow them. If requested, they must identify themselves and whom they represent.

iii) Editors must ensure these principles are observed by those working for them and take care not to use non-compliant material from other sources. "

The Broadcasting Code's practice 8.7 says: 'If an individual or organisation's privacy is being infringed, and they ask that the filming, recording or live broadcast be stopped, the broadcaster should do so, unless it is warranted to continue.'

Under the codes, a journalist should normally respect a person's refusal to answer questions or his/her request to stop photographing, filming or recording him/her. But the public interest exceptions may mean that a journalist could, for example, be justified in returning or ringing again in further attempts to question a fraudster about a fraud or a politician about involvement in a scandal, or pursuing them for a short while with such questions, or photographing or filming them as they walk away. The Impress Code guidance to its clause on harassment says that if a journalist's conduct is 'intimidation' there is no public interest exception.

4.7 Law against harassment

Irrespective of what the codes say, paparazzi who hound people could be prosecuted or sued under the Protection from Harassment Act 1997 which created criminal offences and civil remedies.

The 1997 Act—created to deal with obsessive stalkers rather than journalists— says harassment can include causing alarm or distress and is 'a course of conduct', which means the conduct must have occurred at least twice. It also contains specific stalking offences—following, watching or spying on someone could be stalking if they cause alarm or distress.

 See the Additional Material for ch. 4 on www.mcnaes.com for case studies on harassment law. One concerns a warning given controversially by police to a reporter after he sought comment from a convicted fraudster about a website scam she was running. She had complained he was 'harassing' her.

4.8 Accidents and major incidents

Accidents and major incidents are newsworthy. Photographs and footage help the public to understand what has happened. They may occur in public places, but there are sensitivities in covering them.

👁 Case study

In 2015 Ipso ruled that the *Derby Telegraph* breached three clauses of the Editors' Code because a member of its staff took a photo of two 11-year-old girls—one of them injured—following a traffic accident outside a school and it was published online. It showed the injured girl lying on the pavement, with her face pixelated, a girl next to her, who was identifiable and two passers-by. The newspaper did not know the girls were sisters and therefore that publishing the image was likely to identify both. The girls' mother complained that the photo depicted a distressing incident for her daughters, and was taken when everyone involved was in shock and emergency services had yet to arrive. Publication of the photo added to the family's distress and, as it related to her daughters' welfare, it should not have been used without her consent, she said, adding that she was also concerned that the newspaper had not pixelated the face of her uninjured daughter. The newspaper had not been able to contact the family as the injured girl's name had not been released. After hearing of the complaint, the newspaper immediately removed the image from its website. Ipso said the injured girl had, in the circumstances, a reasonable expectation of privacy. Photographing her breached clause 2 of the Code and publication of the photo, which had risked notifying friends and relatives of the accident, breached clause 4 (intrusion into shock) and clause 6 (children) because it was done without parental consent.

The *Telegraph* suggested that the accident was of public interest, because of previously expressed concerns about the area's road safety. But Ipso said the *Telegraph* had not explained how publishing the photo contributed to that public interest and that no 'exceptional' public interest—it had to be exceptional because children were involved—appeared to exist (*A woman v Derby Telegraph*, adjudication issued 13 February 2015).

 clauses 4 and 6 are explained later in this chapter

Publishing a photo showing identifiably an adult victim at an accident scene is also likely to be deemed a breach of the Code's clause 2, unless consent is obtained. But pixelating the victim's face will help ensure there is no breach.

on 'exceptional', see 4.13, Protecting children's welfare and privacy

Practice 8.16 of the Broadcasting Code says: 'Broadcasters should not take or broadcast footage or audio of people caught up in emergencies, victims of accidents or those suffering a personal tragedy, even in a public place, where that results in an infringement of privacy, unless it is warranted or the people concerned have given consent.'

✳ Remember

Both Ipso and Ofcom will allow exceptions to their normal privacy rules in respect of coverage of major incidents such as terrorist bombings because of the very strong public interest in showing what has happened, including the distress in people's face and that they were injured, even if they have not consented to being photographed or filmed.

See the Additional Material for ch. 4 on www.mcnaes.com, 'Coverage of major incidents'.

4.9 Prohibitions on intrusion into grief or shock

Clause 4 (Intrusion into grief or shock) of the Editors' Code says:

see also 4.17,
Material
from social
media sites,
on needing
to be
sensitive

 In cases involving personal grief or shock, enquiries and approaches must be made with sympathy and discretion and publication handled sensitively. These provisions should not restrict the right to report legal proceedings. 🙶🙶

Ipso guidance issued in 2017 on reporting deaths and inquests says coverage of violent or accidental deaths should not contain graphic information likely to add to the distress of the bereaved.

📖 See Useful Websites at the end of this chapter for this guidance. Ch. 17 covers inquests.

Broadcast of images or descriptions in such coverage could, depending on the context, breach the Broadcasting Code's prohibitions on harm and offence explained in 3.4.5.

The Ipso guidance warns that clause 4 is breached if a media organisation breaks news of a death to the deceased's family either directly by a journalist seeking comment or by publishing some detail about the death. This could happen, for example, if a photo of a fatal road accident scene shows a vehicle's registration number, or some other unique characteristic. The same principle applies to incidents in which someone is or could be badly hurt, because for relatives to hear or realise this from media coverage would be intrusion into shock (a point Ipso made in its ruling in the *Derby Telegraph* case, cited earlier, in which a published photo identified the accident victim). The 'public interest exceptions' in the Editors' Code do not apply to clause 4 and so cannot justify such intrusion.

Practice 8.18 of the Broadcasting Code says broadcasters should take care not to reveal the identity of a person who has died, or of victims of accidents or violent crimes, unless and until it is clear that the next of kin have been informed or unless it is warranted.

4.9.1 Funerals and the bereaved

Ofcom guidance says that at funerals, programme-makers should respect requests to withdraw. Ipso guidance is that the wishes of the family should be taken into account, where they are known or can reasonably be inferred. It notes a funeral procession may happen in public view but says that care should be taken with photographs of people in states of extreme distress.

The Broadcasting Code, section 8, warns broadcasters that the bereaved may need special consideration as a 'vulnerable person' who may not be able to give informed consent to be featured in a programme.

See the Additional Material for ch. 4 on www.mcnaes.com for what the Broadcasting Code says about programmes covering traumatic past events.

see too 4.14, Vulnerable people

4.10 Privacy in hospital and institutions

Clause 8 of the Editors' Code says journalists must identify themselves and obtain permission from a responsible executive of hospitals or similar institutions before entering non-public areas to pursue inquiries. This reflects that all patients have a reasonable expectation of privacy during their treatment, and that a patient may not be well enough to make the best decision if approached for an interview. The Code allows this clause to be overridden if there is a sufficient public interest for a journalist to go into a non-public area—see the Additional Material case studies. The Impress Code guidance says people in hospitals, private clinics and residential homes may reasonably expect a high level of privacy, and that journalists should 'take great care' when conducting any inquiries there, but that these can be justified in the public interest.

The Broadcasting Code practice 8.8 says: 'When filming or recording in institutions, organisations or other agencies, permission should be obtained from the relevant authority or management, unless it is warranted to film or record without permission. Individual consent of employees or others whose appearance is incidental or where they are essentially anonymous members of the general public will not normally be required. However, in potentially sensitive places such as ambulances, hospitals, schools, prisons or police stations, separate consent should normally be obtained before filming or recording and for broadcast from those in sensitive situations (unless not obtaining consent is warranted). If the individual will not be identifiable in the programme then separate consent for broadcast will not be required.'

By 'separate consent', the Broadcasting Code means there needs to be a two-stage consent—for example, consent must normally be obtained before filming/recording begins, and then further consent must be obtained from those individuals for the broadcasting of footage or audio which identifies them. Broadcasters may need to ask the people filmed or recorded to sign consent forms so that, should there be a complaint, there is proof of consent.

4.11 Health information

Information about anyone's health, such as a serious illness or condition, is normally private, unless the individual chooses to disclose it. If details leak out, publishing them would almost certainly breach each code's provision about privacy, unless a strong public interest justification applied, such as—the Editors' Codebook suggests—demonstrating poor health was affecting a senior politician's performance. The Codebook warns that early speculation about whether a woman is pregnant, or accurately reporting a pregnancy before the normal 12-week ultra-sound scan confirms it, can be intrusive.

> The Codebook is introduced in 2.4, The scope of the Editors' Code, and see Useful Websites at the end of this chapter. See too the *Soames v The Sunday Times* case study in the Additional Material for ch. 4. Publication of medical or therapy details without the individual's consent could breach data protection law or lead to a privacy lawsuit, see 26.2, 27.6.1 and 28.5.2.

4.12 Relationships, correspondence, communications

Ipso, Impress and Ofcom are likely to adjudicate that publishing intimate details of a person's sex life breaches the relevant code, unless the person aired them or there is a public interest justification, when the 'proportionality' principle could still mean little detail should be published.

see 4.1.1, Proportion-ality. See 27.6.3 for privacy law on relationships

In 2016 Ipso rejected a complaint from a woman that a newspaper's publication of details from a 'swingers' website—including her 'profile' photo—revealed to family members that she was a swinger. Anyone with an email address could access on the site details—'which most people would consider to be highly private'—she had disclosed about herself, so she had no reasonable expectation of privacy in respect of them, Ipso said (*Pearce v Daily Star Sunday*, 19 September 2016).

Clause 2 of the Editors' Code seeks to protect the privacy of correspondence and digital communications.

👁 Case study:

In 2017 Ipso ruled that the *Daily Star Sunday* breached clause 2 by publishing the content of phone texts a woman alleged were sent to her by an 'England ace' celebrity (apparently the woman revealed the private texts to the newspaper—they were not 'hacked'). But Ipso ruled that the paper's coverage of her account of the alleged relationship—in which she said where they kissed, when they first had sex and that he misled her by not telling her he was still in another relationship—did not otherwise breach clause 2. Ipso said the detail given was 'limited' and she had a right to freedom of expression to tell her story (*A man v Daily Star Sunday*, 21 June 2017).

---

see 2.4.4.2, Recording interviews and phone calls

Clause 10 of the Editors' Code bans the 'interception' of phone calls. That clause too is covered by the Code's public interest exceptions. But a journalist who hacks phone and emails risks being prosecuted for a criminal offence, as the Editors' Codebook and Impress Code guidance warn.

Ch. 35 outlines the 'phone-hacking' scandal in which people's private voicemail messages were illegally accessed ('intercepted') by or on behalf of journalists seeking stories. But recording your own phone calls is not 'hacking'.

4.13 Protecting children's welfare and privacy

The Editors' Code, clause 6 (Children), says:

" i) All pupils should be free to complete their time at school without unnecessary intrusion.

ii) They must not be approached or photographed at school without permission of the school authorities.

iii) Children under 16 must not be interviewed or photographed on issues involving their own or another child's welfare unless a custodial parent or similarly responsible adult consents.

iv) Children under 16 must not be paid for material involving their welfare, nor parents or guardians for material about their children or wards, unless it is clearly in the child's interest.

v) Editors must not use the fame, notoriety or position of a parent or guardian as sole justification for publishing details of a child's private life. "

By 'custodial' the clause means, if parents have split, the parent with whom the child usually lives (this is what this chapter means by 'parent'). Clause 6 means that the school's permission is normally needed for a journalist to approach, photograph or film a pupil of any age on school premises.

The clause is subject to the Code's public interest exceptions. But the Code warns: 'An exceptional public interest would need to be demonstrated to override the normally paramount interests of a child under 16'.

👁 Case study

In 2007 the Press Complaints Commission ruled that a Scottish newspaper breached clause 6 because of the way it published on its website mobile phone footage shot by a 16-year-old girl showing disruptive behaviour by classmates. The PCC accepted it was in the public interest to use the footage to show the behaviour, because the girl said lax discipline in the class contributed to her poor exam results. But the PCC criticised the paper for failing to change the images to conceal the children's identities (*Gaddis v Hamilton Advertiser*, 30 July 2007).

Ipso has warned that clause 6 i) might be breached if what is published about a child has an adverse effect on the child's time at school, even if the subject matter is not about the school.

The Editors' Code *may* not be breached by a photo or footage which has a focus on a child in public place, but the definition of 'welfare' in clause 6 is wide. Ipso and PCC adjudications make clear that publishing images in which children are identifiable concerns their welfare if they are shown in a way or circumstance which may cause them distress, embarrassment, humiliation or have another adverse effect on them, and that in such circumstances a parent's or legal guardian's consent is normally needed to obtain the image and to publish it.

Case study

The PCC in 2001 upheld a complaint by author J. K. Rowling that *OK!* magazine breached clauses 2 and 6 by using 'long lens' photos of her eight-year-old daughter on a public beach wearing a swimsuit. The PCC said she was vulnerable to comments from her peers and that J.K. Rowling's solicitors had stated the girl was embarrassed by attention as a result of the photographs.

 See *Derby Telegraph* case, 4.8, Accidents and major incidents, for another example of breach of clause 6.

Some celebrities ask Ipso to record that they do not want their children's faces shown in media coverage. The Editors' Codebook says the responsibility is for editors to determine the position in any particular case.

Under clause 6, a parent or guardian's consent is needed before interviewing any child about a matter which concerns his or her welfare—for example, health or family life—as the child might say something he or she could regret after publication. The interview itself could distress the child. Asking a child questions by email or via social media would be an interview. Ipso warned in 2017 that the term 'interview' includes a media organisation's publication of a statement a child under 16 has posted online, even if it has not contacted the child. So parental consent may be needed before reporting or reproducing an online post, even though the child has already published it.

Impress Code clause 3.1 has provision to protect children's welfare, including about when they can be photographed. Its guidance says a family may have a reasonable expectation of privacy in a public place, for example when on a shopping expedition.

For privacy law, see *Weller* case, 27.7, Children's own privacy rights.

The Broadcasting Code has protection for children's welfare in section 8, on privacy. This too is subject to public interest exceptions. Practice 8.20 says: 'Broadcasters should pay particular attention to the privacy of people under 16. They do not lose their rights to privacy because, for example, of the fame or notoriety of their parents or because of events in their schools.'

Practice 8.21 says:

> Where a programme features an individual under 16 or a vulnerable person in a way that infringes privacy, consent must be obtained from:
>
> - a parent, guardian or other person of eighteen or over in loco parentis; and
> - wherever possible, the individual concerned;
> - unless the subject matter is trivial or uncontroversial and the participation minor, or it is warranted to proceed without consent.

This Code, like the Editors' Code, states that normally broadcasters must get a school's permission before filming pupils—see practice 8.8, cited earlier in 4.10, Privacy in hospitals and institutions. The Broadcasting Code's section 3 also has general protection for under-18s involved in programmes, covered in 3.4.4 and 3.4.13.1.

4.13.1 Children in crowds and at public occasions

Publishing innocuous photos or footage of crowds does not normally intrude into the lives of children shown in them at random. A regulator will probably accept a parent's consent for a child being a spectator or participator at an event which is likely to be photographed or televised by the media as implied consent for the child to appear in coverage. A code could be breached if there is a particular focus on a child and it could be foreseen that publishing the image could affect his/her welfare. For example, the Impress Code clause 3.1 does not apply to use of images of children in 'general scenes'—such as street fairs or protests—unless there is a 'detriment' to their well-being or safety.

 The Additional Material for ch. 4 on www.mcnaes.com has other case studies of adjudications concerning children, including about two brothers filmed in a mosque's youthclub and a boy filmed in a football crowd.

4.14 Vulnerable people

The Broadcasting Code's practice 8.21, cited earlier, gives a 'vulnerable person' the same protection as a child under 16. It says those vulnerable may include those (over 16) with learning difficulties, mental health problems, the bereaved, the traumatised and the sick.

4.15 Relatives and friends of those accused or convicted of crime

Clause 9 i) of the Editors' Code says: 'Relatives or friends of persons convicted or accused of crime should not generally be identified without their consent, unless they are genuinely relevant to the story.'

Ipso has ruled that a defendant's children, if mentioned in court proceedings, are 'genuinely relevant' and that a person who attends court in support of a defendant is too—see the Additional Material for ch. 4 for cases.

 see also 5.15, Juveniles under investigation on other parts of clause 9

4.16 User-generated content

Pictures and footage supplied by readers and viewers, including from mobile phones, often feature in media coverage, particularly of major events such as the aftermath of terrorist atrocities. Journalists handling this 'user-generated content' (UGC) should realise it might breach the privacy of those depicted, or intrude into grief or shock.

Also, some UGC pictures published have turned out to be faked or supplied in breach of someone else's **copyright**.

→ glossary

4.17 Material from social media sites

ch. 29 explains copyright

Journalists routinely search social media sites, including Facebook, Flickr, Tumblr, Instagram and Twitter, for pictures or footage of people in the news, or for news. Publishing this material may breach copyright.

Publishing it might also be an intrusion into privacy, particularly if the person portrayed did not know he/she was being photographed or filmed, or did not know that the material was on the social media site. If there is a complaint, Ipso will decide if the person had a reasonable expectation of privacy in relation to the material. For example, who uploaded it to the internet? Was the material hidden behind privacy settings on the social media site? If it was, Ipso will ask how the media organisation obtained it. Ipso will consider too if it showed information intrinsically private, such as medical information or private activities.

see Useful Websites at the end of this chapter for this Ipso guidance

In guidance issued in 2017 on use of social media material, Ipso suggested that journalists should take screenshots of the material to be published, showing the dates and any privacy settings, if possible; keep contemporaneous notes of any discussion around the public interest in publishing information, where relevant; and pixelate or remove any individuals who might feature in the photo to be published but are not relevant to the story. The notes would be needed for the 'audit trails'. The Impress Code guidance also says privacy settings should be respected unless a public interest exception applies.

audit trails are explained in 2.4.1

 Case study

In 2017 a woman complained that a *Mail Online* article about controversy in which she was involved had featured, without her consent, a photo of her in a Hallowe'en costume. Ipso said clause 2 of the Editors' Code was not breached because the photo was not private information. It noted that before the complained-of article appeared the woman had placed the photo in the public domain by posting it on her Twitter account, which had some 36,000 followers, so she did not have 'a reasonable expectation of privacy' in respect of the photo (*Bryan v Mail Online*, 5 October 2017).

In some circumstances, even if the person in the image is the one who placed it in the public domain, journalists must consider if it is ethical to use it in the context of a news story projected to a different, and probably much bigger, audience. For example, the grieving family of a teenager who has died might be even more distressed if media reports include a social website picture showing the youngster apparently drunk on a social occasion, which Ipso might consider to be an insensitive use of the photo—a breach of clause 4 of the Editors' Code.

Ipso's position is that publishing an innocuous image, obtained from a publicly accessible page on a social media website, of someone who died in a shocking event or who is a crime victim does not breach the Code provided that the manner of publication is sensitive to people's grief or shock—for example, see *Cross v Airdrie and Coatbridge Advertiser*, 12 February 2015.

 see 4.9, Prohibitions on intrusion into grief or shock, for clause 4

Ipso has also ruled that the Editors' Code is not normally breached by a media organisation quoting comments or messages—such as tributes to someone who has died—which people make on publicly accessible pages of social media sites (*Hodder v Dorset Echo*, 16 April 2015) but see 4.13 on quoting postings by children.

> For further case studies about media publication of social media or user-generated content, see the Additional Material for ch. 4 on www.mcnaes.com.

➡ Recap of major points

- Media regulators and civil courts use the criterion of 'a reasonable expectation of privacy' when deciding if the media have intruded into person's private life.

- Intrusion into privacy can be ethical and lawful if there is a public interest justification.

- The regulators' codes require journalists to have parental consent for photographing, filming or recording a child if his/her welfare or privacy is involved.

- Journalists should not intrude into shock or grief—for example, when publishing images of accident scenes, photographing funerals or publishing photos from social media sites.

- Journalists must take care when deciding whether to publish pictures or footage supplied by the public or copied from social media sites, as publication may breach privacy or copyright.

((•)) Useful Websites

www.ipso.co.uk/editors-code-of-practice/
   Editors' Code of Practice

www.editorscode.org.uk/
   Editors' Codebook

www.ipso.co.uk
  Independent Press Standards Organisation (Ipso)

**www.ipso.co.uk/press-standards/guidance-for-journalists-and-editors/
deaths-and-inquests-guidance/**
  Ipso guidance on deaths and inquests

www.ipso.co.uk/harassment/
  Information about Ipso's 'harassment' phone line for people to ask for its help

www.ipso.co.uk/press-standards/guidance-for-journalists-and-editors/social-media-guidance/
  Ipso guidance on use of social media material

https://impress.press/standards/impress-standards-code.html
  Impress Standards Code and guidance

http://stakeholders.ofcom.org.uk/broadcasting/broadcast-codes/broadcast-code/
  Ofcom Broadcasting Code

**www.ofcom.org.uk/tv-radio-and-on-demand/information-for-industry/guidance/
programme-guidance**
  Ofcom's guidance on the Code

www.bbc.co.uk/editorialguidelines/guidelines/privacy
  BBC Editorial Guidelines on filming in public places, sensitive places and private
  property and use of social media material

www.bbc.co.uk/editorialguidelines/guidance/social-media-pictures
  BBC editorial guidance on use of social media pictures

www.bbc.co.uk/editorialguidelines/guidelines/children-young-people/impact-of-contribution
  BBC Editorial Guidelines on children as contributors

Part 2

Crime, courts and tribunals

Crime—media coverage prior to any court case

Chapter summary

This chapter explains how police investigations are driven by the standard of proof needed to convict someone of a crime. Reporters should understand police powers to arrest and detain. There is a strong public interest in media reporting of crime and police investigations, but journalists must be wary of contempt of court law, made 'active' when a suspect is arrested and in other circumstances. There may be libel risks in identifying suspects before they are charged.

5.1 Standard of proof in criminal law

Those accused of crime enjoy 'the presumption of innocence'. This legal principle means that those charged with crimes are not required to prove themselves innocent—the prosecution has to prove guilt 'beyond reasonable doubt', the standard of proof required for a conviction. Police and other agencies which investigate crime need clear evidence to meet this standard.

5.2 Arrests

Under the Police and Criminal Evidence Act 1984 a police officer can arrest a person who has committed, is committing or is about to commit an offence (however minor), or anyone of whom there are reasonable grounds for suspicion. But the officer must have reasonable grounds for believing the arrest is necessary to achieve one of the purposes specified in the Act—for example, to allow 'prompt and effective investigation' of a crime, or to stop a person from obstructing the highway. Police may use 'reasonable force' to make an arrest. An arrest automatically makes the case 'active' under the Contempt of Court Act 1981, limiting what can be published about it.

✳ Remember

The 1981 Act, explained in ch. 19, safeguards the fairness of trials. That chapter explains what types of material, if published about an active case, can amount to a contempt, for which a media organisation can be heavily fined.

5.3 Police questioning of suspects

An arrested person is usually taken to a police station. A suspect who goes to a police station voluntarily may be arrested there. Police sometimes tell the media that someone is 'helping with inquiries'.

- Journalists should check whether the suspect is helping police voluntarily or is under arrest, as newsrooms need to know if the case is 'active'. If it is 'active', contempt law affects what can be published.

5.3.1 Limits to detention by police, prior to any charge

The law says no one should normally be held under arrest for more than 24 hours—they must be released if they have not been charged within that period. The time limit runs from the time of arrest or from when the suspect arrived at the police station, depending on circumstances. A police superintendent can authorise a further 12 hours' detention of someone suspected of an **indictable offence**. Police can then ask a magistrates' court to authorise the person's detention for another 36 hours. If a further application is made, the court cannot extend this detention beyond a maximum total of 96 hours. But people suspected of terrorism can be detained for 14 days without charge.

→ glossary

5.3.2 False imprisonment

An arrested person who later sues the police for damages, alleging unlawful arrest or 'false imprisonment', must prove that the police grounds for detaining him/her were unreasonable.

 Ch. 36 explains that photo-journalists covering tense incidents may be threatened with arrest.

 The Additional Material for ch. 5 on www.mcnaes.com explains the *habeas corpus* procedure in which police and official agencies can be required to justify to the High Court why a person is being detained.

5.4 The Crown Prosecution Service

Most prosecutions are the responsibility of the Crown Prosecution Service (CPS), a Government department, with bases serving each of the 43 police areas in England and Wales. The head of the CPS is the Director of Public Prosecutions.

(((•))) See Useful Websites at the end of this chapter for the CPS site.

The CPS is independent of police, but has a duty to advise and direct them in investigations, except into the most minor crimes. It decides, in all major cases involving police investigation, whether a suspect should be prosecuted, and if so, on what charge(s).

- A charge is a formal accusation, giving the alleged offender basic details of the alleged crime, including, for example, the date, place, details of property allegedly stolen, its value and the owner's name, and, for a violence offence, the name of the alleged victim. It means the case will be prosecuted and go to court.

Usually a suspect is charged at a police station. He/she should be given the charge in written form, but may already have been charged orally, before the document was ready. A charge makes a case 'active' under the Contempt of Court Act 1981 if it is not active already because of an arrest.

The case ceases to be 'active' if an arrested person is released without charge, unless he/she is released on **police bail** because officers want more time to complete investigations. A suspect on police bail must return to a police station on a specified date, when he/she may be charged or released without charge.

 → glossary

The duration of police bail is limited initially to 28 days, but a police superintendent can authorise it to be extended for a further three months if no decision has been taken on whether the suspect should be charged. Any further extension has to be approved by magistrates. Police should tell the media whether a suspect who has not been charged remains on police bail, because journalists need to know—to comply with contempt law—if the case is 'active'.

> For more context, see 19.4.3, When do criminal proceedings cease to be active? and 5.12, Police guidelines on naming of suspects and victims.

5.4.1 Decisions on whether to prosecute

When considering if a suspect should be prosecuted, CPS lawyers assess whether there is 'a realistic prospect of conviction'. If the case passes that test, they consider if it is in the public interest to prosecute. In almost all serious cases, consideration of the public interest leads to a decision to prosecute.

5.5 Limits to detention by police, after any charge

Once someone is charged police must stop questioning him/her, except in limited circumstances. The person, if under arrest, must by law be taken before a magistrates' court on the day he/she is charged or on the following day, except Sundays, Christmas Day or Good Friday. Alternatively, after being charged the person may be released on police bail to attend court.

In all major cases lawyers employed by the CPS conduct the prosecution in court, although police have power to prosecute in some cases.

5.6 Other prosecution agencies in the public sector

Various other governmental agencies investigate and prosecute offences—for example, local authorities may investigate and prosecute landlords for breach of tenants' rights, and the Serious Fraud Office, a Government department, investigates and prosecutes serious and complex fraud.

> ((•)) The www.mcnaes.com chapter on Scotland provides an outline of its prosecution system.

5.7 Laying or presenting of information; summonses; service of written charge

The decision whether to prosecute may be taken quickly—for example, soon after an arrest. But it might not be taken for months if time is needed to gather evidence. A prosecution can begin with a charge. It can also begin by 'laying' or 'presenting'—either term is used—'information' before a magistrate. In this procedure an allegation that a crime has been committed is made orally or in writing to a magistrate who will, without at that stage full consideration of evidence, issue a summons to be served on the alleged perpetrator.

- A summons is a formal document, issued by a magistrates' court, setting out one or more crime allegations in similar detail to a charge. It requires attendance at court on a specified date to respond to the allegation(s).

The issue of a summons makes the case active under the Contempt of Court Act 1981, as ch. 19 explains.

For public prosecutors—including the CPS—laying or presenting 'information' has been replaced with a streamlined procedure called 'written charge and requisition' in which the prosecuting agency serves (usually by post) such documents on the accused. The requisition is formal notification of the date he/she must appear at the magistrates' court. Summonses and requisitions are used routinely for minor offences if these cannot be resolved by a 'fixed penalty'. The 'single justice procedure' (SJP) involves service of 'written charge and notice'. Any type of service of a written charge makes a case 'active' under the 1981 Act.

for context, see 7.7 on 'fixed penalty' and 7.8 on SJP

5.8 Arrest warrants

Magistrates can issue an arrest warrant if sworn, written information is laid before them that a person has committed an indictable offence, or any **summary offence** punishable by imprisonment, or in relation to any offence if the suspect's address is not sufficiently established for a requisition or summons to be served.

→ glossary

for offence categories see 6.1

- An arrest warrant is a formal document in which a magistrate empowers any police officer to arrest a suspect, wherever he/she is in England or Wales, to be taken to the magistrates' court.

It can be used for a suspect 'on the run'. The terms of an arrest warrant may allow for a person to be released on bail, after being arrested and completing formalities at a police station, to appear at the magistrates' court at a future date.

The issue of an arrest warrant makes the case 'active' under the 1981 Act if it has not already become active because of the issue of a summons or service of a written charge. A UK arrest warrant is needed for police to get a European Arrest Warrant for the extradition to the UK of a suspect who has fled to another EU state.

5.9 'Private prosecutions'

Any citizen can, by laying information before a magistrate, start a prosecution, seeking to prove that an accused individual has committed a specified crime. The police and the CPS may have been aware of the allegation but concluded there was no or insufficient evidence. The capacity for any citizen to start a 'private prosecution' is seen as a fundamental right to counter-balance any inertia or partiality by police or other official agencies. But a magistrate can refuse to issue a summons if the allegation is deemed frivolous. A private prosecution may quickly become unsustainable because, for example, an individual citizen lacks the investigatory powers of the police. The CPS can take over a 'private prosecution', and withdraw the case, and the Attorney General can also stop private prosecutions.

 the Attorney General's role is explained in 1.6

The Royal Society for the Prevention of Cruelty to Animals regularly conducts private prosecutions for cruelty to or neglect of animals.

5.10 The risk of libel in media identification of crime suspects

The media may discover that someone is being investigated by police or another agency—for example, that the person is under arrest. A media report which includes the suspect's name, or other detail identifying him/her in this context, may allow that individual successfully to sue the publisher for libel if the investigation does not lead to a prosecution. Publishing a statement that someone is under investigation, even when this is factually correct, may be defamatory because it creates an inference that he/she is guilty.

 chs. 20 and 21 explain defamation dangers

👁 Case study

In 2011 Bristol landlord Chris Jefferies won 'very substantial' settlements in libel actions against eight national newspapers for articles published after one of his tenants, landscape architect Joanna Yeates, was found dead. Police arrested Mr Jefferies at one stage, but later released him. The newspapers published defamatory material about him. But then another man was charged with murdering Joanna and subsequently convicted. Louis Charalambous, Mr Jefferies' solicitor, said of the libellous coverage: 'Christopher Jefferies is the latest victim of the regular witch hunts and character assassination conducted by the worst elements of the British tabloid media' (*Media Lawyer*, 29 July 2011).

As 19.6.2 explains, what was published about Mr Jefferies also led to two newspapers being convicted of contempt of court.

The media can safely publish the name of a person under investigation or arrest if the name is officially supplied by a spokesperson for a governmental agency—for example, the police, CPS or a local council—because the report will be protected by the defamation defence of qualified privilege, as 22.7.2.5 explains.

In reality, media organisations reporting high-profile investigations, especially if a celebrity or public figure is a suspect, may choose—because of the fierce competition to break news—to publish the suspect's name before it is known if he/she will be charged and without any qualified privilege. They might decide that the person is unlikely to sue for libel because, for example, a celebrity or politician may not wish to alienate the media or stir up more publicity. Or the media might take the risk of naming the person because police leaks indicate that a charge is sure to follow. If the person is charged, a libel action over pre-charge publicity becomes less likely as any damage it caused to the person's reputation will usually be outweighed by, or indistinguishable from, damage caused by reports of the consequent court case, which—as ch. 22 shows—the media can safely publish.

5.11 Privacy law

Wealthy people and celebrities who have been arrested, or questioned by police, or who are under investigation, may try to persuade the High Court to issue injunctions to prevent the media reporting the facts, arguing that any coverage would be an infringement of their rights to respect for privacy and family life under Article 8 of the European Convention on Human Rights. Financial news and information service Bloomberg defeated one businessman's attempt to make it take down a story about a law enforcement agency's investigation into his company and its activities (*ZXC v Bloomberg LP* [2017] EWHC 328 (QB)). But in *ERY v Associated Newspapers Ltd* ([2016] EWHC 2760 (QB)) Mr Justice Nicol granted a prominent and wealthy businessman—who was questioned under caution in a police investigation—an injunction banning the *Mail on Sunday* from reporting the fact that he had been quizzed. The judge ruled that ERY had a reasonable expectation of privacy which was likely to trump the media's Article 10 rights to freedom of expression.

 for context, see 1.3.2, Convention rights. Ch. 27 explains privacy law

5.12 Police guidelines on naming of suspects and victims

The College of Policing, which sets standards for police forces, says that:

- police should not tell the media the name of a suspect unless naming him/her is justified by 'a policing purpose' such as avoiding a threat to life, preventing or detecting crime, or warning the public about a 'wanted' person.

- police can release an arrested person's age and gender, what the alleged offence is and a general location of the arrest; and say whether he or she is in custody, released on police bail (and if so to which date), or without bail or with no further action being taken.

The College says that, unless legal restrictions apply, after an adult is charged or summoned his/her name, date of birth, address, details of the charge(s) and date of court appearance should normally be released, with his/her occupation if relevant to the alleged crime.

The guidance says a crime victim's name will not normally be released unless he/she consents and no reporting restriction applies.

It also says that the identities of people dealt with by cautions, speeding fines and other fixed penalties—out-of-court disposals—should not be released.

5.13 Automatic anonymity for victims of some crimes

It is illegal to identify a victim or alleged victim of a sexual offence, an offence of trafficking for human exploitation or of female genital mutilation. This lifelong automatic anonymity is explained in ch. 11.

5.14 Teachers given anonymity

Section 13 of the Education Act 2011 gives automatic lifelong anonymity to teachers in respect of any allegation that they have or may have committed an offence against a pupil at their school.

The ban makes it illegal to publish anything likely to lead members of the public to identify the teacher as being the subject of the allegation.

Section 13 makes it unlawful, for example, to identify a teacher accused of assaulting or sexually abusing a child at his or her school if that teacher has not been charged with a criminal offence—even if the accusation is referred to in public, for example at an employment tribunal hearing at which the teacher claims unfair dismissal.

But the anonymity ends if the teacher is charged with an offence or a court agrees to an application that it should be lifted in the interests of justice. It also ends if the Education Secretary publishes information about the individual in connection with an investigation or decision relating to the allegation, or if the General Teaching Council for Wales publishes information about the individual in connection with an investigation, hearing or decision on the allegation.

This law was created because teachers complained that they were vulnerable to false allegations. A teacher may waive his/her anonymity, by giving written consent—for example, to a media organisation—to being identified. The consent is not valid if it is proved that it was obtained by unreasonable interference with his/her peace or comfort. The anonymity also ends if the teacher himself/herself publishes information about the allegation—for example, on a social media page.

see also 28.4.1, Getting information from police, on data law and victims

see Useful Websites at the end of this chapter for the College guidance

→ glossary

ch. 18 covers tribunals

Publication of anything which breaches the anonymity is punishable by an unlimited fine. Those liable to be prosecuted are the same as for breach of the anonymity provision for victims of sexual offence victims—see, Liability for breach of the anonymity provision. It is a defence for anyone accused of publishing such information to show that at the time he or she was not aware, and did not suspect or have reason to suspect, that the publication included the information in question, or that the allegation had been made.

5.15 Juveniles under investigation

Codes used by regulators are relevant to media coverage of police investigations, because they provide safeguards against publicity for juveniles who are victims, witnesses and defendants at a stage before automatic anonymity begins for them when a charged juvenile appears at a youth court, or before a magistrates' or Crown court can decide whether to make an order granting anonymity. That anonymity law is explained in ch. 10. As already mentioned, juvenile (and adult) victims of some types of crime have automatic anonymity from the time an allegation is made.

Part of clause 9 (Reporting of crime) of the Editors' Code says: 'Particular regard should be paid to the potentially vulnerable position of children under the age of 18 who witness, or are victims of, crime. This should not restrict the right to report legal proceedings.'

The clause also says: 'Editors should generally avoid naming children under the age of 18 after arrest for a criminal offence but before they appear in a youth court unless they can show that the individual's name is already in the public domain, or that the individual (or, if they are under 16, a custodial parent or similarly responsible adult) has given their consent. This does not restrict the right to name juveniles who appear in a Crown court, or whose anonymity is lifted.'

Clause 9 is subject to the Code's public interest exceptions. Ch. 2 introduces the Code and the exceptions. Another part of clause 9 relevant to the ethics of who should be identified in crime reporting is covered in 4.15, Relatives and friends of those accused or convicted of crime.

The Broadcasting Code, which is introduced in ch. 3, says in rule 1.9: 'When covering any pre-trial investigation into an alleged criminal offence in the UK, broadcasters should pay particular regard to the potentially vulnerable position of any person who is not yet adult who is involved as a witness or victim, before broadcasting their name, address, identity of school or other educational establishment, place of work, or any still or moving picture of them. Particular justification is also required for the broadcast of such material relating to the identity of any person who is not yet adult who is involved in the defence as a defendant or potential defendant'.

((•)) See the Additional Material for ch. 5 on www.mcnaes.com for law banning the disclosure of identities of police informants, including 'investigation anonymity orders', and for legal and ethical considerations when journalists accompany police 'raids' to arrest or search.

➡ Recap of major points

- Covering crime stories presents contempt of court dangers for the media, because an arrest, an oral charge, service of a written charge, or the issue of a summons or an arrest warrant makes a case 'active' under the Contempt of Court Act 1981.

- There could be libel risks if a suggestion is published, prior to any charge, that a suspect may be guilty of a crime if what is published identifies the suspect.

- Teachers accused of an offence against a pupil have anonymity in law unless they are charged.

- Police should normally release the name of a person charged.

- Codes used by media regulators have provision to protect juveniles from publicity if they are involved in a police investigation into crime.

((•)) Useful Websites

www.cps.gov.uk/
Crown Prosecution Service

www.cps.gov.uk/about/principles.html
Code for Crown Prosecutors

www.app.college.police.uk/app-content/engagement-and-communication/media-relations/
College of Policing guidance

6

Crimes—categories and definitions

Chapter summary

All criminal cases begin in magistrates' courts. The most serious, such as murder, rape or robbery, progress to a Crown court. Journalists must know the different categories of crimes to understand when reporting restrictions affect what can be published in court stories, and the legal definitions of some crimes to avoid libel problems when referring to offences.

6.1 Categories of criminal offences

Criminal charges are grouped into three categories: indictable-only, either-way and summary.

→ glossary

(1) Indictable-only offences are the most serious crimes, punishable by the longest prison terms—for example, murder, rape, **robbery**. Such cases are processed initially by a magistrates' court, but cannot be dealt with there. The maximum jail sentence which magistrates can impose (six months) would be too lenient for a defendant convicted of a serious offence. So indictable-only cases progress quickly to a Crown court, as explained in ch. 8. If the defendant admits the charge there, or a jury finds him/her guilty, the judge passes sentence. The term 'indictable-only' derives from 'the indictment', the document used at a Crown court to record the charge(s).

→ glossary

→ glossary

(2) Either-way offences include **theft**, sexual assault and assault causing grievous bodily harm. These charges can be dealt with either at a Crown court or by magistrates, hence the term 'either-way'. For this category, magistrates may—after hearing an outline of a case—decide that it is so serious that only a Crown court can deal with it. As ch. 8 explains, even if magistrates decide they can deal with the case, the defendant can exercise the right to choose trial by jury at Crown court. Either-way offences are regarded as being less serious than indictable-only offences, but nevertheless include distressing, harmful crimes.

ch. 9 explains Crown courts

(3) Summary offences are comparatively minor offences such as common assault, drunkenness and speeding offences. Summary charges are dealt with in magistrates' courts, except in some cases in which a defendant faces both summary and either-way or indictable-only charges arising from the same event, in which instance a Crown court may deal with all of them. People charged only with a summary offence have no right to a jury trial. 'Summary proceedings' means 'proceedings in a magistrates' court', with the term 'summary' indicating the relative speed of the process.

✳ Remember

Confusingly, indictable-only and either-way charges are sometimes referred to collectively as 'indictable' charges, because they both share the possibility of jury trial at Crown court. But, as stated earlier, magistrates can decide to deal with an either-way case in their summary proceedings—that is, as if it were a summary offence.

6.2 Defining criminality

There are two elements in most crimes:

- an act which is potentially criminal—which lawyers refer to as the *actus reus*; and
- a guilty mind—the *mens rea*, which means that the act was carried out, or planned or attempted, with guilty intention—that the perpetrator knew he/she was acting, or intending to act, unlawfully.

Generally, the prosecution must prove both elements. In the crime of murder, the *actus reus* is that of unlawfully killing someone, and the *mens rea* is that the act was done with intent to kill or cause grievous bodily harm. If there is no such intent, a killing may be a lesser crime—for example, manslaughter.

6.2.1 Strict liability

Some offences are of **strict liability**. Strict liability, when it applies in law, removes or limits the defences to the charge. Strict liability means that a motorist who exceeds the speed limit commits an offence even if he/she did not realise how fast he/she was driving. A motorist who drives with too much alcohol in his/her blood commits an offence even if he/she did not intend to breach the alcohol limit. Strict liability can be seen as a practical, societal solution to deter dangerous or anti-social conduct for which, in many cases, it would be impossible to prove that *mens rea*—a guilty mind—existed.

→ glossary

Journalists must understand this concept, not least because some criminal offences arising from publishing material are strict liability offences, meaning it is not a defence to say 'Sorry, I didn't intend to . . .'—for example, publishing material which breaches the Contempt of Court Act 1981.

see 19.4, Contempt of Court Act 1981—strict liability

6.3 Definitions of crimes

chs. 20 and
21 explain
defamation

A victim of theft may tell friends he/she has been 'robbed'. A journalist who makes this colloquial error when reporting a court case will seem foolish and—worse—the error could lead to a defamation action.

Reporting that a defendant who is guilty of a minor theft was guilty of robbery suggests to the public that he/she committed a much worse crime, as robbery—which involves violence or threatened violence—is generally regarded as worse than theft.

The crime definitions in the following list are simplified. For fuller definitions, see the Crown Prosecution Service's Prosecution Guidance section, listed at the end of this chapter under Useful Websites, or *Blackstone's Criminal Practice*.

6.3.1 Crimes against people

Murder The unlawful killing of a human being with the intention of killing or causing grievous bodily harm. An adult convicted of murder must be sentenced to life imprisonment. Indictable-only.

Manslaughter Killing by an unlawful act likely to cause bodily harm but without the intention to kill or cause grievous bodily harm. Manslaughter can be a charge in its own right. A jury in a murder trial might in some circumstances find the defendant not guilty of murder but convict him/her of manslaughter as an alternative. Indictable-only.

Corporate manslaughter An organisation such as a company, a police force or a Government department can be convicted of this offence if the way in which its activities were managed or organised caused someone's death and amounted to a gross breach of a duty of care the organisation owed to the deceased. Indictable-only.

Infanticide The killing of an infant under 12 months old by its mother, when her mind is disturbed as a result of the birth. Indictable-only.

Assault; common assault; battery; assault by beating The way these offences evolved in **case law** led their definitions to overlap. These charges are likely to be used in cases in which no, or only transient or trifling, bodily injury is allegedly caused. 'Assault' and 'common assault' can mean an unlawful infliction of force/violence, or a hostile act—for example, a threatening gesture—which puts another person in fear of immediate violence. Journalists should not assume that an assault charge necessarily alleges that a physical attack occurred. Either type of act must be proved as intentional or reckless. A push can be a common assault. Battery can also be expressed as a charge of 'assault by beating'. They are summary offences, unless the assault allegedly involved racial or religious motives, when they are either-way.

➔ glossary

Assault occasioning actual bodily harm (ABH) An assault—that is, a threat and/or attack, see earlier—which caused more than transient and trifling harm. The harm could be psychiatric illness. Either-way.

Wounding or inflicting grievous body harm (GBH) These charges are in section 20 of the Offences against the Person Act 1861. It must be proved that the defendant intended or foresaw causing some harm and—depending on which charge the prosecution sees as accurately describing the injury—that the harm caused was a wound or grievous (that is, serious) harm which was not, or not only, a wound. Either charge, in full form, includes the term 'malicious'—for example, 'malicious wounding'. A 'wound' is the slicing through or breaking of skin and can be a mere cut. But a wounding charge tends to be used only if the wound is serious. A GBH charge tends to be used, for example, if the harm includes broken bone, or led to substantial loss of blood and/or extended medical treatment and/or permanent disfigurement and/or permanent disability. These charges are either-way.

Wounding 'with intent'/inflicting grievous body harm 'with intent' Under section 18 of the 1861 Act, the wounding or GBH is deemed to have been 'with intent' if there is intent to cause GBH or to resist 'lawful apprehension'. Such a charge is indictable-only. It carries a maximum penalty of life imprisonment.

Rape Indictable-only. See definitions of sexual offences in ch. 11, which also explains that victims of these offences must have anonymity in media reports.

6.3.2 Crimes against property or involving gain

Theft Dishonest appropriation of property belonging to another with the intention of permanently depriving the other of it (Theft Act 1968). Either-way. The act of theft is stealing. Do not refer to this offence as robbery.

Robbery Theft by force (that is, violence), or by threat of force. Indictable-only.

Handling Dishonestly receiving goods, knowing or believing them to be stolen, or dishonestly helping in the retention, removal, disposal or sale of such goods. Either-way.

Burglary Entering a building as a trespasser and then

- stealing or attempting to steal from it; or
- inflicting or attempting to inflict grievous bodily harm to anyone in it; or
- making trespassing entry to a building with:
  - intent to steal; or
  - intent to inflict GBH; or
  - intent to do unlawful damage.

Generally, burglary is an either-way charge, but in some circumstances it is indictable-only.

Aggravated burglary Burglary while armed with a firearm, imitation firearm, or any other weapon or explosive. Indictable-only.

Fraud Under the Fraud Act 2006, there are now general offences of fraud, defined as conduct 'with a view to gain or with intent to cause loss or expose to a risk of loss' involving either:

- dishonestly making a false representation (for example, using a credit card dishonestly or using a false identity to open a bank account); or
- dishonestly failing to disclose information when under a legal duty to disclose (for example, failure when applying for health insurance to disclose a heart condition);
- dishonestly abusing a position (for example, an employee swindling money from his/her employer).

The Act also includes a fraud offence of obtaining services dishonestly. These statutory fraud offences are either-way, but if deemed to be of sufficient 'seriousness or complexity', they are treated procedurally as indictable-only (as explained in 8.3.1.1). Conspiracy to defraud is indictable-only.

Blackmail Making an unwarranted demand with menaces with a view to gain. This offence could be a threat to disclose embarrassing secrets or photos involving the victim unless money is paid, or another type of extortion such as a threat to contaminate goods on a supermarket company's shelves unless money is paid. Indictable-only.

Taking a vehicle without authority Sometimes referred to as 'taking without owner's consent' (TWOC). It can cover conduct known as 'twocking' or 'joy-riding' in which offenders abandon a car after using it. This offence does not involve an intention to deprive the owner permanently of the vehicle and so should not be described as theft. Summary.

Aggravated vehicle taking When a vehicle has been taken (as above) and someone is injured, or the vehicle or other property is damaged because of how it was driven. Either-way.

6.3.3 Motoring crimes

Driving under the influence of drink or drugs Driving a motor vehicle when the ability to do so is thus impaired. Summary.

Driving with excess alcohol When alcohol in the driver's body exceeds the prescribed limits—80 milligrammes of alcohol in 100 millilitres of blood; 35 microgrammes of alcohol in 100 millilitres of breath; or 107 milligrammes of alcohol in 100 millilitres of urine. Summary.

Causing death by careless driving when under the influence of drink or drugs The driver is unfit to drive as a result of drink or drugs, or has consumed excess alcohol or failed to provide a specimen. Indictable-only.

✳ Remember

It may not be fair or accurate (and therefore could be a libel problem) to describe a driver with more than the prescribed limit of alcohol as 'drunk'. He/she may only be marginally over the limit. It is safe to use the term 'drunk' if and as it is expressed in evidence or if—in the case of a convicted defendant—the evidence clearly supports this.

6.3.4 Other noteworthy crimes

Perjury Knowingly giving false evidence after taking an oath as a witness to tell the truth in court, or in an affidavit, or to a tribunal. Indictable-only.   →glossary

Perverting the course of justice Concealing evidence or giving false information to police. Indictable-only.

Wasting police time A lesser offence, committed by a person knowingly making a false report that a crime has been committed or falsely claiming to have information material to an investigation.

➡ Recap of major points

- There are three main categories of criminal offences:
  - indictable-only, which can only be dealt with by a Crown court;
  - either-way, dealt with by a Crown court or a magistrates' court—see ch. 8;
  - summary—almost all such cases are dealt with by magistrates.
- If an offence is of 'strict liability', the defendant can be convicted even if he/she had no clear 'intention' to do wrong.
- A media organisation which fails to report an offence or charge accurately might be successfully sued for libel by the defendant.

((•)) Useful Websites

www.cps.gov.uk/prosecution-guidance
   Crown Prosecution Service, 'Prosecution guidance'

7

Magistrates' courts— summary cases

Chapter summary

Magistrates' courts deal with about 95 per cent of all criminal cases and send the rest—the most serious—to Crown courts. Hearings in which magistrates try or sentence defendants are called 'summary proceedings'. Offences with which they deal include burglaries, sexual assault and dangerous driving. Magistrates can jail convicted defendants for up to six months for a single offence. This chapter also explains bail and details the automatic reporting restrictions on what the media can publish from pre-trial hearings at magistrates' courts.

7.1 Who are magistrates?

The role of magistrates originated in the twelfth century. They still use the ancient title of 'justice of the peace'. Most are volunteers and part-time—that is, lay magistrates. There are about 17,500 lay magistrates, who are trained and paid expenses. In 2018 there were around 160 magistrates' courts in England and Wales.

 → glossary

At least two lay magistrates must sit to try a criminal case. A trial in a magistrates' court is known as a **summary trial**, reflecting the fact that magistrates dispense quick and relatively informal justice whereas the higher courts, handling more serious and complex cases, have slower processes.

One magistrate is sufficient for some court duties. When a court hearing has more than one magistrate, one acts as chair and announces decisions. Magistrates are advised on law by a justices' clerk or one of his/her staff of legal advisers, who sits in front of the magistrate(s) in court.

> See the Additional Material for ch. 7 on www.mcnaes.com, 'More about magistrates'.

7.1.1 District judges

About 140 professional district judges, appointed after at least five years' experience as a lawyer or legal executive, also sit in magistrates' courts. Most are in city districts with high caseloads. A district judge tries cases on his/her own. For convenience, this book refers to 'magistrates' (that is, plural) sitting in court, because two or three lay magistrates sit in many hearings.

7.2 The taking of pleas

Defendants facing summary charges are asked, usually during their first appearance in the magistrates' court, how they plead. Pleading guilty to a charge means they are convicted of it. Sentencing usually takes place at a later date, to enable preparation of a 'pre-sentence report'.

 For detail on sentencing and 'pre-sentence reports', see 7.6. For categories of charges, see 6.1.

A contested case will in most instances be adjourned for summary trial. When it is first adjourned, the magistrates must decide, unless the charge is a minor one, whether to grant **bail**.   → glossary

Defendants who deny **either-way** charges can ask magistrates to try them. The   → glossary
allocation (mode of trial) procedure is outlined in the next chapter, which explains   → glossary
that a denied either-way charge is tried at a Crown court if the defendant wishes or if magistrates decide it is too serious for them to try.

A defendant under arrest or previously denied bail may not be brought to court for a pre-trial hearing but appear there via a video link from a police station or prison.

7.3 Bail

Bail is the system by which a court grants a defendant his/her liberty until the case's next hearing.

The court may impose conditions—for example, that the defendant should live at home, and/or surrender his/her passport and/or report to a police station once a week and/or not contact someone who is a witness.

The Bail Act 1976 has a general rule that a defendant must be granted bail unless:

- the court is satisfied there are substantial grounds for believing that if bail is granted, the defendant
  - will abscond, or
  - commit another offence, or
  - obstruct the course of justice (for example, by interfering with witnesses), or
  - will, or will be likely to, cause mental or physical injury to an associated person or cause him/her to fear such injury;
- the court decides the defendant should be kept in prison for his/her own protection (for instance, if the alleged crime has so angered the community that a mob may attack him/her);

- the defendant is alleged to have committed an **indictable** offence when he/she was on bail granted in an earlier case;
- the defendant is already serving a jail sentence;
- there is insufficient information to decide on bail.

A court must give reasons for refusing bail.

A defendant charged with murder can only be given bail by a Crown court judge.

7.3.1 Evidence and previous convictions aired

When deciding on bail, the court is told of the defendant's relevant previous conviction(s) and some details of prosecution evidence about the charge(s) faced. A defence lawyer arguing for bail may outline defence evidence.

7.3.2 Surety

In some cases, a court will insist that the defendant has a surety before bail is granted. A surety is someone—for example, a relative or friend of the defendant—who guarantees that the defendant will 'surrender' to bail—that is, appear at court as required.

The surety agrees to forfeit a sum of money, fixed by the court, if the defendant absconds. If the defendant absconds, a surety who fails to pay the sum can be jailed.

7.3.3 Failure to surrender

Failing to surrender to bail is a criminal offence which will probably result in the court issuing an arrest warrant.

7.3.4 Appeals

Defendants refused bail by magistrates can apply to a Crown court judge for bail. The prosecution, if the alleged offence is serious, can appeal to a Crown court judge to challenge a decision by magistrates to grant bail.

7.4 Reporting restrictions for pre-trial hearings

When a denied charge is heading for a summary trial, magistrates may hold at least one pre-trial hearing to consider and decide any dispute between prosecution and defence on admissibility of evidence or other questions of law, and to decide on bail.

Section 8C of the Magistrates' Courts Act 1980 imposes **automatic** restrictions limiting contemporaneous reporting of these pre-trial hearings. These are intended to prevent the risk of prejudice should a case originally due to be tried by magistrates end up being tried by a Crown court jury. Parliament anticipated that, because of changes to integrate the courts' system, a case—even if a magistrates' court starts preparing to try it—may end up being tried at a Crown court with a 'related' either-way or indictable-only case. A magistrates' court might also initially agree in the allocation procedure to try an either-way case but later in a pre-trial hearing decide that a Crown court should try it after all because the alleged offence is more serious than it first appeared.

The type of material aired in a pre-trial hearing which could, if published contemporaneously by the media, subsequently prejudice a jury's verdict at Crown court is outlined in 8.2.1—for example, defendants' previous convictions.

7.4.1 The scope of the section 8C reporting restrictions

The section 8C restrictions automatically apply to reports of pre-trial hearings at magistrates' courts in cases due for summary trial.

They ban publication of:

- any ruling by magistrates on admissibility of evidence and other questions of law, and of any order to discharge or vary such a ruling;
- applications for such rulings and for such orders, including legal argument and discussion about whether such a ruling or order should be made.

The Act defines a pre-trial hearing as one relating to a charge due to be tried by magistrates to which the defendant has pleaded not guilty and which takes place before magistrates start hearing prosecution evidence at the trial. So section 8C could cover a defendant's first appearance at court, as well as any other pre-trial hearing, but does not prevent contemporaneous reporting of the plea.

While the restrictions are in force, the media can only report seven categories of information from pre-trial hearings which consider admissibility of evidence or other questions of law. These are (in simplified form):

- the names of the court and magistrates;
- the names, ages, home addresses and occupations of the defendant(s) and witnesses;
- the charge(s) in full or summarised;
- the names of solicitors and barristers in the proceedings;
- if the case is adjourned, the date and place to which it is adjourned;
- arrangements as to bail;
- whether **legal aid** was authorised.	→ glossary

It is also safe to publish that reporting restrictions are in force—this is not prejudicial.

The effect of the restrictions is to ban publication of any reference to evidence, except as it is encapsulated in the wording of the charge(s), or to other potentially prejudicial matter aired in the hearing—again, 8.2.1 explains what such matter is.

As regards 'arrangements as to bail', it will be safe to report, unless the court orders otherwise, whether bail was granted, and, if it was granted, any bail conditions and **surety** arrangement.	→ glossary

But if bail is refused the media should *not* report in most instances that the prosecution opposed bail, and in particular should not report why it was opposed, or the reasons magistrates gave for refusing it, as this could be prejudicial.

It would be safe to report that someone was remanded in custody for his/her own protection. The home addresses which may be published are those current when the report is published and former addresses which were current during events that gave rise to the charge(s).

✳ Remember

A report which refers to a defendant's former address or includes a photo or footage of it should make clear that he/she no longer lives there. Failing to do so could cause the current occupants to sue for libel because the report will link them to the court case.

The explicit ban in section 8C on publishing pre-trial argument and rulings about admissibility of evidence and other questions of law is a 'belt and braces' approach, since limiting reports to the seven categories cited earlier has the same effect.

A media report of a pre-trial hearing can safely include neutral descriptions of the court scene and neutral background information.

 See 8.2.2, The scope of the section 52A restrictions, about such neutral material.

7.4.2 When do the section 8C restrictions cease to apply?

The court can lift the section 8C reporting restrictions, wholly or in part, to allow the media to publish contemporaneously fuller reports of these pre-trial applications and of any ruling or order made in them. If any defendant objects, the court can lift the restrictions only if satisfied that doing so is in the interests of justice. If there are objections, these applications and any representations made to the court about them (that is, argument in court about whether the restrictions should be lifted) cannot be reported until the case is 'disposed of', even if restrictions are lifted earlier in other respects.

The section 8C restrictions automatically lapse when the case is 'disposed of', which happens when all defendants in the case are acquitted or convicted of all charges in the case, or if the court dismisses the case or the prosecution decides not to proceed with it.

So, at the end of the trial, a media organisation could publish a report of evidence ruled inadmissible some weeks or months previously in a pre-trial hearing, or of any ruling made in it. A report of a pre-trial hearing published as soon as practicable after the section 8C restrictions are lifted or expire will be regarded as a contemporaneous report and so enjoy the protection of section 4 of the Contempt of Court Act, explained in 19.10, and absolute privilege in defamation law, explained in 22.5, if the report is fair and accurate, and other requirements of those defences are met.

7.4.3 Liability for breach of the section 8C restrictions

A proprietor, editor or publisher can be prosecuted and, if convicted, face an unlimited fine for breaching these restrictions.

7.5 Procedure in summary trials

Though reporting restrictions cover pre-trial hearings, what is said in a trial at a magistrates' court can usually be reported fully as it occurs.

No restrictions under the 1980 Act apply, but they could apply under other law, explained in chs. 10–12. Again, to be legally safe the reporting must be fair and accurate.

The usual summary trial procedure is as follows.

- The prosecutor makes an opening speech, describing the alleged crime.
- Witnesses testify, after swearing an oath or affirming that their evidence is true.
- Prosecution witnesses are called first. Each is asked questions by the prosecutor to elicit their **evidence-in-chief** (that is, evidence given during questioning by the side which called them). The defence can cross-examine them. The prosecution may then re-examine them. → glossary
- When prosecution evidence ends, the defence may submit, for any or all charges faced, that there is no case to answer—that is, that the prosecution cannot meet the standard of proof required.
- If the magistrates agree with this submission, they dismiss the charge. Otherwise, or if there is no such submission, the trial continues.
- Defence witnesses are called. These may include the defendant, though he/she cannot be compelled to testify.
- Defence witnesses are questioned to elicit their evidence-in-chief. They can be cross-examined by the prosecutor and then re-examined by the defence.
- When the court has heard all witnesses, the defence may address the court in a closing speech, arguing how facts and law should be interpreted. Either side can address the court twice in total, in opening or closing speeches. The defence has the right to make the last speech.
- If the magistrates feel a charge is not proved, they acquit the defendant.
- If they find him/her guilty on any charge, he/she is convicted of it, and the magistrates sentence the defendant, or adjourn to sentence at a later date.

the standard of proof in criminal law is explained in 5.1

! Remember your rights

There are court rules on what case material journalists can see to help them report a trial and a national protocol on what prosecution material can be released to them to help coverage of cases—see 15.13, Journalists' access to case material in court proceedings.

7.5.1 **Hostile witnesses and leading questions**

Normally, to ensure witnesses tell of events in their own words, lawyers are not allowed to put leading questions to them when they give evidence-in-chief.

- But a witness who refuses to testify or retracts a statement made to investigators can be ruled by the court to be 'a hostile witness'—and can then be asked leading questions by the side which calls him/her.
- A leading question is one which suggests what answer is expected. 'Did anything happen after that?' is not a leading question; 'Did you then see a man with a knife?' is.

7.5.2 **'Bad character'**

the presumption of innocence is explained in 5.1

As a general rule, prosecutors in trials cannot refer to a defendant's previous 'bad character' because—to comply with the principle of the presumption of innocence—the focus is on evidence for the charge(s) being tried, not any past crime.

But evidence of previous offences and other reprehensible behaviour can be introduced to correct a false impression given by the defendant, or as evidence that he/she follows a distinctive method when committing offences of the kind with which he/she is charged, or if the defendant's evidence has attacked another person's character.

7.6 **Sentencing by magistrates**

→ glossary

At sentencing hearings for an admitted offence, the prosecution tells magistrates details of the crime. If there is dispute about the facts of an admitted offence, the magistrates must accept the defence version unless the prosecution proves its version in a **Newton hearing**.

Otherwise, defendants who admit an offence and those convicted at trial are sentenced in the same way, as follows.

The court will consider any written statement from the victim of the crime. Before sentence is passed, the defendant's lawyer can make a speech in mitigation, citing any extenuating circumstances while asking for leniency.

A defendant may ask for other offences to be 'taken into consideration'.

- Offences to be 'taken into consideration', which should not be confused with previous convictions, are crimes which the defendant admits although he/she has not been charged with them.

The defendant brings these to the court's attention to be sentenced for them as well as for the charged offence(s). By admitting uncharged crimes—for example, burglaries—the defendant removes the possibility of being prosecuted for them in future, giving the opportunity of a fresh start.

Magistrates may also consider a 'pre-sentence report' about the defendant's background, prepared by a probation officer. A defendant being sentenced may appear in court via a video link from a prison if he/she has been denied bail or jailed because of an earlier conviction.

> See Useful Websites at the end of this chapter for the Government's guide to probation.

7.6.1 Jail sentences

Magistrates can jail a defendant for up to six months for a single offence and for up to 12 months for more than one offence if they decide that jail terms should run consecutively, depending on penalties specified for an offence.

- Consecutive sentences are two or more jail terms ordered by the court to run one after the other, imposed when the defendant is convicted of more than one crime. If a sentence of six months is made consecutive to one of three months, the defendant is sentenced overall to nine months.

- Concurrent sentences are those where the defendant is sentenced overall only for the length of the longest sentence imposed. In the example just given, this would be six months.

Courts can give a suspended sentence to a defendant deserving leniency.

- A defendant given a suspended sentence does not have go to jail unless he/she commits a further offence or breaches a requirement of the suspended sentence—for example, that he/she should do unpaid community work—during the period for which the sentence is suspended.

So, a jail term of six months can be suspended for two years. If the defendant commits no other offence in that time and does not breach any requirement, the suspended sentence lapses.

✳ Remember

A report which inaccurately portrays a suspended sentence as an immediate jail term could create a libel problem, as an offender might sue for the inference that the crime was worse than it was.

see 22.5 and 22.7 for defamation considerations in court reporting

7.6.2 Committal for sentence

Magistrates dealing with a defendant who has pleaded guilty to an either-way charge or one convicted of an either-way charge in a summary trial can, in most instances, send the case to the Crown court for a judge to sentence there, if the magistrates have decided—because of the case's details or any previous conviction(s) the defendant has—that their punishment powers are insufficient. This sending is called 'committal for sentence'. A Crown court judge can impose longer jail terms.

7.6.3 Fines

Some offences can be punished by a fine but not by a jail sentence, though failure to pay the fine could lead to such a sentence.

For years it was the case that, broadly speaking, the maximum fine which magistrates could impose was £5,000, where law specifies this. Most fines are much lower. But for decades there have been exceptions in certain statutes—for example, an employer could be fined up to £20,000 for a health and safety breach. Now there are more exceptions, because in 2015 a section of the Legal Aid, Sentencing and Punishment Act 2012 was put into effect to abolish the general £5,000 limit on magistrates' fining power. This means that for a wide range of offences, including health and safety breaches, there is now no specified limit on the fine.

7.6.4 Other types of sentence

- *A community order, sometimes referred to as a 'community sentence' or 'community punishment'*—The court orders a defendant to obey one or more requirements, at least one of which (for an adult defendant) should normally be deemed by the court to be punitive, which could include:
  - unpaid work in the community under a probation officer's direction, now branded 'community payback';
  - a curfew, with a requirement that the offender wears an electronic 'tag' to monitor whether he/she obeys it;
  - a fine;

  and one or more non-punitive elements, for example a requirement to attend treatment for drug or alcohol dependency.

  Failure to comply with any requirement in the order could be punished by a jail sentence of up to six months.

- *A conditional discharge*—This means that the court has not immediately imposed or specified punishment, but states that if the offender commits any other offence within a period specified by the court, such as a year, he/she is liable to be punished for the first offence as well as for the subsequent conviction.

- *An absolute discharge*—This means that the court feels that no punishment, other than the fact of the conviction, is necessary.

As well as imposing a sentence a court can order an offender to pay compensation to a crime victim.

((•))　See Useful Websites at the end of this chapter for more detail on sentencing, including on community orders.

7.6.5 Binding over and restraining orders

Since the fourteenth century, courts have had power to 'bind over' a person 'to keep the peace'. This can be used to resolve, without trial, minor allegations of assault, threatening behaviour or public disorder, in that the prosecution may drop a charge if the defendant agrees to be 'bound over'. A binding over can also follow a conviction. A witness too can be bound over, if, for example, he/she seems to have been involved in a fracas.

When binding over, the court specifies an amount which the person must pay if he/she breaches the peace—for example, by violent or threatening conduct—within a specified period. The order is a preventative, civil law measure, not a punishment, and is *not* a conviction and should not be reported as such.

A court may impose a restraining order on a defendant, even one acquitted at trial, to protect another person—for example, an ex-partner—from harassment. The order may ban the defendant from any contact with that person.

7.6.6 Section 70 committal

Magistrates can make an order under section 70 of the Proceeds of Crime Act 2002 committing the case of a convicted offender to a Crown court hearing to assess what money or property he/she has gained from crime and, if necessary, to make a confiscation order. No automatic reporting restrictions apply to the committal hearing or the Crown court hearing.

7.7 Many cases dealt with by post or online

For 'fixed penalty' offences a defendant need not appear at court if he/she, having received written notice of the charge, returns a form admitting guilt and pays the fine. For such traffic offences—including speeding and driving without insurance—pleas can be made online, and many such cases are dealt with in the 'single justice procedure'.

7.8 Single justice procedure

Law allowing a single lay magistrate or a district judge to deal with some types of case in private came into force for magistrates' courts on 13 April 2015. By 15 June 2017, this procedure was 'live' in 57 magistrates' courts as a national rollout progressed.

This law is in sections 16A–16F and other amended sections of the Magistrates' Courts Act 1980, created by Part 3 of the Criminal Justice and Courts Act 2015.

The procedure means that trials for such offences and the sentencing of defendants convicted at trial or by guilty plea are conducted in private, in the absence of the defendant and solely by consideration of documents (that is, without any oral evidence or oral submissions) if all the following conditions are met:

- the alleged offence is summary and not punishable by imprisonment;
- the defendant was 18 or older at the time of the alleged offence;
- the defendant pleads guilty or has not responded to a 'written charge and notice' asking for an indication of plea and served on him/her by the relevant prosecuting agency;

- the defendant or his/her representative has not objected before the hearing to this procedure being used.

If no plea is indicated or there has been no response to the 'written charge and notice', the magistrate decides whether guilt is proved. A legal adviser (a court official) must be present, but a prosecutor does not have to be. This type of trial—because it involves a district judge or only one lay magistrate and only documents—is officially referred to as 'trial by single justice on the papers'. It means the defendant—having agreed to it or having not responded—might not know the date or venue of the private hearing, because cases can be quickly switched from one courthouse to another if the first is too busy. After a conviction, the court can decide to sit in open court to sentence if it considers it is no longer 'appropriate' to deal with the case in private, and if so, the defendant must be summoned to appear.

! Remember your rights

Journalists may feel the single justice procedure, introduced to save costs, breaches the fundamental principle of open justice. Ch. 15 covers open justice matters including in 15.12.3, Getting information about single justice procedure cases, the rights journalists have to discover the outcome of these cases.

7.9 Appeal routes from magistrates' courts

The defence or prosecution may contest a ruling on law by a magistrates' court by appealing to the High Court by means of the 'case stated' procedure. In other types of challenge, the defence can ask the High Court for a **judicial review**.

 →glossary

A defendant appealing against a conviction by a magistrates' court or the severity of the sentence imposed appeals to a Crown court.

These High Court and Crown court roles are explained in 9.12 and 9.13.

➡ Recap of major points

- Trials and sentencing at magistrates' courts are known as summary proceedings.
- Automatic reporting restrictions under section 8C of the Magistrates' Courts Act 1980 limit what the media can report from pre-trial hearings.
- Magistrates can jail a convicted offender for up to six months for one offence and for up to 12 months for two or more offences.
- Many trials at a magistrates' court can be reported fully and contemporaneously, though some trials are, in the 'single justice on the papers' procedure, now being conducted in private if the case cannot lead to a prison sentence.

((•)) Useful Websites

www.magistrates-association.org.uk/
Magistrates Association

www.gov.uk/guide-to-probation
Government guide to probation

www.sentencingcouncil.org.uk/
Sentencing Council website which explains types of sentence

8

Magistrates' courts—the most serious criminal cases

Chapter summary

Those charged with the most serious crimes—such as murder and robbery—make their first court appearance in a magistrates' court, usually having been held since arrest in police cells. Journalists may be on the court's press bench. But automatic reporting restrictions are in force in these preliminary hearings, to safeguard the defendant's right to fair trial by jury, because the case is bound for the Crown court. It is illegal for the media to breach the restrictions, but some newsworthy facts can be reported immediately from the magistrates' court. The restrictions also apply in preliminary hearings for either-way charges, such as sexual assault. Magistrates try some either-way cases.

8.1 Processing of indictable-only and either-way charges

Defendants charged with the most serious crimes cannot be tried by magistrates. These cases are, as ch. 5 explains, **indictable-only**. They have an initial phase in the magistrates' court, where decisions on bail and case management may be made, but are quickly 'sent for trial' to a Crown court where, if the defendant denies the offence, a jury trial will take place. For most indictable-only cases magistrates can decide on bail. But only a Crown court judge can decide on bail if the charge is murder (when bail is exceptional).

bail is explained in 7.3

A hearing at which a defendant on an indictable-only charge appears in a magistrates' court is only a preliminary hearing, known as a 'sending' hearing. But it will be newsworthy if the alleged crime is already notorious. Usually a 'sending' hearing is the defendant's first—and only—appearance before magistrates.

Some **either-way** cases are also sent to the Crown court for trial if in the 'allocation' procedure—explained later in this chapter—magistrates do not offer the defendant the option of **summary trial** or if the defendant wants trial by jury.

→ glossary
→ glossary
→ glossary

8.2 Section 52A automatic reporting restrictions

Automatic reporting restrictions tightly limit what the media can publish contemporaneously from a **preliminary hearing** at a magistrates' court concerning any indictable-only case, or an either-way case which retains potential for trial. These restrictions are in section 52A of the Crime and Disorder Act 1998. Their scope is set out in the next section. They restrict media reports of 'allocation' and 'sending' hearings from disclosing information which could create a risk of prejudice to jury trials—and cover *any* hearing of such cases at the magistrates' courts which occurs before 'allocation' or 'sending'.

The concern is that people reading or hearing information given at preliminary hearings may include some who months later will be called to be jurors in the cases. Justice demands that jurors try the case only on the evidence presented at the trial and should not be influenced by what they remember from pre-trial coverage.

the jury system is explained in ch. 9

8.2.1 Types of prejudicial matter

The section 52A restrictions are designed to prevent publication from preliminary hearings of:

- any reference to evidence in the case, apart from what is encapsulated in the wording of the charge(s);
- a defendant's previous conviction(s);
- any other material with potential to create prejudice.

Evidence Some evidence might be referred to in detail in an allocation or sending hearing—for example, magistrates may need to hear it to assess the risk of a defendant re-offending if given bail or, in an either-way case, to assess whether he/she should be offered the option of summary trial. But some evidence mentioned by the prosecution or defence might not figure in the trial. When the case reaches the Crown court a judge might rule, before the trial, that some evidence is inadmissible—for example, evidence that a defendant confessed to the crime will be ruled inadmissible if the judge accepts that the confession was made under duress. Reports of a preliminary hearing at a magistrates' court which air such evidence could be recalled by jurors at the trial and so contaminate their deliberations and lead to a defendant being wrongly convicted.

Previous convictions Generally, because of the principle of the 'presumption of innocence', a Crown court jury is not told if a defendant has previous conviction(s). But a defendant's criminal record may be referred to in a 'sending' hearing—for example, to help magistrates decide on bail. Magistrates will also be told about a defendant's criminal record in the allocation procedure, which will precede any 'sending' in an either-way case. A juror could be prejudiced against the defendant by recalling a media report of allocation or sending proceedings if it disclosed that criminal record.

presumption of innocence is explained in 5.1

Other potentially prejudicial material could include suggestions by the prosecution in a 'sending' hearing that a defendant is guilty of more offences than the crime alleged in the charge(s). For example, in a rape case police might check other unsolved rapes if they suspect that the defendant is a serial rapist, and magistrates might hear of those inquiries from a prosecutor opposing bail. The inquiries might come to nothing, but allowing media reports to air those suspicions could lead to a juror remembering them and telling fellow jurors at the trial.

8.2.2 The scope of the section 52A restrictions

The section 52A restrictions list categories of information from preliminary hearings at a magistrates' court which can be published. The list is expressed here in simplified format:

- the name of the court and the magistrates' names;
- the name, age, home address and occupation of the accused;
- in the case of an accused charged with a 'serious or complex' fraud, any 'relevant business information'—see later;
- the charge(s) in full or summarised;
- → glossary   • the names of **counsel** and solicitors engaged in the proceedings;
- if proceedings are adjourned, the date and place to which they are adjourned;
- → glossary   • arrangements as to bail'—whether bail was granted, and if it was, any conditions and **surety** arrangement;
  - if bail is refused, the usual approach is that media organisations do *not* report that the prosecution opposed bail, and in particular should not report why it was opposed, or the magistrates' reasons for refusing bail, as such information might be prejudicial—but it would be safe to report that someone was remanded in custody for his/her own protection;
- → glossary   • whether **legal aid** was authorised to pay for the defendant(s) to be represented by a lawyer.

Section 52A says that if the case in the preliminary hearing is classed as 'serious or complex' fraud, a report of the hearing can include 'relevant business information'. This business information is the same as that which can be reported from Crown court hearings dealing with applications for such fraud charges to be dismissed.

 For 'serious or complex' fraud, see also 8.3.1.1, Two types of either-way case are simply 'sent', and 9.4.3, 'Relevant business information'.

The scope in section 52A for reporting the place to which the case has been adjourned permits, on any logical interpretation, saying that a case has been 'sent for trial' to the relevant Crown court.

The fact that reporting restrictions are in force can be reported. Section 52A does not specify this, but it cannot be prejudicial to publish this fact.

If there is argument in court about whether the section 52A reporting restrictions should be lifted, any defendant's objections to lifting should not be reported contemporaneously even if the court decides to lift them—see 8.2.7.1.

8.2.3 Reporting denials of guilt and choice of jury trial

When reporting preliminary hearings covered by section 52A the media routinely publish:

- *basic protestations of innocence* made by the defendant from the dock or through a solicitor—in an indictable-only case no formal plea is taken at the magistrates' court, but it may be made clear there that the charge is denied; in either-way cases defendants are asked to indicate how they will plead;
- *that a defendant, in an either-way case, has chosen trial by jury.*

Although publication of protestations of innocence and choice of jury trial is beyond what strict application of section 52A would permit, the media are safe in reporting these facts, because:

- it seems only fair to the defendant to quote his/her denial of guilt—if made in relation to the only charge faced or to all charges—and choice of jury trial, which too indicates denial of the charge(s);
- publishing such matter cannot be prejudicial—a jury, obviously, will know if a charge is denied.

But the media should be wary, when the restrictions apply, of reporting anything suggesting that a defendant will later enter a mixture of pleas—for example, quotes suggesting he/she is likely to admit one charge while denying another. This could be prejudicial if at trial jurors are not told of the admission but remember it from pre-trial coverage.

8.2.4 Describing the courtroom scene

The media routinely report, even when section 52A restrictions apply, scene-setting information: that the hearing lasted 10 minutes; what the defendant wore; that he/she 'spoke only to confirm his/her name and address'; that guards stood on either side of him/her. Such bland material will not cause prejudice.

8.2.5 Background material

Media organisations publishing reports of preliminary hearings usually add some background material about the defendant and/or the alleged crime. Background material, from sources other than the court hearing, is not itself a report of those proceedings and so does not contravene section 52A. But the Contempt of Court Act 1981 would cover such material, so nothing should be published which creates a substantial risk of serious prejudice or impediment—see ch. 19. Mingling background material into a court report without sufficient care could create such a risk—for example, potential jurors who see/hear the report could draw wrong inferences about the evidence.

An option for the media, when they want to report on an alleged crime committed, say, in the previous 24 hours, but for which the alleged perpetrator has already appeared in court in a preliminary hearing, is to publish items segregated by page design or separate narrative. Each item could have its own headline/introduction—a story on the alleged incident, conforming to contempt law, not citing material from the court hearing, and, somewhere else, a separate report solely of the preliminary hearing, conforming to the section 52A restrictions.

8.2.6 Liability for breach of the section 52A restrictions

Section 52B of the 1998 Act says 'any proprietor, editor or publisher' of a newspaper or periodical can be prosecuted if it breaches the section 52A restrictions. If the breach is published in any other type of written report—for example, on a website not linked to a newspaper—'the person who publishes it' can be prosecuted.

In the case of a TV or radio programme, 'the body corporate which provides the service' and any person 'having functions in relation to the programme corresponding to those of an editor of a newspaper' can be prosecuted. The penalty is an unlimited fine.

👁 Case study

In 2013 *The Sun* newspaper was fined £3,350 after it admitted breaching the section 52A restrictions in its report of the hearing in which Oldham magistrates' court sent the case of Andrew Partington, charged with manslaughter and criminal damage, to Manchester Crown court for trial. The report—including its headline 'Gas pipe's cut, boom . . . you bitch'—quoted evidence from texts, described as the crux of the prosecution case, in which Partington threatened his girlfriend. Fining *The Sun*, District Judge Jonathan Taaffe said at Manchester magistrates' court that this was 'shoddy' journalism. He endorsed the view that it went way beyond what was permitted, and that its content and tone created a substantial risk of prejudice. At Crown court Partington, 28, of Buckley Street, Oldham, was jailed for 10 years after admitting causing the gas blast which destroyed houses and killed a neighbour's child (Judiciary of England and Wales press release, *The Independent* and BBC online news, 5 April 2013). See Useful Websites at the end of this chapter.

✳ Remember

If a breach of the section 52A restrictions occurs after a trial has begun and is serious enough—because of what is published—to cause the trial to be aborted, a media organisation might also become liable for huge costs under section 93 of the Courts Act 2003 which can punish 'serious misconduct'.

 This risk of liability for huge costs if 'serious misconduct' affects a case is explained in 19.9.

8.2.7 When do the section 52A restrictions cease to apply?

The restrictions cease to apply in three sets of circumstances.

8.2.7.1 A magistrates' court can lift the restrictions

Magistrates' courts have a discretionary power to lift the restrictions, including at the request of a defendant. If any defendant objects, the restrictions may only be lifted if the magistrates decide that doing so is in the interests of justice. A defendant might want restrictions lifted so his/her solicitor can publicise an appeal for witnesses through a full media report of the hearing—for example, the defence solicitor may be seeking witnesses to help corroborate the defendant's **alibi**: 'My client was at the funfair, not the crime scene. Did anyone see him at the fair?' →glossary

Section 52A says that if any defendant, whether a sole defendant or a co-accused, objects to the restrictions being lifted, his/her representations to magistrates on this issue, even if a lifting order is then made, should not be reported until the end of the case, including any trial. But whether an order lifting restrictions was made or not can be reported contemporaneously.

Once these reporting restrictions have been lifted they cannot be re-imposed (*R v Blackpool Justices, ex p Beaverbrook Newspapers Ltd* [1972] 1 All ER 388, [1972] 1 WLR 95). If magistrates decide, after a request from one defendant, to lift the restrictions, they are lifted in respect of all defendants in the hearing—even if any objected (*Leeds Justices, ex p Sykes* [1983] 1 WLR 132).

> ((•)) For an example of a report of a hearing in which the restrictions were lifted, see *Express* and *Star* report in Useful Websites at the end of this chapter.

8.2.7.2 The restrictions lapse if it becomes clear there will be no trial

The restrictions cease to apply to a report of an allocation hearing if the sole defendant, or all the defendants in the case, plead guilty to each either-way charge faced (and there are no indictable-only charges in the case). This means there will be no trial and no 'sending' of the case to Crown court.

8.2.7.3 The restrictions lapse after the last trial ends or if the case does not proceed

The Act says restrictions on a report of the sending and/or allocation proceedings cease to apply 'after conclusion' of the trial of the defendant(s) or—if there is more than one trial—the last trial in the case. This means that if an either-way case is tried summarily, the restrictions automatically cease to apply at the end of that trial if that is the only one in the case (they do not apply to reporting of the trial itself).

They also cease to apply if the sole defendant in a case 'sent' to Crown court pleads guilty, or, if there is more than one defendant, they all plead guilty to all charges.

The restrictions also finish if in either court all the charges are discontinued or withdrawn, and the court therefore formally acquits the defendant(s). Otherwise, the restrictions cease to apply after delivery of the last verdict in the only or last trial in the case.

The section 52A restrictions affect only what can be reported from the earlier allocation and sending proceedings, and do not affect reporting of the trial.

Criminal Practice Direction I General Matters 5B.22 says that if the case does not result in a guilty plea, a finding of guilt or an acquittal, the 52A restrictions do not cease to apply automatically and an application to lift them must be made to the court.

 For context, see 15.10.1 about what the Practice Directions are.

When the restrictions cease to apply, the evidence aired or submissions made at any preliminary hearing at a magistrates' court weeks or months earlier may be fully reported. For example, the media may wish to highlight evidence which, for legal reasons, the jury did not hear, which might give a fuller picture of the defendant or throw light on how the crime was investigated.

 See the Additional Material for ch. 8 on www.mcnaes.com for an example of a newspaper reporting evidence aired at a preliminary hearing months after it occurred.

8.2.7.4 Contempt and defamation considerations

A report of preliminary proceedings published as soon as practicable after the section 52A restrictions are lifted or expire will be regarded as a contemporaneous report and so enjoy the protection of section 4 of the Contempt of Court Act 1981, explained in 19.10, and absolute privilege in defamation law, explained in 22.5. To be legally safe the reporting must be fair and accurate, as these chapters explain.

8.3 Procedure in allocations hearings and whether section 52A applies

An either-way case will have at least one preliminary hearing in a magistrates' court, and if the defendant denies the charge, the allocation procedure will take place. Either-way cases include **theft**, burglary and sexual assault charges. A defendant in an either-way case has a right to jury trial, but may choose not to exercise it. An allocation hearing determines whether a defendant who intends to deny the charge will be tried summarily or by a jury. For as long as an either-way case retains potential for trial, the section 52A restrictions apply to reports of the allocation hearing. See Figure 8.1, which shows how an either-way case is processed.

8.3.1 Allocation procedure in either-way cases

In an either-way case, the defendant is asked, usually in its first hearing in the magistrates' court, to indicate how he/she intends to plead.

- *A defendant's indication of an intention to plead guilty* is automatically treated as a formal plea of guilty, convicting him/her of that offence. If this is the only charge in the case, the section 52A restrictions automatically

Figure 8.1 Processing of either-way cases in magistrates' courts

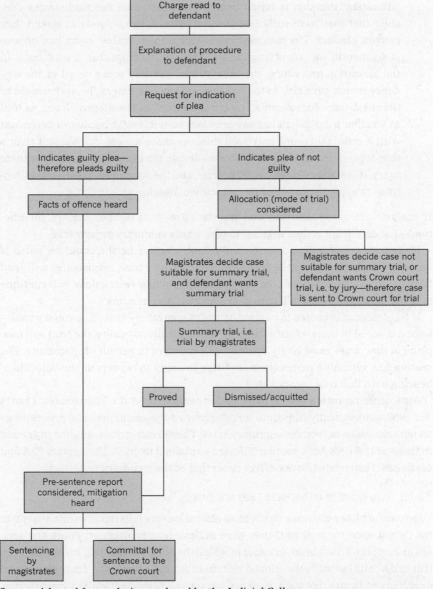

Source: *Adapted from a design produced by the Judicial College*

lapse, as there will be no trial. The magistrates will sentence the defendant at that hearing or a later one. But they may decide, after hearing more detail of the offence and of the defendant's previous conviction(s), that their powers of punishment are insufficient and that the case should be committed for sentence to the Crown court for the defendant to be sentenced there. Magistrates' sentencing powers are explained in ch. 7.

- *If the defendant indicates that he/she will plead not guilty*, magistrates will decide whether he/she should be offered the option of summary trial. This 'allocation' decision is based primarily on whether the magistrates consider that they have sufficient power to punish the defendant, should they convict him/her. The maximum sentence a magistrates' court can impose is six months for one offence and 12 months for more than one offence. In the allocation procedure, the magistrates are told some detail of the evidence which gave rise to the charge, so they can assess the seriousness of the allegation—for example, the crime's effect on the alleged victim, as well as whether a defendant has any previous conviction(s), because a defendant with a criminal record may well deserve more severe punishment than a first-time offender. If the magistrates decide the case is too serious for them to try, it is sent to Crown court for trial, and the section 52A restrictions continue to apply to reports of the 'allocation' hearing and 'sending'.

If magistrates agree that they can try the case—that is, they 'accept jurisdiction'—the defendant is then asked if he/she wants summary or jury trial.

Magistrates may indicate to the defendant whether he/she could be jailed if convicted at their court. If the defendant chooses jury trial, magistrates will send the case to Crown court, and the section 52A reporting restrictions will continue to apply to reports of the 'allocation' hearing and the 'sending'.

If the defendant chooses to be tried by the magistrates—that is, summary trial—he/she is asked to enter a formal plea. If he/she pleads not guilty, the trial will take place in that court, most likely after an adjournment to permit preparations. The section 52A reporting restrictions continue to apply to reports of the 'allocation' hearing until that trial is concluded.

Also, other reporting restrictions, under section 8C of the Magistrates' Courts Act 1980, automatically come into force to cover subsequent pre-trial proceedings which take place before the summary trial. These restrictions, similar in format to those of the 1998 Act's section 52A, are explained in ch. 7. The section 52A and section 8C restrictions do not affect reporting of the summary trial itself.

8.3.1.1 Two types of either-way case are simply 'sent'

Two types of either-way case do not have allocation hearings but are simply 'sent' to the Crown court for trial, as if they were indictable-only offences. These are 'serious or complex' fraud cases, or cases in which the alleged offending is sexual or violent *and* a child (possibly the alleged victim) is due to be a witness. This streamlined procedure indicates that such cases are too serious to be dealt with by magistrates.

➡ Recap of major points

- An indictable-only case will be 'sent for trial' to the Crown court.
- A denied either-way offence can in most instances be tried by magistrates or by a jury. The defendant can choose trial by jury.

- Reporting restrictions in section 52A of the Crime and Disorder Act 1998 automatically apply to media reports of 'allocation' and 'sending' hearings in the magistrates' court.

((•)) Useful Websites

www.expressandstar.com/news/crime/2013/02/08/halesowen-murder-suspect-acted-in-self-defence-claim/
Express and Star newspaper report of a preliminary hearing in which reporting restrictions were lifted

www.judiciary.gov.uk/judgments/r-v-news-grp-newspapers-ltd/
District Judge Jonathan Taaffe's remarks when fining *The Sun* for breach of the section 52A restrictions in the Andrew Partington case

www.independent.co.uk/news/media/press/sun-fined-3000-for-oldham-gas-explosion-reporting-breach-8562354.html
The Independent's report of *The Sun* being fined

www.bbc.co.uk/news/uk-england-21499501
BBC report of Partington being sentenced

9

Crown courts and appeal courts

Chapter summary

Crown courts deal with the most serious criminal cases, including murder. Their trials lead to the tense moment when the jury announces the verdict, with the press bench full for major cases. This chapter details the work of Crown courts, the jury's role and how reporting restrictions ban the media from publishing full reports of pre-trial hearings. It also outlines the work of the High Court, Court of Appeal and Supreme Court.

9.1 Roles at Crown courts

There are Crown courts at 38 locations in England and Wales, in administrative regions referred to as 'circuits'. The most famous is the Central Criminal Court in London—known as the Old Bailey.

In Crown court trials:

- juries decide if each charge is proved;
- judges rule on law and sentence convicted offenders.

In exceptionally rare circumstances—for example, if there is a real risk that criminals could intimidate jurors to acquit a defendant—a Crown court trial can proceed with no jury, leaving the judge to decide the verdict(s).

9.1.1 Who are jurors?

A Crown court jury consists of 12 people, aged between 18 and 75, selected randomly from electoral rolls for the local districts and summoned to appear for jury service. Some categories of people, such as anyone jailed in the previous 10 years, are barred from being jurors.

9.1.1.1 Types of Crown court judge

Three types of judge sit in Crown courts:

- High Court judges—those who can sit in the High Court and Crown courts. They are referred to as, for instance, 'Mr Justice Smith' or 'Mrs Justice Smith', and wear red robes for criminal cases. Only they can try the most serious offences, such as murder, as they are the most experienced judges.

- Circuit judges, referred to as 'Judge John Smith' or 'Judge Mary Smith', are barristers of at least 10 years' standing or solicitors who have been Recorders.

- Recorders—part-time judges—are barristers or solicitors who have held 'rights of audience' (that is, the right to represent clients) at Crown court. Recorders are usually referred to as 'the Recorder, Mr John Smith' or 'the Recorder, Mrs Mary Smith'.

✳ Remember

Some cities have bestowed the title of 'Honorary Recorder of—' on the senior circuit judge, who carries out ceremonial duties.

9.1.2 Lawyers at Crown court

Prosecutions at Crown court are conducted by barristers. Barristers also usually appear for the defence. Barristers are referred to as **'counsel'**. Solicitors have 'rights of audience' in some circumstances. A court clerk sits in each Crown court in front of the judge, to assist in procedures.

→ glossary

see also the roles of solicitors and barristers, explained in 1.5

9.2 Routes to Crown court

A case yet to be tried reaches a Crown court because it has been sent for trial by a magistrates' court or youth court—see 8.1, Processing of indictable-only and either-way charges and 10.2.4, 'Sending for trial' for homicide, 'grave' and other cases—or by a High Court judge by means of a voluntary bill of indictment, a rare legal process explained in the Additional Material for ch. 9 on www.mcnaes.com.

A case may also be heard by the Crown court if it has been committed by a magistrates' court for sentence or subject to 'section 70' committal—see in 7.6.2, Committal for sentence and 7.6.6, Section 70 committal—or is an appeal—see later, 9.12, The Crown court as an appeal court.

9.3 Arraignment

A defendant whose case is sent to a Crown court for trial is there asked to plead guilty or not guilty to each charge on the **indictment**, so formal pleas can be recorded.   → glossary

glossary This process is known as **'arraignment'**. At Crown court charges are referred to as 'counts'. See also 9.5, Reporting the arraignment.

9.4 Hearings prior to jury involvement—automatic reporting restrictions

 glossary

In cases in which a defendant denies guilt, there will be at least one hearing at Crown court before the jury is involved. In a pre-trial hearing the defendant may appear there via a video link from prison, if **bail** has been denied previously.

 glossary

Statutes impose **automatic** reporting restrictions on media coverage of some of these hearings. The hearings are for the judge to make rulings, some of which may determine what the jury will be told if the case goes to trial, or make bail decisions.

bail deci-
sions are
explained
in 7.3

The reporting restrictions are to prevent publication of information which could prejudice a trial. The principle is that potential jurors should not learn about information discussed in hearings held before the trial in which they will sit. Potentially prejudicial material which could be discussed at these hearings includes a defendant's previous conviction(s), or evidence ruled inadmissible. For examples of what can cause prejudice if published, see 8.2.1, Types of prejudicial matter, which also explains similar restrictions in section 52A of the Crime and Disorder Act 1998 which apply—for the same reason—to media coverage of

 glossary

preliminary hearings in magistrates' courts.

9.4.1 The scope of the automatic reporting restrictions

The automatic restrictions limiting media reports of some types of pre-trial hearing at Crown courts are in various statutes, but of the same format. They restrict these reports to seven categories of information:

- the name of the Crown court and judge;
- the names, ages, home addresses and occupations of defendant(s) and witness(es);
- the charge(s), or a summary of it/them;
- the names of solicitors or barristers in the case;
- if proceedings are adjourned, the date and place to which they are adjourned;
- arrangements as to bail—that is, whether bail was granted, and if it was, any bail conditions and **surety** arrangement;

 glossary

- whether **legal aid** was authorised.

 glossary

Witnesses are unlikely to take part in a hearing before trial. But if they do, or are mentioned in court, under these restrictions they can be named in reports, unless other law gives them anonymity.

 Chs. 11–12 explain anonymity law, and ch. 10 explains that it may cover juveniles in Crown court cases.

In cases in which bail is refused, the usual interpretation of the restrictions is that the media should not report if and why the prosecution opposed bail or the reasons the judge gave for refusing it, as such information could be prejudicial.

Home addresses can include past addresses in events which gave rise to the charges. To avoid defamation, care is needed in references to former addresses—as explained in 7.4.1.

9.4.2 Which types of hearing?

The types of hearing for which the above format of restrictions apply are:

Unsuccessful applications for a case to be dismissed, prior to arraignment A defendant whose case is sent for trial to Crown court may apply to a judge, before arraignment, for it to be dismissed because of insufficient evidence. The reporting restrictions on such hearings are detailed in Schedule 3 to the Crime and Disorder Act 1998.

'Preparatory hearings' A Crown court may hold a 'preparatory hearing' in a case involving a serious offence or which will involve a complex or lengthy trial. A preparatory hearing must be held in a terrorism case. The hearings are so the judge can rule on case management issues. Such a hearing, if held, marks the start of the trial and takes place shortly before the jury is sworn. If the arraignment has not yet been held, it must take place at the start of the preparatory hearing. The reporting restrictions—again, in the format set out earlier—are in section 11 of the Criminal Justice Act 1987 for preparatory hearings in 'serious or complex fraud' cases, and in section 37 of the Criminal Procedure and Investigations Act 1996 in respect of preparatory hearings in other types of case.

the meaning of 'sworn' is explained in 9.6.1

The same restrictions apply, generally under section 37 of the 1996 Act and—for serious or complex fraud cases—under section 11 of the 1987 Act to media reports of any application to a Crown court judge for leave to appeal against rulings made at a 'preparatory hearing' and to any such appeal in a higher court.

9.4.3 'Relevant business information'

Section 11 of the Criminal Justice Act 1987 allows journalists covering an unsuccessful application for a 'serious or complex' fraud case to be dismissed or covering a preparatory hearing in such a case to include 'relevant business information' in reports of the hearing even when the automatic restrictions are in place. This means the media can include in the report:

- any address used by the defendant for carrying on business on his/her own account;
- the name of the business at 'any relevant time'—that is, when events which gave rise to the charge(s) occurred;
- the name and address of any firm in which he/she was a partner, or by which he/she was engaged, at any such time;

- the name of any company of which he/she was a director, or by which he/she was otherwise engaged, at any such time, and the address of its registered or principal office;
- any working address of the defendant in his/her capacity as a person engaged by any such company.

'Engaged' means under a contract of service or a contract for services.

9.4.4 What else can be reported?

In addition to the information which the format of restrictions lists as safe to publish, it is safe to include in reports of pre-trial Crown court hearings neutral descriptions of the court scene and non-prejudicial background facts of the type outlined in ch. 8 in relation to preliminary hearings before magistrates—see 8.2.2, The scope of the section 52A restrictions.

9.4.5 'Pre-trial' hearings—automatic reporting restrictions

The Criminal Procedure and Investigations Act 1996 defines a 'pre-trial hearing' as any hearing at a Crown court before a guilty plea is accepted (that is, before it becomes clear there will be no trial), or—in cases which remain contested—all hearings which occur before a jury is sworn or before the beginning of a 'preparatory' hearing. Reporting restrictions in section 41 of the Act automatically ban publication, before the conclusion of all proceedings in the case, of what is said at a 'pre-trial hearing' in:

- applications for rulings on the admissibility of evidence or any other question of law, including any rulings made by the judge;
- applications for such a ruling to be varied or discharged, including any order made.

9.4.6 The safest course to obey the restrictions

The law enshrining these various sets of restrictions developed piecemeal. Their definitions of hearings held at Crown court before a trial overlap, and the extent to which the restrictions apply to all types of these hearings is unclear.

- A journalist's safest course, to avoid breaching the law in a contemporaneous report of a Crown court hearing held before a jury becomes involved— that is, a contested case—is to check, by asking the court clerk, what type of hearing the judge considers it to be and, unless advised it is a pre-trial hearing under the 1996 Act, to include only the categories of information listed under the heading 'The scope of the automatic reporting restrictions' plus in fraud cases 'relevant business information', and non-prejudicial background information. If told simply that it is a 'preliminary hearing', the journalist should ask for a more specific definition.

see also 9.5,
Reporting the
arraignment

9.4.7 When do the automatic reporting restrictions cease to apply?

A Crown court judge can lift the restrictions, or lift them in part, to allow the media to publish contemporaneously fuller reports of such hearings.

If any defendant objects to this, the judge may lift them only if satisfied that doing so is in the interests of justice. Argument in court about whether the restrictions should be lifted cannot be reported until the 'conclusion' of all relevant trials, even if restrictions are lifted in other respects.

If the judge leaves the restrictions in place, they automatically cease to apply at the 'conclusion' of relevant proceedings. The statutes state that this is, or it can safely be construed to be, the acquittal or conviction of a sole defendant or, for multiple defendants, of all defendants in respect of all charges in all trials in the case, or when it becomes clear that, for some other reason, no relevant trial remains pending, which might be when the prosecutor decides not to proceed with the case or when all charges are dismissed for lack of evidence. But reporting restrictions under other law may still apply—see chs. 10–12.

 For a case study on how in 2014 a judge at Southwark Crown court agreed to lift reporting restrictions covering a pre-trial hearing, see the Additional Material for ch. 9 on www.mcnaes.com.

9.4.8 Liability for breach of the automatic reporting restrictions

Liability and penalty for breach of the reporting restrictions under the Acts cited earlier are the same as for breach of restrictions in section 52A of the Crime and Disorder Act—see 8.2.6, Liability for breach of the section 52A restrictions. If a breach occurs after a trial has begun, and is serious enough—because of what is published—to cause it to be aborted, a media organisation may also become liable for huge costs under section 93 of the Courts Act 2003—see 19.9, Media could face huge costs if 'serious misconduct' affects a case.

9.4.9 Appeals against rulings by judge—reporting restrictions

The Criminal Justice Act 2003 gives the prosecution the right to appeal against a ruling by a Crown court judge which would terminate all or part of the case—for example, that there is no case to answer—no matter what stage the case has reached when the ruling is made. Section 71 of the Act, intended to prevent prejudice to the trial or to any linked trial, automatically bans reporting of any Crown court discussion (which, if the trial has begun, would be in the jury's absence) about such an appeal. It also restricts reports of the Court of Appeal hearing, and of any further appeal made to the Supreme Court, to the same seven categories of information listed earlier under the heading 'The scope of the automatic reporting restrictions'. These restrictions apply, unless lifted earlier, until the conclusion of all trials in the case.

 In the proceedings featured in the 2014 case study, the Court of Appeal lifted the section 71 restrictions. See the Additional Material for ch. 9 on www.mcnaes.com.

9.5 Reporting the arraignment

If, at the arraignment, defendants in a case plead guilty to each charge, they are convicted of each charge, in which case the restrictions detailed earlier in this chapter cease to apply as there will be no trial.

If, at the arraignment, a sole defendant or all defendants deny the charge or charges, the media can safely report those pleas contemporaneously if there will be just one trial in the case.

But if a defendant or co-defendants enter a mixture of guilty and not guilty pleas, or if denied charges are to be dealt with in more than one trial, a judge may—to avoid what he/she considers a substantial risk of prejudice—make an order under section 4(2) of the Contempt of Court Act 1981 postponing publication of some of that information. A judge could do this, for example, to ban media reports of an arraignment from mentioning, until the trial ends, any charge which has been admitted (if the jury is not to be told about it) or—if the case will involve more than one trial—any charge not due to be dealt with in the first trial. Or the judge could use section 4(2) to ban any reporting of the arraignment, and of the first trial, until any further trial in the case is concluded.

For detail on section 4(2) orders and for considerations to be borne in mind even if a judge does not make such an order, see, Section 4(2) orders.

9.6 Procedure in Crown court trials

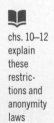

chs. 10–12 explain these restrictions and anonymity laws

The media can publish full, contemporaneous reports of what the jury is told at a Crown court trial once it has started, but must comply with any discretionary reporting restriction or any automatic anonymity for a complainant of a sexual offence.

✳ **Remember**

Until the jury has returned all verdicts, no report of a trial should include—unless the judge says otherwise—any ruling, discussion or argument which takes place in the jury's absence. This is explained in 19.11.3, concerning the law of contempt of court. To comply with that law and defamation law, reporting of the trial must be fair and accurate—19.10, 22.5 and 22.7.

9.6.1 Selection of the jury and the giving of evidence

A Crown court trial is under way when the jury is 'empanelled'—that is, when a group of potential jurors is taken into the courtroom and the court clerk selects 12 at random. These will be 'sworn'—required to swear an oath that they will try the case according to the evidence.

Soon after this prosecution counsel 'opens the case' by outlining it. Prosecution witnesses then testify. A Crown court trial usually follows the same sequence used in magistrates' trials as regards the giving of evidence, including cross-examination, and speeches by lawyers.

At Crown court defence counsel may choose to make a speech 'opening' the defence case prior to calling defence witnesses. After all these have been heard, prosecuting counsel in most cases makes a closing speech to the jury, which is followed by the defence's closing speech.

procedure in summary trials is explained in 7.5

The judge then sums up the case, to remind jurors of evidence and direct them on the law. The judge will, if he/she decides that evidence is not sufficient to support a charge, direct the jury to bring in a verdict of not guilty on that charge.

Otherwise, and to consider any other charge, the jury 'retires' to a jury room to decide the verdict(s). A jury **bailiff** escorts jurors to and from the room, and is the only official allowed contact with them in it. The jury will have been directed to elect a foreperson to speak on its behalf.

→ glossary

9.6.2 **Majority verdicts**

A judge initially asks a jury to reach a unanimous verdict on each charge—that is, a unanimous decision to acquit or convict.

- But if a jury has deliberated the case for at least 2 hours and 10 minutes and has failed to reach a verdict, the judge can recall it to the courtroom to tell it that a majority verdict is acceptable (for each charge).
- For a full jury of 12, majority verdicts of the ratios 11–1 or 10–2 are acceptable.
- If a jury is reduced in number for any reason—for example, because one or two jurors have fallen ill during the trial—a majority of 10–1 or 9–1 is allowed.
- If a defendant is convicted by a majority, rather than unanimously, the media should report the fact that it was by a majority decision, as this indicates that one or two people in the jury disagreed with the guilty verdict.

the legal ban on interviewing jurors about verdicts is explained in 12.4

If the verdict is an acquittal, the court asks no questions of the jury about the ratio of the vote—so usually no indication of how many jurors concurred in the verdict is given. But if the foreperson volunteers in court the fact that acquittal was by a majority, it is by convention regarded as unfair to publish this fact, because stating that one or two jurors voted against acquittal could leave a stain on the defendant's character even though he/she is cleared of the charge.

A jury which cannot reach a verdict by a sufficient majority is known as a 'hung jury'. The prosecution then has to decide if it wants to seek a re-trial.

❗ Remember your rights

There are court rules on what case material journalists can see to help them report a trial and a national protocol on what prosecution material can be released to them to help coverage of cases—see 15.13, Journalists' access to case material in court proceedings.

9.7 Sentencing at Crown court

If a defendant pleads guilty at a Crown court to all charges, the judge will pass sentence, often after an adjournment. First, the judge will hear the prosecution's summary of the facts, and be told if the defendant has previous convictions and

→glossary

of any offences to be **taken into consideration**. The judge will also consider any statement from the victim(s) about the impact of a crime or—in a homicide case— a statement by bereaved relatives about the crime's effect on them. The judge will

→glossary

also hear **mitigation**.

Sentencing after a Crown court trial follows a similar pattern, though the judge, having presided at it, will not normally need to hear again detail of the offence(s).

The same sentencing procedure is used for a defendant who, after conviction in a magistrates' court, has been committed for sentence to the Crown court. A defendant may appear at a sentencing hearing via a video link from prison, if he/ she has been denied bail or is already serving a jail term.

Crown courts frequently impose jail terms, but have the same range of other sentencing options as magistrates—see 7.6.

If no other factors apply—for example, the defendant is not sentenced to life or to an 'extended' sentence—he/she can expect, if he/she behaves well in prison, to be released 'on licence' halfway through the term imposed by the court, which means that after release he/she will monitored by a probation officer and may be returned to prison to serve the remainder of the jail term if a licence condition is broken.

9.7.1 Life sentences and extended sentences

Life sentences are imposed for murder and other serious offences. The sentencing judge will state a minimum term of the sentence which the defendant should serve—the tariff—and may pass 'a whole life order', meaning the sentence will actually be for life.

A defendant convicted of a sexual or violent offence can be categorised as a 'dangerous offender'. This law is complex, but in summary an offender can be categorised as 'dangerous' if a Crown court judge considers there is significant risk of him/her committing further offences which might cause members of the public serious harm. The offender could incur a life sentence. Other categories of 'dangerous offender' receive 'extended' sentences, meaning they will not be considered for release from prison until they have served two-thirds of their sentence.

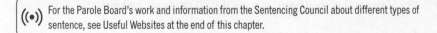 For the Parole Board's work and information from the Sentencing Council about different types of sentence, see Useful Websites at the end of this chapter.

9.8 The Court of Appeal

A defendant who wishes to appeal against a conviction or the severity of the sentence imposed by a Crown court can seek permission to appeal to the Court of Appeal Criminal Division, based in London. Permission to appeal can be granted by the Crown court trial judge or the Court of Appeal itself, or a case may later be referred to the Court by the Criminal Cases Review Commission.

The Court of Appeal may, if it allows the appeal, quash a conviction. It may decide there must be a re-trial of the case, by another Crown court jury.

Appeals are usually heard by three judges. A reporter covering a Court of Appeal hearing in which its judgment is delivered may, in cases decided by a majority rather than a unanimous decision, have to wait until each of the three judges has announced his/her own decision for that majority, and therefore the appeal result, to be revealed.

The Court has a similar procedure in appeals in civil cases. Appeals beyond the Court of Appeal go to the Supreme Court.

Figure 1.1 in 1.2.3, shows the hierarchy of the court system

9.9 Journalists can visit prisoners

The right of a convicted prisoner to be visited in jail by a journalist investigating whether there has been a miscarriage of justice was upheld in *R v Secretary of State for the Home Department, ex p Simms* [2000] 2 AC 115.

> See also 'Visiting prisoners' in the Additional Material for ch. 9 on www.mcnaes.com.

9.10 The Supreme Court

In 2009 the Supreme Court replaced the appellate committee of the House of Lords (also known as the Law Lords) as the highest court in criminal and civil law. Its judges are referred to as 'Justices of the Supreme Court'. It only hears appeals of high significance, usually no more than 40–50 each year. Appeals are heard by several Justices, with a majority decision being binding. The court sits in the former Middlesex Guildhall.

9.11 Re-trials after 'tainted acquittal' or after compelling new evidence emerges—reporting restrictions

Under what is known as the 'double jeopardy rule', the law usually prevents someone acquitted of an offence being tried for it again. But there are two major exceptions.

- If a Crown court trial convicts a person of interference with or intimidation of a juror, witness or potential witness in an earlier trial in which the same or another defendant has been acquitted, the prosecution can apply to the High Court for an order quashing that acquittal, to allow a re-trial.

see Useful Websites at the end of this chapter for CPS guidance on section 82

- Under the Criminal Justice Act 2003, if 'new and compelling evidence' emerges after a defendant has been acquitted at Crown court of a serious charge as defined by the Act, the prosecution can apply to the Court of Appeal for the acquittal to be quashed and a new trial to be held.

The Court of Appeal, when dealing with applications under the 2003 Act, can make an order under the Act's section 82 imposing reporting restrictions which make it an offence to publish anything which would create a substantial risk of prejudice to a re-trial. This can ban the media from reporting the application to quash the acquittal, or anything relating to it—for example, reporting that there are ongoing police investigations about the new evidence. The restrictions can be in force until the end of any re-trial or the matter is dropped.

9.12 The Crown court as an appeal court

Defendants can appeal to a Crown court judge against refusal by magistrates to grant bail.

Defendants can appeal to the Crown court against conviction by magistrates, including in youth courts. In the appeal there is no jury—a judge will sit normally with two lay magistrates. The Crown court also hears appeals against the severity of sentences imposed by magistrates and may confirm a sentence, substitute a lesser penalty or increase it, but not to more than the highest sentence magistrates could have imposed.

9.13 The High Court

The High Court Queen's Bench Division, which deals with criminal and other matters, has about 70 judges and sits in major cities.

A defendant convicted by magistrates, or who has appealed unsuccessfully to the Crown court, may appeal to the Queen's Bench Division on the grounds that a decision was wrong in law. This procedure is known as appeal by way of 'case stated', because no evidence is given verbally to the High Court, which considers a written record of the case. The prosecution can also use this procedure to challenge an acquittal by magistrates. The High Court has wide powers to reverse, affirm or amend magistrates' decisions, including those of youth courts. It can order the case to be re-tried summarily.

for the High Court's role in civil law, see 13.3

9.13.1 Judicial reviews

Part of the High Court's work involves **judicial reviews**, hearings which can consider other types of challenge to decisions made by magistrates. The media can use the judicial review procedure to challenge discretionary reporting restrictions imposed by magistrates or coroners—as explained in 16.4.2.1.

9.14 Courts martial

People in the armed forces are subject to UK law in the courts martial system, even if the alleged offence was committed in another country. These military courts are usually open to the public and media—for example, when in 2013 a Royal Marine was convicted of murdering an insurgent in Afghanistan.

 For more information on courts martial, see Useful Websites at the end of this chapter and the Additional Material for ch. 9 on www.mcnaes.com.

➡ Recap of major points

- Crown courts deal with the most serious criminal cases.
- Crown court judges rule on law and decide on punishment, and in trials juries decide whether each charge is proved.
- Automatic reporting restrictions limit what the media can report from most Crown court hearings held prior to trial.
- A defendant convicted in a Crown court may seek to appeal to the Court of Appeal and thereafter to the Supreme Court.
- Crown courts hear appeals from magistrates' courts against conviction or sentence.
- The High Court is also an appeal court for certain matters.

((•)) Useful Websites

www.gov.uk/jury-service
  Government guidance on jury service
www.gov.uk/guide-to-probation
  Government guidance on probation
www.gov.uk/government/organisations/national-probation-service
  National Probation Service
www.gov.uk/government/organisations/parole-board
  Parole Board
www.sentencingcouncil.org.uk/
  Sentencing Council website which explains sentences
www.supremecourt.uk/
  Supreme Court
www.cps.gov.uk/legal/p_to_r/retrial_of_serious_offences/
  Crown Prosecution Service guidance on section 82
www.judiciary.gov.uk/about-the-judiciary/the-justice-system/jurisdictions/military-jurisdiction/
  Courts martial

10

Juveniles in court proceedings

Chapter summary

Most juveniles charged with crimes are dealt with in youth courts by magistrates. The public cannot attend these courts, but journalists can. Reporting restrictions automatically ban identification of the juveniles involved, to protect their welfare. The term 'juvenile' covers those aged under 18. Juveniles are involved in cases in adult courts too—these courts may ban media reports from identifying such juveniles. The media may argue against this—for example, if the juvenile is a persistent offender.

10.1 Juveniles and the age of criminal responsibility

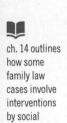

ch. 14 outlines how some family law cases involve interventions by social workers

Children under the age of 10 have not reached 'the age of criminal responsibility', so cannot be prosecuted for a crime as they are considered too young to distinguish between right and wrong. But they may be placed under the supervision of social workers.

The distinction between a 'child' (a person aged under 14) and a 'young person' (a person aged 14–17) is not important for journalists reporting courts, although some statutes use both terms. Lawyers, courts and this chapter use the term 'juvenile' broadly to describe anyone under the age of 18.

10.2 Juveniles in youth courts

Most juveniles who are prosecuted are dealt with by youth courts, presided over by magistrates or a district judge. Youth courts are usually in the same building as magistrates' courts (where adult defendants appear) but have smaller courtrooms to make juveniles feel less nervous than they might be in an adult court.

Magistrates who sit in youth courts receive special training. Procedures there, including trials, are similar to those in adult magistrates' courts, described in chs. 7 and 8.

A juvenile denied **bail** may be sent to non-secure accommodation run by the   →glossary
local authority, or—if the alleged offending is persistent or serious—to custody, as
explained later in this chapter.

10.2.1 Youth courts' powers

Most offences dealt with by youth courts are minor. Because youth courts' sentencing powers are limited they cannot try extremely serious cases, such as homicide, and must send such cases to a Crown court, in a procedure discussed later.
But a youth court has discretion, if it considers its punishment powers sufficient
in a particular case, to try other offences—such as rape or **robbery**—which, had   →glossary
the defendant been adult, could only be tried by a Crown court.

10.2.2 Sentencing

A youth court can impose **community sentences, absolute** and **conditional**   →glossary
discharges —sentences explained in 7.6.4, Other types of sentence—and can fine.
A parent must pay this fine if the offender is aged under 16. A youth court can
also make a 'youth rehabilitation order', a type of community sentence which
can involve several requirements, such as a curfew, unpaid work or a requirement for mental health treatment.

Many young offenders who admit a first offence are merely made subject to an
order which means they must cooperate with a referral to a youth offender panel
of trained youth workers. This seeks to get the offender to address his/her offending behaviour and repair harm it caused. An offender who fails to cooperate can
be given a more severe punishment.

In serious cases, youth courts can make 'detention and training orders' of
between four months and two years. Normally this means that the juvenile spends
half the period in custody with training and the other half being supervised in the
community.

The court may make 'a parenting order' requiring, for example, a parent to
attend counselling and guidance sessions.

10.2.3 Juveniles in custody

A juvenile refused bail by a youth court, or sentenced to detention and training,
can be held on **remand** or, for that sentence, in a secure children's home, a secure   →glossary
training centre or a young offenders' institution.

10.2.4 'Sending for trial' for homicide, 'grave' and other cases

A juvenile charged with a homicide offence, such as murder, or one of a range of
firearms offences cannot be tried or sentenced by a youth court because of the
seriousness of the charge, and there are other categories of offence—for example,
what is alleged to be a serious or complex fraud—which only a Crown court can

deal with. Juveniles facing such a charge initially appear in a youth court for decisions on bail and procedure but these cases are then sent for trial to a Crown court.

10.2.4.1 Grave offences

the allocation
procedure
is explained
in 8.3

→ glossary

→ glossary

The law on juvenile defendants allows some crimes to be classified as 'grave'—those for which an adult offender could be jailed for 14 years or more (apart from the homicide and firearms offences referred to earlier) and some sexual offences. In such cases the youth court considers whether its maximum power of punishment—a two-year detention and training order—would be sufficient if the defendant were to be convicted. This is allocation procedure similar to that for **either-way** charges in an adult magistrates' court—it determines which court is the venue for the trial. If the youth court considers its sentencing power insufficient, the case is sent to a Crown court for trial if the offence is denied, or sent there by **committal for sentence** if the defendant admits guilt.

10.2.4.2 Extended sentences and co-accused with an adult

The youth court will also send a case for Crown court trial if it considers that the defendant would, if convicted, be classed as a 'dangerous offender' for sentencing—see 9.7.1, Life sentences and extended sentences—or because the juvenile is to be tried there co-accused with an adult defendant.

10.2.4.3 Section 52A reporting restrictions

→ glossary

Unless guilt is admitted for the sole charge or all charges—by the juvenile formally indicating the intention to plead guilty—the **automatic** reporting restrictions of section 52A of the Crime and Disorder Act 1998 apply to the allocation hearing and any sending hearing in such a case, and to any preceding hearing. These restrictions normally stay in force until the trial concludes. For a case the Crown court must deal with, no indication of plea is taken in the youth court.

See 8.2 and 8.3 for details of the section 52A restrictions and how on rare occasions they may be lifted. They are explained in relation to cases in the (adult) magistrates' courts—but apply identically in respect of such preliminary hearings at youth courts. Their effect is to ban the contemporaneous reporting of prejudicial matter.

for explanation of these
1980 Act
restrictions,
see 7.4

10.2.4.4 Section 8C restrictions

Pre-trial hearings of a case to be tried by a youth court are covered by the automatic reporting restrictions in section 8C of the Magistrates' Courts Act 1980.

! Remember your rights

Other reporting restrictions, preventing identification of juveniles, normally apply automatically to cases at youth courts, as explained later in this chapter. So, for some hearings, section 52A of the 1998 Act or section 8C of the 1980 Act *and* anonymity will apply.

10.2.4.5 Committal for sentence—'dangerous offenders'

A youth court which convicts a juvenile of a serious crime can also consider at this stage whether he/she should be classed as a 'dangerous offender'. If the answer is 'yes', there will be a committal for sentence—that is, the youth court will commit him/her to Crown court for a judge there to decide the sentence.

❗ Remember your rights

The reporting restrictions in section 52A of the 1998 Act or section 8C of the 1980 Act do not affect the reporting of a trial at a youth court or Crown court, or a youth court hearing which decides whether to commit for sentence. These restrictions only apply to reports of preliminary/pre-trial hearings.

ch. 9, p. 106, Life sentences and extended sentences

10.3 Admission to youth courts

Parliament has decided that the public should not be allowed inside youth courts, to avoid juveniles suffering adverse contemporaneous publicity from their involvement in the proceedings, whether they are defendants facing allegations or convicted of immature law-breaking, or witnesses or victims/alleged victims of the crime.

- But journalists are allowed into youth courts to cover cases—section 47 of the Children and Young Persons Act 1933 gives 'bona fide representatives of newspapers or news agencies' the right to attend.

Reporters may need to assert their right to be in court.

👁 Case study

In February 2017 District Judge Julia Newton banned a Press Association (PA) reporter from a hearing at Highbury Corner youth court, after the defence said the reporter's presence would be detrimental to the welfare of the defendant, a teenager accused of assault and possessing an offensive weapon. After PA protested that its reporter was excluded, a Judicial Communications spokesman said of the judge: 'In hindsight she realises this was an error and that she had no legal authority to exclude the press and they should have been allowed to attend under section 47 the Children and Young Persons Act 1933.' The prosecutor did not challenge the defence application for the reporter to be kept out. A Crown Prosecution Service spokesman said, of that lack of a challenge, that the CPS did not believe that its general guidance to prosecutors was correctly applied (*Media Lawyer*, 28 March 2017).

The Youth Court Bench Book, guidance for magistrates published by the Judicial College in 2017, says: 'Fair and accurate reports of proceedings, even where individuals are not identified, should be encouraged where appropriate as they can help promote public confidence.'

 CPS guidance to prosecutors about reporting restrictions is outlined in 16.4.1.1, 16.7.2 and 16.8. See Useful Websites at the end of this chapter for the Bench Book.

There can be exceptions to the ban on the public attending a youth court—for example, an adult or child who is the victim of the crime may be allowed to see an offender being sentenced.

10.4 Section 49 automatic restrictions on identifying juveniles

Parliament decided to shield all juveniles 'concerned in the proceedings' in youth court cases—defendants, victims/alleged victims and witnesses—from adverse publicity by banning, until they reach the age of 18, the media from identifying them in any publication referring to their cases. This automatic anonymity is bestowed by section 49 of the Children and Young Persons Act 1933.

Section 49 says that (here summarised):

- no matter relating to any juvenile concerned in proceedings shall, while he/she is under the age of 18, be included in any publication if it is likely to lead members of the public to identify him/her as someone concerned in the proceedings.

It also says that the following matters in particular should not be included if likely to identify the juvenile:

- his/her name;
- his/her address;
- the identity of any school or other educational establishment he/she attends;
- the identity of any place of work; and
- any still or moving picture of him/her.

The definition 'concerned in the proceedings' includes a juvenile 'in respect of whom the proceedings are taken', which means that section 49 anonymity applies to a juvenile who is the victim/alleged victim in the case even if he/she is not a witness—for example, because he/she is too young to give evidence.

for context, see 16.3 about the, Judicial College guidance for criminal courts

But a juvenile victim/alleged victim who is dead *can* be identified by the media, because a dead juvenile is not 'concerned in the proceedings'. This point is made in the Judicial College guidance on reporting restrictions—see Useful Websites at the end of this chapter.

Section 49 says 'publication' includes 'any speech, writing, relevant programme or other communication in whatever form, which is addressed to the public at large or any section of the public'.

👁 Case study

In October 2016 Thomas Sinclair, editor of the *Pembrokeshire Herald*, was fined £500 at Llanelli magistrates' court because a *Herald* report named a juvenile defendant when referring to a youth court case, breaching section 49 of the Children and Young Persons Act 1933. Sinclair admitted this. The juvenile, the 17-year-old skipper of a trawler, had been fined in February that year by Haverfordwest youth court for local bye-law offences because of an accident in November 2015 when the trawler ran onto rocks. The prosecutors in that case—Milford Haven Port Authority—issued a press release which referred to the fines and identified the trawler, but did not name the juvenile or specify that the Haverfordwest magistrates were sitting as a youth court. The *Herald*'s report, based on that release, included the teenager's name. Mr Sinclair, 37, of Hamilton Terrace, Milford Haven, said the juvenile had been widely identified as the trawler's skipper in coverage of the accident after it took place, and added: 'I thought that because it was a private prosecution brought by MHPA it was in the adult court'. District Judge Neil Evans told Sinclair that anonymity for juveniles appearing in youth court was a fundamental pillar of the British legal system. 'You as the editor knew this defendant was a youth and at the very least you ought to have made proper enquiries', the judge said, adding: 'This was a cavalier approach to reporting.' The skipper, Jake Bowman-Davies, was named in coverage of Sinclair's conviction because by then the section 49 anonymity had lapsed as he had turned 18 (*Holdthefrontpage* and *Western Telegraph*, 6 October 2016; *Media Lawyer*, 11 October 2016).

10.4.1 No identifying detail should be published

The section 49 restrictions mean that media reports of youth court cases should not include any detail which could identify a juvenile concerned in the proceedings. Describing a defendant as 'a 14-year-old Bristol boy' would not identify him because Bristol is large. But naming a small village as a defendant's home could well identify him/her to people who know he/she lives there. Reporting a juvenile's nickname or an unusual physical characteristic might identify him/her to some people. Reporting that he is the 12-year-old twin son of a policeman will identify him to anyone who knows of such twins. The test is always whether, as a result of the report, any member of the public could realise who the juvenile is. Adults who figure in youth court cases as witnesses or are mentioned in evidence can be named, as long as this does not identify a juvenile (or breach any discretionary restriction imposed by the court in respect of the adult). But a journalist may need to leave a name and detail identifying an adult out of a report to avoid identifying a juvenile—for example, a father who gives evidence about his son, the defendant, cannot be named: see 10.11 about jigsaw identification, and see the Additional Material for ch. 10 on www.mcnaes.com.

👁 Case study

In 2003 a district judge fined the *Plymouth Evening Herald* £1,500 for publishing a photograph of a 15-year-old boy convicted at a youth court of stabbing a fellow pupil. The district judge said evidence by friends and relatives that they had recognised the boy, even though his face was pixelated, meant that the paper had breached section 49 (*Media Lawyer*, 4 March 2004).

✳ Remember

Section 49 does not only apply to reports of youth court cases. It bans any publication (e.g. a feature on crime, or a tweet about an individual) from identifying a juvenile as being concerned in a youth court case.

Section 49 is not a blanket ban on identifying the juvenile's school, in that it may be possible for a report to identify the school if it is large, without being likely to identify the juvenile. But journalists should err on the side of caution, and the safest course is to ask the court for specific permission to identify the school if this is 'in the public interest'—see 10.4.5, When section 49 anonymity ceases to apply. The court might give permission, for example, to let the media highlight a problem of drug-dealing at a particular school, because the court can disapply section 49 'to any specified extent'.

10.4.2 When does the section 49 anonymity begin?

Section 49 refers to court proceedings. Therefore, strictly speaking, its anonymity does not take effect until the first hearing begins in the youth court. Journalists may decide, to avoid a defamation risk—see 5.10, The risk of libel in media identification of crime suspects—not to identify a juvenile being investigated by police even though section 49 applies only if or when the case reaches a youth court hearing. Another consideration is that clause 9 of the Editors' Code or rule 1.9 of the Broadcasting Code may be breached if a juvenile being investigated by police is identified in reporting—see 5.15, Juveniles under investigation.

10.4.3 Anonymity retained for appeal and youth rehabilitation order hearings

these Crown court and High Court appeal routes are explained in 9.12 and 9.13

- Section 49 anonymity also applies to reports of Crown court hearings of appeals from the youth court against conviction or severity of sentence, and to reports of High Court hearings of appeals from the youth court (or from the Crown court appeal hearings) by 'case stated' (that is, an appeal about how law should be interpreted), and to reports of appeal hearings in higher courts, should either type of appeal go higher, so the anonymity travels up with the appeal.

- The anonymity also applies to reports of proceedings in a magistrates' court for breach, revocation or amendment of youth rehabilitation orders if the court announces that section 49 applies, and to reports of the hearings in higher courts of appeals from such proceedings, including by 'case stated'.

- The section 49 restrictions do *not* apply to reports of the Crown court proceedings involving a juvenile sent there for trial or committed there for sentence. But the Crown court may make a discretionary order giving him/her anonymity under section 45 of the Youth Justice and Criminal Evidence Act 1999, as explained later.

10.4.4 Breaches of section 49 and who can be liable

Publishing material which breaches section 49—identifies a juvenile who should have anonymity—is a criminal offence, for which the punishment is an unlimited fine.

Section 49 says that the proprietor, editor or publisher of a newspaper or periodical can be prosecuted for a breach. For a TV or radio programme the prosecution can be of 'the body corporate' which provides the programme service and 'any person having functions in relation to the programme corresponding to those of an editor of a newspaper', and in the case of any other publication, any person publishing it. The Attorney General must consent to such prosecutions.

Section 49 says it is a defence for someone prosecuted for breaching the anonymity to prove that at the time of the alleged breach he/she was not aware, and neither suspected nor had reason to suspect that the publication included the matter in question. But in essence the offence is one of 'strict liability'.

'strict liability' is explained in 6.2.1

10.4.4.1 Readers' comments which breach anonymity

It is possible that a reader might post directly onto a media organisation's website a comment identifying a juvenile who should have anonymity. Law which can protect the organisation from any liability includes regulation 19 of the Electronic Commerce (EC Directive) Regulations 2002, provided the comment was deleted expeditiously when the organisation became aware of its unlawful content.

see 22.12 for detail of regulation 19

10.4.5 When section 49 anonymity ceases to apply

The section 49 anonymity automatically expires when the juvenile reaches the age of 18. Legislative amendments to section 49 made this clear, following *R (on the application of JC & RT) v Central Criminal Court* [2014] EWCA Civ 1777.

Section 49 allows a youth court to lift a juvenile's anonymity—that is, before he/she turns 18—to allow the media to identify him/her 'to any specified extent' in three types of circumstance.

(1) *To avoid injustice*—This power is rarely exercised. A youth court could use it to allow a media report of a preliminary hearing to identify a juvenile defendant whose lawyer says he/she wants publicity to help trace witnesses

→ glossary

to prove an **alibi**—'My client John Doe was at the funfair that night, not the crime scene. Did anyone see him at the funfair?' The court might also do so to quash rumours suggesting that the victim was in fact the defendant.

(2) *Unlawfully at large*—A youth court can lift section 49 anonymity, if asked to do so by or on behalf of the Director of Public Prosecutions, to help to trace a juvenile who is 'unlawfully at large' after being charged with or convicted of a violent or sexual offence, or any offence for which a person aged 21 or more could be jailed for 14 years or more. This would let the media name and publish a photograph of a juvenile who has failed to answer bail or who escaped from secure accommodation and may be a threat to public safety.

(3) *In the public interest*—A youth court can lift the anonymity of a juvenile it convicts of any offence if satisfied that doing so is 'in the public interest'.

- Before taking this decision it must give the prosecution and defence the opportunity to argue for or against lifting the anonymity.

The power to lift the anonymity can be used when a youth court feels that the media should be able to identify—for the benefit of the community—a juvenile who has persistently offended or committed a notorious crime.

 See also 16.8, Challenges to youth court anonymity, for the 'public interest' grounds the media can cite to argue in court for a convicted juvenile's anonymity to be removed.

❗ Remember your rights

A court can only lift section 49 anonymity 'in the public interest' if the juvenile is a convicted defendant. Remember too that though section 49 anonymity expires when a juvenile turns 18, law created in 2015 means a youth court can give lifetime anonymity to a juvenile witness or victim/alleged victim in a case, as this chapter explains later.

👁 Case study

The ability of youth courts to lift section 49 'to any specified extent' is illustrated by a 2006 decision of Newbury youth court, which ruled it was in the public interest to allow media reports to name a 14-year-old girl convicted of drink-driving. But it banned publication of recent photographs of her and the naming of her school. Shortly after the court decided this, the girl, who was first convicted of drink-driving when she was 12, threw a punch at the prosecutor and hurled a 2 litre jug of water at the magistrates (*Media Lawyer*, 28 March 2006).

10.5 Juveniles in adult courts

A juvenile may appear in the (adult) magistrates' court if jointly charged with an adult. The juvenile may be tried there as a co-accused, or the magistrates can remit the juvenile's case to the youth court for trial or sentencing. If the adult's case is sent for trial to the Crown court, the juvenile's case may be sent there too if the magistrates think a joint trial is in the interests of justice—for example, to avoid making witnesses testify in two trials. Youth courts may also send a juvenile defendant to a Crown court for trial or to be sentenced, as explained in 10.2.4.

10.6 Section 45 reporting restrictions in adult criminal courts

There is no automatic ban on identifying any juvenile as being 'concerned in the proceedings' of an adult criminal court—magistrates', Crown or higher court—whether as a defendant, witness or victim/alleged victim.

But adult criminal courts have discretion under section 45 of the Youth Justice and Criminal Evidence Act 1999 to give such juveniles anonymity.

A section 45 order should specify the individual it covers. Its scope normally is that (here summarised):

- no matter relating to the juvenile shall be included in any publication while he/she is under the age of 18 if it is likely to lead members of the public to identify him/her as someone concerned in the proceedings.

Section 45 says that the following matters in particular should not be included if likely to identify the juvenile:

- his/her name;
- his/her address;
- the identity of any school or other educational establishment he/she attends;
- the identity of any place of work; and
- any still or moving picture of him/her.

A section 45 anonymity order covering a juvenile defendant, witness or victim/alleged victim may well mean that some details in the charge(s) or some details of evidence cannot be published and, possibly, that an adult defendant or adult witness in the case also cannot be identified.

For example, if a father is charged with assaulting his child, whose identity is protected by a section 45 order, the relationship cannot be included in any report naming the father as the defendant, as this would identify the child. Even mentioning the child's age in such reports could inadvertently reveal a familial relationship and so unlawfully identify the child.

see also 10.12 on cases of abuse within a family

The types of detail which could breach section 45 anonymity are the same as those which could breach the automatic anonymity provided in respect of youth court cases under section 49 of the Children and Young Persons Act 1993.

See 10.4.1 for examples of such detail. Also, media organisations must guard against 'jigsaw identification' occurring—see 10.11.

! Remember your rights

A section 45 order can apply to a juvenile 'in respect of whom the proceedings are taken'. It therefore can be used to prevent a media report of a truancy case from identifying a child whose parent is prosecuted in the adult magistrates' court for failing to ensure the child attends school. The effect would be that the report could not identify the parent either and should not identify the school if there is any likelihood of this identifying the child.

10.6.1 When section 45 anonymity ceases to apply

Anonymity under a section 45 order automatically expires when the juvenile turns 18. The Court of Appeal has said the section makes that clear (*R (on the application of JC & RT) v Central Criminal Court* [2014] EWCA Civ 1777). A criminal court can at an earlier stage revoke the order, so lifting the anonymity provision, or relax the order's scope by making an 'excepting direction' (another order).

As ch. 16 explains, media organisations sometimes argue in court for section 45 orders to be lifted so—for example—reports can identify defendants convicted of serious crime. See 16.7 and its sub-sections for detail about a court's power to revoke such an order, and for case law which the media can cite to challenge the provision or continuation of section 45 anonymity.

10.6.2 The 2015 changes

Section 45 of the 1999 Act was brought into force on 13 April 2015. In the criminal courts, it replaced—as the discretionary power to provide anonymity for juveniles—section 39 of the Children and Young Persons Act 1933. Use of section 39 is now restricted to non-criminal proceedings, as explained later in this chapter.

10.7 Invalid anonymity orders

- A court, to pay proper heed to the principle of open justice, should not make a section 45 order under the 1999 Act or a section 39 order under the 1933 Act merely because of the juvenile's age or as an order arbitrarily covering all juveniles in the case. It should consider for each whether there is good reason for anonymity.
- These sections can only provide anonymity for a living juvenile, not one who is dead—for example, a murder victim.
- A court cannot use either type of order to specifically give anonymity to an adult.

See 16.7 and its sub-sections for guidance and case law on media challenges to section 45 or section 39 orders which are invalid or unnecessary.

10.8 Lifetime anonymity for a juvenile witness or victim/alleged victim

Since 13 April 2015, any criminal court—youth court, magistrates' courts and Crown court—can make an order under section 45A of the Youth Justice and Criminal Evidence Act 1999 to provide:

- lifetime anonymity for a juvenile witness or a juvenile victim/alleged victim so that he/she is not identified as having been 'concerned in the proceedings'. This anonymity cannot be given to a defendant, even if he/she is also a witness.

The scope of this anonymity is the same as that under section 45, except that a section 45A order means the anonymity does *not* expire when the juvenile reaches 18. A court can make such an order when it is satisfied that the juvenile is in 'fear or distress' about being publicly identified as being concerned in the case and that without the anonymity the quality of his/her evidence or level of cooperation with the party (defence or prosecution) which wants him/her to give evidence is likely to be diminished.

 See 16.9.2 for grounds on which a section 45A order can be challenged. For example, it may be invalid or so substantially restrict what can be reported that there is a public interest justification to challenge it. But the welfare of such a juvenile must be considered.

Section 50 of the Act says that a person protected by this anonymity provision can waive it by giving written consent to be identified. There is no requirement for a court to approve this consent, which can be given direct to a journalist. But the consent is not valid unless the person who gives it has reached the age of 18. Also, the consent will be invalid if it was obtained by interfering with the person's 'peace or comfort'.

Section 45A makes clear it cannot be used to protect any defendant's identity.

10.8.1 'Publication' and liability for breach of section 45 or 45A anonymity

The law about who can be prosecuted for breaching anonymity under a section 45 or 45A order under the 1999 Act is the same as for breaching section 49 anonymity under the Children and Young Persons Act 1933, and the definition of 'publication' is the same in both Acts. The punishment is the same too for those convicted of breach—an unlimited fine.

 for this law, see 10.4 and 10.4.4

see too
10.4.4.1 about
readers'
posted
comments
which breach
anonymity

Section 50 of the 1999 Act says a person accused of publishing information which breached section 45 or 45A anonymity shall have a defence if it can be proved that he or she was not aware, and neither suspected nor had reason to suspect, that the publication included the matter or report in question.

10.9 Section 39 reporting restrictions in civil proceedings and coroners' courts

→ glossary

ch. 13
explains
civil courts
and ch. 17
explains
coroners'
courts

When juveniles are 'concerned' in civil law proceedings—for example, in the High Court or a county court as **claimants**, defendants or witnesses—or in a coroner's court as a witness, they *can* be identified in the media as being involved in the case unless the court specifically forbids it.

A court which wants, 'in relation' to any such proceedings, to ban the media from identifying such a juvenile can make an order under section 39 of the Children and Young Persons' Act 1933.

The scope of a section 39 order is normally that no publication referring to the case shall reveal:

- any particulars 'calculated' (that is, likely) to lead to his/her identification as being concerned in the proceedings, and could specifically ban publication of;
  - the juvenile's name;
  - his/her address;
  - his/her school;
  - a picture of or including the juvenile.

see 10.4.1,
No identify-
ing detail
should be
published

The wording of section 39 has yet to be fully standardised with that of the other reporting restrictions explained earlier. The section 39 wording means that, unless the court decides otherwise, the order may well ban identification of the juvenile's school in any publication referring to the case, irrespective of whether identifying the school is likely to identify the juvenile, and ban publication of a picture of or including the juvenile, irrespective of whether it is likely to identify him/her.

As with section 49 anonymity in respect of youth court cases, see 10.4.1, a journalist must take care not to breach a section 39 order made by a civil or coroner's court by including too much detail about any juvenile protected by it.

Section 39 says 'any person' who includes in a publication material which breaches the anonymity is liable for the breach. The definition of 'publication' is the same as in section 49 of the Act—see explanation earlier in this chapter. Breach of section 39 anonymity, as with section 49 anonymity, is punishable by an unlimited fine.

 For an example of illegal identification of a juvenile's school, see the *Newcastle Journal* case study in the Additional Material for ch. 10 on www.mcnaes.com.

10.9.1 When does section 39 cease to apply to a juvenile?

In 2014 the Court of Appeal, upholding previous case law, ruled that section 39 anonymity automatically expires when the juvenile reaches the age of 18 (*R (on the application of JC & RT) v Central Criminal Court* [2014] EWCA Civ 1777).

A civil court wanting to extend the juvenile's anonymity provision beyond this age—that is, into adulthood—could make an order drawing directly on powers derived from the European Convention on Human Rights. Civil courts also have a specific power in the Civil Procedure Rules (CPR) to order that the identity of a witness or party should not be disclosed.

 See 12.10, Other anonymity orders, on the CPR and 16.5, Rights to anonymity are limited. See too 16.7, Court orders giving juveniles anonymity, and its subsections for guidance and law on how the media can challenge section 45 or section 39 orders which are invalid or unnecessary.

10.10 Anti-social behaviour injunctions and criminal behaviour orders

A court imposing or considering imposing an anti-social behaviour injunction may make an order under section 39 of the Children and Young Persons Act 1933 to give anonymity to a juvenile who is the subject of the hearing. A juvenile who is the subject of an application to impose a criminal behaviour order (CBO) may have anonymity under section 49 of the same Act. A juvenile accused of breaching a CBO may be given anonymity by an order made under section 45 of the Youth Justice and Criminal Evidence Act, but does not have automatic anonymity under section 49 of the 1933 Act. For explanations of the relevant law, including anonymity provision for juvenile witnesses in respect of such injunction or CBO proceedings, see the Additional Material for ch. 10 on www.mcnaes.com.

10.11 Jigsaw identification

- 'Jigsaw identification' describes the effect when someone to whom the law has given anonymity is nevertheless identifiable to the public because of a combination or accumulation of detail published.

It can occur when two or more media organisations cover the same case. Each may publish a report which in itself preserves the anonymity. But jigsaw identification will occur if someone who reads, views or hears the reports of more than one organisation can, by combining the different detail in each, recognise the person who should be anonymous.

Jigsaw identification can also occur through publication of a series of sequential reports which allow too much detail to accumulate. The term is also used to describe such an accumulation in a *single* report.

The examples given below relate to anonymity for juveniles. But jigsaw identification can also destroy anonymity the law grants to others, such as victims and alleged victims of sexual offences.

 Sexual offences law is explained in ch. 11. Other law giving anonymity is explained in chs. 12, 13, 14, 17 and 18.

Example 1 A juvenile in a youth court, who has anonymity under section 49 of the Children and Young Persons Act 1933, admits causing criminal damage to a sports car owned by local millionaire John Doe. One local paper reports: 'A 15-year-old boy vandalised a sports car owned by London tycoon John Doe, costing him £5,000 in repairs.' Another local paper reports: 'A 15-year-old boy vandalised his rich neighbour's sports car, causing £5,000 damage.' Neither paper names the boy, and the second paper does not name Doe. But anyone reading both will know the boy is Doe's neighbour, which will identify the boy locally.

Example 2 A juvenile granted anonymity by an order under section 45 order of the Youth Justice and Criminal Evidence Act 1999, testifies at Crown court in a murder trial. A local radio station describes her as 'a 16-year-old who works as a shop assistant in London'. Another radio station does not mention her job but describes her routine as 'commuting each morning to work in Charing Cross'. A newspaper reports that she lives in Islington. This accumulation of detail could lead those who know her, and who listen to both stations and read that newspaper, to realise that she is the witness.

10.12 Cases of abuse within a family

There is a particular danger of jigsaw identification in reporting court cases concerning violence or sexual abuse allegedly inflicted on a child by a relative or family 'friend'—for example, when a father, stepfather or a mother's live-in partner is the adult defendant. In such cases, when the abuse is physical but not sexual, it is standard practice for magistrates or the Crown court judge to make a section 45 order. In cases where the charge is of sexual abuse, the child has automatic anonymity under other law—see ch. 11.

When covering such abuse cases in courts, a media organisation has two options.

(a) *The report can name the adult defendant*—but if the defendant is a relative, the report must not include any detail of his/her relationship to the child, to protect the child's anonymity. This can severely restrict what is published—for example, about how the defendant had opportunity to abuse the child, or even the child's age. Lord Justice Maurice Kay made this comment in the Court of Appeal in 2005, alluding to a case in which a father was convicted of conspiracy to rape a child and of distributing indecent photographs of her: 'Offences of the kind established in this case are frequently committed by fathers and step-fathers. . . . If the offender is named and the victim is described as "an 11-year old schoolgirl", in circumstances in which the offender has an 11-year old daughter, it is at least arguable that the composite picture presented embraces "particulars calculated (likely) to lead to the identification' of the victim" (*R v Teesside Crown Court, ex p Gazette Media Company Ltd and others* [2005] All ER (D) 367 (Jul)).

(b) *If the report does not identify the adult defendant in any way*, it can therefore refer to the familial or household relationship between the defendant and child, can definitely refer to the child's age and can include greater detail of evidence, while preserving the child's anonymity.

An editor's instinct is usually that it is in the public interest for people charged with crime—and particularly those convicted of it—to be named, as a deterrent and so that a community can be wary of that individual. This is achieved by the approach in (a), if it is possible to construct a meaningful report without revealing the family relationship. But another editor may feel that the public interest is best served by the approach in (b), which can make clear that the alleged abuse was, for example, by a relative. Approach (b) allows publication of more evidential material and more questions to be raised about why the community, social services or the police remained unaware of the abuse within the household.

Jigsaw identification may occur if two media organisations covering the case adopt different approaches. If one follows policy (a), naming the adult defendant but obscuring his relationship to the child victim, and the other follows approach (b), not identifying the defendant but reporting, for example, that he was the child's father, anyone reading both reports will be able to identify the child even though neither report names him/her. To avoid jigsaw identification of the child, all the newsrooms involved need to adopt the same approach.

 See 11.9, Ethical considerations, on the ethical ban on identifying children in sexual cases, including those who are defendants.

➡ Recap of major points

- Most juveniles charged with a crime are dealt with by youth courts. The public cannot attend these courts, but journalists can.

- Section 49 of the Children and Young Persons Act 1933 bans media reports from identifying anyone aged under 18 as being involved in a youth court case, whether as defendant, witness or crime victim/alleged victim.

- This anonymity can be lifted, in the case of a convicted juvenile, to allow the media to identify him/her in the public interest—for example, after persistent offending.

- There is no automatic anonymity for a juvenile involved in adult court proceedings. But an adult court can make an order under section 45 of the Youth Justice and Criminal Evidence Act 1999 to give the juvenile anonymity.

- There is no automatic anonymity for a juvenile involved in civil proceedings or inquests at coroners' courts. But these courts can make an order under section 39 of the Children and Young Persons Act 1933 to give the juvenile anonymity.

((•)) Useful Websites

www.gov.uk/browse/justice/young-people
Government guidance on the youth justice system

www.judiciary.gov.uk/publications/reporting-restrictions-in-the-criminal-courts-2/
Judicial College guidance, *Reporting Restrictions in the Criminal Courts*, 4th edition, as revised in May 2016 by the Judicial College, Media Lawyers Association, News Media Association and Society of Editors.

www.sentencingcouncil.org.uk/wp-content/uploads/youth-court-bench-book-august-2017.pdf
Youth Court Bench Book

www.gov.uk/government/publications/review-of-the-youth-justice-system
Review of the youth justice system, published by the Ministry of Justice in 2016

Sexual offences, human trafficking and female genital mutilation

Chapter summary

The law gives victims and alleged victims of sexual offences, including rape, lifetime anonymity in media reports of these crimes and any subsequent prosecutions. Several media organisations have been fined for publishing material which breached this anonymity and so caused considerable distress to those identified. As this chapter explains, the anonymity may be removed in some circumstances, allowing the media to identify the individual, but a journalist should consider if this would be ethical. The law also gives anonymity to victims/alleged victims of female genital mutilation, and of human trafficking for sexual and non-sexual exploitation, including slavery or forced labour.

11.1 Automatic, lifelong anonymity for complainants of sexual or trafficking offences

Section 1 of the Sexual Offences (Amendment) Act 1992 says that after an allegation of a sexual or human trafficking offence is made:

- no matter relating to that victim/alleged victim shall, during his/her lifetime, be included in any publication if it is likely to lead members of the public to identify him/her as the victim/alleged victim of the offence.

It says the ban includes in particular, if likely to identify that person:

- his/her name;
- his/her address;
- the identity of any school or other educational establishment he/she attends;
- the identity of any place of work;
- any still or moving picture of him/her.

Section 6 of the Act defines publication as any speech, writing, relevant programme or other communication in whatever form addressed to the public at large or to any section of the public, and a 'picture' as 'a likeness however produced'.

The anonymity is automatic and lifelong, and applies from the time an allegation is made by the alleged victim or anyone else—for example, when a parent complains to police, or to a journalist, that a child has been sexually abused—and remains in place regardless of whether the allegation is later withdrawn, or the police are told, or an alleged offender is prosecuted, or anyone is convicted.

The anonymity also applies to anyone who is the target of any attempt or conspiracy to commit a sexual or human trafficking offence.

In rare circumstances a court may lift the anonymity or the individual concerned may waive it, as this chapter explains. But it usually applies.

 See the Additional Material for ch. 11 on www.mcnaes.com, Newspaper breached anonymity after the rape charge was dropped.

11.2 The wide application of the anonymity

Parliament decided in 1976 that the violation of rape, and the potential for victims to suffer embarrassment and further trauma when testifying in court, justified giving them anonymity. This anonymity is provided by the 1992 Act. It since been extended to victims/alleged victims of other sexual offences, and recently to victims/alleged victims of offences of 'human trafficking for exploitation'—including non-sexual offences—in section 2 of the Modern Slavery Act 2015. The anonymity applies to crime stories as well as court reports—for example, to a news website report that police are investigating a rape. Nothing should be published which is likely to reveal the identity of the victim/alleged victim, such as a picture of the house where the sexual offence is said to have taken place or the victim/alleged victim of human trafficking lived.

 For detail of the 2015 Act, see 11.6, Trafficking offences for which victims/alleged victims have anonymity.

The anonymity also applies to reports of the trials of those accused of these offences, although the defendant can be named, as well as to reports of courts martial and civil cases. So a woman who alleges she was raped or subject to trafficking and who sues the alleged perpetrator in a civil court must remain anonymous in reports of that lawsuit.

Similarly, anyone who claims at an employment tribunal that he/she was the victim of a sexual or a trafficking offence must be anonymous in reports of the case.

 Ch. 9 outlines the courts martial system, ch. 13 explains civil courts, and ch. 18 and its Additional Material on www.mcnaes.com cover employment tribunals.

A person who says, when being interviewed for a biographical feature, that he/she was at some time sexually attacked or molested, or trafficked for exploitation, cannot legally be identified in it as being a victim/alleged victim of this crime, unless he/she gives valid written consent for such identification, as this chapter explains later. Similar anonymity under other law applies for anyone who says she is a victim of female genital mutilation, as this chapter also explains.

Case study

Trinity Mirror Southern Ltd was fined a total of £10,000 in 2011 after admitting that the *Aldershot News and Mail, Farnborough News and Mail, Fleet News and Mail* and *Yateley News and Mail* had published in a report of a court case the names of two women who were victims of sexual assault. Human error was blamed for this breach of the Sexual Offences (Amendment) Act 1992. *(Hampshire Constabulary's Frontline* magazine, issue 163, July 2011).

> For more detail of this case, and others in which media organisations were fined for breach of the 1992 Act, see the Additional Material for ch. 11 on www.mcnaes.com.

11.3 Care needed with detail

Section 1 of the 1992 Act prohibits publication of matter 'likely to lead' to identification. A report of a sexual or trafficking offence which refers to the alleged victim's school or workplace and gives his/her age could prompt speculation likely to lead to identification. For example, although saying the victim is a student at a specific university is unlikely to identify him/her, giving further detail, such as that the victim is a 25-year-old music student, is likely to do so. In 1983 the then Solicitor General said that a report of a rape case could break the law if it included sufficient detail to identify the victim in the minds of some people even though not in the minds of the community generally.

Case study:

In 2016 the Telegraph Media Group was fined £80,000—the highest fine yet imposed for breach of the 1992 Act, or any statutory reporting restriction—because the *Daily Telegraph* published a photo which could have identified a teenager as a victim of sexual offences. It was published with a report of the conviction at Bradford Crown court of Adam Johnson, the former England and Sunderland football player, on a charge that he had sexual activity with the girl, aged 15. He had admitted grooming her and one lesser charge of sexual activity. The photo was copied from a Facebook page image which, in its original form showed Johnson with the girl. The *Telegraph* is understood to have 'significantly modified' the image before publication to disguise her identity. But, after being charged under the 1992 Act, it accepted at Westminster magistrates' court that publication of the modified version was likely to identify her, although there was no evidence that this had happened because of that publication. As well as being fined, the *Telegraph* was ordered to pay £1,473 in prosecution costs, and £10,000 in compensation to the girl *(Media Lawyer,* 10 October 2016).

11.3.1 Jigsaw identification

Jigsaw identification must be avoided whenever reports refer to an offence for which the law gives the victim/alleged victim anonymity. It may occur if a newspaper reporting a rape trial describes the alleged victim as 'a mother of three' who lives and works locally, a TV station describes her as 'a nurse', and a radio station describes her as 'a woman in her 30s' who works nights—an accumulation of detail which could identify her to colleagues and acquaintances—see also 10.11, Jigsaw identification.

see also 10.12, Cases of abuse within a family

Media organisations covering cases involving sexual abuse of a child by an adult in the same family or household should agree whether their reports (a) name the adult defendant, but omit any detail of any relationship to the child, or (b) do not identify the adult defendant and report that the alleged abuse was familial or within the household.

Journalists should also pay heed to relevant parts of the Editors' Code or the Broadcasting Code, which are explained later in this chapter.

👁 Case study

see 11.7, Liability for breach of the anonymity provision

for Mr Sinclair's conviction for breach of a juvenile defendant's anonymity, see 10.4

In 2017 *Pembrokeshire Herald* editor Thomas Sinclair, 37, was convicted of breaching the 1992 Act because of detail in a report of a court case published in the sister paper, the *Ceredigion Herald*. Llanelli magistrates' court heard that the report named a man convicted of voyeurism, gave his age and occupation and detailed his 'familial links' to the victim. The Crown Prosecution Service said that the report made 'jigsaw identification' of her likely, which is unlawful under the Act. District Judge David Parsons was told that the trainee journalist who wrote the report was sent to the voyeurism case without training, supervision or support. The judge ruled that Sinclair, as editor, had breached the 1992 Act, which he denied. He was fined £1,500 and ordered to pay £1,500 compensation, £500 costs and £150 surcharge. Sinclair, of Hamilton Terrace, Milford Haven, maintained that there was no likelihood of the report leading members of the public to identify the voyeurism victim. He said that at the time of the report he had already booked staff onto a media law course (*Western Telegraph*, 20 April 2017; *Ceredigion Herald*, 20 April 2017; *Media Lawyer*, 12 May, 2017).

11.4 Invalid orders purporting to give a defendant anonymity

The media may decide, particularly when covering a court case involving alleged sexual abuse within a family, that the only way to preserve anonymity for the alleged victim(s) is not to publish anything identifying the adult defendant. But occasionally magistrates' courts and Crown court judges have sought to make that choice for the media by making an order, purportedly under the Sexual Offences (Amendment) Act 1992, stating that the defendant should not be identified. There is no power in the Act to make such an order. It should be challenged, because it is invalid—see 16.10, Sexual offence law does not give anonymity to defendants.

11.5 Sexual offences for which victims/alleged victims have anonymity

The 1992 Act, as amended by the Sexual Offences Act 2003, applies the anonymity for victims and alleged victims as regards virtually all offences with a sexual element. The most serious are **indictable-only**, with a maximum sentence of life imprisonment. These include: →glossary

- *rape*—penetration of vagina, anus, or mouth without consent, by penis—if the victim is aged under 13, any such conduct is defined as rape, even if the victim says there was no compulsion, because the victim is so young (Note that males and females can be rape victims but only males can be rapists; females can be guilty of inciting or aiding rape);
- *assault by penetration*—of vagina or anus, without consent and otherwise than by penis—for example, by finger or object;
- *causing or inciting a child under 13 or a person who has 'a mental disorder impeding choice' to engage in sexual activity* in which the activity caused or incited involves penetration by penis or otherwise;
- *an attempt, conspiracy, or incitement* to commit any of the above offences;
- *aiding, abetting, counselling, or procuring* the commission of any of them.

Some sexual crimes are **either-way** charges. For some, an offender can be sentenced to a jail term of up to 14 years. Either-way charges include: →glossary

- *sexual assault*—intentional sexual touching, without consent;
- *administering a substance with intent to engage a person in sexual activity*—for example, spiking someone's drink with a drug;
- *trespass with intent to commit a sexual offence*;
- *sexual intercourse with a girl who has reached the age of 13 but who is under 16*—this offending is not classed as rape if there is no compulsion, but could be very serious and exploitative if the perpetrator is much older;
- *abuse of a position of trust, through sexual activity with someone aged under 18*—so, for example, a male teacher having consensual sex with a 17-year-old girl who is not a school pupil is not committing a crime as she is over 16, the age of sexual consent, but if she is a pupil at the school where he works, the sexual relationship is criminal abuse of his position of trust as a teacher;
- *sexual activity by a care worker*—for example, in a hospital—if it involved such activity with a person in his/her care who has a mental disorder and but did not involve penetration (which would be indictable-only);

- *engaging in sexual activity in the presence of a child*, or causing a child to watch a sexual act, for the perpetrator's sexual gratification;
- *arranging or facilitating commission of a sexual offence against a child*, anywhere in the world;
- *meeting or intending to meet a child following sexual grooming*—for example, an adult contacting a child over the internet—in which case the child has anonymity even if no meeting takes place;
- *sexual activity by an adult with a child family member* (note that it is incorrect to describe such an offence as incest, because incest is a consensual relationship);
- *taking an indecent photograph of a child; paying for the sexual services of a child; causing, inciting, arranging or facilitating the sexual exploitation of a child or controlling a child for this purpose*;
- *causing or inciting or controlling prostitution for gain*—some journalists may not realise that anonymity has been extended to cover adults who are or have allegedly been, for example, 'controlled' prostitutes;
- *exposure* (colloquially called 'flashing') of genitals with the intent to cause alarm or distress;
- *voyeurism*—observing for sexual gratification someone else or people doing something private (for example, taking a shower, or having sex), knowing they did not consent to being observed because, for example, a hidden camera was used.

Buggery is no longer illegal between consenting adults, but is an offence if perpetrated on someone aged under 16—who is a victim and therefore has anonymity.

A sexual offence which allegedly occurred before 1 May 2004 will be charged according to older definitions, but anonymity applies. One such older offence is 'indecent assault'.

The anonymity does not apply to two adult relatives who are charged with consensual, illegal sexual activity with each other—which would have been charged as 'incest' under the old law—or to adults accused of consensual sexual activity in a public lavatory. But if only one of them is charged, the other retains anonymity. It also does not apply in cases involving a person accused of sexual activity with an animal.

11.6 Trafficking offences for which victims/alleged victims have anonymity

The Modern Slavery Act 2015 was created to clarify and consolidate the law on slavery, forced labour and human trafficking, and to increase the penalties for such offences—which for some is a life sentence. The Act's Explanatory Notes say: 'Modern slavery takes a number of forms, including sexual exploitation, forced labour and domestic servitude, and victims come from all walks of life.'

The 2015 Act amended section 1 of the Sexual Offences (Amendment) Act 1992 so that the lifelong automatic anonymity given to victims of sexual offences in general, explained earlier, now covers all victims/alleged victims of 'human trafficking for exploitation' offences in section 2 of the 2015 Act. These—defined in section 3 of the 2015 Act—are (summarised):

- arranging or facilitating the travel of another person with a view to that person being exploited
  - by being held in slavery or servitude, or
  - being required to perform forced or compulsory labour, or
  - because something is done to or in respect of the person which involves or would involve the commission of an offence listed in Part 1 of the Sexual Offences Act 2003, or in section 1(1)(a) of the Protection of Children Act 1978 (indecent photographs of children), or
  - by being encouraged, required or expected to donate or sell an organ from his/her body, or
  - when the person being exploited is a child, or is mentally or physically ill or disabled, or has a family relationship, being subject to force, threats or deception designed to induce him/her to provide any kind of service, or to provide or enable someone else to obtain benefits of any kind, in circumstances when an adult who was not ill or disabled or did not have that family relationship would be likely to refuse to be thus exploited.

Sexual offences listed earlier in this chapter are in Part 1 of the 2003 Act, so the trafficking could include travel being arranged for children for them to be sexually exploited, or arranged to control people for prostitution, and the anonymity would apply even if, as events turned out, the victims did not suffer the sexual offences—because, for example, police intervened.

For there to be a trafficking offence, there must be the element of 'arranging or facilitating of travel'. This covers arranged or actual travel within the UK, another country or from one country to another, or merely recruiting someone for such travel. For a journalist, recognising that a person is the victim/alleged victim of such a trafficking offence—and therefore should have anonymity—should be straightforward if police say this or after the alleged perpetrator is charged. And if the person is also the victim/alleged victim of a sexual offence, it should be clear that anonymity applies. But otherwise a journalist learning of or interviewing an exploited person, or one for whom exploitation was planned, will need to understand how such trafficking offences are defined, and that an element may be forced labour or another form of exploitation and that there may not be a sexual element.

The anonymity will cover, for example, a trafficked woman forced to work as a household maid, or trafficked immigrants or mentally vulnerable people being compelled to work by threats of violence, or anyone for whom such a destiny was knowingly planned, irrespective of whether anyone was prosecuted for the offence. If the journalist suspects anonymity may apply, yet the person is willing to be identified in an account of such an ordeal or plan, the best course is to obtain his/her written consent to be identified—if the victim/alleged victim gives written consent.

11.7 Liability for breach of the anonymity provision

Section 5 of the 1992 Act says that those who can be prosecuted if a publication/ broadcast breaches the anonymity are the newspaper or periodical's proprietor, editor and publisher, or any 'body corporate' (for example, a company) providing the programme service and any person whose functions in relation to the programme correspond to those of an editor of a newspaper, or as regards any other form of publication, any person publishing it.

It is a defence for the person accused to show that he/she was not aware, and neither suspected nor had reason to suspect, that the material published would be likely to identify the victim/alleged victim of the sexual or trafficking offence. The punishment is a fine for which the Act does not specify a maximum amount.

 See the Additional Material for ch. 11 on www.mcnaes.com for case studies of media organisations being fined for breaching the anonymity of victims of sexual offences. For the 'regulation 19' defence if a reader's online comment breaches anonymity, see 22.12, General protection in regulation 19.

11.8 When does the anonymity cease to apply for victims/alleged victims of a sexual or trafficking offence?

The anonymity does not apply to dead people—for example, a murdered rape victim.

11.8.1 By court order, at the request of a defendant

- A court due to try someone for a sexual or trafficking offence can, on the application of a defendant or a co-defendant, remove an alleged victim's anonymity if it is satisfied that:
  - it should be lifted to induce people likely to be needed as witnesses to come forward; and
  - otherwise the conduct of the applicant's defence at the trial is likely to be substantially prejudiced.

→ glossary

A defendant may argue that he/she needs witnesses to come forward to support an **alibi**. For example, allowing the media to identify the alleged victim of a sexual offence when reporting the alibi defence could jog the memories of members of the public about where and when he/she was seen, and who, if anyone, was with him/her at the time of the alleged offence.

Courts are rarely asked to lift anonymity on this ground, specified in section 3 of the 1992 Act. If the alleged offence is indictable-only a magistrates' court does not have power to waive the anonymity.

11.8.2 By court order, to lift 'a substantial and unreasonable' restriction on reporting

- The court trying a sexual or trafficking offence can lift an alleged victim's anonymity if it is satisfied that:
  - the anonymity would impose a substantial and unreasonable restriction on media reporting of the trial; and
  - it is in the public interest to remove or relax it.

If the alleged offence is indictable-only, a magistrates' court does not have power to waive the anonymity. Cases in which courts are asked to lift anonymity on the above ground, specified in the Act's section 3, are very rare.

 For an example of this power being used, see the *Hutchinson* case study in the Additional Material for ch. 11 on www.mcnaes.com

11.8.3 If the victim/alleged victim gives written consent

The media may identify someone as being the victim/alleged victim of a sexual or trafficking offence if he/she consents. But section 5 of the 1992 Act specifies that:

- the consent must be in writing;
- the person waiving his/her anonymity must be aged 16 or over; and
- the consent will not be valid if it is proved that anyone 'interfered unreasonably with the peace and comfort' of the person, with the intention of obtaining it.

This wording of the law guards against anyone being pressured into giving consent and makes clear that anyone under 16 is too young to consent. Parents of victims/alleged victims under 16 cannot consent on their behalf.

A court's permission is not needed for this consent to be given. Victims of sexual offences have often given written consent, particularly after the offender is jailed. For example, a woman who has been raped may feel that letting the media identify her sends a powerful signal to other rape victims that they can find the courage to seek justice and that there is no stigma in being a victim. Some trafficked victims may feel the same.

11.8.4 If the case is 'other than' the sexual or trafficking offence alleged

 for definitions of perjury and these other offences, see 6.3.4

People alleged to have falsely claimed to police that they have been a victim of a sexual or trafficking offence may be charged with wasting police time, or perjury, or perverting the course of justice.

- A person appearing in court on such a charge—for example, perjury—in relation to what is said to be a false allegation of a sexual or trafficking offence can be identified in reports of those proceedings as someone who was previously said to be the victim of that offence.

This is because section 1(4) of the 1992 Act says that an alleged victim of a sexual or trafficking offence can be identified in material which consists 'only of a report of criminal proceedings other than' proceedings for that offence.

The 'other than' definition means it would be legal for media covering a burglary trial to identify a woman home owner when reporting that she had asserted in court that the alleged burglar raped her, although the media would need to check that those proceedings at no time included a charge alleging she was a sexual offence victim—see the Additional Material for ch. 11 on www.mcnaes.com, Newspaper breached anonymity after the rape charge was dropped. The 'other than' definition would also allow the media to identify a woman defendant, charged with assaulting a man, as having said in those assault proceedings that the man had tried to rape her. But in both such instances there would still need to be ethical consideration of whether the report should identify her as regards such statements.

Case study

In 2017 the Court of Appeal removed any doubt that criminal proceedings in which a rape complainant is accused of perjury or wasting police time fall into the category of 'other proceedings' under section 1(4). The Court said that the section's meaning was 'plain and obvious', and that the Judicial College guidance about it is accurate. The Court's ruling arose in a successful challenge by *The Sun* against a Crown court judge's decision that the media could not identify Jemma Beale in reports of her trial that year in which she was convicted of perjury and attempting to pervert the course of justice for making false allegations of rape and sexual assault, including one which had led to a man being jailed for seven years. He was subsequently acquitted on appeal. (*R v Jemma Beale in the matter of an appeal by News Group Newspapers* [2017] EWCA 1012 (Crim)).

For the Judicial College guidance, and for context about it see 16.3 and Useful Websites at the end of this chapter.

 Courts can make prevention orders to restrict the activity of sexual or trafficking offenders. For detail, including how the media may oppose anonymity provision for the offender in respect of the order, see 16.6.2.8, Civil orders imposed on sexual or trafficking offenders or suspects, and the Additional Material for ch. 11 on www.mcnaes.com, which also covers sexual and trafficking risk orders.

11.9 Ethical considerations

The combined effect of clause 7 'Children in Sex cases' and clause 11 'Sexual Assault' of the Editors' Code, overseen by the Independent Press Standards

Organisation, is to impose an ethical ban on media organisations who are Ipso members, or any others which adhere to the Code, from identifying any victim or alleged victim of a sexual offence unless the law permits identification. So, breach of anonymity provided by the 1992 Act's section 1—for example, by publication of too much detail from a court case—can lead to Ipso ruling that the Code was breached too. But Ipso has also ruled that these clauses were breached in reports which did not—for whatever reason—result in the media organisations concerned being prosecuted under the 1992 Act.

 ch. 2 introduces the Code, which is set out in full in this book's Appendix, pp. 457–462

If the law permits identification of any such victim or alleged victim, clauses 7 and 11 of the Code mean that the anonymity should be preserved in coverage of the case, on an ethical basis, unless an exception stated in the relevant clause applies.

 For case studies on PCC and Ipso adjudications about breach of these clauses, see the Additional Material for ch. 11 on www.mcnaes.com, which also outlines ethical guidance about referring to relatives and friends of people accused of paedophile offences.

11.9.1 'Children in sex cases'

Clause 7 ('Children in sex cases') says: 'The press must not, even if legally free to do so, identify children under 16 who are victims or witnesses in cases involving sex offences.'

It adds that in any press report of a case involving a sexual offence against a child:

- the child must not be identified;
- the adult may be identified;
- the word 'incest' must not be used where a child victim might be identified;
- care must be taken that nothing in the report implies the relationship between the accused and the child.

The clause applies to any context from the time a sexual offence is alleged, including to coverage of criminal and civil proceedings, and tribunal cases.

ch. 18 covers tribunals

A primary aim of the clause is to help ensure that when more than one media organisation covers a criminal court case concerning children being allegedly sexually abused in a family or household, all organisations adopt a common approach of, for example, identifying the adult defendant, if this can be done without identifying the victims/alleged victims. The aim is to avert 'jigsaw identification', see 11.3.1, which could occur if some organisations decide not to identify the adult defendant but to air evidence of his/her relationship with the alleged victims.

see 10.12, Cases of abuse within a family

Clause 7 is subject to the Code's public interest exceptions, which means there may be rare circumstances in which Ipso accepts it is ethical for the press to identify a child who is a witness, victim or alleged victim in a sexual offence case (if the law permits identification). But the Code says there would have to be 'exceptional public interest' to override the normally paramount interests of a child under 16.

see Useful
Websites at
the end of
this chapter
for the
Codebook

The 2016 edition of the Editors' Codebook, produced to aid interpretation of the Code, says that clause 7 also means that defendants aged under 16 accused of sexual offences should not be identified in coverage of their case, unless the court permits identification but that, if it does, there could be an exceptional public interest in reports identifying such a child convicted of a sexual assault. As ch. 10 explains, juvenile defendants usually have anonymity in law but a court can permit them to be identified. The 1992 Act does not give them anonymity, see 11.4.

The Codebook also notes that girls who become mothers after having under-age sex sometimes put their motherhood into the public domain, but points out—in this context—that no-one under 16 can in law give valid consent to be identified in a publication as a victim of a sexual offence, and that parents cannot give this consent on their behalf.

> To interview an under-age mother may breach the Editors' Code because the interview or publishing it could affect her welfare. See 4.13, Protecting children's welfare and privacy.

11.9.2 'Adequate justification'

The Code's clause 11 says: 'The press must not identify or publish material likely to lead to the identification of a victim of sexual assault unless there is adequate justification and they are legally free to do so'.

Clause 11 covers all victims or alleged victims of sexual offences, whatever their age, and whatever the context or legal forum in which the allegation arises. But the particular, (in effect) overriding provision in clause 7 as regards the identification of those under 16 means that clause 11's term 'adequate justification' applies to editorial decisions on the identification of those aged 16 or older. If such a person has given valid, written consent for their own identification, that would normally under the Code justify such lawful identification.

Clause 11 is not formally subject to the Code's public interest exceptions, but the term 'adequate justification' embraces public interest considerations.

> In a 2016 case Ipso interpreted 'adequate justification' when ruling that the *Daily Record's* lawful identification of a sexual assault victim breached clause 11. See the case study in the Additional Material for ch. 11 on www.mcnaes.com.

11.9.3 Ofcom and Impress Codes

Rule 1.8 of the Broadcasting Code says broadcasters should 'be particularly careful not to provide clues' which may lead to the identification of children when by law they should have anonymity 'as a victim, witness, defendant or other perpetrator in the case of sexual offences featured in criminal, civil or family court proceedings'. This rule also warns against jigsaw identification and that inadvertent use of the term 'incest' may identify such a child.

The Impress Standards Code says that publishers must preserve the anonymity of victims of sexual offences, but that (adult) victims can agree to be identified. For context about the Impress code, see 2.5. Ch. 3 which introduces the Broadcasting Code.

for these codes in full, see Useful Websites at the end of this chapter

11.10 Lifetime anonymity for victims/alleged victims of female genital mutilation

Part 5 of the Serious Crime Act 2015 amended the Female Genital Mutilation Act 2003, making it a criminal offence, punishable by an unlimited fine, to publish anything likely to lead members of the public to identify someone as a victim/alleged victim of female genital mutilation (FGM).

This lifetime anonymity provision, in section 4A and Schedule 1 of the 2003 Act, has in effect the same scope as the anonymity provision in the Sexual Offences (Amendment) Act 1992 for victims/alleged victims of sexual or trafficking offences. A journalist covering an actual or alleged case of FGM must take the same care about what detail is published, and to avoid jigsaw identification, as when covering those other offences detailed earlier in this chapter.

The anonymity also covers victims/alleged victims of offences of aiding, abetting, counselling and procuring the main FGM offence, as well as victims/alleged victims of the new offence of failing to protect a girl from the risk of FGM. It also covers a victim who agreed to undergo FGM.

FGM is a cultural tradition in some East African and Middle East nations—for example, Somalia and Yemen. There is evidence that it is inflicted on some UK girls and young women from ethnic communities which share that culture.

see Useful Websites at the end of this chapter for information about FGM

FGM is usually arranged by the victim's parents or another adult relative, so a report which can identify a defendant without identifying the victim may well be rare. FGM has been illegal in the UK since 1985, but by early 2018 there had not been any successful prosecutions.

Paragraph 1(4)–(8) of Schedule 1 to the Act allows a trial judge to lift the anonymity on what are, essentially, the same grounds on which a judge can lift the anonymity in proceedings for sexual and trafficking offences. One ground is that the judge is satisfied that the anonymity should be lifted to avoid the conduct of a person's defence at the trial of an FGM offence being substantially prejudiced—for example, the judge may accept that such publicity is needed for alibi witnesses for the defence to come forward. The other ground is to enable the media to produce a full report of a particular trial because this would be 'in the public interest'—see 11.8.2, By court order, to lift a 'substantial and unreasonable' restriction on reporting. But it will be very rare for the anonymity to be lifted for such reasons.

The victim herself may consent to waive her anonymity. For that consent to be legally valid, she must be aged 16 or over, give written consent, and not have consented as a result of unreasonable interference with her peace and comfort.

Those who can be prosecuted for breaching a victim's anonymity are the same as for breach of anonymity of a victim/alleged victim of a sexual or trafficking offence—see 11.7, Liability for breach of the anonymity provision—but could also include in some circumstances a 'senior officer' (for example, a director) of a media company, as well as the company.

It is a defence for a person to prove that he/she did not know or suspect the publication included 'the matter in question' or to prove there was valid waiver of the anonymity.

11.11 'Revenge porn'

The new offence of publishing so-called revenge porn came into force in April 2015. The offence, under section 33 of the Criminal Justice and Courts Act 2015, consists of disclosing a 'private sexual photograph or film' without the consent of the person depicted in the content and with the intent to cause him/her distress. Victims of the offence do not have automatic anonymity in law—but many editors have decided against naming them, taking the view that it is not the media's job to achieve the offender's objective by adding to the victim's embarrassment and humiliation. Section 33 contains a defence for publishing such a photo or film within 'journalistic material' if done with a reasonable belief that this was in the public interest—a defence which is a safeguard for investigative journalism.

➡ Recap of major points

- It is illegal for the media to identify the victims/alleged victims of sexual offences— including rape and sexual assault—in reports of these crimes or of court cases which follow.

- The same anonymity applies for the victims/alleged victims of offences of 'human trafficking for exploitation' and, under other law, for the victims/alleged victims of female genital mutilation.

- A court can remove the anonymity in certain circumstances, but this rarely happens.

- There is a danger of 'jigsaw identification', particularly when several media organisations are covering a case of alleged sexual abuse within a family.

- A victim/alleged victim who is aged 16 or over can waive the anonymity by giving a media organisation written consent for her/him to be identified.

((•)) Useful Websites

www.cps.gov.uk/legal-guidance/rape-and-sexual-offences
   Crown Prosecution Service guidance on prosecution of sexual offences

www.legislation.gov.uk/ukpga/2015/30/notes/contents
   Explanatory Notes to the Modern Slavery Act 2015

www.editorscode.org.uk/the_code_book.php
The Editors' Codebook provides detailed advice on clauses 7 and 11 of the Editors' Code

http://stakeholders.ofcom.org.uk/broadcasting/broadcast-codes/broadcast-code/
Ofcom Broadcasting Code

https://impress.press/standards/impress-standards-code.html
Impress Standards Code

www.impress.press/downloads/file/code/impress-code-guidance.pdf
Impress guidance on its code

www.gov.uk/government/uploads/system/uploads/attachment_data/file/300167/ FGM_leaflet_v4.pdf
Guidance on female genital mutilation, published by the Home Office

12

Court reporting— other restrictions

Chapter summary

Earlier chapters have shown that reporting crime and courts is not a job for an untrained amateur. Reporting restrictions can dictate what is published; breaching them is an offence. This chapter details more restrictions, including permanent bans on using cameras and audio-recording devices in any court. Revealing how individual jurors voted in verdicts is also illegal. Reporting what a court has heard in private can be punished as contempt of court. The chapter also outlines how courts can stop the media identifying some adult witnesses and blackmail victims, or postpone reporting of a case. Chapter 16 shows how to challenge a reporting restriction as invalid or unnecessary. Chapter 22 deals with defamation dangers in court reporting.

12.1 Ban on photography and sketching in courts and precincts

In 1925 Parliament banned photography in courts. Case law means the ban includes filming (that is, any method of shooting footage) in courts. A primary reason for the ban is that use of cameras, and any publication of images gained, would put added strain on witnesses, defendants and jurors.

Section 41 of the Criminal Justice Act 1925 makes it illegal to:

- take or try to take any photograph of or shoot footage or try to shoot footage of; or
- make or try to make—with a view to publication—any portrait or sketch of:
  - 'any person' in any court, its building, or within its precincts;
  - 'any person' who is 'entering or leaving' a court building or its precincts;
- publish such a photo, footage, portrait or sketch.

Section 41 applies to criminal, civil and family courts, coroners' courts and any tribunal classed as a court. In the Act 'any person' includes judges, magistrates, coroners, jurors, witnesses, defendants and any other party in a case.

- The Act does not define 'precincts', which causes practical difficulties. The term includes rooms, foyers or corridors within the courthouse building, but it is unclear to what extent it includes areas immediately outside. If unsure, check with the particular court.

Journalists standing on the public pavement frequently photograph and film judges, lawyers, defendants and witnesses entering or leaving court buildings—for example, the Royal Courts of Justice in London. Where this practice has become customary, it is rare for a court to object, though it would seem to breach the section 41 ban on showing people 'entering or leaving'. Jurors should not be photographed, as this might be regarded as a contempt in common law, as explained later in this chapter. Breaches of section 41 can be punished with fines of up to £1,000. Criminal Practice Direction I 6C.4 says that in court 'any equipment which has photographic capability must not have that function activated'.

for what the Directions are, see 15.10.1

12.1.1 Artists' sketches of court cases

The media publish artists' sketches of scenes in court, including the face of the defendant, to illustrate newsworthy cases. To comply with section 41, these artists visit the court's public gallery or press bench, memorise the scene and characters, but do the actual sketching elsewhere. A Government Consultation Paper made no objection to sketching in a courthouse press room.

12.1.2 Jury visits to the scene of crime or death

If a judge or coroner decides that jurors should visit an outside location such as a crime or accident scene to help them understand evidence, the visit should not be filmed, photographed or sketched without the court's permission. The judge or coroner may allow this, as long as no juror can be identified through what is published. The visit means the court has moved temporarily to that location.

12.1.3 Photography and filming could be contempt of court

- Although the 1925 Act bans photography or filming in a court or in its precincts, such activity can also be treated as a contempt of court in common law. If a person is ruled to have committed such contempt, he or she can be fined a greater sum than the 1925 Act permits, or be jailed—see *H M Solicitor General v Kyle Cox and Damien Parker-Stokes* [2016] EWHC 1241 (QB).

see also 19.3, Contempt in common law

The level of fine to punish such a contempt is at the judge's discretion. If the punishment is a jail sentence the term could be as much as two years. Some members of the public have been jailed for using a mobile phone to take photos or film in courts. Notices there warn such activity is banned.

👁 Case study

On 20 February 2017 a member of the public, David William Davies, 39, sitting in Cardiff Crown court's public gallery, began using his mobile phone to film a person giving evidence in a trial of another man for dangerous driving. Davies streamed the footage live on Facebook. More than 650 people saw it, some commenting on it online. Davies, of Llanwit Fardre, Rhondda Cynon Taff, posted an invitation for people to 'tune in' for further footage. Someone alerted police to the streaming. Davies was arrested the next day when he returned to the court. Judge Greg Bull QC jailed him for 28 days for contempt. PC Richard Sellek said: 'Unfortunately, cases such as this are becoming more and more commonplace' (*Wales Online, BBC online and South Wales police press release,* 22 February 2017).

A media photographer's conduct could be regarded as contempt if it amounts to 'molestation'—interference with the administration of justice—even if the activity is some distance from the courthouse. Case law suggests that running after a defendant for a short while in order to photograph him/her would not usually be seen as molestation (*R v Runting* [1989] Crim LR 282). But stalking a defendant or witnesses further, or jostling them, could be contempt as it might deter them or other witnesses from giving evidence.

👁 Case study

In 2009 Mr Justice Keith warned photographers to stop taking pictures of two young brothers as they arrived at Sheffield Crown court in cars, under blankets, saying he would take action if he thought a contempt had taken place. The brothers had admitted inflicting, when aged 10 and 11, horrific violence on two boys in Edlington, near Doncaster (*Press Gazette,* 7 September 2009).

12.1.4 Broadcasting from highest courts allowed

ch. 9 explains the work of the Court of Appeal and the Supreme Court

Provisions in other statutes mean the Supreme Court and Court of Appeal can allow broadcasting of their proceedings which, being concerned with points of law, are argued from documentary evidence and so are unlikely to involve witnesses in person and do not have jurors.

See the Additional Material for ch. 12 on www.mcnaes.com for law which permits broadcasting of these courts' proceedings and for detail of a pilot scheme to film the sentencing remarks of Crown court judges.

12.2 Ban on audio-recording in court

It is illegal to use any audio-recording device in a court, including a tape-recorder, or a mobile phone's recording facility, without the court's permission.

The ban is in section 9 of the Contempt of Court Act 1981, which makes it a contempt to:

- use a tape-recorder or any other audio-recording device in court, or take one into a court for use, unless the court gives permission;
- broadcast any audio-recording of court proceedings, or play any of it in the hearing of any section of the public;
- make any unauthorised use of a recording, if recording has been allowed.

The penalty for breaching section 9 of the 1981 Act is a jail term of up to two years and/or an unlimited fine.

- One purpose of this ban is to prevent witness testimony being broadcast, which for some witnesses would increase the strain of giving evidence.
- Another is to stop secret recordings being made in the public gallery by, for example, a defendant's criminal associates, who could use them to intimidate or humiliate a prosecution witness, or to help dishonest witnesses collude in false corroboration. For example, a witness could listen to a recording of another's evidence and repeat the same information in his/her own evidence, but claim to have recalled it independently.

12.2.1 Permission to audio-record

A court has discretion to allow audio-recording, including by a journalist—for example, for note-taking—and to allow publication of the sound recording. Rule 6.9 of the Criminal Procedure Rules says that anyone who wants permission to record in a criminal court must apply to it as soon as reasonably practicable, and notify the case's parties and anyone else the court specifies that permission is being sought. An applicant must explain why recording should be permitted and why publication of the recording should be permitted, if this is proposed. Criminal Practice Direction I 6A.2 says that a relevant factor in a criminal court's decision on whether to permit audio-recording may be 'the existence of any reasonable need' on the part of the applicant, whether a litigant or person connected with the media, for the recording to be made, and 6C.5 says this factor is likely to be relevant when a civil or family court considers such an application.

 See 15.10.1 for what the Rules and Directions are. For recording in civil courts, see too Useful Websites at the end of this chapter. On note-taking in courts, see 15.8.

12.3 Tweeting, emailing and texting 'live' reports from court

Reporters should not make or receive calls on mobile phones during court hearings—doing so could be punished as a contempt because it is disrespectful, and potentially disruptive and damaging to the administration of justice. A judge might fine or jail a reporter whose mobile phone ringtone interrupts a witness's testimony, particularly if the witness is already finding testifying difficult. The normal rule is that mobile phones must be turned off in court. The rule derives from the **inherent jurisdiction** courts have to govern their own proceedings.

→ glossary

An exception to this rule is that journalists and legal commentators attending courts are allowed to report cases by tweeting, texting, emailing or posting directly on to the internet with a mobile phone or internet-connected laptop without having to ask the court's permission. This is because in 2011 the Lord Chief Justice issued practice guidance giving a general permission for them to report cases from all types of court by using 'live, text-based communications'. Since 2015 this permission, as regards criminal proceedings, has been set out in Criminal Practice Directions 6C.1–3, 6C.6, 6C.8 and 6C.11–14.

These Directions (and the 2011 guidance) say:

- the devices must be silent and unobtrusive.
- a court can decide 'at any time' to forbid all use of such devices—for example, if there is concern that a witness due to testify could be coached or briefed on what to say by reference to tweets of earlier evidence or that simultaneous reporting from the courtroom may create pressure on witnesses, by distracting or worrying them.

This general permission to use such devices applies only for 'journalistic purposes' and does not extend to members of the public, although they can apply for permission.

The Supreme Court, which is not covered by these Directions, has a policy allowing the use of live text-based communications, though not in some types of case.

> ((•)) See Useful Websites at the end of this chapter for the Criminal Procedure Rules, the Criminal Practice Directions and the Supreme Court's policy.

12.4 Confidentiality of jury deliberations

It is a contempt of court to breach the confidentiality of a jury's deliberations, whether the jury is in a Crown court, an inquest or a civil case. Juries arrive at their verdicts in secret discussions, in rooms guarded against intrusion. The secrecy helps jurors to be frank in discussions, without fear of a public backlash for an unpopular decision or retribution from a vengeful defendant they convict. For the role of juries in criminal trials, civil cases and inquests, see chs. 9, 13 and 17.

- Section 20D of the Juries Act 1974, which applies for Crown courts, the High Court and county courts, makes it contempt of court intentionally to obtain, solicit or disclose (for example, by publication) any detail of
    - statements made,
    - opinions expressed,
    - arguments advanced, or
    - votes cast
  by jurors during their deliberations.

Jurors too breach this law if they disclose such detail.

 For similar law for inquest juries, 17.10, Reporting restrictions.

The ban can be breached even if what is published does not identify an individual juror or even a particular trial. The penalty for a contempt by breaching section 20D is a jail term of up to two years and/or an unlimited fine.

After a trial the media is safe to publish a juror's general impressions of his/her experience of jury service, provided the individual is willing to volunteer these and is not asked about statements made, opinions expressed, arguments advanced or votes cast during the deliberations, and does not refer to such issues in what is published. A juror could be interviewed, for example, on whether he/she felt that evidence was clearly presented. Journalistic investigations of alleged miscarriages of justice such as a controversial murder conviction sometimes prompt jurors from the trial to speak up months or years later. Some have contacted journalists to say that, in the light of new evidence which has emerged, they are no longer certain of the accused's guilt. The safest course is to seek legal advice before conducting or publishing such an interview.

👁 Case study

In 2009 the High Court fined *The Times* £15,000 and ordered it to pay £27,426 costs for breaching the confidentiality of jury deliberations. The newspaper had published an article about the 10–2 majority verdict with which a Crown court jury convicted a childminder of a child's manslaughter. It did not name the jury foreman, who had approached the newspaper, but quoted him expressing doubt about the medical evidence, and as saying that, early in its deliberations, the jury voted 10–2 in an initial indication of its consensus and that the majority of jurors—because of what he called 'common sense' rather than 'logical thinking'—held to their initial view that the defendant was guilty. *The Times* denied contempt, but the High Court ruled that, by using these quotes, it had breached the law banning disclosure of 'votes cast', 'opinions expressed' and 'statements made' during the jury's deliberations, even though jurors' identities were not disclosed, and the foreman's descriptions of the deliberations were brief and possibly inaccurate (*Attorney General v Michael Alexander Seckerson and Times Newspapers Ltd* [2009] EWHC 1023 (Admin)). The jury foreman was fined £5,000 for his part in the breach (*Media Lawyer,* 20 December 2009).

12.5 Contempt risk in identifying or approaching jurors

There is a risk of a media organisation being accused of common law contempt if it identifies a juror against his/her wishes, even after a trial. The disclosure could be ruled to have interfered with the judicial process by putting the juror at risk of harm from anyone unhappy with a verdict and by potentially deterring other people from jury service. A reporter deemed to have harassed a juror for an interview might be ruled to be in contempt, as such harassment too could discourage people from serving as jurors.

 Case study

In 2013 a judge at Oxford Crown court held a hearing to consider an explanation for why Lucy Ford, of the *Banbury Guardian*, photographed two jurors outside the courthouse and had asked them to help her identify a defendant. The judge accepted that their being photographed was an accident because they had walked into her picture and that there was no attempt to intimidate them (*Holdthefrontpage*, 12 February 2013).

> 📖 See ch. 19 about common law contempt. See also 37.4.5.2, Identifying jurors, on the statutory ban on identifying jurors who have served in trials in Northern Ireland.

A juror discharged during a case for late attendance or being drunk may well be named in open court and could be punished by the judge. In the absence of any court order to the contrary, the media can safely identify him/her, if named, and say how he/she was dealt with.

12.6 Section 11 orders—blackmail, secrets, personal safety

A court can ban the media from reporting a person's name, or other information, in coverage of a case.

Section 11 of the Contempt of Court Act 1981 says (here summarised):

- A court can ban the publication of a name or other matter in connection with the proceedings as long as it has first allowed that information to be withheld from the public.

Section 11 orders are not used routinely, but typical uses are as follows.

To protect the identity of victims/alleged victims of blackmail The target of blackmail involving a threat to reveal an embarrassing secret will be less likely to report the threat to police, or give evidence, if it is likely that his/her identity will be given in open court and be reported by the media. In blackmail trials, the alleged victim is usually referred to in open court simply by a letter, for example, 'Ms X'. This protects the administration of justice as a continuing process.

> 📖 The legal definition of the criminal offence of blackmail is given in 6.3.2.

To protect commercially sensitive information or secret processes For example, a company may sue another for damages over breach of confidence about valuable

research data. The court may hear evidence about the data **in private** to preserve its confidentiality—if it does not stay confidential, the case would be pointless. A section 11 order could ban reports of the case publishing leaks of the data.

To protect national security, state secrets For example, a defendant prosecuted under the Official Secrets Act 1911 may be accused of betraying UK military secrets to a foreign power. The court may well go into private session to hear evidence about those secrets. A section 11 order could be used to ban publication of such material, should it leak out. It could also ban the media from identifying intelligence officers who are witnesses, as identification would end their usefulness as undercover agents and put them at risk.

ch. 33 explains official secrets law

To protect a person from the risk of harm A court might be persuaded to ban publication of a witness's name and address, or the address of a defendant—for example, a sexual offender—to prevent an attack on that person by criminals or vigilantes. But the media can oppose such orders on the grounds that they are unnecessary—see, Anonymity, addresses and risk of attack?

12.6.1 Two-stage process

A section 11 order is the second step in a two-stage process. The court first has to rule that a name or other information should not be given in proceedings held in public. Only then it can impose a section 11 order. If the name or information then slips out by mistake in a public session—for example, in what a witness or lawyer says—or if the media discover it by other means, the order makes it illegal to publish it in any context which connects it to the case. Section 11 orders remain in force indefinitely, or until revoked.

the term 'jigsaw identification' is explained in 10.11

When a section 11 order is in force to ban publication of a person's identity, journalists need to guard against 'jigsaw identification'.

Breaching a section 11 order is an offence of contempt of court punishable by a jail term of up to two years and/or an unlimited fine.

But section 11 only bans the reporting of the name or matter 'in connection with the proceedings'.

12.7 Ban on reporting a court's private hearing

Courts sit in private, with the public and media excluded, for some cases, including when considering whether mentally ill people should be confined in hospitals and hearings involving state secrets. The media is **automatically** banned from publishing what is said in some categories of cases heard by a court in private—that is, **in chambers** or **in camera**.

→glossary

→glossary

Section 12 of the Administration of Justice Act 1960 makes it a contempt of court to publish, without the court's permission, a report of proceedings it has heard in private and which:

- relate to the exercise of the inherent jurisdiction of the High Court with respect to children;
- fall under the Children Act 1989 or the Adoption and Children Act 2002, or otherwise relate wholly or mainly to the maintenance or upbringing of a child;

- fall under the Mental Capacity Act 2005, or under any provision of the Mental Health Act 1983 authorising an application or reference to be made to the First-tier Tribunal, to the Mental Health Review Tribunal for Wales or to a county court;
- involve national security;
- involve a secret process, discovery or invention;
- are those, of any kind, where the court expressly bans publication of all or specified information relating to the private hearing.

 Ch. 14 explains children cases in family courts, and ch. 18 covers mental health tribunals.

A reporter may be told what has happened in a private hearing by one of the parties. But in the particular categories of case listed in section 12, it automatically prohibits the publication of anything heard by a court in private, to protect the welfare, including the privacy, of children and the mentally ill or incapacitated, and state or commercial secrets.

A breach of section 12, if proved as contempt, is punishable by a jail term of up to two years and/or an unlimited fine.

- Any document 'prepared for use' in a court's private hearing is deemed to be part of those proceedings. If a case falls into the section 12 categories, the court will regard publication by the media of information or quotations from such a document, such as a psychiatric report or a report on a couple's fitness as parents, as a contempt.

The definition of court in section 12 includes tribunals classed as courts.

 For detail about tribunals classed as courts, see ch. 18 and its Additional Material on www.mcnaes.com.

12.7.1 Some detail can be published about a private hearing

Some material about a private hearing in these types of case can be published. Section 12 makes clear that publishing the text, or a summary, of any order made in such a hearing is not contempt unless the court has specifically prohibited its publication.

In *Re B (A Child)* [2004] EWHC 411 (Fam), Mr Justice Munby stated that section 12 did not itself ban publishing a reference to 'the nature of the dispute' being heard in the private hearing. He added that what could be published without breaching section 12 included:

- the names, addresses or photographs of parties and witnesses involved in the private proceedings;
- the date, time or place of hearings in the case; and
- 'anything which has been seen or heard by a person conducting himself lawfully in the public corridor or other public precincts outside the court'.

But he added that a court could ban publication of even these details, or that automatic restrictions under other law could apply.

If the court hearing in private does not fall into the section 12 categories, a media organisation may safely be able to publish an account of it, for example, if guided by a person who was in it. But a media report of a case heard in private is not protected by any statutory **privilege** in relation to defamation law and will not be protected by section 4 of the Contempt of Court Act 1981 if it creates a substantial risk of serious prejudice or impediment to an 'active' case.

→glossary

12.8 Ban on unauthorised publication of case material

ch. 19 explains contempt law and ch. 22 explains privilege

Even if a case is heard in public, a journalist should exercise care before quoting from a document used in it if the material has not been read out in court.

As explained in ch. 13, civil cases are conducted mainly by reference to documents. It is safe to quote from any document the journalist obtains from court with permission for it to be reported, or from any case document he/she is able to inspect by right. For example, if the civil case is heard in public, it will be safe to quote from any **skeleton argument** provided to a journalist by lawyers involved unless the court forbids this. In criminal cases, the media has a qualified right to see case material, to aid reporting. How journalists can gain access to material in civil and criminal cases is explained in 15.13.

→glossary

Any reporting restriction—for example, protecting the identity of a child or alleged victim of a sexual offence—must be observed when reporting from such documents. And the reporting must be fair and accurate to comply with the Contempt of Court Act 1981 and defamation law.

> For these requirements for reporting to be fair and accurate, see 19.10 about contempt law, and 22.5 and 22.7 about privilege in defamation law.

Journalists should beware of the risk of contempt incurred by publishing material from a document they have obtained irregularly from one side or the other in criminal or civil proceedings, which one party was compelled or had a duty to produce as part of the **disclosure** process and which has not been read out in open court. 'Disclosure' is the pre-trial exchange of evidence and information. Contempt law applies because of the danger that parties who fear that material they provide to the other side might be published, even though it was not used in court, may refuse to cooperate fully with the disclosure process. Also, unauthorised use of material disclosed by the prosecution to the defendant in a criminal case is a contempt under the Criminal Procedure and Investigations Act 1996. Again, publication of material not aired in open court—even if the reporting fairly and accurately reflects the material—is not protected by statutory privilege in defamation law or by section 4 of the Contempt of Court Act 1981, unless sanctioned by a court or its rules.

→glossary

12.9 Lifetime anonymity for adult witnesses

A criminal court can ban the media from disclosing an adult witness's identity if there is concern that he/she is scared or distressed about being identified as a witness. This discretionary power to ban is in section 46 of the Youth Justice and Criminal Evidence Act 1999 (the 1999 Act).

- Section 46 empowers a court to give an adult witness lifetime anonymity in any published reference to or report of the case if it is satisfied that:
  - the quality of his/her evidence, or of his/her level of cooperation in preparations for the case, is likely to be diminished by fear or distress in connection with being identified by members of the public as a witness in that case; and
  - granting anonymity is likely to improve the quality of the witness's evidence or the level of his/her cooperation.

This law is intended to give better protection to witnesses who fear that the fact that they have testified, or are due to do so, will provoke hostility from criminal elements in their communities.

Section 46 says a party in the proceedings in a criminal court—including the defence, though it is usually the prosecution—can ask the court to make the anonymity order, called a 'reporting direction', to cover a witness aged 18 or over. The court may hear this request in camera.

12.9.1 The scope of a section 46 order

The wording of section 46 means that the order's normal scope is that:

- no matter relating to the witness should, during his/her lifetime, be included in any publication if it is likely to lead members of the public to identify him/her as being a witness in the proceedings.

Section 46 says the following matters in particular should not be included if likely to identity the person as being a witness;

- the witness's name;
- his/her address;
- the identity of any educational establishment he/she attends;
- the identity of any place of work; and
- any still or moving picture of him/her.

Any detail which risks revealing the witness's identity should be left out. The witness may be the alleged victim of the offence(s) being tried. If so, the effect on reports will be major and similar to that of the lifetime anonymity automatically given by other law to victims/alleged victims of sexual or trafficking offences, who therefore do not need section 46 anonymity as witnesses. When a section 46 order is made, journalists should ensure they avoid jigsaw identification.

The Act says that a section 46 order *cannot* be used to give a defendant anonymity.

 The term 'jigsaw identification' is explained in 10.11. Law which provides lifetime anonymity for victims/alleged victims of sexual or trafficking offences is explained in ch. 11.

12.9.2 Factors a court must consider

The 1999 Act says that when deciding whether to grant section 46 anonymity, the court must take into account: the witness's view about anonymity; the nature and circumstances of the alleged offence(s) being tried; the witness's age, social and cultural background, and ethnic origins; his/her domestic and employment circumstances, religious beliefs, or political opinions; and any behaviour towards the witness on the part of the defendant, or the defendant's family or associates, or anyone else likely to be a defendant or witness in the proceedings.

The court must also consider:

- whether it would be in the interests of justice to make the anonymity order; and
- the public interest in avoiding imposing a substantial and unreasonable restriction on reporting the proceedings.

12.9.2.1 Breaches of section 46 orders

Publishing material which breaches the section 46 anonymity incurs the same liability as breaching a sexual or trafficking offence victim's anonymity.

Anyone prosecuted for breach of section 46 has a defence if he/she can prove that:

see 11.7, Liability for breach of the anonymity provision

- he/she was not aware, and neither suspected nor had reason to suspect, that the publication included the matter or report in question; or
- the witness concerned gave written consent for the matter to be published.

This 'written consent' defence will fail if it is proved that the consent was obtained by interfering with the witness's 'peace or comfort'. But this written consent by the witness does not have to be approved by a court.

The court which bestowed the section 46 anonymity, or a higher court, can make 'an excepting direction' to remove the anonymity entirely or relax it to some extent, if satisfied that doing so is necessary in the interests of justice, or that the restriction imposes a substantial and unreasonable restriction on reporting the proceedings, and that it is in the public interest to remove or relax the restriction.

> Further detail about section 46 orders and grounds on which the media can challenge their imposition or continuation can be found in 16.9.

12.10 Other anonymity orders

The High Court has power to ban publication of the identities of people concerned in its proceedings and uses it to give anonymity to children involved in high-profile cases. The court also usually gives anonymity to mentally incapacitated adults when protecting their interests in civil cases. A media organisation which publishes information identifying such people in breach of such an order could be punished for contempt of court. The High Court's powers derive from its inherent jurisdiction and from Article 8 of the European Convention on Human Rights, concerning the right to respect for privacy and family life.

> For further detail of use of such orders in family law, see 14.19, Anti-publicity injunctions in family cases. For their use in privacy cases, 27.3.2 and 27.3.3.

The Civil Procedure Rules apply in civil cases in county courts and the High Court. Rule 39.2(4) states: 'The court may order that the identity of any party or witness must not be disclosed if it considers non-disclosure necessary in order to protect the interests of that party or witness.'

see Useful Websites at the end of this chapter for these Rules

The Court of Appeal has ruled that courts dealing with applications to approve settlements in personal injury claims brought by children should normally make anonymity orders, though they should hear representations from a media organisation wishing to argue against such orders being made (*JXMX (by her mother and litigation friend, AXMX) v Dartford and Gravesham NHS Trust, with the Personal Injury Bar Association and the Press Association as interveners* [2015] EWCA Civ 96). But mere embarrassment does not justify anonymity for adults in reports of court cases—see 16.6.2.10.

> See the Additional Material for ch. 5 on www.mcnaes.com about anonymity for police informants. For information on anonymity for persons subject as suspected terrorists to a 'terrorism prevention and investigation measure', see ch. 40, 'Terrorism and the effect of counter-terrorism law', on www. mcnaes.com.

12.11 Indefinite anonymity for convicted defendants and others

→glossary

In exceptional instances, the High Court uses **injunctions** to stop the media publishing the new identities or whereabouts of people who became notorious after committing, or being associated with, horrific crimes. The aim is to protect them from public hostility, safeguard them from possible vengeance attacks and help rehabilitate them after their release from imprisonment. Publication of detail which breaches an injunction is punishable as a contempt of court. These court orders are based on the protected person's human rights—Article 2 (right to life), Article 3 (right not to be subject to torture or other degrading treatment) and Article 8 (right to respect for privacy and family life) of the European Convention on Human Rights.

The first such case concerned Mary Bell. In 1968, when she was 11, she was convicted of the manslaughter of two young boys and sentenced to detention for life. The High Court granted her indefinite anonymity in 1984, four years after her release. In 2001 it granted indefinite anonymity to Jon Venables and

Robert Thompson who in 1993, when they were 11, were convicted of the murder of 2-year-old James Bulger in Merseyside.

> See the Additional Material for ch. 12 on www.mcnaes.com for detail of such cases, including that of Maxine Carr. See there too the Additional Material for ch. 37, 'Bans on identifying defendants'. Law which may protect website operators if a reader posts a comment breaching anonymity law is explained in this book in 22.12.

12.12 Ban on publishing 'indecent' matter

Section 1 of the Judicial Proceedings (Regulation of Reports) Act 1926 prohibits publication in any court report of any 'indecent matter or indecent medical, surgical or physiological details . . . the publication of which is calculated to injure public morals'. It is unlikely that mainstream media organisations would be prosecuted today under this legislation.

12.13 Postponement power in Contempt of Court Act 1981

Section 4(2) of the Contempt of Court Act 1981 gives courts the power to order the postponement of publication of reports of a court case, or any part of a case, where doing so appears necessary to avoid a substantial risk of prejudice to the administration of justice in that case or any other case which is pending or imminent.

This restriction is best understood in the context of contempt law, so is explained in 19.11, Section 4(2) orders. See also 16.6 for grounds on which a section 4(2) order may be challenged as invalid or unnecessary.

12.14 Postponed reporting of 'special measures' and section 36 orders

A court can make a 'special measure' direction (order) under the Youth Justice and Criminal Evidence Act 1999 to help a 'vulnerable' or 'intimidated' witness give evidence. For example, the witness may be allowed to testify from behind a screen or by live video link, or all the reporters but one might be asked to leave court during his/her testimony. Section 36 of the same Act allows a court to bar a defendant representing himself/herself from cross-examining a witness. The Act automatically bans the media from reporting during the trial that a 'special measure' direction or a section 36 order has been proposed or made, and why, because in some cases a jury might be improperly influenced in its verdict if it had such knowledge.

> For more details about these reporting restrictions, see the Additional Material for ch. 12 on www.mcnaes.com.

✳ **Remember**

Decisions on 'special measures' and cross-examination issues are likely to be taken at pre-trial hearings, or when a jury is out of the court, so other statutes, or contempt law, will probably also be in effect to restrict contemporaneous reporting of what is decided about such measures and issues—see 9.4, Hearings prior to jury involvement—automatic reporting restrictions; 19.11.2, Proceedings in court in the absence of the jury; and 19.11.3, The law is not clear.

12.15 Postponing reports of 'derogatory' mitigation

Section 58 of the Criminal Procedure and Investigations Act 1996 allows a court to postpone a media report of a derogatory allegation which is made in a 'speech in mitigation', but has not been given in evidence, if it feels that someone's reputation may have been unfairly besmirched. This restriction is rarely used.

 When mitigation is heard in magistrates' and Crown courts is explained in 7.6 and 9.7. More detail on section 58 is in the Additional Material for ch. 12 on www.mcnaes.com.

12.16 Extradition hearings

Media coverage of hearings in the UK on whether a person should be extradited to another country are not affected by any automatic reporting restrictions. These hearings usually take place in Westminster magistrates' court.

 The media has won the right to see case material to enable full reporting of extradition hearings, See 15.12.7 on documents which must be read aloud in court and 15.13.1 on access to material in criminal cases.

➡ **Recap of major points**

- It is illegal to take photographs of, film or sketch people in a court or its precincts.

- It is also illegal to make an audio-recording of a court hearing without permission.

- Journalists have a general permission to tweet, email or text from the courtroom when reporting, but other use of mobile phones there is punishable as a contempt of court.

- It is illegal to seek to discover, or to publish, what a jury discussed in deliberating on a verdict or how an individual juror voted in the verdict.

- Publication of material identifying a juror may be held to be a contempt of court.

- In certain categories of case it is contempt of court to publish material heard by a court in private.

- An order under section 11 of the Contempt of Court Act 1981 prohibits publication of a name or other matter which has been withheld from the public proceedings of the court—for example, the name of a blackmail victim.

- Section 46 of the Youth Justice and Criminal Evidence Act 1999 allows a court to give an adult witness in a criminal case lifelong anonymity in media reports.

- In exceptional cases, the High Court has given convicted offenders indefinite anonymity, so the media cannot reveal their whereabouts after they are released.

((•)) Useful Websites

www.judiciary.gov.uk/publications/reporting-restrictions-in-the-criminal-courts-2/
Judicial College guidance, *Reporting Restrictions in the Criminal Courts*, 4th edition, as revised in May 2016 by the Judicial College, Media Lawyers Association, News Media Association and Society of Editors.

www.judiciary.gov.uk/wp-content/uploads/JCO/Documents/Guidance/ltbc-guidance-dec-2011.pdf
Practice guidance on 'live text-based communications' issued in 2011 by Lord Chief Justice

www.justice.gov.uk/courts/procedure-rules/criminal/rulesmenu-2015
Criminal Procedure Rules and Criminal Practice Directions

www.jcpc.uk/docs/policy-on-live-text-based-communications.pdf
Supreme Court policy on 'live text-based communications'

www.justice.gov.uk/courts/procedure-rules/civil
Civil Procedure Rules and Practice Directions

www.justice.gov.uk/courts/procedure-rules/civil/rules/part39/pd_part39a
Practice Direction 39A which covers audio-recording in civil courts

13

Civil courts

Chapter summary

Civil law cases are a rich source of news. Civil courts deal with private disputes and wrongs. Some cases involve companies or individuals suing for damages. Some are brought against the state and public bodies—for example, when a patient sues a hospital trust for medical negligence. County courts deal with most civil litigation. The High Court deals with complex or high-value claims. Few civil cases involve juries. Bankruptcies and company liquidations are civil law matters. Magistrates have some civil law functions.

13.1 Types of civil litigation

Most civil litigation is concerned with:

→ glossary

- breaches of contract, including recovery of debt;
- torts—civil wrongs for which monetary damages can be awarded (including negligence, trespass, defamation, infringement of **copyright** and misuse of private information);
- breach of statutory duty;
- proceedings by financial institutions against borrowers;
- possession proceedings by landlords against tenants, usually for failure to pay rent;
- 'Chancery' matters, discussed later;
- insolvency, including bankruptcy and the winding up of companies;

family law is explained in ch. 14

- family law cases, including divorce and disputes between estranged parents over residence arrangements for and contact with their children;
- applications by local authorities to take into care children considered at significant risk of violence or neglect, which are also family law cases.

13.2 **County courts**

County courts deal with most civil cases. They are based in 47 centres in England and Wales.

13.3 **The High Court**

The High Court deals with the most complex or serious civil cases and those of highest value. The administrative centre of the High Court is at the Royal Courts of Justice in London. Outside London it is divided administratively into 'district registries', which have offices and courtrooms, mostly in cities, and share buildings with the larger county court centres.

The High Court comprises three divisions:

- the *Queen's Bench Division* (QBD), within which there are also specialist courts, including the Admiralty Court, the Commercial Court and the Technology and Construction Court;
- the *Chancery Division*, which deals primarily with company work, trusts, estates, insolvency and intellectual property (county courts also have limited jurisdiction in this area);
- the *Family Division*—see ch. 14.

High Court judges normally sit singly to try cases. The High Court is also an appeal court in civil law. In appeals and for some other functions, two or three judges hear the case, and it is then known as the 'Divisional Court'. A QBD court carrying out certain functions is referred to as the 'Administrative Court'. It handles **judicial review** of the administrative actions of Government departments and other public authorities, and of the decisions of some tribunals.

→ glossary

 Ch. 18 explains tribunals. The High Court's role as a criminal court is explained in 9.13.

13.4 **The Court of Appeal**

The Court of Appeal, Civil Division, is for most cases the court of final appeal in civil law. It hears appeals from the county courts and the High Court. Some are heard by three judges, but usually by two. When there are three, each may give a judgment but the decision is that of the majority. In a limited number of cases, appeals can be made to the Supreme Court. The Court of Appeal's procedures in civil cases are similar to those in its criminal cases—for example, how an appeal result is revealed. This is explained in 9.8.

 The hierarchy of the civil and criminal courts is shown in ch. 1, Figure 1.1 on p. 5.

13.5 Types of judge in civil courts

Three types of judge preside in the county courts and High Court.

- *District judges*—These are appointed from among practising solicitors and barristers. Their casework includes many fast-track and small claims cases, discussed later, family disputes and insolvency. They may be referred to in media reports as, for example, 'District Judge John Smith', but are increasingly being referred to as, in this instance, 'Judge John Smith'. Deputy district judges are part-time appointments.
- *Circuit judges*—Busier county courts may have two or more senior judges known as 'circuit judges'; in some regions they travel round a circuit of several towns or cities to hear cases, hence the origin of the title. Circuit judges also sit in Crown courts in criminal cases. Recorders are barristers and solicitors who sit part-time with the jurisdiction of a circuit judge. Retired circuit judges who sit part-time are known as 'deputies'. Circuit judges hear some fast-track and most multi-track trials, discussed later, and may also hear appeals against the decisions of district judges. Appeals from a circuit judge lie direct to the Court of Appeal.
- *High Court judges*—These are more experienced, and so more senior, than circuit judges.

13.6 Legal terms for parties in civil cases

ch. 14 explains divorce law

In most civil actions, the party, whether a person or organisation, who initiates the action—for example, claims damages for a **tort**—is called the 'claimant'. The party against whom the action is taken is the 'defendant'. In some actions—for example, bankruptcy and divorce cases—the person making the claim is the petitioner and the other party is the respondent.

13.7 Media coverage of civil cases

 Fair, accurate and contemporaneous reports of what is said in the public proceedings of a court are protected by the section 4 defence of the Contempt of Court Act 1981, if published 'in good faith', see 19.10; and by absolute **privilege** in defamation law, explained in 22.5. Qualified privilege protects non-contemporaneous reports and those based on case documents made available by the court, if that defence's requirements are met. Qualified privilege is explained in 22.7.

13.7.1 Open justice and case documents

Rule 39(2) of the Civil Procedure Rules says the general rule is that hearings should be heard in public—see ch. 15 for details of these rules, which have some exceptions allowing a court to sit in private.

Practice Direction 27, supplementing the Rules, says that a judge, if the parties agree, may deal with a small claims case in a private hearing. This power to sit in private is in addition to the exceptions to open justice in Rule 39 (2).

A journalist could argue against a decision to hold a hearing in private, citing the benefits of open justice.

small claims hearings are explained in 13.10

! Remember your rights

Journalists have rights to see case documents in civil proceedings as it might otherwise be impossible to report cases, particularly trials, meaningfully, because evidence is presented in documents and may not be aired orally in court. These rights are explained in 15.13.4, Access to registers and documents in civil cases.

13.7.2 Settlements

A case in which one party sues another may well be settled before trial, usually by one side paying the other a sum of money. The settlement means there will be no court judgment on the facts.

- A media report of a settlement should not suggest that the side paying the money has admitted liability—that is, blame—for the wrong allegedly suffered by the other unless liability *is* admitted. Wrongly suggesting that a settlement indicates an admission of liability could be defamatory.

For example, a private health clinic might sue for libel if a report wrongly suggests it has admitted liability for medical complications after cosmetic surgery even though it *has* paid out to a claimant to settle the case.

13.7.3 Reporting restrictions and contempt law

Judges in civil cases can impose reporting restrictions. They can use section 39 of the Children and Young Persons Act 1933 to ban the media from identifying a juvenile as being a claimant, defendant or witness—see 10.9. They can use section 11 of the Contempt of Court Act 1981 to ban indefinitely a name or matter from being included in case reports—see 12.6. They have other powers to ban reports from identifying people on privacy or other grounds—see 12.10 and 16.6.3.

The bans on taking photographs, sketching, filming or audio-recording apply in civil courts, as do other protections in law of the justice process, including jury deliberations, and of jurors and witnesses generally—see chs. 12 and 19. Because the Contempt of Court Act 1981 applies to media reports of civil cases, once a case is 'active' no extraneous material—for example, comment on it—must be published which creates a substantial risk of serious prejudice or impediment to the course of justice in it. But as juries are rarely used in civil cases, the Act is considerably less restrictive of pre-trial coverage than it is for criminal cases.

see too 11.2 on anonymity for victims/ alleged victims of sexual offences

> Ch. 19 explains the 1981 Act, particularly in 19.13 as regards civil cases. Ch. 15 explains the open justice principle. Ch. 16 shows how journalists can challenge invalid reporting restrictions.

13.7.4 'Payments into court'

The defendant in certain types of civil action—for example, a contract dispute or a defamation case—may make a 'payment into court' before or during the trial. This is a formal offer of payment to the claimant to settle the case. Journalists who discover such an offer has been made should not report it unless and until it is referred to in open court at the end of the proceedings. Disclosing at any earlier stage that an offer has been made will probably be regarded as contempt of court as it could prejudice the court's decision. The judge in the case (or jury, if there is one) is not told of the offer before reaching a judgment or verdict. If at the end of the trial the court finds for the claimant, but awards less than the defendant has offered, the claimant will have to pay all of the costs he/she incurred after the first date on which the offer could have been accepted.

13.7.5 Government plans for an 'online court'

In 2017 the Government introduced, in the Prison and Courts Bill, draft legislation to enable the creation of an 'online court' which it said would enable people to resolve civil claims of up to £25,000 'simply and easily' online, with 'virtual' hearings conducted by telephone or some form of 'video conference' unless using a physical courtroom was deemed necessary. The 2017 General Election stalled this plan's progress. Little detail emerged of how the media could report trials conducted online with the judge, parties and witnesses being at different locations. Money claims of up to £10,000 can already be made online in some types of case, but under this existing process there is a hearing in a physical court if the case is defended. Check www.mcnaes.com for updates, and see Joshua Rozenberg's book in the Book list, p. 463.

13.8 Starting civil proceedings

 Most civil actions in the High Court and county courts are begun by the court issuing a **claim form** prepared by the claimant. It details the claim against the defendant and the remedy or remedies sought. The remedy sought might be an **injunction**—an order compelling the other party to do something or stop doing something—or an order for the defendant to pay a debt or to pay damages. The claim form is served on the defendant.

The vast majority of money claims—for example, for debts—do not go to trial as the defendant usually does not file any defence, and in these circumstances the claimant simply writes to the court asking for judgment to be entered 'in default'. If damages are claimed, there might be a hearing to decide the sum. Once a judgment for the claimant is entered in the court's records—which means the defendant has been held 'liable'—the claimant can enforce it, seeking the money from the defendant. The court's enforcement procedures could include **bailiffs** taking the defendant's goods to sell to pay the money owed.

 →glossary

13.9 Trials in civil cases

The general rule is that a defendant who wants to dispute a civil claim must file a defence within 14 days of service of the particulars of the claim (which can be served with the claim form) or, if the defendant files 'an acknowledgment of service', 28 days after service of the particulars of claim.

A civil trial is confined to issues which the parties set out in their **statements of case** which include the claim form, the 'particulars of claim', the defence to the claim, any counter-claims or reply to the defence and 'further information documents'. As a general rule, the public, including journalists, have the right to see these documents.

→glossary

see 15.13.4.2, Civil case documents for which copies can be obtained

Each case is allocated to an appropriate 'track' based upon various factors including the value of the claim and its complexity.

The three tracks are the:

- small claims track;
- fast track;
- multi-track.

While the money value of the claim is not necessarily the most important factor, claims for more than £10,000 but less than £25,000 are generally allocated to the fast track. Claims below these levels—but not possession claims—are allocated to the small claims track. In 2017 the Government said it intended to raise the limit of personal injury claims, which the small claims track could deal with, from £1,000 to £5,000 for road traffic accident related claims, and to £2,000 for all other personal injury claims.

Cases allocated to the fast track are intended to be heard within 30 weeks and to be concluded in a trial lasting no more than one day.

Many multi-track claims are only a little more complicated than those on the fast track. Courts encourage negotiated (or mediated) settlements.

Most civil cases are resolved without reaching trial.

13.10 Small claims hearings

Cases on the small claims track are decided at a county court by a district judge and intended to be heard within a few months. The procedure is designed to allow litigants to present their own case, without the need for a lawyer. Proceedings are informal. The judge must give reasons for the final decision. A public hearing may be in a courtroom but will usually be in the district judge's 'chambers' (that is, a private room) with access allowed. If all parties agree, the judge can deal with the case without a hearing.

13.11 **Full trials**

In fast-track and multi-track claims there is, if necessary, a formal trial. This is by a judge sitting alone, unless the case is in the few categories in which there may be a jury—see later in the chapter.

 →glossary

Most parties involved in trials at county courts and the High Court instruct solicitors to prepare their cases. Solicitors either brief **counsel**—instruct a barrister to advise and to argue the case in court—or represent the client themselves in a county court trial. Solicitor-advocates can appear for their clients in the higher courts without needing to brief a barrister.

 for context see 1.5, The legal profession

Claimants and defendants may represent themselves in court and can be assisted by some other lay person (often called a 'McKenzie friend').

13.11.1 **Full trial procedure**

Unless there is a jury, civil trials are now largely based on documents, read beforehand by the judge, with each party disclosing its documents to the other side before trial. The documents are those listed earlier, plus witness statements. Each party may also supply a '**skeleton argument**' setting out its case. In the trial, witnesses may do no more than confirm that their written statement is true, although usually the judge allows some supplementary questions.

 →glossary

> Journalists' rights to access case material in civil cases are explained in 15.13.4, e.g. they should normally be able to see skeleton arguments and, during the trial, witness statements.

The claimant and his/her witnesses testify first, and are cross-examined by the defendant or his/her advocate, then his/her witnesses testify and are cross-examined by the claimant or his/her advocate. Expert evidence may be admitted only with the court's permission. Often the court appoints a single expert, who is jointly instructed by the parties.

After all the evidence, the parties or their advocates make their submissions on the evidence and law. Finally, the judge gives his/her judgment and the reasons for it.

the standard of proof in criminal law is explained in 5.1

- In civil law, the standard of proof—the criterion used by a judge (or jury—see later) to determine which of any competing pieces of evidence will be accepted as the truth—is that each is to be proved 'on the balance of probabilities'. This means the judge (or jury) decides which version of a disputed event is more likely to be true. This is a lower standard of proof than that needed for criminal convictions.

A judge may 'reserve'—delay—giving judgment, to have more time to weigh evidence and check the law. The judge may read the judgment out in court at a later date or have it printed and 'hand it down' at a subsequent hearing. Court reporters are usually provided with copies of printed judgments. After the judgment (or, in jury trials, the verdict, discussed later) there is usually argument about costs, an issue on which the judge must make an appropriate order, as it is not simply a question of the loser paying the winner's costs, though the loser can expect to pay a major part of these.

 The rights journalists have to see judgments are explained in 15.13.4.2 and 15.13.4.6.

13.11.2 Trials with juries

In civil law, there is a right to apply for trial by a jury if the claim involves:

* an allegation of fraud; or
* false imprisonment; or
* malicious prosecution.

As ch. 20 explains, the Defamation Act 2013 removed the presumption of jury trial in defamation cases, but left the court the discretion to call a jury.

The reasons why juries can be used in these categories of case were described in a House of Lords judgment as 'historical rather than logical'. They include the notion that fraud claims particularly concern allegations against someone's honour and that false imprisonment or malicious prosecution cases usually involve allegations against an arm of the state such as the police, and so a jury is needed to give the public confidence that the case has been independently decided as a judge alone might be seen as another arm of the state.

A judge has discretion to allow jury trial in other types of civil case, but such instances are exceptional.

If there is a jury trial, the judge will sum up the case after each side has made final submissions. In some cases the judge may ask the jury for a general verdict, but in more complicated cases the judge will give the jury a series of questions to answer in the verdict. Juries decide the level of damages if the verdict is for the claimant. Juries in civil cases, like those in criminal trials, are selected at random from the electoral role. A county court jury consists of eight people and a High Court jury of 12.

13.12 Civil functions of magistrates

The role of magistrates' courts in family law cases—a branch of civil law—is outlined in ch. 14. Magistrates also hear appeals from decisions of local authority committees on licensing public houses, hotels, off-licences and betting shops.

13.13 Bankruptcy

The civil courts deal with bankruptcy cases, some of which yield news stories of wild extravagance at the expense of creditors or HM Customs & Revenue. The term 'bankruptcy' only applies to people. Companies go into liquidation—see below.

13.14 Company liquidation

Care should be taken, when reporting that a limited company has gone into liquidation, to make the circumstances clear. There are different types of liquidation.
Misuse of terms could create a libel problem.

 The Additional Material for this chapter on www.mcnaes.com explains bankruptcy procedures; what
being bankrupt means; the defamation danger in wrongly stating someone is bankrupt; that court
documents in a bankruptcy case can be inspected by a journalist; and the different types of company
liquidation.

➡ Recap of major points

- County courts handle most civil litigation. The High Court deals with the more
  serious or high-value claims.

- Civil case hearings are mainly conducted by reference to documents. A journalist
  has rights to see the key documents of cases heard in public.

- Civil courts can impose reporting restrictions. Contempt law applies to media
  coverage of their cases, but is less restrictive if no jury is involved.

- Journalists need to take care before suggesting a person is bankrupt or a company
  is insolvent, because this could be defamatory if untrue.

((•)) Useful Websites

www.citizensadvice.org.uk/law-and-courts/legal-system/taking-legal-action/
courts-of-law/#h-the-county-court
Citizens' Advice guide to county court cases, including small claims

www.judiciary.gov.uk/you-and-the-judiciary/going-to-court/county-court/
Judiciary webpage about the county courts

www.judiciary.gov.uk/you-and-the-judiciary/going-to-court/high-court/
Judiciary webpage about the High Court

Family courts

Chapter summary

Family law, a branch of civil law, includes cases involving disputes between estranged parents after marital breakdown—for example, about contact with a child—and those brought by local authorities seeking to protect children. A court can remove a child from his/her parents because of suspected abuse or neglect. Reporting restrictions and contempt of court law severely limit what the media can publish about most family cases, to protect those involved, particularly children, who in most instances must not be identified. This chapter examines the main restrictions. But because of the complexity of court rules and the restrictions, a fuller version of this chapter is provided on www.mcnaes.com.

14.1 Introduction

The term 'family cases' covers a range of matters in civil law.

A new unified Family Court began in 2014, amalgamating the previously complex and piecemeal system, but continues to operate from existing courthouses throughout England and Wales, with a role for magistrates and with judges continuing to preside in the most complex cases, including in the Family Division of the High Court.

see ch. 13 for an overview of the civil court system

14.2 Types of case in family courts

Two major categories in family court proceedings are 'private' and 'public' law cases.

Private law cases include:

- matrimonial cases—proceedings for divorce, judicial separation or nullity, or to end a civil partnership;
- deciding financial arrangements between estranged or divorced couples;

- disputes between estranged parents about their children—for example, over which parent the children live with or the other parent's rights to contact with them, leading to the courts making 'child arrangement orders' under the Children Act 1989;
- applications for court orders—for example, to enforce the return of a child abducted by one parent in defiance of the other's rights;
- paternity disputes;
- applications in domestic violence cases for 'non-molestation' orders;
- applications to protect a person from a 'forced marriage'.

Public law cases include:

- applications, mainly by local authorities, for court orders allowing social workers to intervene to protect a child they suspect is being neglected or abused in his/her home. This intervention could be supervision if parental neglect makes the child behave badly—such orders are made under the Children Act 1989. Courts can also make emergency protection orders allowing police or social workers to remove children including babies if there is immediate concern for their safety;
- adoptions—a court can sanction adoptions of children who have been removed from their birth parents by a local authority in public law cases. Other adoptions may formalise existing relationships, and therefore are private law cases.

14.3 Reporting family law cases

Rules—currently the Family Procedure Rules 2010—bar the public from family cases involving children but allow journalists to attend these and most types of family case. But reporting family law cases is fraught with difficulties because of anonymity provisions under the Children Act 1989, contempt of court provisions in section 12 of the Administration of Justice Act 1960, and other extremely tight restrictions. As a result, much reporting consists of anonymised articles involving, for example, parents' claims that they have suffered a miscarriage of justice at the hands of social workers, medical experts or the courts.

See the longer version of this chapter on www.mcnaes.com for more about the Rules.

Disputes between parents over where a child lives are almost invariably shrouded in anonymity almost as soon as they arise, because of the 1989 Act's restrictions.

This complex net of restrictions has led to criticism that family courts operate in 'secret'.

14.3.1 Reforms

In 2013 Sir James Munby became President of the Family Division. He pledged to 'improve access to and reporting of' cases in the family court while preserving the privacy of families involved. He said that court rules would change. In January 2014 he issued guidance to judges to increase the number of judgments published by family courts.

((•))
see Useful Websites at the end of this chapter for this guidance

✱ Remember

Ethically journalists should not normally interview children aged under 16 on matters concerning their welfare without the consent of a parent or responsible adult—see 4.13, Protecting children's welfare and privacy.

14.4 Anonymity under the Children Act 1989

Section 97 of the Children Act 1989 makes it an offence to publish:

- a name or other material intended or likely to identify a child—anyone under the age of 18—involved in any current case in a court in which any power under the Act has or may be exercised with respect to that or any other child;
- an address, as being that of a child involved in such an ongoing case;
- detail identifying the child's school.

Section 97 anonymity automatically applies to children in unresolved disputes between parents, and cases involving intervention by social workers. It applies to any report of what is said in court or a written judgment, as well as to any wider feature about a child who is involved in an ongoing case. Clearly, it also means the child's family cannot be identified. Avoid jigsaw identification.

📖
see 10.11, Jigsaw identification, which explains this term

- Breaching section 97 by publishing material identifying a child covered is punishable by a fine of up to £2,500. It is a defence for an accused person to prove that he/she did not know, and had no reason to suspect, that the published material was intended or likely to identify the child.

14.4.1 Adoptions

Section 97 also bans reports of adoption proceedings—which journalists cannot attend—from identifying the child concerned while he/she is under the age of 18.

14.4.2 When does anonymity under the Children Act 1989 cease?

- Section 97 (4) of the Children Act 1989 says a court may waive, to any specified extent, the anonymity otherwise automatically bestowed on a child if his/her welfare requires it.

The Lord Chancellor may also do so, with the Lord Chief Justice's agreement.

Judges have waived the anonymity to allow the media to identify and show pictures of children abducted by a parent or hidden from social workers, in the hope—usually borne out—that the public will help find them.

14.4.3 Anonymity ends when the case concludes

The Court of Appeal held that section 97 anonymity only applies while Children Act proceedings are going on and ends with the case (*Clayton v Clayton* [2006] EWCA Civ 878). The then President of the Family Division said that if a court felt that anonymity should continue beyond a case's conclusion to protect a child's welfare or privacy, it should issue an **injunction** to continue it. The High Court or a county court can order that the anonymity continue until the child is 18.

→ glossary

✳ Remember

A journalist who wants to identify a child as having been involved in a case under the 1989 Act—for example, in a story about a mother's battle with social workers or a parent's account of the break-up of a marriage—should be sure that the proceedings have ended and that no order has been made to continue a child's anonymity.

14.4.3.1 Wards of court

Children who are made wards of court by the High Court, or are the subject of proceedings to make them wards, are automatically protected by section 97 anonymity while the case is ongoing (*Kelly v British Broadcasting Corporation* [2001] Fam 59).

👁 Case study

In 2001 Bobby Kelly, aged 16, ran away from home and joined the 'Jesus Christians' cult. His family made him a ward of court. A BBC reporter traced and interviewed him. Mr Justice Munby ruled in the High Court that the media did not require the court's permission to interview a ward of court or to publish the interview. But he warned that the media should observe reporting restrictions (*Kelly v British Broadcasting Corporation*). Anonymity might apply, and a published interview should not breach contempt law in respect of matter heard by a court in private (as this chapter explains). The BBC was allowed to identify Bobby. He was homesick but said 'you have to give everything up to work for God'.

((•))
see Useful Websites at the end of this chapter for the Bobby Kelly story

14.5 Anonymised judgments

The texts of family case judgments, if published, are usually anonymised to prevent a child or adult being identified. It is a contempt of court to report an anonymised judgment in a way which identifies any protected person.

14.6 Contempt danger in reporting on private hearings

Section 12 of the Administration of Justice Act 1960 makes it a contempt of court to publish, without a court's permission, a report of a private hearing if the case falls into certain categories, including those which:

- relate to the exercise of the **inherent jurisdiction** of the High Court with respect to children; →glossary
- are under the Children Act 1989 or the Adoption and Children Act 2002 or which otherwise relate wholly or mainly to the maintenance or upbringing of a child;
- are under the Mental Capacity Act 2005, or any provision of the Mental Health Act 1983 authorising an application or reference to be made to the First-tier Tribunal, the Mental Health Review Tribunal for Wales or to a county court;
- are of any kind where the court expressly bans publication of all or specified information relating to the private hearing.

The section 12 prohibition applies broadly across family cases heard in private, including wardship cases. The definition of 'private'—see below—includes some cases which journalists may attend. It could also be a contempt to publish information from a document prepared for use in a private hearing (*Re F (A Minor) (Publication of Information)* [1977] Fam 58, [1977] 1 All ER 114). This would include a witness statement in a dispute between parents over contact arrangements regarding children, or a social worker's report for a court about a child, irrespective of whether the information published was anonymised.

ch. 18 explains the tribunal system

It might also be a contempt to publish any of the judgment unless the judge authorises publication.

- But section 12 does allow publication of any order a court makes in private proceedings unless the court specifically bans publication of the order.

Also, section 12 does not stop the media making basic reference to a case being heard in private, although anonymity provisions may be in place under the Children Act 1989 or court order, making it illegal for a report to identify the family involved.

 For more detail on section 12 of the 1960 Act, see 12.7, Ban on reporting a court's private hearing.

14.6.1 The definition of 'private'

Section 12 reporting restrictions apply if a family case is heard in private. The position by late 2017 remained that if a Family Court or the Family Division of the High Court excluded the public from a family case, it was classed as private, even if journalists were able to attend. The section 12 restrictions apply unless the judge lifts them. If they are not lifted, a journalist can only report limited detail about the hearing.

> ((•))　See President's guidance in Useful Websites at the end of this chapter for context.

Following the creation of the unified Family Court, the only access rights for the media in any family case involving children are in the 2010 Rules. This means that the reporting restrictions in section 12 of the 1960 Act apply to cases in which magistrates preside, as the restrictions will apply in all tiers of the Family Court, unless the court lifts them or new rules are introduced. Check www.mcnaes.com for updates.

14.7　Disclosure restrictions

Part 12.73 of the Family Procedure Rules, reflecting section 12 of the 1960 Act, says no information 'relating to' court proceedings concerning children and held in private, whether or not the information is in documents filed with the court, may be communicated to the public, or to anyone other than lawyers, officials or other specified categories of people, without the court's permission. There is a similar ban for adoption cases. These rules therefore implicitly forbid, for example, a parent of a child taken into local authority care, or a lawyer, giving a journalist information about the proceedings (other than the few details permitted by section 12 of the 1960 Act), unless the court authorises it. The ban applies whether or not journalists attend the private hearing.

> 　See the extended version of this chapter on www.mcnaes.com for courts' powers to authorise journalists to see case documents: 'Can journalists see documents?'.

The ban does not stop a parent telling in general terms how he/she feels about the court case or of the wider experience of, for example, a child being removed from him/her—though any anonymity applying under the Children Act 1989, or through a court order, must be preserved in any report.

14.8　Other reporting restrictions in family cases

The reporting restrictions of the Children Act 1989 and those in the Administration of Justice Act 1960 were referred to earlier. Other restrictions can apply in family cases, depending on the type of case.

Automatic reporting restrictions under section 2 of the Domestic and Appellate Proceedings (Restriction of Publicity) Act 1968 cover some types of family case—for example, about failure to pay maintenance—in any court which hears such a case or an appeal.

Divorce cases, referred to later in this chapter, have their own reporting restrictions.

Remember

A full explanation of reporting restrictions and journalists' rights to attend family cases is provided in the longer version of this chapter on www.mcnaes.com. Also, the High Court Family Division has published a detailed guide to reporting family proceedings—see Useful Websites at the end of this chapter.

14.9 Anti-publicity injunctions in family cases

The High Court has inherent jurisdiction to order that a person must be anonymous in published reports of its proceedings and judgments. It is a contempt to breach such an injunction. Injunctions can be issued to protect children and mentally or physically incapacitated adults in family cases, and in other types of case in which the court is ruling on their medical treatment or whether they should be kept alive.

> See the extended version of this chapter on www.mcnaes.com for the procedure to alert the media to applications for family law injunctions, and for instances of injunctions restricting media coverage of a criminal trial and an inquest.

14.9.1 News-gathering activity can be banned

An injunction can forbid news-gathering or other activity which is deemed likely to jeopardise a person's welfare or privacy, or could lead to the subjects feeling harassed. Mr Justice McKinnon made such an order in 2008 banning the media from approaching two women whose father was jailed for life at Sheffield Crown court after repeatedly raping them, as children and adults, and fathering children by them. Nobody involved was named in reports of the father's trial, but it was feared that news-gathering activities could lead to their being identified in local communities.

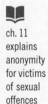
ch. 11 explains anonymity for victims of sexual offences

14.10 Coverage of divorce, nullity, judicial separation and civil partnership cases

Divorce, judicial separation or nullity cases, or proceedings to end a civil partnership, have usually been dealt with by Family Courts, although some are transferred to the High Court.

Most divorce proceedings are uncontested. Lists of petitioners granted a decree nisi—the first stage of a divorce—are read out in open court. The decree ends the marriage when it is made absolute, usually six weeks after being granted. In a contested case, the husband, wife or other witnesses might give evidence in court.

Reporting restrictions, as explained in the longer version of this chapter on www.mcnaes.com, apply to divorce, judicial separation and nullity cases, and proceedings to end a civil partnership—whether the report is of a hearing in a contested case or of case documents open to inspection. Rules on when such cases can be heard in private are also explained in the extended version of this chapter on www.mcnaes.com. In matrimonial cases there may be hearings on financial orders (previously known as 'ancillary relief')—that is, the division of property and other financial arrangements between estranged couples.

14.10.1 Inspection of evidence and copy of decree

Part 7.20 of the Family Procedure Rules 2010 permits anyone, within a period of 14 days after the decree nisi is made, and if it has not been contested, to inspect and make copies of an evidential statement which rule 17.19 requires the petitioner to supply before the decree can be made. This statement must tell the court if there have been any changes in the information given in the application for the divorce. The reporting restrictions covering divorce proceedings may limit what can be published from the statement. Part 7.36 allows anyone to obtain from the court a copy of the decree absolute. For more detail, see the longer version of this chapter on www.mcnaes.com.

14.11 The Court of Protection

The Court of Protection is a specialist court established by the Mental Capacity Act 2005 to make decisions for people who lack the mental capability to decide for themselves—for example, on financial or welfare matters or medical treatment. It makes decisions for some elderly people suffering from dementia, for example. It used to sit in private, but a pilot scheme has now been launched to open its proceedings while regulating reporting by the imposition of restrictions to protect the identities of the individuals and families involved. Its judgments are usually anonymised. For more detail, see the longer version of this chapter on www.mcnaes.com.

➡ Recap of major points

- Family courts are difficult to report as reporting restrictions apply in most cases, because the hearings are classed as private.

- A child involved in ongoing proceedings under the Children Act 1989 should not be identified in media reports of such cases unless the court authorises it.

- The High Court has had for decades wide-ranging powers to protect the welfare of children and others, including anonymity orders. The new, unified Family Court—which has a High Court tier—retains these powers.

((•)) Useful Websites

www.judiciary.gov.uk/wp-content/uploads/JCO/Documents/Guidance/family-courts-media-july2011.pdf

An official guide for journalists, judges and practitioners explaining the law on reporting family courts, endorsed by the President of the Family Division, the Society of Editors and the Judicial College

http://news.bbc.co.uk/1/hi/uk/852109.stm
http://news.bbc.co.uk/1/hi/uk/853876.stm

BBC reports on Bobby Kelly, when he was a ward of court

www.judiciary.gov.uk/Resources/JCO/Documents/Guidance/transparency-in-the-family-courts-jan2014.pdf

The President's 2014 guidance to family courts

15

Open justice and access to court information

Chapter summary

Open justice is vital to a democracy. If justice is done in secret, the public can have no confidence in it, because secrecy may hide injustice. Journalists are the public's eyes and ears in courtrooms, so need to know their rights of admission to courts. This chapter explains them, and refers to case law and statute which journalists can cite to oppose attempts to exclude them from courts. But the law does allow courts to sit in private on occasion. This chapter also explains journalists' rights to see court documents needed to report criminal and civil cases. Other chapters refer to admission rights for particular types of court—youth courts in ch. 10, family courts in ch. 14, coroners' courts in ch. 17 and employment tribunals in ch. 18.

15.1 Open courts—a fundamental rule in common law

In 1913, the House of Lords in *Scott v Scott* [1913] AC 417 affirmed the common law rule that normally courts must administer justice in public. One law lord, Lord Atkinson, said in that case:

> " The hearing of a case in public may be, and often is, no doubt, painful, humiliating, or deterrent both to parties and witnesses, and in many cases, especially those of a criminal nature, the details may be so indecent as to tend to injure public morals, but all this is tolerated and endured, because it is felt that in public trial is to be found, on the whole, the best security for the pure, impartial, and efficient administration of justice, the best means for winning for it public confidence and respect. "

 The Additional Material for ch. 15 on www.mcnaes.com gives more detail of *Scott v Scott* and other cases about open justice.

15.1.1 Benefits of open justice

The benefits to society of open justice include (with examples of the many cases or sources in which they have been listed):

- It promotes public confidence in and respect for the administration of justice in all types of proceedings, civil or criminal; and deters inappropriate behaviour on the part of the court (*Scott v Scott; R v Legal Aid Board, ex p Kaim Todner* [1998] 3 All ER 541). It enables the public to know that justice is being administered impartially (*R v Legal Aid Board, ex p Kaim Todner*).
- Full, contemporaneous reporting of criminal trials in progress promotes the values of the rule of law (*Re S (FC) (A Child)* [2004] UKHL 47, [2005] 1 AC 593).
- It puts pressure on witnesses to tell the truth (Judicial College guidelines, referred to later in 15.5—the premise is that a lie told in public proceedings is more likely to be exposed than one told behind closed doors.
- It allows the public to scrutinise the processes by which criminal cases are investigated and brought to trial (*Khuja v Times Newspapers and others* [2017] UKSC 49).
- It can result in evidence becoming available which would not become available if the proceedings were conducted behind closed doors or with one or more of the parties' or witnesses' identity concealed (*R v Legal Aid Board, ex p Kaim Todner*)—for example, a person who reads a media report of a case may come forward with new evidence.
- Publicity about criminal trials, including convictions, and the identities of defendants, is a deterrent to anyone considering committing crime (*R (Y) v Aylesbury Crown Court and others* [2012] EWHC 1140 (Admin)).
- It reduces the likelihood of uninformed, inaccurate comment and rumours about the proceedings, including about what is said in them (*R v Legal Aid Board, ex p Kaim Todner; PNM v Times Newspapers and others* [2013] EWHC 3177 (QB)).

Lord Woolf noted in *R v Legal Aid Board, ex p Kaim Todner* that any reporting restriction is a departure from the open justice principle and so must have an overriding justification. Ch. 16 provides specific grounds on which journalists can challenge reporting restrictions or decisions to exclude them from hearings. But the foundation of such challenges is that general benefits, including those listed above, always flow to society from open justice.

✳ Remember

Mr Justice Tugendhat said in the High Court: 'It is not necessary, in order for a newspaper to rely on the principle that reporting may encourage witnesses to come forward, for there to be any evidence in support of such likelihood' (*PNM v Times Newspapers and others*, which became known as the *Khuja* case. For more details about this important case, see 16.5.2.

15.2 The media's role in open justice

A journalist's vital role in reporting court cases as trustee for the wider public has been recognised in many judgments. In *R v Felixstowe Justices, ex p Leigh* [1987] QB 582, [1987] 1 All ER 551, Lord Justice Watkins said:

❝ The role of the journalist and his importance for the public interest in the administration of justice has been commented upon on many occasions. No-one nowadays surely can doubt that his presence in court for the purpose of reporting proceedings conducted therein is indispensable. Without him, how is the public to be informed of how justice is being administered in our courts? ❞

for challenge procedure, see ch. 16

Scott v Scott, Attorney General v Leveller Magazine Ltd and other cases referred to in this chapter—rulings which upheld the open justice principle—can also be cited by a journalist when challenging exclusion from a court hearing.

! Remember your rights

The vital role of journalists in reporting court cases is recognised in the general permission for them to use devices in court to tweet, text and email reports. For details of their right to use such devices, unless the court bans this, see 12.3.

15.3 The limited scope of common law exceptions to open justice

It is generally acknowledged that departing from the open justice rule by excluding the press and public from a court case is only justified in common law in three sets of circumstances:

- *when their presence would frustrate the process of justice*—for example, when a woman or child cannot be persuaded to give evidence of intimate sexual matters in the presence of many strangers, or it is feared that some people would try to disrupt the hearing if allowed into the court's public gallery;
- *when unchecked publicity would defeat the object of the proceedings*—for example,
  - when a case concerns a trade secret and publicity would reveal the secret to commercial rivals, or
  - when a case concerns a matter relating to national security which could be damaged by publicity, or
  - when the court is considering granting an order to one party that another party must produce evidence which it might destroy, before the order is served on it, if it were to be tipped off by reports of an open court hearing that such an order was being sought;

- *when the court is exercising a parental role to protect the interests of vulnerable people*—mainly:
  - children, for example, in family law cases, or
  - people with mental incapacity or mental illness—

  and unchecked publicity could harm the welfare of those involved.

ch. 14
explains
family law

→ glossary

Statutes and procedural rules set out in **statutory instruments** allow courts to exclude the public—and in some instances journalists—in specified circumstances, as this chapter explains. These statutory powers cover, to an extent, the same kinds of occasion for which common law justifies exclusion. Common law can be used if no statutory power covers the occasion, but does not give courts a general licence to exclude journalists and/or the public.

Lord Diplock, emphasising that common law departs from its open justice principle only in rare circumstances, said in a 1979 House of Lords judgment that the rule should only be set aside when:

> " … the nature or circumstances of the particular proceeding are such that the application of the general rule in its entirety would frustrate or render impracticable the administration of justice or would damage some other public interest for whose protection Parliament has made some statutory derogation from the rule (*Attorney General v Leveller Magazine Ltd* [1979] AC 440). "

> ◉ The Additional Material for ch. 15 on www.mcnaes.com provides more detail of this case.

15.4 Articles 6 and 10

Article 6 of the European Convention on Human Rights says everyone is entitled to a fair and public hearing. The rights which Article 6 primarily protects are those of parties in civil litigation and defendants in criminal cases rather than those of the media or wider public. A journalist challenging exclusion from a court should cite Article 10 which, by protecting freedom of expression and the right to impart information (in this context, to report the court case) and the public's right to receive it (to know what happened in the case), safeguards the benefits of open justice. But the common law rule of open justice should also be cited—it is independent of Article 6 or 10 rights, is much older, and so is more deeply rooted in case law.

> Ch. 1 explains the Convention's effect, and Article 10 is set out in 1.3.2.

15.5 The 'necessity' test

It is an established principle that any court should only impose the minimum reporting restriction needed to achieve its objective. The 'test' is therefore 'necessity', a point emphasised in *Scott v Scott*. The wording of Article 10 reflects this.

It means that any restriction on journalists' access to a court hearing or on their reporting of it must be limited to that 'necessary in a democratic society'.

Journalists opposing being barred from a criminal court hearing or opposing a reporting restriction can direct the court to guidance issued by the Judicial College, *Reporting Restrictions in the Criminal Courts*—see Useful Websites at the end of the chapter. It states: 'The public and the media have the right to attend all court hearings and the media is able to report those proceedings fully and contemporaneously. Any restriction on these usual rules will be exceptional. It must be based on necessity. The burden is on the party seeking the restriction to establish it is necessary on the basis of clear and cogent evidence'. The guidance says the fact that hearing evidence in open court will cause embarrassment to witnesses or air allegations damaging to an individual's reputation does not justify excluding the press and public, because it does not meet the test for necessity—that is, exclusion or a reporting restriction must be 'necessary' to achieve a purpose permitted by common law or statute and because no other measure can do this. Statutory grounds of exclusion are set out later in this chapter.

 Case study

→ glossary

A High Court judge criticised Malvern magistrates' decision to sit in camera to hear **mitigation** for a woman who admitted driving with excess alcohol. Her solicitor had asked the court to sit in private because she would refer to embarrassing details of her pending divorce which—the court was told—had made her suicidal and drink to excess, and her emotional state meant she could not speak about this in open court. The High Court agreed that magistrates did have power to sit in camera but Lord Justice Watkins said that in this case their reason for doing so was 'wholly unsustainable and out of accord with [the open justice] principle' (*R v Malvern Justices, ex p Evans* [1988] QB 540, [1988] 1 All ER 371).

> A practice direction supplementing the criminal court rules says that a reporting or access restriction must be worded in precise terms and be proportionate. For more detail see 16.2.2.

15.5.1 Journalists can sometimes stay when the public is excluded

If the public are lawfully excluded, it does not follow that journalists must necessarily go too. Rowdy supporters of a defendant may be banned or ejected from a court's public gallery. But journalists are not going to be rowdy. In 1989 a Court of Appeal judgment acknowledged that there might be cases during which the press should not be excluded with the other members of the public (*R v Crook (Tim)* (1989) 139 NLJ 1633).

15.5.2 The exclusion should be no longer than necessary

The Court of Appeal said in 1989 that a judge should be alive to the importance of adjourning into open court as soon as exclusion of the public was not plainly necessary (*Re Crook (Tim)* (1991) 93 Cr App R 17).

15.5.3 Criminal courts cannot sit in private to protect a defendant's business interests

The risk that publicity might severely damage a defendant's business does not justify a criminal court sitting in private (*R v Dover Justices, ex p Dover District Council and Wells* (1991) 156 JP 433).

15.6 In private, in chambers and in camera

The following terms are used of a court not sitting in public.

- The term **in chambers** refers to occasions when a hearing, usually a preliminary one in a case, is held in the judge's chambers or another room rather than a formal courtroom.   → glossary

- The term **in camera** is used when the public and media are excluded from all or part of the main hearing in a case—such as a criminal trial. The hearing is effectively being held in secret.   → glossary

- The term **in private** is used to cover both the above terms. But a hearing may be held in chambers for administrative convenience, rather than because of a decision or rule that it should be private—see later in this chapter.   → glossary

15.7 Contempt and libel issues in reporting of private hearings

If a case being heard in private falls into certain categories—for example, it is about national security or the upbringing of children—it is a contempt for anyone, including a journalist, who discovers what has been said in its private hearing to publish such information or material from documents prepared for use in the case—see 12.7 for explanation of section 12 of the Administration of Justice Act 1960, and for explanation of what limited detail can be reported about such private hearings.

Publishing information from a private hearing in any court case:

- is not protected by section 4 of the Contempt of Court Act 1981 if the publication creates a substantial risk of serious prejudice or impediment to an 'active' case—see 19.10.

- is not protected by **privilege** if someone defamed by it sues for libel—see 22.5 about absolute privilege and 22.7 about qualified privilege.   → glossary

15.8 Note-taking permitted in court

Criminal Practice Direction I General Matters paragraph 6D.1 says that anyone can make notes in a criminal court on paper or by 'silent electronic means'— as long as this does not interfere with 'the proper administration of justice'. The Direction refers to this general permission as a feature of the open justice principle. This part of the Direction came into force in March 2016, after a High Court ruling that note-taking by anyone in the public proceedings of a court must be permitted unless, because of a particular concern, the court bans it in an individual case (*Ewing v Cardiff and Newport Crown Court v DPP* [2016] EWHC 183 (Admin)). So the default position in law permits note-taking by anyone.

Reporters on a court's press bench were already allowed to take notes. But sometimes there are not enough seats there for them and there have been instances of ushers—because of an informal rule at some courts—forbidding reporters or journalism students, and anyone else, from taking notes in the public gallery until the judge or magistrates could be asked to approve it. This stemmed from concern that note-taking by some members of the public could aid improper collusion among witnesses, or be used to intimidate a witness. Her Majesty's Courts and Tribunals Service guidance to court staff says—as the High Court did in *Ewing*—that note-taking in a Crown court's public gallery can only be banned if there is suspicion about its purpose, and then only by the judge. The Criminal Practice Direction says that where there is reason to suspect that note-taking is for an unlawful purpose, or may disrupt the proceedings, court staff can make inquiries, and that the court has power to ban note-taking by a specified individual or individuals if the ban is necessary and **proportionate**.

→glossary

The Direction applies to criminal courts. The High Court ruling was about Crown courts. But both reflect the general, open justice principle, and so could be cited in any court which seeks to ban note-taking without a good reason.

15.9 Statute law on open and private hearings

Magistrates' cases Section 121 of the Magistrates' Courts Act 1980 says magistrates must sit in open court when trying a case or considering jailing someone, or hearing a civil law complaint, unless other enactment (statute law) permits them to sit in private. There is now such an exception in the 1980 Act itself—inserted as sections 16A–16F by the Criminal Justice and Courts Act 2015—which is known as the 'single justice procedure'. In this procedure in some circumstances—if the alleged offence is not punishable by a jail sentence—a case may be tried in private, in the defendant's absence, and a fine imposed if he/she is convicted.

 See also 7.8 about the 'single justice procedure', including when it allows a trial to be conducted in private. See 15.12.3 for how journalists can find out about such cases.

Indecent evidence Section 37 of the Children and Young Persons Act 1933 gives any court the power to exclude the public—but not journalists—when a witness aged under 18 is giving evidence in a case involving indecency.

Sexual history Section 43 of the Youth Justice and Criminal Evidence Act 1999 requires a court hearing an application to introduce evidence or questions about a complainant's sexual history—for example, in a rape case—to sit in private. This reflects the sensitivity of airing in court the sexual history of someone who may have suffered a sexual offence. The court must give in open proceedings its decision on whether such evidence will be allowed.

One journalist can stay Section 25 of the 1999 Act allows a court to make a 'special measures direction' to exclude the public and some journalists when, for example, a witness is due to testify in a sexual offence case or one brought under the Modern Slavery Act 2015 involving alleged slavery, servitude, forced or compulsory labour, or human trafficking for exploitation, or when there are reasonable grounds for believing that someone other than the defendant wants to intimidate the witness. But one journalist must be allowed to stay in court.

 Law in the 1999 Act which postpones the reporting of 'special measures' is outlined in 12.14, with more detail in the Additional Material for ch. 12 on www.mcnaes.com.

The 1999 Act says that even if, under section 25, some journalists and the public are excluded from a court, the proceedings are still deemed to be being held in public 'for the purposes of any privilege or exemption from liability available in respect of fair, accurate and contemporaneous reports'. This is a reference to contempt and defamation law, explained in 19.10 and 22.5.

Official secrets trials If a defendant is accused of spying for a foreign power or disclosing state secrets, journalists and members of the public may be excluded on national security grounds when some evidence is given or discussed—see 33.5 for this exclusion law.

Sentence review for informants Section 75 of the Serious Organised Crime and Police Act 2005 says a Crown court may exclude the public and press when reviewing a sentence previously imposed on a defendant who pleaded guilty, and who has given or offered assistance—for example, information about a crime—to a prosecuting or investigating agency such as the police.

 See the Additional Material for ch. 15 on www.mcnaes.com for detail about section 75, including about circumstances in which a journalist has a strong argument to oppose exclusion.

Closed material procedure Controversial provisions for 'closed material procedure' were enacted in Part 2 of Justice and Security Act 2013 to allow a court considering a civil claim to hear evidence in private—and without the **claimant** → glossary having access to it—if it accepts that disclosing the evidence would damage national security. The Government said this would allow it to contest compensation claims from terror suspects without the security services having to reveal sensitive evidence in open court.

 Detail about Part 2 of the Justice and Security Act 2013, and events which led to this legislation being created, can be read in the Additional Material for ch. 15 on www.mcnaes.com.

15.10 Procedural rules and open justice

Courts have procedural rules set out in statutory instruments. The wording of some rules gives courts wide discretion to sit in private. A journalist facing exclusion because of a procedural rule should argue that the court's interpretation of it must fully recognise the common law protection of open justice and Article 10, and cite *Scott v Scott*, in which Lord Shaw stressed that judges must be vigilant to ensure that the open justice principle is not usurped.

- Lord Shaw said: 'There is no greater danger of usurpation than that which proceeds little by little, under cover of rules of procedure, and at the instance of judges themselves.'

15.10.1 Criminal cases—rules on open and private hearings

Procedure for criminal cases in magistrates' courts, Crown courts and the Court of Appeal (Criminal Division) is governed by the Criminal Procedure Rules, and the Criminal Practice Directions which explain and supplement the Rules.

((•)) See Useful Websites at the end of this chapter for these Rules and the Directions.

Rule 6.2 says a court must have regard to the importance of dealing with criminal cases in public and allowing them to be reported. Rule 24.2 states specifically that the general rule is that a trial or sentencing in a magistrates' court must be in public.

Rule 6.6, for magistrates' and Crown courts, says that if either side wishes to argue that a trial or part of it should be heard in private (that is, in the limited circumstances when a court has power to waive the open justice rule), it must apply in writing to the court no less than five business days before the trial is due to begin—though rule 6.3 allows a court to hear an application sent later than this. The court officer must at once display notice of the application prominently in the courtroom's vicinity and give the media notice of it. The application itself will be heard in private, unless the court orders otherwise, and if in a Crown court will be heard after the **arraignment** but before the jury is sworn. The rule adds that if a court orders that a trial will be heard wholly or partly in private, it must not begin until the day after the application was granted, giving the media some time to challenge the decision.

The term 'court officer' is explained in 15.12

→ glossary

Ch. 16 explains how a journalist can in any court oppose or challenge an access restriction.

The Criminal Procedure Rules allow courts to conduct some procedures in private—for example, an application to a Crown court judge for **bail** after magistrates have refused it. But the presumption in law is that a journalist can be allowed into a bail hearing.

ch. 9 explains Crown court procedure

 For case studies of how reporters challenged exclusion from hearings, including a Crown court bail hearing, see the Additional Material for this chapter on www.mcnaes.com.

15.10.2 Dealing with contempt of court

Criminal and civil courts have particular rules to ensure that if someone is punished for contempt of court—for example, for disobeying a court order or threatening a witness in the courtroom—the court must announce this in public proceedings. See the Additional Material for ch. 15 on www.mcnaes.com.

15.10.3 Civil cases—rules on open and private hearings

The Civil Procedure Rules (CPR) cover civil proceedings in the Queen's Bench and Chancery divisions of the High Court and the county courts.

Rule 39(2) of the CPR says that the general rule is that a hearing is to be in public but that a hearing, or part of it, may be held in private if:

((•))

see Useful Websites at end of this chapter for CPR

- publicity would defeat the object of the hearing;
- it involves matters relating to national security;
- it involves confidential information (including information relating to personal financial matters) and publicity would damage that confidentiality;
- it is necessary to protect the interests of any child or protected party;
- it is an **ex parte** application (one made **without notice**)—that is, one party in the case is not yet aware of the proceedings—and a public hearing would be unjust to any respondent;

→glossary

- it involves uncontentious matters arising in the administration of trusts or of a deceased's estate;
- the court considers a private hearing necessary in the interests of justice.

Civil Practice Direction 39A, which supplements this rule, makes clear that the term 'hearing' includes a trial. It also lists types of case which shall, 'in the first instance', be listed as private. These include a claim by a mortgagee for possession of land, landlords' applications for possession of residential property because rent is owed, and proceedings under the Consumer Credit Act 1974 and the Protection from Harassment Act 1997 (the latter would include some cases in which a civil remedy is sought against domestic violence).

! Remember your rights

A journalist can try to persuade the judge that a case in such a category should be heard in public. The Practice Direction states that the judge should have regard to 'any representations' made. The CPR also provide that other types of hearing may be held in private. A journalist excluded from a civil court should ask which rule applies, and can remind the judge that the fact that a rule or Practice Direction indicates a hearing may be held in private does not mean that he/she should automatically exclude the public and press. The judge must consider the facts of the particular case before deciding about exclusion, and the party requesting such exclusion must have clear and cogent evidence to justify the request (*Registrar of Companies v Swarbrick and others* [2014] EWHC 1466 (Ch)).

 The Additional Material for ch. 15 in www.mcnaes.com provides summaries of civil cases in which media organisations, by referring to Part 39(2) of the Civil Procedure Rules, have successfully argued for their rights to attend the hearings, even when a party asserted this would expose 'confidential' information. See Useful Websites at the end of this chapter for these Rules. For general information on civil courts, see ch. 13. Other rules apply to the family courts—see ch. 14.

15.11 Hearings in chambers are not always private

this part of the 1960 Act is explained in 12.7

A hearing may be in chambers—for example, a judge's office—rather than in public in a courtroom, because of routine administrative convenience. Lord Woolf (later Lord Chief Justice) said in the Court of Appeal in 1998 that members of the public and journalists who ask should be allowed to attend a hearing in chambers if this is practical and the case is not in a category listed in section 12 of the Administration of Justice Act 1960 (*Hodgson v Imperial Tobacco* [1998] 2 All ER 673, [1998] 1 WLR 1056).

15.12 What information and help must criminal courts provide?

Many court clerks—most of whom are now officially called 'legal advisers'—are helpful in giving reporters in court basic detail about a case, such as how to spell the defendant's name. The Criminal Procedure Rules have set out when 'the court officer' must provide certain information on request. They say 'the court officer' is 'the appropriate member of the staff of a court'. If an inquiry has to be made to the court's administration office, staff there will know who has these duties.

15.12.1 Rule 5.8

Rule 5.8 gives members of the public, including reporters—whether in the court-house or phoning—the right to obtain certain details of a case. This applies if the court officer has the details, if the case is ongoing or the verdict was less than six months ago, and if no reporting restriction prohibits supplying the details. The court officer must in these circumstances supply the details verbally or by other arrangements prescribed by the Lord Chancellor.

The details are:

- the date of any public hearing in the case, unless any party has yet to be notified of that date;
- each alleged offence and any plea entered;
- the court's decision at any public hearing, including any decision about bail or the sending of the case to another court;
- whether the case is under appeal;
- the outcome of any trial and any appeal;
- the identity of the prosecutor, the defendant, the 'parties' representatives'—normally lawyers—including their addresses, and name of the judge, magistrate or magistrates, or justices' legal adviser by whom a decision at a hearing in public was made.

a public register shows if a fine imposed by a criminal court is unpaid—see p. 197

Rule 5.8 says a request for these details may be made orally, makes clear that no reasons for the request need to be stated and requires the court officer to supply details of any reporting or access restriction ordered by the court.

The person asking must pay 'any fee prescribed'. As yet there has been no announcement that journalists are expected to pay for these basic details.

But rule 5.8 says that a request for such detail about any other case—which would include those in which the verdict was more than six months ago—must be in writing, unless the court otherwise permits, must explain why the information is required, and should state if a request for the information has already been made under a protocol, and if so, the reason for refusal. It adds that if any other information about a case is requested or a request is made to see a document containing information about the case, the court may decide this at a hearing, public or private, or without a hearing.

❗ Remember your rights

Rule 5.8 means that a reporter in a magistrates' court must be given detail of the charges, from the charge sheet, and that the Crown court must supply detail of charges as listed on the **indictment**. The point is also made in Criminal Practice Direction I General Matters 5B.

> 📖 The 'Publicity and the Criminal Justice System' protocol which can give the media access to case material is explained in 15.13.3. Data protection law must not be used by court staff as a blanket excuse for withholding information from journalists—see 28.4.3.

15.12.2 Protocol on court lists and registers

Under a protocol agreed between the News Media Association, the Society of Editors and Her Majesty's Courts and Tribunals Service (HMCTS), the Service sends

see Useful
Websites at
the end of
this chapter
for the
protocol

see ch. 22
on privilege
and ch. 10
on youth
courts

free of charge and by email to local newspapers copies of the daily lists of defendants due to appear in magistrates' courts and copies of these courts' 'registers', which briefly record each day's details of convicted defendants and punishments.

Home Office Circular no. 80/1989 said the lists should contain each defendant's name, age, address, the charge he/she faces and, where known, his/her occupation.

It is likely that qualified privilege protects a fair and accurate media report of court lists and registers should anyone sue for a defamatory error published by the media but which was in the document when supplied by HMCTS. But a journalist at a court hearing should quote the defendant's details and charge(s) as given at the hearing, and not rely on the list or register. A fair, accurate and contemporaneous report of the hearing will be protected by absolute privilege.

If the register includes details of juvenile defendants, check whether they were dealt with by the youth court, in which case usually they must not be identified in what is published.

Crown court lists can be accessed from an internet service, www.courtserve.net/homepage.htm, as well as seen at the courts, but give less information than those for magistrates' courts.

The protocol agreed between media organisations and the HMCTS says: 'Crown court staff are encouraged to cooperate with local newspapers when they make enquiries.'

> See the Additional Material for ch. 15 on www.mcnaes.com for a case in which a reporter secured such cooperation by citing the protocol.

15.12.3 Getting information about 'single justice procedure' cases

for more
detail on
'single
justice
procedure',
see 7.8

As this chapter has explained, new law in 2015 created—to save costs—the 'single justice procedure' (SJP). It permits a single magistrate to deal with some types of criminal case in private (and possibly in an office, not a courtroom). This practice—as the Magistrates Association and others pointed out—breaches the open justice principle. Such cases could include TV licence evasion, speeding or driving without insurance.

Shailesh Vara, former Under-Secretary of State for Justice, said in 2014 that a local advance list of such cases would only be able to state the date by which they were due to have been heard. This is because under the procedure cases are not allocated specific hearing dates. Also, casework can be transferred from one courthouse to another if the first is too busy. Her Majesty's Courts and Tribunals Service said in 2017 that magistrates' courts should be providing lists of forthcoming SJP cases to the local press in line with the lists protocol, see 15.12.2, and that this SJP list should also be published in the public area of the relevant courthouse. Journalists should be aware too that they should be able to get information about SJP cases under rule 5.8 of the Criminal Procedure Rules, referred to earlier in this chapter.

! Remember your rights

Journalists who learn of a newsworthy case dealt with in the 'single justice procedure' could apply under the 2005 protocol—explained in 15.13.3—for material to help report the case. For example, they could ask for a copy of police footage of a politician's traffic offence.

15.12.4 Magistrates' names

As reflected in Criminal Procedure Rule 5.8, case law says a court *must* give the media and public the names of magistrates—also known as 'justices of the peace' (JPs)—dealing with a case. The High Court made this clear in 1987 in *R v Felix-stowe Justices, ex p Leigh*, cited earlier, in which Lord Justice Watkins said: 'There is, in my view, no such person known to the law as the anonymous JP.'

15.12.5 A defendant's details should be given in court

The Home Office said, in Circular no. 78/1967 and a similar circular in 1969, that defendants' names and addresses should be stated orally in magistrates' courts. The 1967 Circular said: 'A person's address is as much part of his description as his name. There is, therefore, a strong public interest in facilitating press reports that correctly describe persons involved.' The High Court ruled in 1988 that a defendant's address should normally be stated in court (*R v Evesham Justices, ex p McDonagh* [1988] QB 553, [1988] 1 All ER 371).

The Judicial College guidance says: 'Announcement in open court of names and addresses enables the precise identification vital to distinguish a defendant from someone in the locality who bears the same name and avoids inadvertent defamation.'

see Useful Websites at the end of this chapter for this guidance

15.12.6 Facts of an admitted case should be stated

If a defendant pleads guilty to a charge, the prosecution should state the facts of the offence in open court, before any sentence is imposed, so that the public and media know the circumstances. This requirement is imposed by Criminal Practice Direction VII Sentencing D.

see Useful Websites at the end of this chapter for the Directions

15.12.7 Documents which must be read aloud in court

Rules 24.5 and 24.15 of Criminal Procedure Rules say that in a magistrates' court the following documents must, unless the court directs (formally decides) otherwise, be read aloud or summarised aloud if any member of the public, including any reporter, is present:

- any written statement by a witness which is admitted as evidence in a trial—including evidence from an expert witness;

- if the defendant has pleaded guilty in writing (and so is not there), the material on which the prosecutor relies to set out the facts of the offence and to provide information relevant to sentence, and any written representations by the defendant.

Criminal Practice Direction V Evidence 16C.4 says rule 24.5 also applies to the transcript of a police interview with a defendant, even if the magistrates retire from the courtroom to read it.

Rule 25.12, which applies to Crown court trials, says that each relevant part of any written statement by a witness which is admitted as evidence must be read or summarised aloud.

Rule 50.15, which applies to extradition hearings, says that any such written statement by a witness must be read aloud or summarised aloud.

15.12.8 Details of witnesses in criminal cases

see Useful Websites at the end of this chapter for CPS guidance

Ministry of Justice guidance issued in 2011 says a witness should not be asked to give his/her address aloud in court unless for a specific reason. Crown Prosecution Service guidance says prosecution witnesses should not be required to disclose their address in open court generally unless it is necessary (e.g. the locus of a burglary).

15.13 Journalists' access to case material in court proceedings

Journalists can safely report information from documents as read out in a court's public proceedings or officially provided by the court, if any reporting restriction in place is obeyed. But there are contempt risks in publishing information gleaned from case documents in other circumstances, as explained in 12.7 and 12.8.

defamation defences for court reporting are explained in 22.5 and 22.7

A media organisation may face a libel action if it publishes defamatory material from a document not read out in open court, or—see later in this section—treated by the court as having been read out aloud, unless the document was officially made available to be quoted in such reporting under some other arrangement.

15.13.1 Access to material in criminal cases

In 2012 the Court of Appeal ruled that *The Guardian* newspaper should have been given access to documents used in an extradition hearing (*R (on the application of Guardian News and Media Ltd) v City of Westminster Magistrates' Court* [2012] EWCA Civ 420). The ruling, a landmark victory for the media, established a presumption in law that journalists covering hearings in courts should be able to see case material to aid that coverage (unless a rule or direction forbids such access).

15.13.2 Part 5B

Criminal Practice Direction I General Matters 5B (hereafter referred to as Part 5B) reflects the presumption created by the *Guardian News and Media* case.

Part 5B says that the opening notes, written submissions and **skeleton arguments** used by **counsel** in criminal courts should usually, once they have been placed before the court, be provided to journalists who want them. Skeleton arguments are documents in which each side sets out the basis of its case.

→ glossary
→ glossary

Part 5B says other documents and information can also be provided to the public or journalists at the discretion of the courts. 'Documents' include photographic, digital, video, CCTV or any other images.

Part 5B says a request for access to documents should first be addressed to the party who presented them to the court. If the party—for example, the prosecution—refuses, the request can be made to the court.

It adds that in the case of requests for information by reporters or lawyers acting for media organisations 'there is a greater presumption in favour of providing the requested material, in recognition of the press's role as 'public watchdog' in a democratic society', adding: 'The general principle in those circumstances is that the court should supply documents and information unless there is a good reason not to in order to protect the rights or legitimate interests of others and the request will not place an undue burden on the court.'

It goes on:

> " It may be convenient for copies to be provided electronically by counsel, provided that the documents are kept suitably secure.
>
> If there is no opening note, permission for the media to obtain a transcript of the prosecution opening should usually be given—[although a transcript will have to be paid for]. "

Part 5B stresses that the media are expected to be aware of the limitations on the use to which such material can be put—for example, that legal argument in the absence of the jury should not be reported before the trial ends.

see also 19.11.2 and 19.11.3 on proceedings in court in the absence of the jury

It also says some information should be given when sought by a member of the public or a journalist, who could simply ask court staff for it and need give no reason for wanting it. This class of information is detailed in rule 5.8 of the Criminal Procedure Rules, explained earlier.

Applications to the court for other information or material—including evidential documents—must be made in writing and be notified to the other parties.

Skeleton arguments and written submissions are likely to fall into the category of documents which a court treats as having been read aloud in their entirety, even if they were neither read aloud nor summarised aloud, and 'should generally be made available on request', Part 5B adds.

Documents which *have* been read aloud in their entirety—such as opening notes or statements, including experts' reports and admissions—should usually be provided on request unless doing so would disrupt the court proceedings or place an undue burden on the court, advocates or others, Part 5B says.

In the case of documents which are read aloud in part, or summarised aloud, Part 5B says:

> ❝ Open justice requires only access to the part of the document that has been read aloud.
>
> If a member of the public requests a copy of such a document, the court should consider whether it is proportionate to order one of the parties to produce a suitably redacted version. If not, access to the document is unlikely to be granted; however open justice will generally have been satisfied by the document having been read out in court.
>
> If the request comes from an accredited member of the press . . . there may be circumstances in which the court orders that a copy of the whole document be shown to the reporter, or provided, subject to the condition that those matters that had not been read out to the court may not be used or reported. A breach of such an order would be treated as a contempt of court. ❞

✳ Remember

((•))
see Useful Websites at the end of this chapter for the Authority

The term 'accredited' here refers to journalists able to produce a press card recognised by the UK Press Card Authority.

Part 5B says courts considering applications for material will take account of factors including:

- whether a request is for the purpose of contemporaneous reporting— a request after the conclusion of the proceedings will require careful scrutiny;
- the nature of the information or documents sought and the purpose for which they are required;
- the stage of the proceedings when the application is made;
- the value of the documents in advancing the open justice principle, including enabling the media to discharge its public watchdog role by reporting the proceedings effectively;
- any risk of harm which access may cause to the legitimate interests of others;
- any reasons given by the parties for refusing to provide the material sought, as well as any other representations received from the parties.

📖
ch. 19 explains contempt law

It states: 'It is not for the judge to exercise an editorial judgment about 'the adequacy of the material already available to the paper for its journalistic purpose' but the responsibility for complying with the Contempt of Court Act 1981 and any and all restrictions on the use of the material rests with the recipient.'

Part 5B indicates that journalists should only apply to the court for material covered by existing protocols after first trying to obtain that information under those protocols from the relevant organisation(s), which would be from:

- HM Courts and Tribunals Service, as regards information in lists and registers from magistrates' courts—see 15.12.2;
- the Crown Prosecution Service or police for material covered by the protocol entitled 'Publicity and the Criminal Justice System'.

15.13.3 The 'Publicity and the Criminal Justice System' protocol

The Crown Prosecution Service in 2005 issued a protocol on 'Publicity and the Criminal Justice System' which says that material on which the prosecution relied in a trial and which *should* normally be released to the media includes:

- maps and photographs, including custody photos of defendants, and diagrams produced in court;
- videos showing crime scenes;
- videos of property seized—for example, weapons, drugs, stolen goods;
- sections of transcripts of interviews which were read to the court;
- videos or photographs showing reconstructions of the crime;
- CCTV footage of the defendant, subject to **copyright** issues.

((•))
see Useful
Websites at
the end of
this chapter
for the
protocol

→ glossary

The protocol also says that material which *might* be released following consideration by the CPS, in consultation with the police, victims, witnesses, and others directly affected by the case, such as family members, includes:

- CCTV footage showing the defendant and victim, or the victim alone, which the jury and public saw in court;
- video and audio tapes of police interviews with defendants, victims and witnesses;
- victim and witness statements.

The protocol also enables the media to ask the CPS head of strategic communications to become involved in the event of a dispute over disclosure.

! Remember your rights

Despite the reference to copyright considerations in part of the protocol, fears that the media may infringe copyright by using case material should not stop it being provided for reporting of a case. See 29.10 on why copyright is not infringed by that usage.

15.13.4 Access to registers and documents in civil cases

The Civil Procedure Rules (CPR) cover county courts, the High Court and the Court of Appeal (Civil Division).

15.13.4.1 Registers of pending and ongoing civil trials

see Useful
Websites at
the end of
this chapter
for these
Rules

ch. 13
explains
how civil
courts
operate

Rule 5.4 of the CPR says any person who pays the prescribed fee may see a civil court's register of claims—that is, its list of cases. As such registers are open to public inspection, a fair and accurate report of what they say is safe to publish in defamation law—see 22.7.2.4. This inspection right is of limited value to journalists scouting for newsworthy cases, because although the High Court at the Royal Courts of Justice in London has registers for the Queen's Bench Division, Chancery Division and the Admiralty and Commercial Court, which deal with many major cases, no other part of the High Court—for example, its district registries (in other cities)—or any county courts have them at present (Practice Direction 5A).

15.13.4.2 Civil case documents for which copies can be obtained

The CPR allow non-parties, such as journalists, access to specified types of case documents filed with the court in civil claims lodged after 2 October 2006, when rule changes took effect.

This access is important, as civil cases are now largely conducted by reference to documents rather than by the systematic taking of oral evidence. A civil trial may be impossible to report meaningfully if a reporter has not read key documents.

For any civil court, rule 5.4C of the CPR provides that, as a general rule, anyone who pays the prescribed fee can obtain from the court a copy of any 'statement of case':

- if the sole defendant has, or all defendants have, filed an acknowledgement of service or a defence; or
- if there is more than one defendant, at least one defendant has filed such an acknowledgement or a defence and the court specifically permits provision of the copy; or
- if the claim has been listed for a hearing, or
- if judgment has been entered in the claim (a judgment means a part of or all the case is concluded).

This rule also allows anyone to obtain a copy of any judgment or order made or given in public—see too 15.13.4.6.

→ glossary

'Statement of case', which is defined in rule 2.3, means the **claim form**, particulars of claim (if not in the claim form) and defence, and also any additional claim, counter-claim or reply to the defence. For further detail of the nature of these documents, see CPR Parts 16 and 20. 'Further information documents' which the court requires a party to supply under rule 18.1 are also part of a statement of case.

Under rule 5.4C, anyone can—if the court gives permission—obtain from the court a copy of any other document filed by a party, or communication between the court and a party or another person.

Rule 5.4D says requests for copies of any of the documents referred to earlier must be in writing. As regards copies of documents for which the court's specific permission is needed, the requester must give notice to the relevant party in the case in accordance with Part 23 of the CPR, in case they object. A party or any person identified in a statement of case may ask the court to restrict or ban on access to such documents. For access after a case is settled, see 15.13.4.7.

The general right in rule 5.4C to see and have copies of some documents does not cover some types of sensitive, civil cases—for example concerning orders to restrict the activities and movements of suspected terrorists.

 For detail on such orders, see www.mcnaes.com for the online chapter, 'Terrorism and the effect of counter-terrorism law'.

The Court of Appeal has ruled that if a party to a civil court case objects to a document being made available for publication, a court will require 'specific reasons' why the party would be damaged by its publication. 'Simple assertions of confidentiality', even if supported by both parties in the case, should not prevail, it said (*Lilly Icos Ltd v Pfizer Ltd* [2002] EWCA Civ 2).

15.13.4.3 Witness statements

A statement of case does not include witness statements. But rule 32.13 of the CPR says: 'A witness statement which stands as evidence-in-chief is open to inspection during the course of the trial unless the court otherwise directs.' This enables public access during the course of the trial to written evidence relied on in court but not read out. But the court may rule that a witness statement should not be made available because of the interests of justice, the public interest, or the nature of medical evidence or confidential information, or because of the need to protect the interests of any child or protected party. Rule 32.13 does not apply to small claims cases.

 for access to witness statements after the case has ended, see 15.13.4.7

15.13.4.4 Interlocutory hearings and judicial reviews

The CPR rules on access to documents apply to interlocutory hearings and **judicial reviews**.

→ glossary

 The Additional Material for ch. 15 on www.mcnaes.com has case studies of how the media, including a regional newspaper, have used the CPR to gain copies of case documents, and how judges have interpreted the Rules. A case study also warns how to avoid libel pitfalls when basing news reports on case documents.

15.13.4.5 Skeleton arguments

Each side in a civil case draws up a skeleton argument—a document summarising its arguments in law. It is now established principle that a civil court can allow a journalist to see these and 'written openings' used by counsel (*GIO Personal Investment Services Ltd v Liverpool and London Steamship Protection and Indemnity Association Ltd (FAI General Insurance Co Ltd intervening)* [1999] 1 WLR 984 and the *Guardian v Westminster City Magistrates* case cited earlier).

Case study

In 2017 *The Guardian* newspaper asked multinational company Ineos for a copy of the skeleton argument it used to gain an interim **injunction** against protesters opposing its 'fracking' activities. At first the company refused to supply it, saying that although it was referred to in court it was not a 'public document'. It later said the 'skeleton's' contents had been superseded. But after exchanges with the newspaper, Ineos supplied a copy (*The Guardian*, 10 October 2017).

15.13.4.6 Judgments and orders

CPR Practice Direction 39A states that when a hearing takes place in open court members of the public can obtain a transcript of any judgment given or a copy of any order made, subject to payment of the appropriate fee. When a judgment is given or an order is made in a private hearing, a non-party wanting a copy will need permission from the judge involved.

 See the Additional Material for ch. 13 on www.mcnaes.com for information about what bankruptcy records can be inspected and ch. 14 in this book for inspection rights for divorce records.

15.13.4.7 Access to statements of case and witness statements after a civil case concludes

The High Court ruled in 2004 that anyone, including a journalist, could potentially obtain access to the statement of case and witness statements from a case which had concluded—including a case settled without a judgment (*Chan U Seek v Alvis Vehicles Ltd and Guardian Newspapers* [2004] EWHC 3092 (Ch)).

 See the Additional Material for ch. 15 on www.mcnaes.com for an outline of this case.

But a party to the concluded case can object to such access. If a judge holds a hearing to decide the access issue, costs could be awarded against a journalist or media organisation whose application fails.

✳ Remember

In defamation law the defence of qualified privilege *will* protect media reports of documents made available to the media as copies, or for public inspection, by a court if the defence's requirements are met and any reporting restriction is obeyed—see 22.7 on privilege. Family courts have their own procedural rules, which normally mean that no case document's contents can be disclosed other than to a limited range of people—see ch. 14.

A public online register shows, if the relevant sum was not paid quickly, whether a person or business has had a county court or High Court monetary judgment made against him/her/it, or was ordered by a tribunal to pay a sum to another party, or was fined by a criminal court, or if a person has had a Child Support Agency liability order made against him or her. For details see the Additional Material for this chapter on www.mcnaes.com.

ch. 18 covers tribunals

➡ Recap of major points

- A journalist arguing against being excluded from a court represents the wider public's interest in open justice.
- Common law, statute and courts' procedural rules enshrine the open justice principle, but do allow courts to sit in private in some circumstances.
- Criminal courts should give reporters basic details of cases, including magistrates' names. Defendants' details should normally be given in open court.
- Reporters covering criminal trials should be allowed to see case material unless a rule prevents this.
- A protocol enables the media to have access to some types of prosecution material—for example, photos and video footage—to help it report a trial.
- The Civil Procedure Rules enable journalists to get copies of and inspect documents in civil cases.

((•)) Useful Websites

www.judiciary.gov.uk/publications/reporting-restrictions-in-the-criminal-courts-2/
  Judicial College guidance, *Reporting Restrictions in the Criminal Courts*, 4th edition, as revised in May 2016 by the Judicial College, Media Lawyers Association, News Media Association and Society of Editors.

www.justice.gov.uk/courts/procedure-rules/criminal/rulesmenu-2015
  Criminal Procedure Rules and Practice Directions

www.justice.gov.uk/courts/procedure-rules/civil
  Civil Procedure Rules and Practice Directions

www.newsmediauk.org/write/MediaUploads/PDF%20Docs/Protocol_for_Sharing_Court_Documents.pdf
  Protocol agreed by Her Majesty's Courts and Tribunals Service on magistrates' courts lists and registers, and cooperation by Crown courts

www.presscard.uk.com/
  UK Press Card Authority

www.cps.gov.uk/legal/v_to_z/witness_protection_and_anonymity/
   Crown Prosecution Service guidance on witness anonymity and protection

www.cps.gov.uk/publications/agencies/mediaprotocol.html
   'Publicity and the Criminal Justice System'—protocol for release of prosecution
   material to the media, agreed by the Crown Prosecution Service and the Association
   of Chief Police Officers

16

Challenging the courts

Chapter summary

Courts often restrict media coverage of cases and journalists must be prepared to challenge invalid or overly broad restrictions—they may be the only people in court arguing for the open justice principle (see ch. 15). This chapter explains the case law and rules journalists can cite when opposing reporting restrictions, and how to make challenges.

16.1 Why a challenge may be needed

A criminal or civil court may try to restrict reporting of a case when it has no power to do so, or to impose a restriction which is valid but wider than necessary.

A journalist challenging a proposed or existing reporting restriction, or possible exclusion from a court, should remind the court of the societal benefits of open justice—see the list in 15.1.1, Benefits of open justice—as well as raise specific points about the particular case.

16.1.1 The necessity principle and Article 10

It is an established principle that any court should only impose the minimum reporting restriction needed to achieve its objective. The 'test' is therefore 'necessity'. As explained in 15.5, The 'necessity' test, this principle is deep-rooted in **common law** and integral to Article 10 of the European Convention on Human Rights, which protects freedom of information and the right to impart and receive information.

→ glossary

for Article 10's full wording, see 1.3.2, Convention rights

16.1.2 A reporting restriction must be obeyed

Reporting restrictions, even if they are invalid or too broad, must be obeyed unless the court amends or lifts them (*Lakah Group and Ramy v Al Jazeera Satellite Channel* [2002] EWHC 2500, [2002] All ER (D) 383 (Nov) (QB)).

16.2 **The media's right to be heard**

((•))
see Useful
Websites at
the end of
this chapter
for the
Rules and
Direction

Rule 6.2(3) of the Criminal Procedure Rules which cover magistrates' and Crown courts says a court should not impose a restriction on access to the court or on reporting unless each party and any other person directly affected—which would include the media—is present or has had an opportunity to make representations. This is re-stated in Criminal Practice Direction 6B.4 in which the Lord Chief Justice details how the Rules should be applied.

16.2.1 **Notice of applications for restrictions and of opposition to them**

Rule 6.4(3) requires that parties applying for a reporting restriction, or for a court hearing to be held partly or entirely in private, should, if the court directs, give the media advance notice. Rule 6.5(3) imposes obligations on media organisations to apply 'as soon as reasonably practicable' if they wish to oppose a reporting or access restriction, and to notify the parties—the defence and prosecution—that such representations are to be made and why the restriction is opposed or should be amended. But rule 6.3 gives the courts discretion to hear applications for restrictions, or media representations against them, made without notice and made verbally rather than in writing. Practice Direction 6B.4 says the order itself should state that any interested party—which would include a journalist—who was not there or represented when it was made has permission to apply to make representations within a limited period, such as 24 hours.

❗ Remember your rights

Journalists opposing applications for reporting or access restrictions, or their continuation, should tell the court if they were disadvantaged because no notice was given. The court may allow them more time to prepare their argument.

16.2.2 **Proportionality and precision**

Practice Direction 6B.1 says open justice is 'an essential principle' in criminal courts, and 6B.4 says that a court needs to be satisfied that the purpose of the proposed order to restrict reporting or access cannot be achieved by a lesser measure, such as a 'special measure'—for example, allowing a witness to give evidence by a live video link, or clearing the public gallery while allowing media representatives to stay in court.

> Law which postpones reporting of 'special measures' is explained in 12.14. See too 15.5.1 and 15.9 on how journalists can sometimes stay when the public is excluded.

→ glossary   It adds that the terms of any order must be **proportionate** so as to comply with Article 10.

Practice Direction 6B.4 says an order which restricts reporting must be in writing, must be worded in precise terms and must specify the legal power under which it is made, as well as its precise scope and purpose and, if appropriate, the time at which it will cease to have effect. The order must also state 'in every case, whether or not the making or terms of the order may be reported or whether this itself is prohibited'.

16.2.3 A record should be made and the media told

Rule 6.8 of the Criminal Procedure Rules says that if a reporting or access restriction is made, the court officer should record the reason for this.

> For who is 'court officer', see 15.12, What information and help must criminal courts provide?

It adds that notice of the restriction should be displayed somewhere prominent in the courtroom's vicinity and communicated to reporters.

Criminal Practice Directions 6B.6 and 6B.7 say a copy of the restriction order should be provided to any local or national media, and court staff should be prepared to answer any inquiry about a specific case. But 6B.7 says it remains the responsibility of those reporting the case to ensure the order is not breached and to make inquiry in case of doubt.

16.3 Judicial College guidance for criminal courts

Guidance entitled *Reporting Restrictions in the Criminal Courts*, published by the Judicial College, can be cited usefully in challenges to actual or proposed reporting restrictions or threatened exclusions, and is endorsed by the Lord Chief Justice in Criminal Practice Direction 6B.1. The College guidance cites case law and the Rules. It says, for example (its page numbers given), that the necessity for a proposed restriction on access or reporting must be 'convincingly established' by clear and cogent evidence by those arguing for it (pp. 5, 7 and 18), that courts which have imposed or are considering imposing a restriction on access or reporting should hear media representations as soon as possible, because contemporaneous court reporting is important and news is perishable (pp. 6 and 18), and that the media are well placed to represent the wider public interest in open justice (p. 18).

((•))
see Useful
Websites
at the end
of this
chapter for
the College
guidance

16.4 Methods of challenge

Reporters challenging proposed or actual reporting restrictions or exclusion of the media from a court should raise the issue as soon as possible.

16.4.1 An approach to the court by a reporter or editor

In court, the reporter should approach the clerk as the first step—for example, if a hearing is under way, by asking an usher to pass the clerk a note.

- If an order has already been made, the clerk can be asked to:
  - supply it in written form, if this has not already been provided;

– specify in writing why it was made, if the order does not make this clear;

– state in writing the statute and section under which it was made, if the order does not state this.

Such a request might prompt the court to reconsider the order, especially if a reporter—or an editor, by fax, letter or email—quotes case law against it.

Reporters opposing a restriction or exclusion should remind the court of their and the public's Convention rights under Article 10, and refer as appropriate to the 'necessity' principle and Judicial College guidance.

- Raising a query or challenge in person in court, or by an editor writing to the court, has the advantages that doing so may resolve the matter quickly and of being the cheapest method as there is no need to involve a lawyer.

A reporter whose argument is being opposed by both the defence and prosecution should remind the court of the warning by Court of Appeal judge Sir Christopher Staughton that '. . . when both sides agreed that information should be kept from the public, that was when the court had to be most vigilant' (*Ex p P* (1998) The Times, 31 March, quoted with approval by Lord Rodger in the Supreme Court case *Guardian News and Media Ltd's Application* [2010] UKSC 1).

16.4.1.1 Duty of Crown Prosecution Service (CPS) prosecutors

((•))

see Useful Websites at the end of this chapter for CPS guidance

A journalist may need to refer to CPS guidance which says: 'Prosecutors should oppose reporting restrictions that they do not feel are necessary for a fair trial. Prosecutors should not apply for reporting restrictions themselves unless they feel they are essential . . .'

16.4.1.2 Costs

Courts do not normally make costs orders against journalists or a media employer when these informal challenges are made, even if they fail. But it is important to make the challenge as early as possible.

16.4.2 Challenges taken to a higher court

If a challenge by a reporter or an editor fails, the court's decision can be challenged in a higher court.

16.4.2.1 Judicial review by the High Court of restrictions imposed by magistrates or coroners

→ glossary

A journalist or media organisation can apply to the Queen's Bench Divisional Court, part of the High Court, for **judicial review** of a decision by a magistrates' or coroner's court.

- This normally involves hiring lawyers and there is a court fee, and, if the challenge fails, the journalist or media organisation may have to meet some or all of the costs of any party which opposed the application. An applicant may have to bear its own costs even when successful.

16.4.2.2 Crown court restrictions can be challenged at the Court of Appeal

Decisions by Crown court judges to impose reporting restrictions or exclude the media can be challenged under section 159 of the Criminal Justice Act 1988, which gives the media a route of appeal to the Court of Appeal.

- The disadvantages are that the appeal may not be considered quickly, so a story may have lost any news value, and the appeal will normally involve hiring lawyers, paying a court fee and, even if it succeeds, costs.

Part 40 of the Criminal Procedure Rules sets out the procedure for such appeals.

 For the Rules, see Useful Websites at the end of this chapter. See also 9.8, The Court of Appeal, for the Court's role.

16.5 Rights to anonymity are limited

Lawyers acting for defendants or arguing on behalf of witnesses may urge courts to use powers based on Article 2 (the right to life), Article 3 (the right to freedom from degrading treatment including torture) and/or Article 8 (right to respect for privacy and family life) of the European Convention on Human Rights to provide anonymity or otherwise restrict reporting.

In criminal cases the power to make such orders (injunctions) derived directly from Convention rights to restrict reporting rests only with the High Court, or higher courts (*Re Trinity Mirror plc and others* [2008] QB 770, [2008] EWCA Crim 50). Magistrates' and Crown courts can restrict reporting to the extent specified in **statutes** and should take Convention rights into account in decisions on restrictions. This chapter explains the limits of such statutory powers, including when a court is told that a defendant or witness needs anonymity to protect from risk of attack.

 for context, see 1.3 about the Convention

 → glossary

- It is exceptionally rare for criminal courts to use any power to ban the media from identifying a defendant and rare too for them to ban publication of a defendant's address.

16.5.1 Open justice requires that reports should identify the defendant

Case law is that only 'rare circumstances' justify a ban preventing reports identifying the defendant in a criminal trial (*R v Marines A, B, C, D & E* [2013] EWCA Crim 2367).

Lord Steyn said in a judgment in which the House of Lords upheld the media's right to identify a defendant:

" . . . it is important to bear in mind that from a newspaper's point of view a report of a sensational trial without revealing the identity of the defendant would be a very much disembodied trial. If the newspapers choose not to contest such an injunction, they are less likely to give prominence to reports of the trial. Certainly, readers will be less interested and editors will act accordingly. Informed debate about criminal justice will suffer (*Re S (FC) (A Child)* [2004] UKHL 47, [2005] 1 AC 593). 🔊

  See also 15.12.5, A defendant's details should be given in court, for case law that a defendant's address should normally be stated in court.

  See also the case study on the *Incedal* case in the Additional Material for ch. 16 on www.mcnaes. com. In exceptional circumstances, the High Court has used the Convention in the context of family law to ban media reports from identifying a defendant in a criminal case—see the extended version of ch. 14, Family Courts on www.mcnaes.com.

16.5.2 Public proceedings, reputation, family life and the Convention

In 2017 the Supreme Court made clear, upholding the principle of open justice, that a person's general right to respect for privacy and family life in Article 8 of the Convention does not mean that the media can banned from identifying him/her in reports of what is said in public proceedings in a criminal case.

👁 Case study

Tariq Khuja, a prominent figure in the Oxford area, was referred to in evidence and by lawyers in public proceedings in the magistrates' court and Crown court as having been a suspect in Operation Bullfinch, a police investigation into the 'grooming' and sexual abuse, including rape and prostitution, of girls aged between 11 and 15. It led to seven men being convicted of such offences in 2013. Mr Khuja was not one of the men charged and—the Supreme Court said—there was no reason to think he ever would be. But it upheld rulings by the High Court and Court of Appeal that he should not be granted anonymity in media reports of the Bullfinch trials. His lawyers argued that his Article 8 right to respect for privacy and family life meant that he should have anonymity, to protect his reputation and avoid any impact of publicity on his family life. But the Supreme Court ruled that the open justice principle meant he had 'no reasonable expectation of privacy' in respect of what was said about him in public proceedings, and so his Article 8 right was not engaged. The Court said the 'collateral impact' on reputation of 'disagreeable statements' which might be made about people in any high profile criminal trial was 'part of the price to be paid for open justice' and for the freedom of the press to report public, judicial proceedings fairly and accurately (*Khuja v Times Newspapers and others* [2017] UKSC 49).

Part of the significance of the Supreme Court ruling in *Khuja* is that it did not grant him anonymity even though—because he was not a defendant or witness—he did not have the chance to clear his name by testifying in the relevant proceedings, and even though the Court accepted that without anonymity there was a 'real risk' Mr Khuja would suffer reputational damage. It follows that those who *do* have opportunity within criminal or civil cases to reply publicly to allegations made against them—that is, defendants, **claimants** or witnesses—should not on reputational grounds alone be granted anonymity in media reports of such public proceedings.

 →glossary

> Ch. 27 explains Article 8 and 'reasonable expectation of privacy'. There is more detail about *Khuja* in the Additional Material for ch. 16 on www.mcnaes.com.

◉ Case study

The Supreme Court said, in *In re Guardian News and Media Ltd and others; HM Treasury v Ahmed and others* [2010] UKSC 1, that in 'an extreme case' a court has power to ban the media from identifying a witness or 'a party' to a case, such as a defendant, if doing so is necessary to protect that person or his/her family from risks to their lives and safety which could arise, for example, because of what the person had said about 'some powerful criminal organisation'. But it removed the anonymity lower courts had given four men who were appealing against asset-freezing orders made under anti-terrorism law. The Court said that the men's right to respect for privacy and family life under Article 8 did not override the media's rights under Article 10 as there was a 'powerful, public interest' in identifying them. It dismissed the argument that defendants should be given anonymity when accused of serious, unsubstantiated offences, saying members of the public 'are more than capable of drawing the distinction between mere suspicion and sufficient evidence to prove guilt'.

see also 16.6.3, Anonymity, addresses and risk of attack?

16.5.2.1 Limit of common law power

In *Khuja* the Supreme Court confirmed that the common law power of courts to sit in private or anonymise case material used in open court has never extended to restricting reporting of what happens (for example, what has already been said) in open court. Any power to do that must be found in legislation—that is, a power specified in statute (*Independent Publishing Co Ltd v Attorney General of Trinidad and Tobago* [2005] 1 AC 190).

16.6 Challenging restrictions made under contempt law

The statutory, discretionary powers courts have for restricting reports of proceedings include those in sections 4(2) and 11 of the Contempt of Court Act 1981.

16.6.1 Section 4(2) orders

Section 4(2) of the Contempt of Court Act 1981 gives courts the power to postpone publication of media reports of all or part of a case to 'avoid a substantial risk of prejudice' to later stages of the same case or to other cases pending or imminent. See also 19.11, Section 4(2) orders.

Postponement orders frequently mean that when the restriction no longer applies the case receives substantially less coverage than it would otherwise have done, especially if the order means that coverage of a sequence of trials has, because of the practicalities of media production, to be compressed into one day's publication on the day the last trial ends. Many details will never be published and the benefits of open justice will have been eroded.

> See 15.1.1, Benefits of open justice. See too the Additional Material for ch. 19 on www.mcnaes.com for concerns expressed in 2009 by a senior policeman that section 4(2) orders preventing terrorism trials from being reported contemporaneously were fuelling myths that the terrorism threat was being exaggerated.

16.6.1.1 Risk of prejudice in sequential cases

Lord Justice Farquharson said in *R v Beck, ex p Daily Telegraph* [1993] 2 All ER 177 that the fact that an accused expected to face a second **indictment** after a trial of the first did not in itself justify making a section 4(2) order. He said it depended on all the circumstances, including the nature of the charges, and the timing and location of the second trial. If substantial prejudice to the accused could be avoided by extending the period between trials, or transferring the case to another court, that course should be followed, he said.

The Crown Prosecution Service general guidance to prosecutors says: 'The number of complex cases where there are a number of linked trials is increasing. In complex cases where there is more than one trial, reporting restrictions may be required to protect some of the proceedings, but this may not mean a blanket ban is needed. In these cases, prosecutors should consider carefully just how comprehensive the restrictions need to be.'

16.6.1.2 The risk of prejudice must be substantial

A section 4(2) order should only be made if the risk of prejudice to current or pending proceedings is substantial.

In 1993 in the Court of Appeal the Lord Chief Justice, Lord Taylor, said that, in determining whether publication of information would cause a substantial risk of prejudice to a future trial, a court should credit that trial's jury with the will and ability to abide by the judge's direction to decide the case only on the evidence before it. The court should also bear in mind that the staying power and detail of publicity, even in cases of notoriety, were limited and that the nature of a trial was to focus the jury's minds on the evidence put before them rather than on matters outside the courtroom (*Ex p Telegraph plc and other appeals* [1993] 2 All ER 971).

Risk of prejudice if one defendant is sentenced before others are tried In 2006 the Court of Appeal overturned a section 4(2) order postponing reporting of the sentencing of terrorist Dhiran Barot. The Crown court judge had made the order on the grounds that reports would prejudice the forthcoming trial of other defendants. But lawyers for the media successfully argued that five months would elapse before that jury trial and so the 'fade factor' would mean that contemporaneous reporting of Barot's sentencing would not create a risk of serious prejudice. Sir Igor Judge said in the Court of Appeal judgment that the right to a fair trial had to be balanced with the hallowed principle that the media had the freedom to act as the eyes and ears of the public. Juries had 'passionate and profound belief in, and a commitment to, the right of a Defendant to be given a fair trial', he said, emphasising the capacity of juries to concentrate on the trial evidence (*R v B* [2006] EWCA Crim 2692).

see 19.8.2, The 'fade factor' and limited publication, explains the term

For more detail of Sir Igor's remarks in this case, see, Juries are told to put pre-trial publicity out of their minds.

Principles for decisions on section 4(2) orders In *R v Sherwood, ex p Telegraph Group* [2001] EWCA Crim 1075, [2001] 1 WLR 1983, the Court of Appeal set out three principles on section 4(2) orders:

> (1) Unless the perceived risk of prejudice was demonstrated, no order should be made;
>
> (2) The court had to ask whether an order was necessary under the European Convention on Human Rights. Sometimes wider considerations of public policy would come into play to justify refusing to make a section 4(2) order even though there was no other way of eliminating the prejudice anticipated;
>
> (3) Applications for postponement orders should be approached as follows:
>
>> (i) Would reporting give rise to a substantial risk of prejudice? If not, that would be the end of the matter;
>>
>> (ii) if such a risk was perceived to exist, would an order eliminate it? If not, obviously there could be no necessity to impose such a postponement. But even if the judge was satisfied that an order would achieve the objective, he/she would have to consider whether the risk could satisfactorily be overcome by less restrictive means;
>>
>> (iii) the judge might still have to ask whether the degree of risk of prejudice contemplated should be regarded as tolerable in the sense of being the lesser of two evils, when compared to the harm which a 4(2) order could cause to the benefits of open justice.

These *Sherwood* principles were endorsed by the Court of Appeal in 2017 (*R v Beale in the matter of an appeal by News Group Newspapers* [2017] EWCA 1012 (Crim)).

see also
16.2.2,
Proportion-
ality and
precision

16.6.1.3 A section 4(2) order cannot be indefinite or permanent

A section 4(2) order can only be temporary in effect. It can be challenged as invalid if its wording does not specify the duration of its effect—that is, for how long publication of reports must be postponed.

The Court of Appeal said in 2017 that such an order should refer to its 'end point' being a specified date or as being the point at which the particular case will have concluded (*R v Beale*, cited earlier).

16.6.1.4 The possibility of re-trial does not mean a hearing is 'pending or imminent'

see 19.4.5,
Proceedings
become
active again
when an
appeal is
lodged

The mere fact that a defendant has lodged an appeal against a conviction does not mean that a re-trial is 'pending or imminent' and so cannot justify use of section 4(2) to postpone the reporting of another case he/she is involved in (*Beggs v The Scottish Ministers* [2006] CSIH 17).

16.6.1.5 Section 4(2) cannot be used to protect reputation or safety

Magistrates and Crown court judges have occasionally made section 4(2) orders for a purpose other than avoiding a substantial risk of prejudice to a current or future hearing. Such orders are invalid. For example, a section 4(2) order cannot be used to ban publication of a name or material to encourage a witness to give evidence, or to protect a defendant's or anyone's reputation or general welfare or safety. The Court of Appeal made this clear in *Re Trinity Mirror plc and others* and in *Re Times Newspapers Ltd*, cited earlier in this chapter.

 Journalists challenging a section 4(2) order should refer the court to pp. 27–29 of the Judicial College guidance—see Useful Websites at the end of this chapter—and may need to read the Additional Material for ch. 16 on www.mcnaes.com, including 'Section 4(2) orders cannot restrict reports of events outside the courtroom or material already in the public domain'.

16.6.2 Section 11 orders

Courts have common law power to order that a name or other information should be withheld from the public during proceedings. A court which uses this power can then make an order under section 11 of the Contempt of Court Act 1981 indefinitely banning publication of the name or matter in connection with the proceedings. The media generally accept that blackmail victims should have such anonymity, but—as this chapter explains—have opposed defendants being given it, or section 11 being used to ban publication of a defendant's address, and may object if section 11 is used for invalid or insufficient reasons to give anonymity to a witness.

 For context, see 12.6, Section 11 orders—blackmail, secrets, personal safety.

Journalists challenging the imposition or continuation of section 11 orders can cite the general points made in 15.1.1, Benefits of open justice, and as regards defendants, points made earlier in pp. 203–204 16.5.1, Open justice requires that reports should identify the defendant.

16.6.2.1 'In connection with the proceedings'

A section 11 order only bans publication of a name or matter 'in connection with the proceedings'—that is, a particular court case. It does not stop the media referring to someone by name in other contexts.

> See the case study in the Additional Material for ch. 11 on www.mcnaes.com, 'Orders to protect the public from risk of sexual offences', about a man who won section 11 protection to stop a newspaper publishing his address in a report of a court proceedings to impose a sexual offences prevention order on him—but the newspaper was able to report from other sources his previous offences and the view that he remained a danger to women.

16.6.2.2 Has the name or matter been withheld from the public?

A section 11 order cannot be made if the name or matter has already been mentioned in public proceedings in the case. In the case underlying *R v Arundel Justices, ex p Westminster Press* [1985] 2 All ER 390, [1985] 1 WLR 708 magistrates had made a section 11 order banning publication of the name and address of a man charged with burglary offences. The High Court ruled in that judicial review that the magistrates had no power to make the order, as the defendant's details had already been given in public—when the clerk routinely checked that information with the defendant in the first hearing. The Court of Appeal has said: 'Unless the court deliberately exercises its power to allow a name or other matter to be withheld, section 11 of the 1981 Act is not engaged' (*Re Trinity Mirror plc and others*, cited earlier).

> See the *Watson Press Agency* case study in the Additional Material for ch. 16 on www.mcnaes.com.

A court which has made a deliberate decision to withhold a name or matter from its public proceedings can use a section 11 order to forbid its publication after it is mentioned by mistake (*Re Times Newspapers Ltd* [2007] EWCA Crim 1925).

16.6.2.3 Is anonymity necessary for justice to be done?

Section 11 orders may only be made when they are necessary in the interests of the administration of justice. In *Attorney General v Leveller Magazine Ltd* [1979] AC 440, Lord Diplock said that departure from the open justice rule was only justified:

" . . . where the nature or circumstances of the particular proceeding are such that the application of the general rule in its entirety would frustrate or render impracticable the administration of justice or would damage some other public interest for whose protection Parliament has made some statutory derogation from the rule. "

 See the Additional Material for ch. 15 on www.mcnaes.com for this case.

see 16.3
and Useful
Websites at
the end of
this chapter
for this
guidance

16.6.2.4 Someone else may be wrongly perceived as the defendant

Page 34 of the Judicial College guidance warns courts that banning publication of a defendant's address creates the risk of 'inadvertent defamation', in that the public might think, wrongly, that someone entirely unconnected with the case but with the same name is the defendant. A court may need reminding of this.

16.6.2.5 Section 11 is not to protect the 'comfort and feelings' of defendants

A section 11 order should not be made for the 'comfort and feelings' of a defendant (*R v Evesham Justices, ex p McDonagh* [1988] QB 553, [1988] 1 All ER 371). Evesham magistrates had agreed that a defendant's address should not be given in court because he feared harassment by his ex-wife, and made a section 11 order banning its publication. But in a judicial review quashing the order Lord Justice Watkins said 'it is well established practice that, save for a justifiable reason', a defendant's address must be given publicly in court. He said:

> **"** There are undoubtedly many people who find themselves defending criminal charges who for all manner of reasons would like to keep unrevealed their identity, their home address in particular. Indeed, I go so far as to say that in the vast majority of cases, in magistrates' courts anyway, defendants would like their identity to be unrevealed and would be capable of advancing seemingly plausible reasons why that should be so. But section 11 was not enacted for the comfort and feelings of defendants. **"**

16.6.2.6 Section 11 is not to protect a defendant's business interests

A section 11 order cannot be used to protect a defendant's business interests, the High Court ruled in *R v Dover Justices, ex p Dover District Council and Wells* (1991) 156 JP 433.

16.6.2.7 Section 11 anonymity is not to protect a defendant's children

A section 11 order cannot be used in a criminal case to shield a defendant's children from the effects of publicity about the case. The Court of Appeal ruled in 2008 that Croydon Crown court was wrong to use an order to stop the media naming a man who had admitted 20 charges of downloading child pornography from the internet. The judge who made the order justified it by saying the defendant's daughters, aged 6 and 8, who were neither victims nor witnesses in the case, would suffer significant harm if their father were to be identified. The Court of Appeal said the judge was wrong to conclude that the children's privacy rights under Article 8 of the European Convention outweighed those of the media and the public under Article 10. In the Court of Appeal judgment, Sir Igor Judge said 'there is nothing in this case to distinguish the plight of the defendant's children from that of a massive group of children of persons convicted of offences relating to child pornography'. Allowing the defendant anonymity would be 'to the overwhelming disadvantage of public confidence in the criminal justice system' (*In Re Trinity Mirror and others*, cited earlier).

16.6.2.8 Civil orders imposed on sexual or trafficking offenders or suspects

Police or the National Crime Agency can apply in civil law for orders restricting the behaviour of convicted sexual offenders if that behaviour suggests they may reoffend—for example, the order can ban them from loitering near schools. Home Office guidance says that it is 'normal practice' for some police forces to ask magistrates, at the outset of the application hearing, to make a section 11 order to stop the offender being identified in reports. The guidance suggests that any disorder arising from public knowledge of his or her involvement in the hearing would make him or her more likely to abscond. There is similar Home Office guidance about civil orders restraining the behaviour of people convicted or suspected of slavery or human trafficking offences under the Modern Slavery Act 2015. Both sets of guidance say: 'It is for the court to decide whether such a prohibition [a section 11 order] is necessary.' The media can argue that such a hearing in respect of an offender needs unrestricted reporting because the public should be able to know who such offenders are.

 For this Home Office guidance, see Useful Websites at the end of this chapter. For a case study on such an order made against a sexual offender, see the Additional Material for ch. 11 on www.mcnaes.com. It covers too 'sexual risk orders' designed for potential offenders.

16.6.2.9 Anonymity should not be used to spare witnesses in criminal cases from embarrassment

A section 11 order made by a Crown court judge giving anonymity to a witness on the grounds that the stress of publicity might cause her to relapse into heroin addiction was criticised in the High Court. Lord Justice Brown said:

" There must be many occasions when witnesses in criminal cases are faced with embarrassment as a result of facts which are elicited in the course of proceedings and of allegations made which are often without any real substance. It is, however, part of the essential nature of British criminal justice that cases shall be tried in public and reported and this consideration must outweigh the individual interests of particular persons. (*R v Central Criminal Court, ex p Crook* (1984) The Times, 8 November) "

see too 15.5, The 'necessity' test, on embarrassment

16.6.2.10 Section 11 anonymity in civil cases

In *R v Legal Aid Board, ex p Kaim Todner* [1998] 3 All ER 541, Lord Woolf said that, in general, parties and witnesses in civil cases had to accept the embarrassment, damage to their reputation and possible consequential loss which could be inherent in being involved in litigation, and that their protection was that normally a public judgment would refute unfounded allegations.

16.6.3 Anonymity, addresses and risk of attack?

Lawyers sometimes urge courts to give a defendant or witnesses anonymity, or to ban publication of their addresses, on the grounds that they are at risk of violence from criminals or vigilantes.

The grounds of the application may be that the order is necessary to uphold rights set out in Articles 2 and 3 of the European Convention on Human Rights. As this chapter has explained, these Articles protect the right to life and the right to freedom from degrading treatment (for example, vigilante attacks) respectively.

→glossary   **Case law about these Articles says:**

- a court asked to give a defendant or witness anonymity, or to ban publication of his/her address, on safety grounds must be satisfied that the risk to his/her safety is 'real and immediate'; and

- the risk must have an objective, verifiable basis—be backed by evidence to the court and not be assessed merely on the person's subjective fears.

If allegations against a defendant, and his/her identity, are already public knowledge, there is no justification for restricting media reports.

In the House of Lords in 2007 Lord Carswell referred to this established criterion that there should be 'a real and immediate risk' to the person's safety to justify anonymity. A real risk was one which was objectively verified, and an immediate risk was one which was present and continuing, he said, adding: 'It is in my opinion clear that the criterion is and should be one that is not readily satisfied: in other words, the threshold is high' (*Re Officer L* [2007] UKHL 36). The Judicial College guidance says on p. 26 that the person seeking a reporting restriction banning, on safety grounds, publication of his or her identity has to provide clear and cogent evidence to show that such publication 'will create or materially increase a risk of death or serious injury'.

This test is the same whether the person allegedly at risk is a defendant or witness, whether the anonymity is sought for the proceedings—that the person should not be identified in court—or only in respect of media reports, whether the restriction being sought is to cover any identifying detail or just an address, or whether it is sought under section 11 of the Contempt of Court Act 1981 or other law.

ch. 13 covers civil cases, ch., 17 covers inquests and ch. 18 covers tribunals and public inquiries

It may be argued in a civil or tribunal case or a public inquiry or an inquest that the common law should be used to provide anonymity in the proceedings and (consequently) in reports of them, for a witness who fears for his or her safety even though there is not a 'real or immediate risk' to them. Such arguments are based on the common law's protection of the justice process—that unless the witness's fear is allayed, he or she may not willingly give evidence or its quality may be diminished. In common law, the court has 'a duty of fairness' to witnesses, and—if there is an application for anonymity on this basis —is allowed to take into account the witness's subjective fears. Case law is that an assertion that the prospect of being identified has caused a witness to suffer ill-health (for example, depression or anxiety) should be tested by the court considering if medical evidence supports this (*Re Officer L*). Criminal courts have statutory powers in section s 45A and 46 of the

Youth Justice and Criminal Evidence Act 1999 to provide anonymity for a witness 'in fear or distress' about testifying, as explained later in this chapter.

16.6.3.1 Police and prison officer defendants—risk of attack

Lawyers defending police or prison officers often argue that their clients should have anonymity or that the media should not publish their home addresses because—it is said—the charges they face or the general nature of their job or duties puts them at risk of attack or harassment from vengeful criminals.

 Case study

Two senior police officers were charged in 2010 with misconduct in public office after alleged improper interference in prosecutions for speeding. Aldershot magistrates refused to make a section 11 order banning publication of their home addresses. They sought judicial review, arguing that publication would put them at risk because of their past involvement in investigating serious crime. The High Court, refusing to make an order, noted that the Press Association, which with a regional media group had argued against a ban, had shown that anyone could use internet records of electoral registers, at a cost of £4.95, to discover the officers' addresses within five minutes. Any risk to the officers' safety, if it existed, would be from someone who targeted them, who would be not be deterred merely because the media had not published the addresses, it said, adding that the type of charges the officers faced were unlikely to provoke a vigilante attack (*R (on the application of Harper and Johncox) v Aldershot Magistrates' Court and others* [2010] EWHC 1319 (Admin)).

For case studies of the media opposing anonymity for a police officer and prison officers in 2017, see the Additional Material for ch. 16 on www.mcnaes.com.

16.6.3.2 Police firearms officers as witnesses—risk of attack

Police firearms officers involved in fatal shootings while on duty have been given anonymity at inquests (for example, *R (on the application of Officer A and another) v HM Coroner for Inner South London* [2004] All ER (D) 288 (Jun)). But police officers involved in 'tasering' a man who died soon afterwards were not granted anonymity—see the case study in 17.10.

16.7 Court orders giving juveniles anonymity

Chapter 10 explains that section 45 of the Youth Justice and Criminal Evidence Act 1999 is now the power which criminal courts can use to provide anonymity for a juvenile who is a defendant, witness or the victim/alleged victim, replacing section 39 of the Children and Young Persons Act 1933. Section 39 remains the power used by civil courts and coroners' courts to provide such anonymity for a juvenile witness, or—in civil courts—for a juvenile who is a party.

Of the range of orders which can restrict reporting, orders made in criminal courts to give juvenile defendants anonymity are probably challenged the most by the media. Reported cases indicate that most such challenges are made after a conviction for a serious offence.

Crown court judges tend to protect a juvenile defendant's identity with a section 45 order made pre-trial. They may consider lifting it if the juvenile is convicted and should give the media opportunity to argue for this. But a court is less likely to revoke an anonymity order after an acquittal.

16.7.1 Challenging section 45 anonymity

see 16.7.5,
Other case
law on
juvenile
anonymity

Journalists challenging the making or continuation of a section 45 order can consider citing elements of the *Markham* judgment, summarised in the next case study, or other case law outlined later.

They can point out that section 45 states that a court which has made an order can—by making an 'excepting direction' (counter-order)—revoke it completely or vary the scope of the reporting restrictions to any extent it specifies, if it is satisfied—

> (a) that the effect of the section 45 order is to impose a substantial and unreasonable restriction on the reporting of the proceedings; *and*
>
> (b) that it is in the public interest to remove or relax that restriction.

see 16.3 and
Useful Web-
sites at the
end of this
chapter for
the College
guidance

Section 45 requires a court considering whether to make an 'excepting direction' to have regard to the welfare of the juvenile. It states that no 'excepting direction' shall be made merely because the case before the court has been 'determined in any way' or has been 'abandoned'. But, as the Judicial College guidance points out, if the case outcome has been decided (determined), that 'may be a very relevant consideration'.

As indicated earlier, if the outcome is that a juvenile has been convicted of a serious crime, the argument for lifting his/her section 45 anonymity is stronger. In 2017 the Court of Appeal made clear that the section's reference to the case being 'determined' does not mean that the media, having argued unsuccessfully earlier in the case against a section 45 order or for it to be lifted, cannot argue in court again—after 'determination' of a verdict—against the anonymity. The Court said, referring to a trial in which a juvenile defendant was convicted of murder, that at its conclusion there was more up-to-date medical and other evidence in relation to her, and no longer a need for her to have anonymity to protect the 'integrity' of the trial, because it had finished. 'The overall picture (and, thus, the interests of justice) had changed', the Court said, approving the judge's decision to lift the anonymity after his earlier refusal to do so. This was the *Markham* judgment—see the next case study.

16.7.1.1 The public interest in lifting or relaxing an anonymity order

Section 52 of the 1999 Act says that, in considering 'the **public interest**', the court
must have regard, in particular and as relevant, to the interest in the open reporting of crime, in the open reporting of matters relating to human health or safety,
and in the prevention and exposure of miscarriages of justice.

 The general benefits of open justice are explained in 15.1.1, and these can be cited to oppose the
imposition or continuation of a section 45 order.

👁 Case study

In 2017 the Court of Appeal ruled that the media could name Kim Edwards and
Lucas Markham, both 15, who jointly committed a double murder. The Court
said that preserving their anonymity would impose 'a substantial and unreasonable restriction' on the reporting of the case, and that it was in the public
interest to remove that restriction. The murder victims were Kim's mother
Elizabeth, 49, and her sister Katie, 13. Kim Edwards and Markham, who were
in a besotted relationship, plotted to kill Mrs Edwards and Katie because Kim
believed her mother favoured Katie over her. Kim Edwards let Markham into
the family home, in Spalding, Lincolnshire, and he killed Mrs Edwards and
Katie by stabbing them both and smothering Katie as they lay in their beds.
Leaving the bodies upstairs, Kim and Markham stayed in the house for two
days watching films, having sex and drinking. The murders were discovered
when police broke into the house after concerns were raised that no-one had
seen the family for some time. Kim Edwards and Markham said later they had
intended to kill themselves with alcohol and pills after the murders, but in the
end decided against it. Markham admitted the murders. Kim Edwards pleaded
guilty to manslaughter by reason of diminished responsibility but denied the
two murder charges brought because of her involvement in planning and carrying out the killings. At a hearing before her Nottingham Crown Court trial,
Mr Justice Haddon-Cave made an order under section 45 of the Youth Justice
and Criminal Evidence Act 1999 granting anonymity to her and Markham in
respect of any publication about the case. Media organisations opposed this,
citing open justice principles, the gravity of the crimes, that the teenagers had
admitted the killings, that the order placed an unreasonable burden on the
media properly and substantially reporting the case, and that knowledge of the
crimes and identity of both defendants had 'widely travelled among friends,
relatives and wider family'. But the judge made the order on the basis that the
'integrity' of the trial needed to be protected by safeguarding Kim Edwards'
emotional welfare during it, because she would be under increased pressure
as it approached. She had intimated that she might kill herself. He said her
welfare could be adversely affected if she was named in coverage during the
trial, and there was potential for a 'social media storm' if she was known to

be the defendant, or Markham to be the person who had admitted the murders. The judge also referred to 'unwanted press intrusion' at the secure unit in which she was housed. That Mrs Edwards and Katie had been murdered had been publicised after their bodies were discovered. They could be identified as victims in reports of Kim's trial, but the section 45 order meant that media coverage of the trial could not explain that the murders which she—the anonymised defendant—was accused of were of relatives, or detail of motive. Because most references to evidence and psychiatric reports could not be included to preserve her anonymity, anyone reading the restricted coverage would not have known why Mrs Edwards and Katie were murdered. The jury convicted Kim Edwards of the murders, after which Mr Justice Haddon-Cave heard fresh media arguments that she and Markham should be identified as the murderers. News organisations argued that there was no longer any need to protect Kim Edwards' state of mind over her involvement in the trial; there was a strong public interest in people fully understanding the events covered in the trial; and that there was a potentially beneficial effect of public identification of murderers deterring others who might consider committing such a crime. They added that the anonymity would automatically lapse anyway when the pair turned 18. Lawyers for the pair and the local council argued that the order should remain in place. Mr Justice Haddon-Cave rejected the argument about the deterrent effect, but lifted the section 45 order, saying there was a strong public interest in full and unrestricted reporting of the case, and a high public interest in identifying Kim Edwards and Markham because they were guilty of an exceptionally grave crime. If the media were unable to identify them, the trial would be deprived of meaning and context because it would be impossible for the public properly to understand that the murders took place in a closed family context, which would exacerbate 'the risk of uninformed and inaccurate comment' about the case, he said. The judge noted that in any event the section 45 order would expire when each defendant turned 18 and that they would be incarcerated for many years beyond that date.

The anonymity remained in place for a further six months because Kim Edwards and Markham appealed against the lifting of the order. The campaign group Just for Kids Law successfully applied to be an 'intervener' to support their arguments. But the Court of Appeal upheld the decision to lift the anonymity, endorsing Mr Justice Haddon-Cave's approach and saying that no evidence had been produced that reporting the pair's identities before the automatic expiry of the anonymity when they reached 18 would adversely affect their future rehabilitation. The Court of Appeal also considered argument that removing Markham's anonymity would cause a risk of him harming himself, but ruled that the judge was right to rule that the risk was not substantial enough to engage on Markham's behalf rights under Articles 2 or 3 of the European Convention on Human Rights (the right to life and the right against degrading treatment) (*Markham and another v R* [2017] EWCA Crim 739).

16.7.1.2 Substantial

The *Markham* case was exceptional because of the gravity of the offences and the substantial effect of the section 45 restrictions. Judges have, after hearing from the media, revoked section 45 orders in cases where the crime was less grave. It can be argued by the media that a section 45 order creates 'a substantial and unreasonable' restriction' if—by limiting what detail can be published about a convicted juvenile—it prevents the local community understanding the case or knowing of an ongoing crime problem which needs to be tackled in a particular location or school, or that it has been tackled, and how. It can also be argued that identifying a juvenile whose offending has been serious would help maintain public confidence in the justice system and deter him/her or others from offending. Again, these are open justice benefits.

benefits of open justice are listed in 15.1.1

 Case study

In 2017 Calen Gaze—who as a 15-year-old 'repeatedly and viciously' stamped on a 13-year-old's head—was identified by the media as having been convicted at Gloucester Crown court of causing grievous bodily harm with intent in that attack. The Court of Appeal had lifted an anonymity order at the request of the *Gloucestershire Live* news site. The attack broke at least 10 bones in the victim's skull, and consequently he needed surgery to put in place a titanium mesh to support his eye socket, as well as a titanium plate. *Gloucestershire Live* argued that allowing coverage to name Gaze, of Matson, would serve the public interest, including by acting as a deterrent (*Gloucestershire Live*, 10 February 2017).

> The Late News section includes a case in which the judge allowed a juvenile murderer to be named in reports as a deterrent, and other cases in which the media could name juvenile defendants.

Journalists might also argue that 'a substantial and unreasonable' restriction is created if a section 45 order giving anonymity to a juvenile victim/alleged victim prevents an adult defendant from being identified. As this chapter has explained, for an adult defendant to have anonymity is contrary to the established principle of open justice. But the court will consider how media identification of the juvenile could affect his/her welfare.

16.7.1.3 Unreasonable

On the issue of what is 'unreasonable', a journalist can as appropriate cite the case law outlined later in the chapter, that anonymity should not be bestowed merely because of the juvenile's age or for a baby or toddler too young to need it, and that it might be inappropriate to bestow it if previous coverage has already legally identified the defendant; or that an anonymity order is invalid if made in respect of a juvenile who is dead or to specify that an adult defendant must not be identified.

16.7.2 Crown Prosecution Service guidance on anonymity for juveniles

((•))
see Useful
Websites at
the end of
this chapter
for this CPS
guidance

CPS guidance to prosecutors accepts that in some cases letting the media identify a convicted (and therefore disgraced and punished) juvenile can help deter others from committing crime.

Also, CPS guidance to prosecutors in 2011 gave the following examples of types of case in which there is a strong public interest in favour of lifting an anonymity restriction in respect of a convicted juvenile:

- significant public disorder where the public would rightly need to be satisfied that offenders were brought to justice and there was a need to deter others;
- serious offences which undermined the public's confidence in the safety of their communities;
- hate crimes which could have a corrosive impact on the confidence of communities.

✳ Remember

'Hate crimes' include racist attacks or incitement to racial hatred. For the latter, see ch. 38, 'The incitement of hate', on www.mcnaes.com.

16.7.3 International treaties do not trump case law

As explained earlier, rights under Article 8 (privacy) and Article 10 (freedom to impart and receive information) of the European Convention on Human Rights are cited in disputes about reporting restrictions. Parts of two other international treaties have been cited in several cases by lawyers arguing for anonymity for juvenile defendants to remain in place. These are Articles 3 and 40 of the United Nations Convention on the Rights of the Child and Rule 8.1 of the United Nations Standard Minimum Rules for the Administration of Juvenile Justice (known as 'the Beijing Rules'). Rule 8.1, for example, says that juvenile defendants' 'right to privacy' should be respected at all stages in order to avoid their being caused harm by 'undue publicity' or by the process of 'labelling' (stigmatisation). Some emphasis is placed on these treaties in the CPS guidance to prosecutors.

In the *Markham* case—cited earlier in this chapter—lawyers arguing for the juvenile defendants' section 45 anonymity to remain in place submitted that the Crown court judge who had ruled against this had failed to have sufficient regard for these treaties. But the Court of Appeal said that such submissions had ignored the UK's own well-established law which itself took into account the international dimension relating to the protection of children. The Court made clear that citing the two UN treaties did not trump UK case law, saying: 'Furthermore, for the future, submissions in this area of the law should focus on the facts of the particular case relevant to the exercise of the court's judgment, rather than the siren calls of abstract principles that have already informed the approach which the courts adopt.'

16.7.4 Challenges to section 45A lifetime anonymity

As explained in 10.8, in April 2015 the Government inserted a new section—section 45A—into the Youth Justice and Criminal Evidence Act 1999, to give criminal courts a discretionary power, in certain circumstances, to ban any publication from identifying a specified juvenile, in his or her lifetime, as being concerned in a case as a witness or victim/alleged victim.

In the same type of circumstances, section 46 of the same Act empowers a criminal court to grant such lifetime anonymity for adult witnesses. Because of this commonality in circumstantial context, grounds on which section 45A orders or section 46 orders can be challenged are discussed together, later in this chapter.

16.7.5 Other case law on juvenile anonymity

As explained in 10.9, section 39 of the Children and Young Persons Act 1933 remains the power used in civil courts and inquests to ban in any publication the identification of a specified juvenile as being concerning in such proceedings, although in April 2015 it was replaced in criminal courts by section 45 of the 1999 Act.

Case law from challenges made in criminal courts before April 2015 to anonymity orders made under section 39 applies in relation to orders under section 45 of the 1999 Act, as the Court of Appeal has made clear in *R v H* [2015] EWCA Crim 1579.

16.7.5.1 A section 45 or section 39 order cannot be in force if the juvenile has turned 18

The wording of section 45 of the 1999 Act and section 39 of the 1933 Act makes clear that these orders can only be made to give anonymity to a person aged under 18. Case law has made clear that anonymity provided by either power automatically expires when the juvenile turns 18. So neither type of order can validly be made *after* the defendant reaches the age of 18.

 See 10.6.1, When section 45 anonymity ceases to apply and 10.9.1, When does section 39 cease to apply to a juvenile?

16.7.5.2 Principles to decide whether anonymity is justified

Lord Justice Simon Brown in *R v Crown Court at Winchester, ex p B* [2000] 1 Cr App R 11 identified the following seven principles a criminal court should consider when deciding whether to make or revoke such an anonymity order as regards a juvenile defendant.

(1) In deciding whether to impose or lift the reporting restrictions, the court will consider whether there are good reasons for allowing the juvenile defendant to be named.

(2) It will give considerable weight to the offender's age and the potential damage to this juvenile of public identification as a criminal before he/she has the benefit or burden of adulthood.

(3) It must have regard to the juvenile's welfare.

(4) The prospect of being named with the accompanying disgrace is a powerful deterrent and naming a defendant in the context of his/her punishment serves as a deterrent to others. These deterrents are proper objectives for the court.

(5) There is a strong public interest in open justice and in the public knowing as much as possible about what has happened in court, including the identity of those who have committed crime.

(6) The weight to be attributed to different factors may shift at different stages of the proceedings and, in particular, after the defendant has been found, or pleads, guilty and is sentenced. It may then be appropriate to place greater weight on the interest of the public in knowing the identity of those who have committed crimes, particularly serious and detestable crimes.

(7) The fact that an appeal has been made may be a material consideration.

Similar points, including about the juvenile's welfare, and the possible deterrent effect of allowing the juvenile to be identified in respect of the case, were made by the High Court in *R on the application of Y v Aylesbury Crown Court, Crown Prosecution Service, Newsquest Media Group Limited* [2012] EWHC 1140 (Admin). The court said in this judgment that if the arguments for and against the anonymity were evenly balanced, the ruling should be for anonymity.

Journalists arguing against the imposition or continuation of a section 45 order may need to remind the court that the anonymity expires at 18, and therefore—as the Court of Appeal has confirmed—Parliament did not see the anonymity's function as being to help the defendant achieve rehabilitation after reaching adulthood (*R (on the application of JC & RT) v Central Criminal Court* [2014] EWHC 1041 (QB)).

16.7.5.3 Challenges to juvenile anonymity in anti-social behaviour or criminal behaviour cases

 For arguments for identifying juveniles in reports of proceedings related to anti-social behaviour injunctions or criminal behaviour orders, see the Additional Material for ch. 16 on www.mcnaes.com.

16.7.5.4 The identity of the juvenile is already in the public domain

In *R v Cardiff Crown Court, ex p M (A Minor)* (1998) 162 JP 527 (DC) the High Court ruled that if a section 39 order under the 1933 Act was not made when the case was first listed, publicity which has already identified the juvenile might make it inappropriate to make such an order at a later stage. The same reasoning will apply to orders under section 45 of the Youth Justice and Criminal Evidence Act 1999.

16.7.5.5 There must be a good reason for an anonymity order

see 16.3 and Useful Web-sites at the end of this chapter for the College guidelines

As the Judicial College guidelines note, age alone is not sufficient to justify making an order. A court should not make an anonymity order in a civil or criminal case automatically, merely because of a juvenile's age, or unthinkingly as a 'blanket' order covering all juveniles in the case.

- In *R v Lee*, cited earlier, Lord Justice Lloyd pointed out that the 1933 Act made a distinction between section 49 anonymity, automatic under the Act in the juvenile (now youth) court, and section 39 anonymity, which is not automatic, in the Crown court—'a distinction which Parliament clearly intended to preserve'. This distinction was preserved in the creation of section 45 of the 1999 Act to replace—in criminal courts—section 39 of the 1933 Act.

16.7.5.6 Is the juvenile concerned in the proceedings?

see Remember your rights in ch. 10, p. 120, which mentions truancy cases

Neither a section 39 order nor a section 45 order is valid if the juvenile is not 'concerned in the proceedings', so criminal courts should not use section 45 to give a juvenile anonymity merely because his/her parent is the defendant, *unless* the juvenile is 'concerned' because he/she is a witness, or victim/alleged victim of the offence, or is the juvenile 'in respect of whom the proceedings are taken'—for example, in a truancy case in which a parent is prosecuted for failing to ensure a child attends school.

In 2000 Mr Justice Elias said in the High Court:

> Sadly, in any case where someone is caught up in the criminal process other members of the family who are wholly innocent of wrongdoing will be innocent casualties in the drama. They may suffer in all sorts of ways from the publicity given to another family member. But I do not consider that in the normal case that is a relevant factor or a good reason for granting a direction under section 39 (*Chief Constable of Surrey v JHG and DHG* [2002] EWHC 1129 (Admin), [2002] All ER (D) 308 (May)).

The fact that anonymity cannot validly be conferred on children not 'concerned in the proceedings' was also acknowledged in *Re S* [2003] EWCA Civ 963.

Sometimes a defendant's children *are* relevant in a court case even when they are not 'concerned in the proceedings'. Moreover, the media—even if they do not intend to publish the name of a child—may have to challenge a section 45 order if its blanket ban on publication of any detail which could identify the child has a 'substantial and unreasonable' effect of preventing reports from identifying the adult defendant, or a section 39 order which has a substantially restrictive effect on the reporting of a civil case or inquest.

👁 Case study

The Court of Appeal in 2013 said that Recorder J J Wright had been wrong to impose at Swindon Crown court a section 39 order banning the media from identifying a 15-year-old boy whose father—a former Army officer—was on trial for defrauding taxpayers of more than £180,000 to send his three sons to an independent boarding school. The trial was already well under way—the prosecution having already identified in open court all three sons, including the 15 year old, and media reports having mentioned them—when the Recorder made the order. The boy was not a witness or otherwise 'concerned in the proceedings'. The father was convicted on most charges (*R v Robert Jolleys, ex p Press Association* [2013] EWCA Crim 1135).

The High Court ruled in 2008 that section 39 cannot be used to spare the embarrassment of a defendant's children if they are 'not concerned in the proceedings' (*Crawford v Director of Public Prosecutions*, The Times, 20 February 2008).

✳ Remember

It may be unethical to name a child in a report of a court case if he or she was not named in the proceedings. The Editors' Code says that relatives of people convicted or accused of crime should not generally be identified without their consent unless they are 'genuinely relevant' to the story. The Broadcasting Code says that children do not lose their right to privacy because of a parent's notoriety. See 4.13, Protecting children's welfare and privacy and 4.15, Relatives and friends of those accused of or convicted of crime.

16.7.5.7 An anonymity order cannot validly be made in respect of a dead juvenile

((•))
see 16.3 and Useful Websites at the end of this chapter for the College guidance

Orders should not be made under section 45 of the 1999 Act or section 39 of the 1933 Act to give anonymity to a dead child. The Judicial College guidance says that for such an order to be validly made the juvenile 'must be alive', pointing out that the Court of Appeal, referring to earlier case law, stated this in *Re S (A Child) (Identification: Restrictions on Publication)* [2005] 1 AC 593.

But instances continue to occur of magistrates and judges needing reminders of this case law—for an example, see this book's Late News.

Courts have purported to make such orders, following applications by prosecution or defence lawyers, or by a local authority asserting a 'child protection' role, in criminal cases when parents are charged with murdering or causing the death of one of their children. The aim of the application may be to prevent the media identifying the defendants, the argument being that this is necessary to protect the defendants' other, surviving children who are not 'concerned in proceedings' from publicity about the case. But, as explained earlier, neither section 45 or section 39 can be used to protect the welfare of any juvenile not 'concerned' in the case, and—see 16.5.1—it is against the principle of open justice to ban the identification of defendants, not least because such a ban may substantially restrict reporting of evidential detail about how and why the alleged crime occurred.

 See the case study about Eli Cox in the Additional Material for ch. 16 on www.mcnaes.com. The extended version of ch. 14, Family Courts on www.mcnaes.com has detail of cases in which such courts have been asked to use other law to ban the media from identifying an adult defendant, to protect the welfare of his/her child.

16.7.5.8 Statute created to protect juveniles cannot specifically give adults anonymity

The Court of Appeal ruled in 1991 that section 39 orders could not be used to specifically ban the publication of the identity of an adult defendant (*R v Southwark Crown Court, ex p Godwin* [1992] QB 190, [1991] 3 All ER 818), a ruling cited in 2014 by the High Court (*R (on the application of JC & RT) v Central Criminal Court* [2014 EWHC 1041 (QB)). The same reasoning will apply to orders under section 45 of the Youth Justice and Criminal Evidence Act 1999.

Lord Justice Glidewell said in *Godwin*:

> In our view, section 39 as a matter of law does not empower a court to order in terms that the names of [adult] defendants should not be published. . . . If the inevitable effect of making an order is that it is apparent that some details, including names of [adult] defendants, may not be published because publication would breach the order, that is the practical application of the order; it is not a part of the terms of the order itself.

In 2005 the Court of Appeal ruled there was no power under section 39 to prohibit identification of adults charged with sexual offences against children. But it warned of the danger of publishing material which might identify the children if the adult's name were published (*R v Teesside Crown Court, ex p Gazette Media Co Ltd* [2005] EWCA Crim 1983).

see 10.12, Cases of abuse within a family

16.7.5.9 Victim is too young to need anonymity

The Judicial College guidance says of section 45 and section 39 powers: 'Age alone is not sufficient to justify imposing an order as very young children cannot be harmed by publicity of which they will be unaware . . .'

Courts have accepted that a baby or a toddler who is the victim/alleged victim of a crime does not need anonymity, because by the time he/she is old enough to be affected by the case's publicity it is likely to have been forgotten.

👁 Case study

In 2013 the High Court upheld a refusal by Lowestoft magistrates' court to grant section 39 anonymity for a 3-year-old girl in a case in which her mother, Tess Gandy, aged 35, was convicted of being drunk in a public place while in charge of the child. Gandy had been cautioned previously for a similar offence. Section 39 anonymity would have prevented the media identifying Gandy, a local councillor. Her identity in the case was protected by a temporary injunction until the High Court made its decision. It ruled that the child was too young to be directly affected by publicity about her mother's conviction, and that open justice and the Article 10 rights of the media and public should prevail. The court said it was 'speculative' to argue, as Gandy's lawyer had, that the girl might be distressed because she might read a report of the case online when she was older. It noted that Archant Community Media, which argued that it should be able in the public interest to identify Gandy as the defendant, pointed out that its policy was to remove from its websites reports of convictions after they became 'spent', if removal was requested (*R (on the application of A) v Lowestoft Magistrates' Court, with the Crown Prosecution Service and Archant Community Media Ltd as interested parties* [2013] EWHC 659 (Admin)).

see 24.1,
Rehabilitation periods, explains when a conviction becomes 'spent'

16.7.5.10 Which proceedings are covered by an order?

In 1993 Lord Justice Lloyd in the Court of Appeal said the word 'proceedings' in section 39 must mean proceedings in the court making the order and not any proceedings anywhere (*R v Lee* [1993] 2 All ER 170, [1993] 1 WLR 103). So, it can be construed that a section 45 order made in a magistrates' court does not apply to reports of the case when it reaches Crown court—but that the Crown court can make a new section 45 order.

16.7.5.11 An order must be clear about whom it protects

The child or children covered by an anonymity order should be clearly identified in it, so the media can be clear about who it covers (*R v Central Criminal Court, ex p Godwin and Crook*, cited earlier, which concerned a section 39 order).

16.8 Challenges to youth court anonymity

see 10.5.1,
When section 49 anonymity ceases to apply

As 10.4 explains, section 49 of the Children and Young Persons Act 1933 gives all juveniles 'concerned' in youth court proceedings, or in appeals from youth courts, automatic anonymity in media reports of or referring to such cases.

A youth court which convicts a juvenile can, by using section 49(4A), lift the anonymity if satisfied that it is 'in the public interest' to do so.

In 1998 the Home Office and Lord Chancellor's Department issued a joint Circular, *Opening up Youth Court Proceedings*, which said that lifting the anonymity would be particularly appropriate in respect of a juvenile defendant:

- whose offending was persistent or serious; or
- whose offending had had an impact on a number of people; or
- in circumstances when alerting people to his/her behaviour would help prevent further offending.

It said occasions when it would not be in the best interests of justice to lift section 49 anonymity included:

- when publicity might put the offender or his/her family at risk of harassment or harm;
- when the offender was particularly young or vulnerable;
- when the offender was contrite and ready to accept responsibility for his/her actions;
- when public identification of the offender would reveal the identity of a vulnerable victim and lead to unwelcome publicity for that victim.

Case study

In 2001 the High Court upheld a youth court's decision, in the public interest, to lift the section 49 anonymity to allow the media to report the name of a 15-year-old offender who had admitted taking a car without the owner's consent. The reason given was that he 'constituted a serious danger to the public'. He had previous, similar convictions for 'joy-riding', and the media had been told he had been arrested 130 times. But the youth court did not allow the media to report his address, publish a photo of him or identify his school. The High Court said that it would be wholly wrong for any court to dispense with a juvenile's anonymity to 'name and shame' as an additional punishment, but that the youth court no doubt had in mind that members of the public, if they knew the 15-year-old's name, would enjoy a measure of protection because they would be on their guard if they met him and knew who he was, and would be slow to grant him any favours of which he could take advantage (*McKerry v Teesdale and Wear Valley Justices* (2000) 164 JP 355, [2000] Crim LR 594).

The guidance issued in 2011 by the CPS on circumstances in which there is a strong public interest in favour of lifting anonymity also applies to the lifting of section 49 anonymity for a convicted juvenile—see 16.7.2, Crown Prosecution Service guidance on anonymity for juveniles.

> See also 16.7.3, International treaties do not trump case law, which may be relevant to challenges to youth court anonymity. For arguments for identifying juveniles prosecuted for breach of criminal behaviour orders, see the Additional Material for ch. 16 on www.mcnaes.com.

16.9 Lifetime anonymity for witnesses and juvenile victims

Section 46 of the Youth Justice and Criminal Evidence Act 1999 gives criminal courts the power to stop the media identifying an adult witness in reports of or references to that case during his/her lifetime. Applications for a witness to have this anonymity are most likely to be made by the prosecution, but can be made by the defence.

16.9.1 Necessary conditions

Section 46 says that before a court makes such an order, these conditions must be met (summarised here):

- The court must be satisfied that
  - the quality of the witness's evidence, or level of cooperation in connection with preparations for the case, is likely to be diminished by reason of his/her fear or distress in connection with being identified as a witness by members of the public, and
  - that giving the witness anonymity in reports of or referring to the case is likely to improve the quality of his/her evidence or the level of his/her cooperation.
- The court must consider whether it is in the interests of justice to make the order, as well as the public interest in avoiding imposing a substantial and unreasonable restriction on reporting of the case.

the Act applies what section 52 says about 'public interest' to sections 45, 45A and 46—see 16.7.1.1

A court's failure to follow this process means the order can be challenged as invalid. See too 12.9, which explains what else the court must consider before making the order; that the effect of the order may be very restrictive on reporting of the case's evidential detail, because of the need to avoid publication of any detail identifying the witness; and that the witness can agree to waive the anonymity by giving written consent, to a publisher, to being identified.

Section 46 says that a court can revoke—or relax the scope of—an order if satisfied that its effect is to impose 'a substantial and unreasonable restriction' on the reporting of the case *and* that it is in the public interest to revoke or relax it. What is said earlier in this chapter about grounds of challenge to the imposition or continuation of a section 45 order may be relevant to challenges to a section 46 order, including what is said about the interpretation of 'substantial', 'unreasonable' and 'public interest'.

✳ Remember

A section 46 order cannot validly be made specifically to give a defendant anonymity. But the effect of the order may be to prevent reports of the case identifying the defendant—for example, if he/she was in a relationship with the witness—and/or meaningfully conveying to the public the circumstances of the crime. See also—16.1, Why a challenge may be needed, and 16.5.1, Open justice requires that reports should identify the defendant.

A journalist wishing to challenge the imposition or continuation of a section 46 order should follow the rule 6.5(3) procedure in the Criminal Procedure Rules, explained in this chapter at 16.2.1, and—as relevant for the particular case—can make the following arguments.

16.9.1.1 Is there 'fear' or 'distress' and would the quality of evidence really be diminished?

Home Office Explanatory Notes to the 1999 Act state: 'Neither "fear" nor "distress" is seen as covering a disinclination to give evidence on account of simple embarrassment.' Under Criminal Procedure Rule 6.4, the party asking the court for the anonymity must explain why it is needed.

16.9.1.2 Does the section 46 order serve much purpose?

If a prosecution witness's identity is known to the defendant—almost always the case—the defendant will tell associates who he/she is. In such cases, the only purpose of section 46 anonymity would be to shield the adult witness's identity from the rest of the population. A journalist can ask the court why a witness's identity has to be shielded if the defendant already knows it and can tell others.

16.9.1.3 Is the person due to give evidence?

There have been occasions when judges have made section 46 orders although it was already clear at that point that the people whose identities were protected would not be giving evidence because the defendants had pleaded guilty—so there would not be any trials. Such orders can be challenged because section 46 was created to safeguard the quality of evidence and level of cooperation provided by a witness in a trial. But if the order is made before the defendant pleaded guilty, it cannot be challenged merely on the ground that the guilty plea means there is no longer a need for it—section 46 says the order cannot be revoked or relaxed 'by reason only of the fact that the proceedings have been determined in any way or have been abandoned'.

 See the Additional Material for ch. 16 on www.mcnaes.com for cases studies on successful challenges by the media to prosecutions requests for section 46 anonymity.

16.9.2 Section 45A anonymity for juvenile witnesses and juvenile victims

The Criminal Justice and Courts Act 2015 inserted a new section—section 45A—into the 1999 Act to give criminal courts a discretionary power to provide a juvenile witness or juvenile victim/alleged victim—that is, a person aged under 18—with the lifetime anonymity a section 46 order can give to adult witnesses.

A section 45A order made unnecessarily or invalidly can be challenged on the same grounds as a section 46 order, see earlier, although the fact that juvenile witnesses may be more vulnerable than adult witnesses are to the effects of publicity should make the media cautious in instigating such challenges.

The conditions which have to be met by the court for a section 45A order to be valid are the same as for a section 46 order to be valid. And under Criminal

Procedure Rule 6.4 the party asking the court for the section 45A anonymity must explain why it is needed. So a court's failure to go through the right process—for example, it has not considered if the witness is in 'fear' about being identified, or has not considered the public interest in avoiding a 'substantial' reporting restriction—is a ground for challenging the order. A court can revoke or relax a section 45A order in the same circumstances as for a section 46 order.

A person whose identity is protected by a section 45A order can, after he/she reaches the age of 18, waive the lifetime anonymity by giving written consent. For more detail, see 10.8, Lifetime anonymity for a juvenile witness/alleged victim.

16.10 Sexual offence law does not give anonymity to defendants

((•))
see 16.3 and
Useful Web-
sites at the
end of this
chapter for
the College
guidance

As ch. 11 explains, the Sexual Offences (Amendment) Act 1992 automatically bans the media from identifying victims and alleged victims of sexual offences. Occasionally magistrates and judges assert that the Act allows them to ban the media from identifying a defendant, insisting that anonymity for a defendant is necessary as an extra precaution to prevent media reports including detail likely to identify a victim/alleged victim. But there is no such power in the Act. The Judicial College guidance states this. The point was also made by the Court of Appeal in *R (on the application of Press Association) v Cambridge Crown Court* [2012] EWCA Crim 2434 and in *R v Jemma Beale* [2017] EWCA Crim 1012. See too 11.4.

16.11 Postponement of reports of derogatory mitigation

→ glossary

Section 58 of the Criminal Procedure and Investigations Act 1996 allows courts to ban, for 12 months, publication of an assertion which is derogatory of a person's character and which is made during a speech in **mitigation**. But such an order cannot validly be made if the assertion was aired during the trial or at any other stage of the proceedings before the mitigation speech.

> ⦿ See the Additional Material for ch. 12 on www.mcnaes.com for more details of this restriction and grounds of challenge if it is made invalidly.

➡ Recap of major points

- Challenges to reporting restrictions can be made by a reporter addressing the court or by an editor writing to it. If this fails, the challenge can be taken to a higher court.

- An order under section 11 of the Contempt of Court Act 1981 should only be made if the relevant name or matter has already been deliberately withheld by the court from its public proceedings.

- A court order bestowing anonymity on safety grounds is only justified if the risk which publicity would create for that person is 'real and immediate', verified by evidence.

- An order under section 4(2) of the Contempt of Court Act to postpone media reporting of a case should only be made to avoid a substantial risk of prejudice to a pending or imminent hearing.

- A section 45 or section 39 anonymity order cannot be made in respect of an adult or a dead juvenile. It can be argued that a baby or toddler is too young to need it.

- Journalists arguing for a youth court, magistrates' court or Crown court to permit reports of a case to identify a juvenile defendant can cite Home Office and CPS guidance on this.

- An anonymity order under sections 45A or 46 of the Youth Justice and Criminal Evidence Act 1999 should only be made if the witness is eligible and if the order is needed to achieve the relevant section's purpose.

((•)) Useful Websites

www.justice.gov.uk/courts/procedure-rules/criminal/rulesmenu-2015
Criminal Procedure Rules and Practice Directions

www.judiciary.gov.uk/publications/reporting-restrictions-in-the-criminal-courts-2/
Judicial College guidance, *Reporting Restrictions in the Criminal Courts*, 4th edition, as revised in May 2016 by the Judicial College, Media Lawyers Association, News Media Association and Society of Editors.

www.cps.gov.uk/legal/p_to_r/prosecuting_advocates_instructions/
Crown Prosecution Service (CPS) general guidance to prosecutors on reporting restrictions

www.cps.gov.uk/legal/p_to_r/reporting_restrictions/
Crown Prosecution Service (CPS) guidance to prosecutors 'Reporting Restrictions—Children and Young People as Victims, Witnesses and Defendants'

www.gov.uk/government/uploads/system/uploads/attachment_data/file/576226/Guidance_on_part_2_of_the_sexual_offences_act_2003_2.pdf
Home Office guidance on sexual harm prevention and sexual risk orders November 2016

www.gov.uk/government/uploads/system/uploads/attachment_data/file/610015/110417_-_statutory_guidance_part_2_-_GLAA_updates-_Final.pdf
Home Office guidance on slavery and trafficking prevention and risk orders April 2017

www.cps.gov.uk/legal/p_to_r/reporting_restrictions/
CPS guidance to prosecutors on reporting restrictions concerning juveniles

www.holdthefrontpage.co.uk/2011/news/under-18s-involved-in-riots-could-be-named/
Report of CPS 2011 guidance to courts on lifting anonymity for juvenile offenders

17

Coroners' courts

Chapter summary

Coroners investigate certain types of death to establish the cause. The inquests they hold are court hearings, often newsworthy. This chapter outlines coroners' duties and explains why some inquests have juries. The Contempt of Court Act 1981 affects what can be reported, and coroners can impose reporting restrictions to give witnesses and children anonymity. Media coverage of inquests must be sensitive to the grief of the bereaved. In another role, coroners' courts decide whether a found object should be classed as historical 'treasure'.

17.1 Overview of the coroner system

A coroner—the office dates from the twelfth century—is appointed to serve a district. Coroners must have practised as a barrister or solicitor for five years (in 2013 the Government agreed that suitably qualified legal executives could also become coroners). There remain some who are not lawyers but practised as doctors. The Coroners and Justice Act 2009 says new coroners must be legally qualified. Coroners investigate the causes and circumstances of certain types of death, in some cases having hearings in their courts to do so. The other role of the coroner system is to decide whether found historical objects should be classed as 'treasure'. Both types of hearing are called 'inquests'.

Coroners' districts are known as 'areas'. The former offices of coroner, deputy coroner and assistant deputy coroner are now, respectively, senior coroner, area coroner and assistant coroner.

17.2 Chief Coroner

The 2009 Act created the national post of Chief Coroner, currently held by Mark Lucraft QC, whose duties include providing leadership for coroners, setting national standards for their work, approving coroner appointments (which are made by local authorities) and reporting annually to the Lord Chancellor on how the coroner system is performing.

17.3 Investigations into deaths

Under the 2009 Act a coroner must investigate certain categories of death: those for which he/she has reason to suspect the cause is unknown; those which are 'violent or unnatural'; and those of people in custody or otherwise held in state detention, which includes people held in police stations, prisons, immigration detention centres and mental hospitals. 'Violent or unnatural' deaths include those caused by crime, accidents, suicide, neglect or lack of care, excessive alcohol, drug abuse or any other form of poisoning. Police and doctors have a duty to report such deaths to the local coroner. Anyone concerned about the circumstances of a death can report it.

A coroner has the right at **common law** to take possession of a body to make his/her inquiries.

→ glossary

17.4 Inquests into deaths

Not all investigations require an inquest. There may be no need if, for example, a post-mortem examination shows that someone died of natural causes. But holding an inquest means a coroner can require witnesses to testify. Inquests help keep communities and institutions vigilant about fatal dangers, and reassure the public that suspicious deaths are investigated. Inquest decisions on how people died are included in national statistics such as those for road accidents.

✳ Remember

An inquest is a fact-finding hearing to establish the reason for a death. It does not decide who, if anyone, might be criminally responsible—that is the role of the criminal courts in, for example, murder cases. The civil courts decide if any party must pay damages to a deceased person's family.

A coroner's jurisdiction to hold an inquest arises from the fact that the body is in his/her area. A coroner must hold an inquest if a body has been brought into his/her area from abroad and he/she has reason to suspect the death was violent or unnatural—which is why the deaths of UK service personnel overseas lead to inquests in the UK.

17.4.1 Purposes of inquests into deaths

The purposes of an inquest into a death are to:

- determine who the deceased was;
- determine how, when and where he/she came by his/her death; and

- make 'findings' on the particulars about the death which have to be registered according to statute.

Establishing a deceased's identity is usually straightforward, but may require lengthy investigation if, for example, a decomposed body is found. The particulars, which have to be communicated to the Registrar of Births, Marriages and Deaths, include the deceased's name, the date and place of death, and his/her gender, age, address and occupation.

In most inquests a coroner sits alone. But juries are called in some, to decide on facts, with the coroner presiding to rule on law and procedure.

17.4.2 Inquests which have juries

The practice of having juries in some types of inquests helps safeguard civil liberties and public health—for example, by providing outside scrutiny of police, prisons and workplace safety.

Under the 2009 Act, an inquest must be held with a jury if the senior coroner has reason to suspect that the death falls into one of these categories:

- the deceased was in custody or otherwise in state detention *and* the death was either violent or unnatural or the cause is unknown;
- the death resulted from an act or omission of a police officer or member of a police force of the armed services in the execution of his/her duty;
- the death was caused by those types of accident, poisoning or disease, such as workplace fatalities, which by law must be notified to a Government department or inspector.

An inquest into any other type of death may also be held with a jury if the senior coroner thinks there is 'sufficient reason'. An inquest jury, selected randomly from electoral rolls, comprises at least seven and not more than 11 people.

17.5 Rules and Chief Coroner's guidance

The Coroners (Inquests) Rules 2013 govern inquest procedure. They are set out in a **statutory instrument** (SI 2013/1616).

→ glossary

((•))

see Useful
Websites at
the end of
this chapter
for the Rules

A coroner investigating a death by means of an inquest may hold three types of hearing—'a pre-inquest review hearing' (rule 6), the inquest opening, and the full hearing, also known as a 'final' hearing (which may take place over more than one day and, in complex cases, last for weeks).

The 'opening' is usually an initial, brief hearing for the coroner formally to ascertain the deceased's identity. The inquest can then be adjourned—there having already been a post-mortem examination and possibly burial or cremation—and is usually resumed after some weeks or months to hear evidence gathered about the circumstances of the death.

17.5.1 Advance information about inquests

Rule 9 says that the date, time and place of the inquest hearing must be 'publicly available' before it starts. Guidance issued to coroners by the Chief Coroner says:

see Useful Websites at the end of this chapter for this guidance

- the coroner must, in advance of a 'final' inquest hearing, and where possible seven days before it, publish (preferably online) certain details including the date, time and place of the inquest, name and age of the deceased, and date and place of their death.

- where possible such advance notice should be given for pre-inquest review and 'opening' hearings, and that it is 'good practice' to use email to update the media about forthcoming cases.

 There is a case study in 17.5.4.4 on lack of advance notice.

17.5.2 Open justice at inquests

Rule 11 says that generally any pre-inquest hearing and the inquest hearings must be held in public but that:

- a coroner may direct that the public be excluded from a pre-inquest review hearing if he/she considers it would be in the interests of justice to do so;

- a coroner who does not have immediate access to a courtroom or other appropriate place in which to open the inquest may open it privately and then announce that it has been opened at the next hearing held in public;

as regards exclusion, see too 17.9, Defamation and contempt issues in media coverage

- as regards a pre-inquest review hearing or any inquest hearing, a coroner can direct that the public (a term which here would include journalists) should be excluded from all or part of it if he/she considers it would be in the interests of national security to do so.

The Chief Coroner's guidance says that any consideration of excluding the public and media from a hearing or of imposing a reporting restriction should, when possible, be addressed at a pre-inquest review hearing, with the media given notice of the issue so they can object there to exclusion or restriction if they wish to, and that if the public and media are excluded from a hearing 'brief reasons' must be given publicly.

 See 17.10, Reporting restrictions, about media challenges to them. Arguments for open justice, which can be made against exclusion from any court, are shown in 15.1.1.

17.5.3 'Live, text-based communications'

The Chief Coroner's guidance says journalists and legal commentators attending inquests are permitted to use phones and laptops for 'live, text-based communications'—that is, to tweet, text, email and post to the internet—for the sole purpose of reporting the proceedings, but that it must be done silently. The source of this permission is the Lord Chancellor's 2011 guidance. The coroner can ban such use of devices in a particular case if he or she decides this is necessary. For context, including why such a ban could be imposed, see 12.3.

 See too 17.10 for the Chief Coroner's guidance on journalists using audio-recorders.

17.5.4 The airing of evidence and access to inquest material

Unlike the criminal courts, where the process is accusatorial, adversarial and subject to strict rules on how evidence is given, an inquest is inquisitorial. The coroner can 'lead' witnesses through their evidence.

17.5.4.1 Written evidence

Rule 23 allows a coroner to take written rather than oral evidence from any witness if satisfied that the evidence is unlikely to be disputed, or that it is not possible for the witness to attend, or to do so within a reasonable time, or that there is a 'good and sufficient reason' why he/she should not attend or to believe that he/she will not attend. For example, the coroner may decide that a busy hospital doctor need not attend an inquest to testify in person.

But the rule says that the coroner must, when accepting written evidence, announce the nature of the evidence and the witness's full name at the inquest. It also says any 'interested person' is entitled to see a copy of any written evidence. Definitions of 'interested persons' are listed in section 47 of the Coroners and Justice Act 2009, and include relatives of the deceased.

Rule 23 adds that: 'A coroner may direct that all or parts only of any written evidence submitted under this rule may be read aloud at the inquest hearing.'

17.5.4.2 Inspection or copying

Coroners generally read written evidence aloud. But if it is not read out, a journalist covering an inquest—despite the fact that he or she cannot qualify as an 'interested person'—would have a strong argument to be allowed to see it, because of Article 10 rights, the open justice principle and the decision of the Court of Appeal in *R (Guardian News and Media) v City of Westminster Magistrates' Court* [2011] 1 WLR 3253, [2011] EWCA Civ 1188 which acknowledged the media's 'watchdog role'.

 This watchdog role is explained in 15.2. Article 10 rights are covered in 15.4. More detail of the *Guardian News and Media* case is in 15.13.1.

The Chief Coroner's guidance cites this case when telling coroners the presumption should be that journalists can inspect or make copies of documents referred to or shown in the inquest proceedings—for example, a statement from a witness who cannot attend; video and photographic evidence; '**skeleton arguments**' and written legal submissions. The guidance also makes clear that journalists can use their phones to photograph such documents in order to make a copy.

→ glossary

A coroner may refuse the media access to any document if the open justice principle was satisfied by it being read out in the proceedings, or if there is another, 'compelling' reason to refuse. The guidance's examples of such a reason include national security, to protect 'sensitive' personal information, to protect someone from a risk of harm arising from disclosure, or to protect a family's privacy. The latter may be a good reason for refusing to allow the media to see a suicide note—such notes are rarely read out verbatim, to spare the bereaved anguish.

The guidance says it may be a good reason to refuse access if granting it would 'place a great burden' on the court in practical arrangements. It is advisable to make requests in writing.

The rules permit a coroner to redact a document before disclosure—for example, to avoid prejudice to related criminal proceedings.

 See too 17.7, Related criminal proceedings. Prejudice is covered in ch. 19 on contempt of court.

Any concern about potential breach of copyright is not a good reason to refuse a journalist access to an inquest document. Copyright law has an exception for court reporting—see 29.10, Copying to report Parliament and the courts.

17.5.4.3 Names

The guidance also says that the first and last names of the deceased, of witnesses (unless granted anonymity) and of 'interested persons' should be given in open court and therefore to the media.

17.5.4.4 Official recordings of inquest proceedings

The 2013 Rules require coroners to keep an audio-recording of every inquest hearing, including 'pre-inquest reviews'. The Coroners (Investigation) Regulations (SI 2013/1629) allow a copy of such a recording to be provided to anyone considered by the coroner to be 'a proper person to have possession of it'. The Rules allow this too. The Chief Coroners' guidance says 'members of the media should normally be expected to be considered proper persons', and that a £5 charge can be made for the copy.

 see Useful websites at the end of this chapter for specific guidance on recordings

A media organisation has, for example, used a copy of a recording when defending itself again a complaint made to the Independent Press Standards Organisation (Ipso) that a report of an inquest was inaccurate (*Corbin v Kent Online*, 9 June 2017). As 12.2 explains about audio-recording in any court, it would be a contempt of court to broadcast or webcast the official or any unauthorised (illegal) recording, or to play it to any section of the public.

 ch. 2 explains the Ipso system

👁 **Case study:**

In 2017 Southwark Coroners' Court agreed to share with the media the recording of the opening of an inquest into the deaths of three terrorists shot dead by police, after media organisations complained they were given no advance notice of the hearing (*Press Gazette*, 27 June 2017).

17.5.4.5 'Record of inquest'

The Chief Coroner's guidance says the media should be allowed to inspect and copy the completed 'Record of Inquest'—that is, the official document recording the findings (particulars to be registered, see 17.4.1) the 'determination' and 'conclusion' of an inquest.

17.6 Inquest determinations and conclusions—formerly 'verdicts'

An inquest into a death produces a categorising decision on what caused it, reached by the coroner, or the jury if there is one. These decisions, announced at the inquests, are traditionally referred to as 'verdicts'. It has become the convention to report that a coroner's jury *returns* a verdict and that a coroner sitting without a jury *records* a verdict. The 2009 Act uses the term 'determination' to denote other decisions as to the identity of the deceased and how, when and where he/she died. It seems likely that 'verdict' will continue to be used colloquially, though 'conclusion' is now the official term for the categorising decision.

Conclusions can, as was the case with verdicts, be expressed in 'short-form', comprising single words or short phrases including 'natural causes', 'accident', 'road traffic collision', 'misadventure', 'drug-related', 'industrial disease', 'unlawful killing' or 'suicide'. An 'open' conclusion is recorded or returned when an inquest decides there is insufficient evidence for any other conclusion.

17.6.1 Narrative conclusions

→ glossary

Recent years have seen increasing use of **narrative verdicts**—brief statements expanding on the coroner's or jury's conclusion on how the deceased came to die, referring to factual context. A 'short-form' term may be included.

The use of such narrative conclusions also fulfils a requirement that a coroner should allow a jury to express a brief conclusion about disputed facts at the centre of the case, so that inquest procedure complies with Article 2 of the European Convention on Human Rights, the right to life, on the principle that a jury must be able to express conclusions in a way which can help avoid similar loss of life. Coroners also usually make concluding remarks to focus public attention on lessons to be learnt from a death and have a legal duty to produce reports for the Chief Coroner if an inquest has revealed circumstances which could continue to place lives at risk.

The European Convention on Human Rights is introduced in 1.3

17.7 Related criminal proceedings

When someone is suspected of crime in connection with a death, an inquest is usually opened, then adjourned until after any criminal proceedings have ended. The inquest may then be resumed if there is sufficient cause. For example, if someone accused of a murder is acquitted, an inquest may subsequently return a conclusion of 'unlawful killing' while not attributing blame. If a public inquiry is instigated under the Inquiries Act 2005 to consider why a person or people died—for example, in a rail crash—the Lord Chancellor can direct that any inquest should be adjourned. It will not be reopened unless there is an exceptional reason.

the law on public inquiries is outlined in ch. 18 and its Additional Material on www. mcnaes.com

17.8 Review of inquest decisions

There is no direct route of appeal against an inquest decision, but an aggrieved person with sufficient legal interest in the case—for example, a deceased's next of kin—can apply to the High Court for **judicial review**. This could result in that court making an order to quash an inquest's decisions and to order that a fresh inquest should be held.

→ glossary

17.9 Defamation and contempt issues in media coverage

An inquest is a type of court proceeding, so in defamation law the defence of absolute **privilege** will protect, from libel actions, fair, accurate and contemporaneous reports of inquests held in public. Non-contemporaneous reports are protected by qualified privilege if the requirements of that defence are met.

→ glossary

privilege is explained in 22.5 and 22.7

   Publication of material heard in any part of an inquest held in private will not be protected by privilege in libel law and—if the inquest is being conducted in private on national security grounds—could be deemed a contempt of court as a breach of section 12 of the Administration of Justice Act 1960, which is explained in 12.7.

   An inquest is covered by the Contempt of Court Act 1981 (the 1981 Act). As explained in ch. 19, it is a contempt to publish material which creates 'a substantial risk of serious prejudice or impediment' to an active case. The Court of Appeal has ruled that an inquest becomes 'active' when it is opened (*Peacock v London Weekend Television* (1986) 150 JP 71). It seems unlikely that a coroner, being an experienced professional, could be prejudiced in his/her considerations by media coverage. But the media should take care, in a case in which a jury is or could be involved, not to publish material which creates a substantial risk of serious prejudice to its deliberations. The media should also avoid publishing material which could breach the Act by affecting a witness's testimony.

   An inquest might precede a hearing in a criminal court into the same events—for example, an inquest might be opened, then adjourned, because someone is charged with murdering the deceased. The media can safely report that inquest hearing contemporaneously if it is held in public, because the report—provided it is fair, accurate and published in good faith—will be protected by section 4 of the 1981 Act unless the coroner has made an order under section 4(2) postponing reporting of the hearing.

these parts of the 1981 Act are explained in 19.10 and 19.11

17.10 Reporting restrictions

Coroners can make orders restricting media reports of inquests—for example, by using section 39 of the Children and Young Persons Act 1933 to give a juvenile witness anonymity, a power explained in 10.9.

Coroners also have **inherent jurisdiction** in common law and under Articles 2 and 3 of the European Convention on Human Rights to order that a witness should have anonymity at inquests—for example, to prevent a real and immediate risk to his/her life (*R (on the application of Officer A) v HM Coroner for Inner South London and others* [2004] EWHC Admin 1592). Article 8 rights—for example, for the protection of family life—may also be cited in favour of anonymity.

Powers coroners can use to restrict reporting include some listed in ch. 12, Court reporting—other restrictions. The Chief Coroner's guidance tells coroners that when possible the media must be given opportunity to argue against a reporting restriction—see too 17.5.2, Open justice at inquests. Ch. 16, Challenging the courts, lists grounds on which invalid or over-broad restrictions can be challenged by the media and explains the significance in this context of Convention Articles 2, 3, 8 and 10.

👁 Case study

The media successfully opposed an attempt by Greater Manchester Police force to preserve anonymity for five officers due to give evidence at an inquest in 2015 into the death of factory worker Jordon Begley, aged 23. Mr Begley, who had a history of alcohol and drug abuse, died in hospital from a cardiac arrest about two hours after police were called to his home and one of the officers shot him with a police-issue 50,000 volt Taser electric stun gun for nine seconds. Manchester coroner Nigel Meadows lifted a temporary anonymity order, agreeing with media organisations that there was no specific evidence of any 'real and immediate' risk to the officers' safety if they were identified in reports of the inquest. The policeman who fired the Taser said he feared that Begley, who began to walk towards him despite being told to stand still, had a concealed weapon. The inquest jury concluded that the restraint methods and use of the Taser 'more than materially contributed' to a 'package' of stress factors which caused Mr Begley's death (*Media Lawyer*, 3 February 2015; *BBC*, 2 June 2015; *The Guardian*, 6 July 2015).

Common law and statutory protections of witnesses and jurors apply to inquest proceedings, as does the automatic ban on photography, filming and audio-recording in courts. Ch. 12 explains these laws. The Chief Coroners' guidance says that if 'appropriate' a coroner can permit a journalist to record proceedings but only as an 'aide memoire' for reporting, and that the recording must not be used for broadcast or any other purpose.

Part 1A of Schedule 6 to the Coroners and Justice Act 2009, inserted by the Criminal Justice and Courts Act 2015, protects the confidentiality of an inquest jury's deliberations. This law is, in essence, the same as law in the Juries Act 1974, which covers other courts—see 12.4, Confidentiality of jury deliberations.

17.10.1 Media challenges to reporting restrictions or lack of access

A media challenge to reporting restrictions imposed by a coroner, or to a decision to exclude the media from an inquest, must—if the coroner refuses to reconsider—be made to the High Court as an application for judicial review—see, Judicial review by the High Court of restrictions imposed by magistrates or coroners.

17.11 Ethical considerations when covering deaths

The Editors' Code and the Broadcasting Code set out ethical standards, explained in 4.9, to minimise media intrusion into bereaved people's grief or shock.

 Chs. 2 and 3 introduce these codes and the Impress code. It too seeks to miminise intrusion.

These code provisions are particularly pertinent to coverage of inquests. Also, each code has content on coverage of suicide cases.

Clause 5 of the Editors' Code says: 'When reporting suicide, to prevent simulative acts care should be taken to avoid excessive detail of the method used, while taking into account the media's right to report legal proceedings'. The clause is covered by the Code's public interest exceptions.

Rule 2.5 of the Broadcasting Code says that methods of suicide must not be included in programmes except when justified editorially and by context. This too is to avoid people copying such methods when feeling suicidal.

 For what Ipso and Ofcom may regard as excessive detail about suicide methods, see case studies in the Additional Material for ch. 17 on www.mcnaes.com. For guidance published by Ipso in 2017 on deaths and inquests, and The Samaritans charity's guidance to the media on covering suicides see Useful Websites at the end of this chapter.

17.12 Treasure inquests

The Treasure Act 1996 empowers coroners' courts to determine whether historical objects found on or buried in the ground should be classed as 'treasure'. Those who find such objects—for example, who use metal-detectors—must declare discoveries so that museums can decide if they want the articles. If they do, a reward based on the find's value is paid to the finder and, possibly, the landowner. The Act has various definitions of treasure, including:

* a found object which is not a single coin, which contains at least 10 per cent of gold or silver and which is at least 300 years old, and any other object found with it.

 For more detail on treasure inquests, see the Additional Material for ch. 17 on www.mcnaes.com.

➡ **Recap of major points**

- The purposes of an inquest into a death are to find out who a deceased person was and how he/she died.

- A coroner can exclude the public and journalists from an inquest on the ground of national security.

- Coroners can impose reporting restrictions.

- Inquests are court hearings and so are covered by the law of contempt of court, which can affect media coverage.

- A treasure inquest decides if a found historical object should be classed as 'treasure', in which case a museum is given the opportunity to acquire it.

((•)) **Useful Websites**

www.legislation.gov.uk/uksi/2013/1616/article/34/made
Coroners (Inquests) Rules 2013

www.gov.uk/after-a-death/
Government guidance on inquests into deaths

www.judiciary.gov.uk/related-offices-and-bodies/office-chief-coroner/
Information about the Chief Coroner

www.judiciary.gov.uk/wp-content/uploads/2016/10/guidance-no-25-coroners-and-the-media.pdf
Chief Coroner's general guidance to coroners on media matters

www.judiciary.gov.uk/wp-content/uploads/2013/09/guidance-no-4-recordings.pdf
Chief Coroner's guidance to coroners about official recordings

www.coronersociety.org.uk/
The Coroners' Society of England and Wales

www.courtsni.gov.uk/en-GB/Services/Coroners/Pages/default.aspx
Coroners Service for Northern Ireland

www.ipso.co.uk/press-standards/guidance-for-journalists-and-editors/
deaths-and-inquests-guidance/
Independent Press Standards Organisation guidance on deaths and inquests

www.samaritans.org/media-centre/media-guidelines-reporting-suicide
Samaritans' media guidelines on reporting suicides

www.inquest.org.uk/
Inquest—a charity providing free advice to the bereaved on contentious deaths

www.gov.uk/treasure
Government guidance on treasure, including definitions

18

Tribunals and public inquiries

Chapter summary

Tribunals are specialist judicial bodies which decide disputes in particular areas of law. The UK has a wide range of tribunals with a huge annual caseload which can yield news and human interest stories. For example, tribunals adjudicate in asylum and immigration cases, on rents tenants can be charged, on benefit entitlements and in employment disputes, and on whether a patient in a secure mental health hospital is safe to return to the outside world. Some tribunals are termed a 'commission' or 'panel'. Some regulate professions and decide, for example, whether doctors or lawyers should be banned from practising because of misconduct. The term 'public inquiry' denotes other kinds of legal investigatory process.

18.1 Introduction

There is a wide range of tribunals. Details in their rules and in those of public inquiries, and in relevant statute are very important for journalists. These laws cover, for example, when tribunals can sit in private or ban publication of specified information relating to their proceedings, and powers an inquiry chair has to restrict reporting. To supply that detail, there is an extended version of this chapter on www.mcnaes.com.

18.2 Tribunals in the administrative justice system

Most tribunals are official bodies which make decisions determining someone's legal rights. There are more than 70 types of tribunal. The majority rule on disputes between an individual, or a private organisation, and a state agency—for example, about tax obligations, benefit entitlements or immigration status. The annual workload of tribunals in the UK's 'administrative justice' system can exceed 700,000 cases.

Tribunals listed here are among those which may be of particular interest to journalists.

Health, Education and Social Care Chamber of the First-tier Tribunal This hears, for example, appeals from people who have been banned from working for organisations concerned with children and vulnerable adults, and includes the First-tier Tribunal (Mental Health) for England, which hears appeals from patients detained under the Mental Health Act 1983 for release from secure mental hospitals. Wales has a separate Mental Health Review Tribunal.

Property Chamber (Residential Property) of the First-tier Tribunal This hears, for example, appeals against rent levels fixed by a rent officer for regulated tenancies.

The First-tier Tribunal is a generic tribunal created to merge the administration of most tribunals dealing with appeals against decisions made by state officials. First-tier Tribunal decisions may, in some instances, be appealed to, or be reviewed by, the next tier of the administrative justice system, known as the Upper Tribunal.

Special Immigration Appeals Commission (SIAC) This hears appeals against Home Office decisions to deport, or exclude, people from the UK on national security or public interest grounds and appeals against decisions to deprive people of UK citizenship.

18.3 Examples of disciplinary tribunals

The disciplinary tribunals of regulated professions are not part of the 'administrative justice' system. Examples are:

Medical Practitioners Tribunal Service This tribunal of the General Medical Council hears complaints against doctors in its fitness to practise panels. These normally sit in public, but can sit in private—for example, when considering confidential information concerning a doctor's health.

Solicitors Disciplinary Tribunal This must, in general, sit in public to hear allegations of professional misconduct against solicitors. But it can in some circumstances exclude the public from all or any part of a hearing.

 For these two tribunals, see Useful Websites at the end of this chapter. For more detail on the administrative justice system and disciplinary tribunals or panels for professions—for example, barristers, nurses and police—see the extended version of this chapter on www.mcnaes.com.

18.4 Defamation and contempt issues in reporting tribunals

A tribunal is classed as a court if it exercises 'the judicial power of the State'—a definition in section 14 of the Defamation Act 1996 and section 19 of the Contempt of Court Act 1981. Many tribunals do have this power.

18.4.1 Privilege

If a tribunal is classed as a court, then under the Defamation Act 1996 a fair and accurate media report of its proceedings held in public, if published contemporaneously, is protected by absolute **privilege**, and if non-contemporaneous, such a report is protected by qualified privilege under Part 1 of the Act's Schedule 1, with no requirement to publish 'explanation or contradiction'. These defamation defences are explained in 22.5 and 22.7.

→ glossary

In the case of any tribunal constituted by or under, or exercising functions under, statutory provision, a media report of its public proceedings will be protected by qualified privilege bestowed by paragraph 11 of Part 2 of Schedule 1 to the Defamation Act 1996 if all the requirements of that defence are met. One requirement is that, at the request of anyone defamed by the published report, a reasonable letter or statement of explanation or contradiction must be published. This type of qualified privilege also protects fair and accurate reports of the findings (but not of the proceedings) of the disciplinary committees of certain private associations—for example, in the field of sport, business and learning.

There is more detail about this 'Part 2' type of qualified privilege in 22.7.

18.4.2 Contempt of Court Act 1981

If a tribunal is classed as a court, the Contempt of Court Act 1981 applies, which means that the media should not publish material which could create 'a substantial risk of serious prejudice or impediment' to any of the tribunal's 'active' cases. Contempt law is explained generally in ch. 19. Under the Act a tribunal case is 'active' 'from the time when arrangements for the hearing are made or, if no such arrangements are previously made, from the time the hearing begins'. It remains 'active' until 'the proceedings are disposed of or discontinued or withdrawn'.

18.4.3 Other restrictions

Unauthorised use of cameras or audio-recorders at a tribunal classed as a court could be punished as common law contempt or a breach of the 1981 Act or—as regards cameras—the Criminal Justice Act 1925. If such a tribunal holds a hearing in private, it may be held to be contempt under section 12 of the Administration of Justice Act 1960 to report what was said in that hearing in a case concerning mental health, national security, the welfare or upbringing of children, or secret processes and in any other case in which the tribunal expressly prohibited publication of information. These restrictions are explained in 12.1, 12.2 and 12.7.

 See the extended version of this chapter on www.mcnaes.com for further detail of laws affecting coverage of tribunals.

18.5 Employment tribunals

Employment tribunals adjudicate on complaints against employers—for example, of unfair dismissal or of 'constructive dismissal' in which a person claims that he/she had to quit the job because of improper conduct by another/others in the workplace. They also adjudicate on complaints that employers discriminated on grounds of gender, race or age.

Employment tribunal hearings in England, Wales and Scotland are governed by rules set out in the Employment Tribunals (Constitution and Rules of Procedure) Regulations 2013. Northern Ireland has its own system of employment tribunals.

18.5.1 Rules of employment tribunals

Rules allow employment tribunals to sit in private for some reasons—for example, national security or to protect a person's privacy.

Rule 50 empowers employment tribunals to make an order 'with a view to preventing or restricting the public disclosure of any aspect of those proceedings' if the tribunal considers this necessary 'in the interests of justice' or in order to protect the rights in the European Convention on Human Rights—including privacy rights—of any person, or in the circumstances described in section 10A of the Employment Tribunals Act 1996. Rule 50 gives employment tribunals discretionary power to make temporary anonymity orders in cases involving allegations of sexual misconduct—for example, that a woman was forced to leave her job because her boss sexually harassed her—and in disability cases.

✳ Remember

The Sexual Offences (Amendment) Act 1992 means that anyone in employment tribunal proceedings who states that he/she is, or who is alleged to be, a victim of a sexual offence—for example, rape or sexual assault—must not be identified in media reports of the case in his/her lifetime, unless he/she has given valid written consent for this. This law is explained in ch. 11.

The extended version of this chapter on www.mcnaes.com gives more detail of employment tribunal rules, including the rights they give journalists to challenge restrictions.

18.6 Public inquiries

Public inquiries can be broadly categorised either as local inquiries, set up routinely in certain circumstances, or those which are set up ad hoc to consider a matter of national concern.

A local inquiry might be held, for example, before planning schemes are approved. Public inquiries initiated ad hoc by Government Ministers have in recent years included the inquiry chaired by Sir Brian Leveson into the culture, practices and ethics of the press, which was established under the Inquiries Act 2005 (the 2005 Act).

The extended version of this chapter on www.mcnaes.com sets out the reporting restrictions which can be imposed under the Act, outlines the powers of an inquiry chair to compel production of evidence, including from a journalist, and explains how the Act gives journalists some rights to view an inquiry's documents.

for context about the Leveson inquiry see 2.1.1

18.6.1 Coverage of public inquiries—defamation law

Reports of the public proceedings of public inquiries held under the Inquiries Act 2005 have the same privilege as reports of court cases—absolute privilege if contemporaneous and qualified privilege if non-contemporaneous, if the respective requirements of these defences are met. The Defamation Act 1996 also provides qualified privilege for reports of a public inquiry's public proceedings, though such reports of inquiries of the type defined in paragraph 11 in Part 2 of the Act's Schedule 1 enjoy that privilege subject to the additional requirement to publish 'explanation or contradiction' if this is requested.

 Absolute and qualified privilege are explained in 22.5 and 22.7. The extended version of this chapter on www.mcnaes.com has more detail of the law affecting media coverage of public inquiries.

➡ Recap of major points

- Most types of tribunal adjudicate in disputes in specialist areas of law. Some are regulatory tribunals for professions—for example, doctors or lawyers.

- Employment tribunals can make permanent anonymity orders in some circumstances, but some anonymity orders are temporary.

- Media reports of the public proceedings of tribunals are protected by qualified privilege and, as regards those classed as courts, by absolute privilege when reports are contemporaneous.

- For any tribunal classed as a court, contempt law applies.

- Media reports of the public proceedings of public inquiries are, as regards defamation actions, protected by either qualified privilege or absolute privilege.

((•)) Useful Websites

www.gov.uk/government/publications?departments per cent5B per cent5D=tribunal-procedure-committee
Procedural rules for the First-tier Tribunal and the Upper Tribunal

www.mpts-uk.org/
   Medical Practitioners Tribunal Service

www.solicitorstribunal.org.uk/
   Solicitors Disciplinary Tribunal

www.justice.gov.uk/tribunals/employment
   Government guidance on employment tribunals

www.gov.uk/government/publications/employment-tribunal-procedure-rules
   Procedural rules for employment tribunals

19

Contempt of court

Chapter summary

The law of contempt protects the integrity of the administration of justice and the fundamental principle that a defendant is presumed innocent until proven guilty. Contempt law most affects journalists when they publish material which might affect a trial by making a jury more likely to find a defendant guilty—or innocent—or by influencing a witness's evidence. Publications might also 'impede' the course of justice by creating a risk that witnesses will refuse to come forward to help the prosecution or defence. Media organisations which have committed contempt by publishing prejudicial material have been fined heavily. The law of contempt applies as much to material on the internet as to other coverage.

19.1 What does contempt of court law protect?

The law of contempt protects the judicial process. Anyone who is disruptive or threatening in a courtroom can be punished immediately for contempt by being sent by the magistrates or judge to the court's cells, and in some cases subsequently to jail, as contempt is a criminal offence.

The greatest risk of the media committing contempt is by publishing material which could prejudice a fair trial by:

- giving the impression that a defendant or suspect is likely to have committed the crime, or vilifying a suspect to the extent that witnesses might refuse to come forward to help his/her defence or the prosecution case;
- seeking to discover or publishing information from the jury's confidential discussions about a verdict—see 12.4, Confidentiality of jury deliberations;
- publishing material which breaches the **common law** of contempt—for example, by 'vilifying' a person for being a witness at a trial—see later in this chapter;   → glossary

- contaminating a witness's evidence by interviewing him/her in detail or offering payment for his/her story before a trial—see later in this chapter;

- publishing material in breach of an **injunction** or other type of court order— for example, by naming a blackmail victim in reports of a trial—see 12.6, Section 11 orders—blackmail, secrets, personal safety.

✳ Remember

The Court of Appeal has ruled that the punishment for publishing material in breach of an order made under a statute other than the 1981 Act—for example, under the Youth Justice and Criminal Evidence Act 1999 explained in ch. 10—should be that specified by that statute, rather than as a contempt (*R v Tyne Tees Television* [1997] EWCA Crim 2395, The Times, 20 October 1997).

19.2 Types of contempt

There are two types of contempt—common law contempt and **strict liability** contempt. Common law contempt consists of publishing material which creates a substantial risk of serious prejudice to proceedings which are pending or imminent with the intention of creating that risk, or of behaviour or conduct which interferes with the administration of justice.

Strict liability contempt, which is governed by the Contempt of Court Act 1981, consists simply of publishing material which creates a substantial risk of serious prejudice or impediment to 'active' proceedings—the court decides whether the publication has created the risk and the writer or publisher's motives are irrelevant. In March 2011, the Attorney General, Dominic Grieve QC, expressed alarm about the media's approach to crime reporting, saying there was 'frenzied interest' in high-profile arrests which stopped only when a suspect was charged or released, and warned that arrested people might have to be given anonymity until they were charged.

📖 See 19.6, What type of material can cause a substantial risk of serious prejudice or impediment?

19.3 Contempt in common law

Common law contempt makes it an offence to publish material which creates a substantial risk of serious prejudice to legal proceedings which are imminent or pending if it can be proved that there was intent to create such a risk.

- The term 'intent' could mean either deliberate intention to create such a risk or recklessness in publishing material which the person responsible for the publication should have foreseen would create such a risk.

The Contempt of Court Act 1981 largely superseded the common law by creating the strict liability rule in respect of a case which is 'active' under the Act. Common law contempt still applies to material published before proceedings become active (and arguably may apply to material published at later stages in the proceedings). Prosecutions of the media for common law contempt are extremely rare as the prosecution must prove that the journalist or editor intended to create a serious risk of prejudice.

 Case study

In 2010 the Police Service of Northern Ireland sought a High Court injunction to stop the BBC broadcasting a documentary about the 1972 bombings in the village of Claudy in which nine people died and 30 were injured. Police argued that even though no proceedings were active, the programme—which the BBC refused to allow an officer to see before it was broadcast—was a contempt, would interfere with the administration of justice or could breach confidentiality. Mr Justice Seamus Treacy rejected the 'unprecedented' application, saying it was based on pure speculation, was not supported by any legal authority and, if allowed, would significantly extend the boundaries of the law (*Media Lawyer*, 3 November 2010).

19.3.1 Witness interviews and 'molestation'

Publishing detailed accounts of a witness's evidence while a case is active could breach the 1981 Act. But even if the intention was not to publish an interview with a witness until after the trial, a reporter who interviews a witness about a case before he/she testifies might be held guilty of common law contempt for having contaminated the witness's memory—for example, by telling him/her what other witnesses said, or by influencing what the witness remembered, or otherwise affecting his/her testimony.

It could also be a contempt by 'molestation' for a journalist to pester a witness so much for a pre-trial interview, or by photographing him/her, that he/she decides against testifying. A media organisation's offer to 'buy up' a witness who has yet to give evidence to tell his/her story after the trial could amount to common law contempt if it were held to have influenced how the witness testified.

 2.4.7, Payments to witnesses, shows how clause 15 of the Editors' Code governs this practice. There is similar provision in the Broadcasting Code—see 3.3, Ofcom—its role and sanctions.

19.3.2 Vilifying a witness

Media organisations which, after a trial has ended, publish criticism of a witness which was so abusive that a judge could rule that it was likely to deter others from being witnesses in future could be punished for common law contempt for 'vilifying' the witness.

 Ch. 12 explains that publishing information from some types of court document, photography or filming in a courtroom, or harassment of a defendant or witness by photographers or film crews, could be ruled to be a contempt in common law.

19.4 The Contempt of Court Act 1981—strict liability

A primary purpose of the Contempt of Court Act 1981 was to replace some aspects of common law contempt and to give greater certainty about what constitutes a contempt. Section 1 of the Act made contempt by publication a strict liability offence in the case of 'active' criminal or civil proceedings.

- The Act makes it a contempt to publish material which creates a substantial risk of serious prejudice or impediment to 'active' legal proceedings.

The strict liability rule means that the prosecution, when seeking to prove that a contempt was committed, does not have to prove that the editor or media organisation responsible intended to create the risk. The court simply judges the actual or potential prejudicial effect of what was published. Prosecutions for contempt are usually of the relevant publishing company.

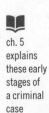

see 1.6, High offices in law, which explains the Attorney General's role

- The Act defines publication as any writing, speech, broadcast or other communication addressed to any section of the public—and includes material on websites.

Breaching the Act is punishable by an unlimited fine and/or a maximum of two years' in jail.

19.4.1 Who can prosecute for contempt of court?

Proceedings for contempt caused by a publication can be initiated only by a Crown court or higher court, or by or with the consent of the Attorney General. Crown court judges usually refer such matters to the Attorney General to decide if the case should be referred to the High Court.

Magistrates cannot punish a contempt of their courts caused by a publication. It would have to be dealt with by the High Court (although no such case concerning their courts has yet been recorded).

19.4.2 When are criminal proceedings active?

The strict liability rule applies only if proceedings are 'active'.

The Act says a criminal case becomes active when:

ch. 5 explains these early stages of a criminal case

- a person is arrested;
- an arrest warrant is issued;
- a summons is issued;
- a person is charged orally; or
- a document specifying the charge is served on the accused.

These steps all mean that there is a definite prospect of an individual facing trial.

A potential problem for the media is that the police may not make clear, after a crime is committed, if a person is under arrest or simply 'helping police with their inquiries'. Journalists must seek clarification.

19.4.3 When do criminal proceedings cease to be active?

Criminal proceedings cease to be active when any of these events occurs:

- the arrested person is released without being charged (except when released on **police bail**);
- no arrest is made within 12 months of the issue of an arrest warrant;
- the case is discontinued;
- the defendant is acquitted or sentenced; or
- the defendant is found unfit to be tried or unfit to plead, or the court orders the charge to lie on file.

→ glossary

Changes to the rules which have stopped police from keeping people on bail for weeks, months or even years have led forces to say that arrested people have been released but remain 'under investigation'. As they are not on bail and have not been charged, this means that the case ceases to be active until such time as the individual is arrested again, or a new suspect is arrested or charged.

ch. 5 explains police bail

A defendant can be ruled to be unfit to stand trial, or to plead, if he/she suffers acute physical or mental illness. An order that a charge should 'lie on file' means that the defendant has not been acquitted or convicted, but the court agrees that the charge is no longer worth pursuing. For example, if after a lengthy trial a defendant is convicted on four charges but the jury cannot agree on the fifth, the judge may order that charge to 'lie on file' because the expense of a re-trial for it would be excessive or a conviction would not lead to a longer prison sentence.

19.4.4 Period between verdict and sentence at Crown court

A Crown court case remains active, even though all the verdicts have been reached, until the defendant is sentenced. It is technically possible for a media organisation to publish material during this period which breaches the 1981 Act even though the jury's involvement has ended. But Crown court judges are regarded as too experienced to be influenced by media coverage, so it is thought unlikely that there can be any substantial risk of serious prejudice, whatever is published, after all verdicts but before an adjourned sentencing. Media organisations are therefore generally safe in publishing background features about such a case, including material which did not feature in the trial, as soon as the last verdict is given, although judges have been known to order the postponement of publication of such material until after sentencing.

19.4.5 Proceedings become active again when an appeal is lodged

The 1981 Act says that:

- when an appeal is lodged, the case becomes active again, so strict liability contempt resumes;
- the case ceases to be active when the hearing of any appeal is completed—unless in that appeal a new trial is ordered or the case is remitted to a lower court.

Lawyers often announce at the end of a criminal or civil case that their clients will appeal, but it usually takes some weeks for an appeal to be prepared and lodged, so there is a time when the case is not active between, in a criminal case, the sentence and the lodging of an appeal.

- Even if an appeal is lodged against a Crown court conviction, the media still have considerable freedom on what can be published about such a case, although it has become active again, as the appeal will be heard by the judges of the Court of Appeal.

see 9.8,
Court of
Appeal

It can safely be assumed that nothing the media publishes will create a substantial risk of serious prejudice to the way these experienced judges approach the case. But if they order a re-trial—that is, another jury trial—the media must be wary of publishing anything which creates a risk of serious prejudice to the re-trial, as witnesses and potential jurors will be considered susceptible to publicity about the case before and during the re-trial.

19.4.5.1 Where to check if an appeal has been lodged

→ glossary

Appeals to the Court of Appeal from Crown courts may be lodged at the Crown court office. Appeals on a point of law to the Queen's Bench Divisional Court (the High Court) from a Crown court appeal hearing must be lodged at the Royal Courts of Justice in London. Appeals from magistrates' court **summary trials** may be lodged at a local Crown court office.

> See 16.6.1.4, The possibility of re-trial does not mean a hearing is 'pending or imminent'.

19.4.6 Police appeals for media assistance

Sometimes, after obtaining a warrant for someone's arrest, police seek media help in tracing the suspect. The warrant makes the case active under the 1981 Act. Police may supply the suspect's photograph and/or description for publication, even though visual identification evidence may figure in the case. If the person is armed or likely to be violent, police may say so, to warn the public.

- Technically, a media organisation publishing such a photograph, description or warning about the person's character could be accused of creating a substantial risk of serious prejudice or impediment to such an active case—see explanations below.

- But the then Attorney General said in the House of Commons during the debate on the Contempt of Court Bill in 1981:

  > " The press has nothing whatever to fear from publishing in reasoned terms anything which may assist in the apprehension of a wanted man and I hope that it will continue to perform this public service. "

- There is no known case of a media organisation being held in contempt for publishing such a police appeal. But there is no defence in the 1981 Act for assisting the police in this way.

The Attorney General's comments would not apply to information supplied by police which was published or repeated after the person's arrest.

19.5 Section 3 defence of not knowing proceedings were active

Section 3 of the 1981 Act provides a defence for an alleged breach of the Act by what has been published. The defence applies if:

- the person responsible for the publication, having taken all reasonable care, did not know and had no reason to suspect when the material was published that relevant proceedings were active.

The person accused of contempt must prove that all reasonable care was taken. So, to be sure that the section 3 defence can be used, a journalist reporting a crime story must check regularly with police, especially before a deadline, about whether someone has been arrested or charged, as either event would make the case active and the story would need to be re-edited to remove any detail likely to breach the strict liability rule. For some news stories journalists might need to check with magistrates' courts whether arrest warrants or summonses have been issued.

If the police or court spokesperson says the case is not active, the journalist should keep a note of what was said, by whom and when, to show that he/she took reasonable care to establish if the case was active.

 See 19.3, Contempt of civil proceedings under the Act, for when a civil case is active. See 17.9, Defamation and contempt issues in media coverage, for when an inquest is active, and 18.4, Contempt issues in coverage of tribunals, for detail of when cases before certain types of tribunal are active.

19.6 What type of material can cause a substantial risk of serious prejudice or impediment?

The 1981 Act does not define what creates a substantial risk of serious prejudice or impediment to an active case. But cases in which editors and media organisations have been convicted of contempt show that material which could be held to be a contempt in active cases includes:

- references to a suspect or defendant's previous convictions;
- information suggesting he/she is dishonest or of bad character in other ways;
- any evidence seeming to link him/her directly to the crime of which he/she is suspected or accused;
- any other suggestion that he/she is guilty.

ch. 7 explains when 'bad character' evidence is admissible

If the person is tried, the magistrates or jury will probably not be told of his/her previous convictions, while character evidence may be admissible only in certain circumstances.

As this chapter explains, it could also be strict liability contempt in an active case to publish:

- a witness's detailed account of a relevant event after a case becomes active;
- a photograph or footage or physical description of a suspect when visual identification of the alleged perpetrator is or is likely to be an evidential issue because:
  - a police identity parade is to be held; and/or
  - a witness is expected to testify at the trial on such identification.

✳ Remember

Contempt law is enforced more strictly in Scotland. This means particular care must be taken in cross-border publication, including on the internet. See the chapter on Scotland on www.mcnaes.com.

19.6.1 References to a defendant's previous convictions

Coverage in *The Times* of a knife attack in which one woman died and another was injured which reported the attacker's previous conviction for the manslaughter of her own mother did not amount to a breach of the Act, the High Court ruled in February 2013. But it was 'deeply regrettable' that the newspaper had detailed Nicola Edgington's previous conviction, said Sir John Thomas, the then President of the Queen's Bench Division, sitting with Mr Justice Eady. The court stressed that those who reported crime should recognise that they published articles making assumptions about the extent of the issues likely to be disputed in forthcoming criminal trials at their peril. Sir John added: 'If there is created a substantial risk of serious prejudice, the danger is that those most immediately concerned in the case, not only any accused person but also the victims and their families, may unnecessarily be deprived of access to justice. That should be a danger no editor wants to create.' The court said it had 'narrowly reached the conclusion' that Attorney General Dominic Grieve QC had failed to prove that *The Times* breached the Act with its coverage of the incident in Bexleyheath in which Nicola Edgington attacked and injured Kerry Clark before stabbing and killing grandmother Sally Hodkin nearby. Edgington was convicted on 7 February 2013 of having murdered Mrs Hodkin and attempting to murder Ms Clark on Monday 10 October 2011 (*Attorney General v Times Newspapers Ltd* [2012] EWHC 3195 (Admin)).

19.6.2 Information suggesting a suspect or defendant is dishonest or of bad character

The *Daily Mirror* and *The Sun* were fined £50,000 and £18,000 respectively in July 2011 over their coverage the previous December of the arrest of former teacher Chris Jefferies, the landlord of murdered landscape architect Joanna Yeates. The court heard that one *Daily Mirror* front page carried the headline 'Jo Suspect is Peeping Tom' beneath a photograph of Mr Jefferies, and another front-page headline read 'Was Killer Waiting in Jo's Flat?', with sub-headings below reading 'Police seize bedding for tests' and 'Landlord held until Tuesday'. *The Sun*'s front-page headline read 'Obsessed by Death' next to a photograph of Mr Jefferies and below the words 'Jo suspect "scared kids"'. Attorney General Dominic Grieve QC said material in the articles gave an 'overall impression' that Mr Jefferies had a 'propensity' to commit the kind of offences for which he had been arrested. The Lord Chief Justice, Lord Judge, said section 2(2) of the Contempt of Court Act 1981 provided that the strict liability contempt rule applied only to a publication which created a substantial risk that the course of justice in the proceedings in question 'will be seriously impeded or prejudiced' and went on: 'Dealing with it briefly, impeding the course of justice and prejudicing the course of justice are not synonymous concepts. If they were, they would not have been identified as distinct features of the strict liability rule.' The issue of impeding the course of justice outside the trial process was 'less well trodden'. Vilification of a suspect under arrest was a potential impediment to the course of justice, he said, adding:

> At the simplest level publication of such material may deter or discourage witnesses from coming forward and providing information helpful to the suspect, which may, (depending on the circumstances) help immediately to clear him of suspicion or enable his defence to be fully developed at trial.

It was not an answer, he said, to argue that, on the evidence actually available, the combination of the judge's directions and the integrity of the jury would ensure a fair trial—the evidence at trial might be incomplete 'because its existence may never be known, or indeed may only come to light after conviction' (*Attorney-General v MGN Ltd and another* [2011] All ER (D) 06 (Aug)). Mr Jefferies was released without charge after his arrest. Another man was convicted of murdering Ms Yeates.

 Mr Jefferies won damages from newspapers for libel—see 5.10, The risk of libel in media identification of crime suspects.

👁 Case study

In 2011 the *Daily Mail* and *The Sun* were found guilty of strict liability contempt after both mistakenly published on their websites a photograph, taken from a social networking website page, showing a man who was on trial for murder posing with an automatic pistol. The case was the first time website operators in the UK had been found guilty of contempt. Lord Justice Moses said in the High Court: 'This case demonstrates the need to recognise that instant news requires instant and effective protection for the integrity of a criminal trial.' The newspapers were found to have created 'a substantial risk' of prejudicing Ryan Ward's trial. He was eventually convicted of murdering father-of-two Craig Wass by hitting him on the head with a brick when he intervened in a row to protect Ward's girlfriend. The offending photograph of Ward appeared on the two newspapers' websites alongside their reports of the first day of the trial. They were removed immediately the newspapers were alerted to the risk—the *Daily Mail* had used the picture uncut, but *The Sun* had cropped it, although part of the barrel of the gun could still be seen. No juror saw the pictures. The High Court said that although the jury was warned against researching material on the internet, a juror would not have understood the trial judge's instructions to have prohibited reading online news reports of the case (*Attorney General v Associated Newspapers Ltd and Another* [2011] All ER (D) 45 (Mar)). The court fined each paper £15,000 and ordered them to pay the Attorney General's costs of £28,117 (*Media Lawyer*, 19 July 2011).

19.6.3 Publishing a witness's detailed account

Publishing a witness's detailed account of a relevant event after a case becomes active may be deemed a contempt because of the risk that:

- the witness may, because such a detailed account has been published, feel obliged to stick to it and therefore less able honestly to retract or vary some detail after further reflection; or
- the witness's evidence may not figure in the trial at all, because it is ruled inadmissible or has been retracted—but if it has already been published, other witnesses or jurors in the case may have read or heard it and been influenced by it.

19.6.4 Visual identification evidence

Publishing a photo or footage or description could influence or confuse a witness who gives identification evidence so that the court might not be sure if the witness's evidence—for example, from an 'identity parade'—is based on what was seen during the crime or on recollection of a subsequently published photograph or footage or description.

Police investigating crimes often ask the media to publish a sketch or computer-generated image of an alleged offender's face as described by one witness—for example, the alleged victim—or to issue a physical description in an attempt to get members of the public to give information about who the alleged offender might be, or whether they too witnessed such a person being at or near the crime scene.

The need to avoid breaching 1981 Act—that is, to avoid creating a substantial risk of serious prejudice—means that the image and description must usually not be published again after the case becomes active, to protect the validity of the provision, particularly by other witnesses, of visual identification evidence in respect of the arrested or charged person, if it is necessary in the case.

👁 Case study

In 1994 *The Sun* was fined £80,000 and its editor Kelvin MacKenzie, £20,000, after it published a photograph of a man charged with murder. The picture was published before an identity parade in which he was picked out by witnesses (*The Independent*, 6 July 1994).

✳ Remember

The examples of prejudicial material in this chapter relate mainly to the contempt risk of saying or suggesting that a suspect or defendant is guilty—but the Act can be breached by publishing material suggesting or asserting a suspect's innocence.

The High Court and Crown courts can grant injunctions to prevent the media publishing material deemed capable of creating a substantial risk of serious prejudice or impediment to a criminal case, or to restrain reporters' attempts to interview witnesses before a trial—see the Additional Material for ch. 19 on www.mcnaes.com.

19.7 What can be published after a criminal case becomes active?

Contempt law does not mean that the media cannot publish anything about a crime after a case becomes active.

Non-prejudicial basic information about the crime can be published—for example, that there was a robbery, where it took place and that later someone was arrested. Media organisations should not report that 'the robber was later arrested' as this says the arrested person is guilty of the offence.

In most cases, it will not be contempt to name the arrested person, because he/she will be named at the trial. But it may be unsafe in defamation law to name an arrested person before he/she is charged. Ch. 5 explains that risk and other law which gives pre-charge anonymity to teachers accused by pupils.

In contempt law it is safe to identify the alleged victim(s) of crime before a prosecution begins. But a reporting restriction may apply to media reports of the court case, as chs. 10 and 12 explain. Victims/alleged victims of sexual offences and slavery and trafficking offences have automatic anonymity from the time the offence is alleged—see ch. 11.

19.7.1 Common ground

It is not prejudicial to publish material which will be common ground between the defence and prosecution at the trial, such as non-prejudicial background material about a defendant or victim. Also, in a murder case, there is rarely a dispute about where the body was found. In contested cases, the nature and extent of a victim's injuries will probably be common ground because much of the forensic or medical evidence will be beyond dispute—the trial issue will be how the injuries were caused or who caused them.

19.8 How the courts interpret the 1981 Act

In *A-G v MGN Ltd* [1997] 1 All ER 456 Lord Justice Schiemann set out the principles a court should follow when deciding whether published material created a substantial risk of serious prejudice in cases with a potential for jury trial. The court, he said, should consider what risk occurred at the time the material was published. The mere fact that by reason of earlier publications there was already some risk of prejudice did not in itself prevent a court finding that the later publication had created a further risk. The court should consider:

- the likelihood of the publication coming to a potential juror's attention;
- its likely impact on an ordinary reader; and
- crucially, the residual impact on a notional juror at the time of the trial.

The court will also consider whether the publication would have given rise to a seriously arguable ground of appeal if the trial had been allowed to continue and ended with a conviction.

19.8.1 Juries are told to put pre-trial publicity out of their minds

At the start of Crown court trials judges tell juries to reach verdicts only on the evidence presented to them and to put pre-trial publicity about the case, or media coverage of the trial, out of their minds. They are also warned not to research the internet for material.

Judges have made clear that juries must be trusted and more recently have firmly re-stated the view that jurors given directions by a judge are capable of looking at the evidence fairly. In *Re B* ([2006] EWCA Crim 2692, [2007] EMLR 145, [2007] HRLR 1, [2007] UKHRR 577) Sir Igor Judge, as he then was, presiding at the Court of Appeal, stressed the robustness and independence of juries in a case in which the Court lifted an order postponing reporting of a hearing at which Dhiren Barot, self-confessed terrorist, was to be sentenced.

He said, at paragraphs 31 and 32 of the judgment, that 'juries up and down the country have a passionate and profound belief in and a commitment to' the defendant's right to a fair trial and went on:

> " They know that it is integral to their responsibility. It is, when all is said and done, their birthright; it is shared by each one of them with the defendant. They guard it faithfully. The integrity of the jury is an essential feature of our trial process. Juries follow the directions which the judge will give them to focus exclusively on the evidence and to ignore anything they may have heard or read out of court. "

The judge at the trial would give the jury appropriate directions, he said, adding:

> " We cannot too strongly emphasise that the jury will follow them, not only because they will loyally abide by the directions of law which they will be given by the judge, but also because the directions themselves will appeal directly to their own instinctive and fundamental belief in the need for the trial process to be fair. "

There were, he added, at least two safeguards against the risk of prejudice—the media's responsibility to avoid inappropriate comment, which might interfere with the administration of justice, and the trial process, including the integrity of the jury.

19.8.2 The 'fade factor' and limited publication

The 'fade factor' recognises that by the time a jury is selected the public will probably have forgotten detail in reports published in the early stages of a criminal case—for example, soon after the crime, or about the time that someone is arrested or charged. Others factors a court takes into account include the area where the material was published and the likely extent to which it was read—or, if broadcast, seen or heard—in that area.

But some material may be so striking, even when published some time before a trial, as to create a substantial risk of serious prejudice or impediment to the trial. This has been said to include, especially, disclosure of a defendant's criminal record.

 see 19.6.1, References to a defendant's previous convictions

---

👁 Case study

The lapse of time was a factor in assessing the substantial risk of serious prejudice in a contempt case in 1997. The *Daily Mail* and *Manchester Evening News*, which reported how a home help was caught on video film stealing from an 82-year-old widow, were found not guilty of contempt of court by the High Court. Mr Justice Owen said his initial view was that the stories were a plain contempt of court as they carried the clearest statements that the accused was guilty at a time when proceedings against her were active. The key issue was whether the stories created a substantial risk that the criminal proceedings against her would be seriously prejudiced. But the stories were several months old by the time of the trial, and Mr Justice Owen had concluded that the contempt allegation was not made good. But Lord Justice Simon Brown warned the media against thinking that when someone was apparently caught red-handed there was no possibility of a not guilty plea at trial (*A-G v Unger* [1998] 1 Cr App R 308).

✳ Remember

The 'fade factor' alone might not be enough to avoid liability for contempt if the court holds that published material has created an impediment to the course of justice—see the Jefferies case at 19.6.2, Information suggesting a suspect or defendant is dishonest or of bad character.

19.8.3 Publishing material shortly before or during a trial

The 'fade factor' offers no protection for material published shortly before a trial, or after it has started. In 2008 ITV Central was fined £25,000 for contempt for broadcasting an item on the morning on which the trial of five men was due to start which reported that one defendant was in jail serving a sentence for murder.

◉ Case study

The *Sunday Mirror* was fined £75,000 in 2002 over articles which led to the collapse of the first trial of two Leeds United footballers on assault charges. The two-page spread—published while the jury was deliberating and had been sent home for the weekend—contained an interview in which the victim's father said his son was the victim of a racial attack, although the jury had been told that there was no evidence of a racial motive, and a story commenting on a major witness's credibility. In the contempt proceedings, **counsel** for the Attorney General estimated the cost of the aborted trial at £1,113,000 and the cost of the subsequent re-trial at £1,125,000 (*Attorney General v Mirror Group Newspapers Ltd* [2002] EWHC 907 (Admin)).

→ glossary

In November 2015 the magazine *GQ* was found to have committed strict liability contempt by publishing an article by New York-based journalist and media commentator Michael Wolff during the trial of former News International chief executive Rebekah Brooks, former *News of the World* editor Andy Coulson and others on charges of conspiracy to hack phones.

see ch. 35 on the hacking allegations

GQ's publisher Conde Nast was fined £10,000 for the contempt and ordered to pay the Attorney General's costs of nearly £50,000. Nearly 100,000 copies of the magazine were withdrawn from sale and destroyed after concerns were raised about the article (*Attorney General v The Condé Nast Publications Ltd* [2015] EWHC 3322 (Admin); *Media Lawyer*, 4 February 2016). Coulson was convicted of hacking. Ms Brooks was acquitted and later reappointed as chief executive of News UK (formerly News International).

 For more detail of the *GQ* case see the Additional Material for this chapter on www.mcnaes.com.

19.8.4 Archive material on news websites

'Fade factor' protection does not apply to material which, since it was originally published, remains accessible to the public in a media organisation's online archive. Jurors might find stories in news archives referring to a defendant's previous convictions, or accounts of the crime they are trying, which were published before the case became active. They might also find accounts published by foreign media which ignore UK contempt law.

But if a UK media organisation's attention is drawn to archived material which, in the view of the defence or prosecution, creates a substantial risk of serious prejudice or impediment to a particular active case, the safest course to avoid a contempt problem is to remove it or block public access to it until the case is no longer active.

In 2012 a woman juror who used the internet to research the defendant, despite the judge's direction forbidding it, was jailed for six months for contempt. The trial at Luton Crown court had to be halted and the defendant re-tried.

In April 2015 new provisions inserted into the Juries Act 1974 by sections 69–73 of the Criminal Justice and Courts Act 2015 made it a criminal offence, punishable by up to two years in jail and/or an unlimited fine, for jurors to do any kind of research, including on the internet, into a case on which they are sitting.

19.8.5 Readers' comments

Media organisations must be wary of allowing readers to post comments online about an 'active' criminal case, as they might contain facts or allegations—for example, about the character or appearance of an arrested person or a defendant's criminal history—which could create a substantial risk of serious prejudice or impediment, because of the risk of witnesses or jurors reading them.

Best practice includes not providing any place for comments under a report of an arrest or ongoing jury trial. The media might be able to rely on the defence in 'regulation 19'—for example, if a reader posts such a comment elsewhere on the site. See 22.12, General protection in regulation 19.

19.9 Media could face huge costs if 'serious misconduct' affects a case

Under the Courts Act 2003 the Lord Chancellor made regulations in 2004 allowing a magistrates' court, a Crown court or the Court of Appeal to order a third party (which could be a media organisation) to pay costs which were incurred in a court case as a consequence of that party's 'serious misconduct'—the Costs in Criminal Cases (General) (Amendment) Regulations 2004. The 'serious misconduct' could be held to have occurred through publication of material or through a reporter's action even if there was no strict liability contempt. The measure was largely inspired by the costly abandonment of the trial in the Leeds footballers case following a *Sunday Mirror* article, referred to earlier. If 'serious misconduct' not amounting to a contempt were held to have occurred in future, the media organisation involved could become liable for huge costs.

Regulation 3F(4) says the court must allow the third party against whom such a costs order is sought to make representations and may hear evidence. An appeal against such an order made by magistrates may be made to the Crown court; an appeal against a Crown court order may be heard in the Court of Appeal. There is no appeal against such an order made in the Court of Appeal.

19.10 Court reporting—the section 4 defence

In some circumstances, a media report of a court hearing might create a substantial risk of prejudice to a later stage of the same case or to another case due to be tried.

Before the Contempt of Court Act 1981, even a fair and accurate report of proceedings in open court could be held to create such risk of prejudice and so be contempt. But section 4 of the 1981 Act gives the media a defence, saying a person cannot be found guilty of breaching the strict liability rule in respect of a report of a court hearing which is held in public which is:

- a fair and accurate report of that hearing;
- published contemporaneously; and
- in good faith.

> 📖 See 22.5.1.4, Reports must be contemporaneous, for definition of the term.

The Act does not define 'good faith', but the overall effect of section 4 is that courts are expected to make a specific order restricting the media if they do not want all or part of any hearing in public to be reported contemporaneously.

 → glossary   The section 4 defence does not protect reports of a court hearing held **in private**—see also 12.7, Ban on reporting a court's private hearing.

19.10.1 Inaccurate reporting of a current jury trial

The section 4 defence does not protect an unfair or inaccurate court report. The High Court fined the BBC £5,000 in 1992 for an inaccurate report of a continuing trial before a jury, saying it contained errors which created a substantial risk of serious prejudice since it was foreseeable that publication would delay and obstruct the course of justice (*A-G v BBC* [1992] COD 264).

19.11 **Section 4(2) orders**

In some circumstances, it might be argued that fair, accurate and contemporaneous reporting of a trial could prejudice a later stage of that case or another, linked, case.

If several defendants are to be dealt with in a series of trials, reports of the first trial could arguably influence people who read or see them and are then selected as jurors for the next or subsequent trials, concerning different allegations against the same defendant(s).

The jury in the second trial, because of the principle of the presumption of innocence for defendants, might well be told nothing about the earlier trial.

But a juror in the second trial who remembers media reports of the first might be more likely to find a defendant guilty, especially one who was convicted at the first trial.

 see 5.1, Standard of proof in criminal law, which explains this principle

To avoid this danger, section 4(2) of the 1981 Act gives a court power to postpone publication of reports of a hearing or trial. In the earlier example, a judge could order that no report of the first trial should be published until the second has finished.

Section 4(2) says a court may order the postponement of the reporting of a case or part of a case:

- where this appears to be necessary for avoiding a substantial risk of prejudice to the administration of justice in those proceedings; or
- in any other proceedings, pending or imminent; and
- that the period of postponement may be as long as the court thinks necessary for this purpose.

Note that a court may make a section 4(2) order if there is a substantial risk of any prejudice, not necessarily 'serious' prejudice. Publishing material which breaches a section 4(2) order is punishable as contempt, with an unlimited fine and/or up to two years in jail.

Normally all charges against a defendant can be reported prior to any trial, even under the **automatic** reporting restrictions of other **statutes** as described in chs. 7–9. But in cases involving a defendant facing more than one trial, a Crown court judge may at a stage prior to trial—for example, at the **arraignment**—make a section 4(2) order postponing publication of the charge(s) the defendant is due to face in any subsequent trial until after the end of the first trial, to stop potential jurors in the first trial knowing that the same defendant is to face another trial.

→glossary

→glossary

 See 16.6.1, Section 4(2) orders, explains the grounds on which the media may challenge the imposition of an order.

19.11.1 **What if a section 4(2) order is not made?**

Sometimes a defendant facing a number of charges will, when arraigned, plead guilty to some but deny the others, so the jury will try him/her on the charge(s) he/she has denied. If a media organisation carries a report before the end of that trial which mentions that the defendant has admitted, or faces, other charge(s), and if the jury has not been told of other charges and/or any such guilty plea (that is, a previous conviction), the judge might feel obliged, to ensure fairness to the defendant, to stop the trial and order a re-trial before a fresh jury elsewhere. Had the judge made a section 4(2) order before the trial began, postponing reporting of the other charge(s) or guilty plea(s), the media's position would have been clear and they would have obeyed the order. But if the judge did not make such an order, the legal position would be less clear on whether reporting the other charge(s)/guilty plea(s) during the trial would be a contempt.

Some experts say the section 4 defence should protect the media in such circumstances, arguing that the defence should apply unless the court makes it clear that information aired in open court should not be contemporaneously reported by making a section 4(2) postponement order. But the section 4 defence is subject to 'good faith' in publishing, so would fail if it could be proved that the person responsible for publication intended to create prejudice to the subsequent trial. Proof of such intent could lead to the offence being regarded not as a breach of the 1981 Act but as a graver contempt at common law.

19.11.2 Proceedings in court in the absence of the jury

During trials judges often have to rule on the admissibility of evidence or other matters after hearing argument from defence and prosecution lawyers in the absence of the jury (which is kept out of the courtroom). The process of making such a ruling is still classed as a public proceeding. But the judge may tell the lawyers not to mention the matters discussed to the jury—for example, if knowledge of them could prejudice its deliberations on the verdict(s). Publishing reports of those discussions and rulings—creating a risk that the jury can quickly become aware of them—before the verdicts are given could lead to the trial being aborted. Judges may not make section 4(2) postponement orders covering such discussions or rulings in the jury's absence, because the expectation is that the media will realise that these should not be published prematurely.

19.11.3 The law is not clear

The application of the law of contempt in both the circumstances outlined earlier—that is, publication before a trial of any guilty plea(s)/other charge(s), or contemporaneous reporting of discussions held or rulings made in a jury's absence during a trial—is unclear if no section 4(2) order has been made.

But specialists suggest that journalists would have a defence by arguing that a court could have made an order under section 4(2), that it should have done so if it wanted material kept from potential jurors and that if it failed to do so, it made that decision on good and sufficient grounds.

Journalists should not, even if no section 4(2) order is made, contemporaneously report things discussed or rulings made in the absence of the jury at a Crown court trial. Even if the publication cannot be held to be contempt, there is a risk—explained earlier in this chapter—that a media organisation might be accused of 'serious misconduct' under section 93 of the Courts Act 2003 and be held liable for the costs of an aborted or delayed trial. The material can be published after all verdicts are reached unless the judge orders otherwise. But judges have been known to make clear on occasion that they have no objection to contemporaneous reporting of what happened in the jury's absence because they did not think it would be prejudicial. Arguably, a cautious approach should be taken to publication of any other charge(s) faced, or guilty plea(s) entered, by a defendant who is shortly to be tried on other matters unless it is clear that the jury will be told about them.

19.12 Section 5 defence of discussion of public affairs

Section 5 of the Contempt of Court Act 1981 says:

> " [A] publication made as, or as part of, a discussion in good faith of public affairs will not be treated as contempt of court under the strict liability rule if the risk of impediment or prejudice to particular legal proceedings is merely incidental to the discussion. "

The defence was introduced because of complaints that freedom of expression in the UK was unnecessarily restricted by a ruling in a case in 1973.

👁 Case study

The *Sunday Times* wanted to publish an article raising important issues of public interest about the way the drug thalidomide was tested and marketed—at a time when civil actions were pending against the manufacturer, Distillers Company (Biochemicals) Ltd, on behalf of children born with deformities because their mothers took the drug during pregnancy. The House of Lords ruled that the proposed article would be contempt in respect of those pending cases. The government-appointed Phillimore Committee said of the decision: 'At any given moment many thousands of legal proceedings are in progress, a number of which may well raise or reflect such issues (matters of general public interest). If, for example, a general public debate about fire precautions in hotels is in progress, the debate clearly ought not to be brought to a halt simply because a particular hotel is prosecuted for breach of the fire regulations.'

The European Court of Human Rights held in 1979 that the Lords' ruling violated the right to freedom of expression under Article 10 of the European Convention on Human Rights.

The government's response was to introduce the section 5 defence. The time of liability for contempt in civil proceedings, explained later in this chapter, was also changed.

👁 Case study

Two newspapers were prosecuted in 1981 for contempt arising from comments published during the trial of Dr Leonard Arthur, a paediatrician accused of murdering a newborn baby with Down's syndrome. It was alleged that the doctor, complying with the parents' wishes, let the infant starve. Dr Arthur was acquitted of murder. The *Sunday Express* admitted that a contempt was committed in a comment article by the editor, John Junor, which said the baby was drugged instead of being fed and died 'unloved and unwanted'. The editor was fined £1,000 and Express Newspapers, £10,000.

But the *Daily Mail* denied contempt, arguing that its article was protected by section 5. The House of Lords ruled on appeal that while the article, which trenchantly considered whether severely disabled babies should be allowed or encouraged to survive, did create a substantial risk of serious prejudice to Dr Arthur's trial, it was written in good faith and was a discussion of public affairs because it was written in support of a 'pro-life' candidate at a by-election. Lord Diplock said the article made no express mention of Dr Arthur's case and the risk of prejudice would be properly described as merely incidental (The Times, 16 and 19 December 1981; *Attorney General v English* [1983] 1 AC 116).

19.12.1 Safest course

To be sure of section 5 protection a media organisation should not, when publishing a general feature or discussion about a societal issue, refer in it to any active case in which the issue figures and in particular should not suggest that the defendant in such a case is or is not guilty.

19.13 Contempt of civil proceedings under the 1981 Act

Under the strict liability rule:

- civil proceedings are deemed to be active from the time a date for the trial or a hearing is fixed;
- a civil case ceases to be active when it is disposed of, abandoned, discontinued or withdrawn.

ch. 13 explains civil courts and which cases could involve juries

There is generally less possibility of media coverage creating a substantial risk of serious prejudice to active civil cases, as most of them are tried by a judge alone, and judges are regarded as highly unlikely to be affected by media coverage.

But there remains the possibility that witnesses in a civil case could be affected by media coverage if it delves so deeply into the circumstances of the case that witnesses' evidence given in advance of or at the trial could be coloured, or their memories be contaminated, by detail they read or see in reports.

When a jury is involved, particular care must be taken not to breach the strict liability rule, and material aired in court in the jury's absence should not be published while the jury is involved in the case.

 Case study

Mr Justice Poole, in the High Court sitting in Birmingham in 1999, reminded reporters that civil proceedings remained active until a case ended. A jury had decided in favour of a man claiming damages from West Midlands Police for malicious prosecution. Before the jury decided on the amount of damages, the *Birmingham Post* suggested he would get £30,000. The judge said the proceedings were therefore tainted. The **claimant** abandoned his case rather than go through a re-trial (*Media Lawyer*, Issue 25, January/February 2000).

→glossary

Sometimes, when a journalist seeks a comment about a civil case, a lawyer involved will insist that little can be published because it is **sub judice**—a term indicating merely that the legal action has begun. But this is not the same as the case being active: a civil case becomes active at what may be a later stage, when a date is fixed for the trial or hearing—and even then, media coverage is not prohibited, provided the strict liability rule is obeyed.

→glossary

> See 13.7.4, 'Payments into court', for an explanation of the contempt danger of reporting that such an offer has been made in a civil case.

19.14 Other contempts under the 1981 Act and other Acts

Section 9 of the 1981 Act says it is a contempt to use or take into court for use any audio-recorder (except with the court's permission), and to broadcast any such recordings.

Section 11 of the Act gives courts powers, when they allow a name or other information to be withheld from the public, to prohibit publication of that name or material in connection with the proceedings. Breach of a section 11 order would be a contempt.

It is a contempt under other statutes to seek to discover or to publish how an individual juror voted in a verdict, or what was discussed by a jury to reach a verdict. That law is explained in 12.4, Confidentiality of jury deliberations.

Section 12 of the Administration of Justice Act 1960 makes it a contempt for the media to publish an account of what was said or done at a court hearing held in private if the case falls within certain categories. The ban also covers quoting from court documents—see 12.7, Ban on reporting a court's private hearing.

 ch. 12 explains these sections in the 1981 Act

➡ Recap of major points

- For the media, the greatest danger of committing contempt of court lies in publishing material which, under the Contempt of Court Act 1981, could be ruled to have created a substantial risk of serious prejudice or impediment to an 'active' case.

- Certain types of information are more likely than others to be regarded as creating such risk—for example, details of a suspect or defendant's previous convictions.

- Journalists should know when, under the 1981 Act, a criminal or a civil case becomes active and when it ceases to be active—because the 'active period' determines what can be published.

- Juries are rarely used in civil cases, so the media have greater leeway about what can be published about active civil cases than in relation to active criminal cases.

- In prosecuting under the Act for strict liability contempt the Attorney General does not have to prove intent to cause prejudice.

- Under section 4(2) a court can order the media to postpone a report of a court case, or part of it, to avoid a substantial risk of prejudice.

- Section 5 provides a defence for a published discussion in good faith of public affairs where the risk of prejudice is merely incidental to the discussion.

- The media should not report legal discussions held or rulings made in the jury's absence during a trial until all the verdicts are reached.

- Under the Courts Act 2003, any party, including a media organisation, held to have committed 'serious misconduct' affecting a court case could be liable for huge costs.

((•)) Useful Websites

www.judiciary.gov.uk/publications/reporting-restrictions-in-the-criminal-courts-2/
Judicial College guidance, *Reporting Restrictions in the Criminal Courts*, 4th edition, as revised in May 2016 by the Judicial College, Media Lawyers Association, News Media Association and Society of Editors.

Part 3

Defamation and related law

Defamation—definitions and dangers

Chapter summary

This chapter explains defamation and why it is of such concern to journalists and publishers. It covers the risks of being sued for libel and losing, and so having to pay huge costs and damages. The chapter explains the definitions of what is defamatory. The following chapters explain who can sue for defamation, what the **claimant** must do to bring an action, the defences and reforms in the Defamation Act 2013, which came into effect in England and Wales on 1 January 2014, meaning that there are now radical differences between libel laws in England and Wales, in Scotland, and in Northern Ireland, which rejected the English reforms. Defamation is one of the greatest legal dangers for anyone who earns a living with words and images—so handling a complaint or drafting an apology about something published is not a job for an inexperienced journalist.

→ glossary

20.1 Seeking legal advice

Defamation law is complex, so this book can provide nothing more than a rough guide. While media organisations can sometimes safely go further than many journalists suppose, they also need to stop and reflect before taking what might be a dangerous course of action.

The golden rule for the journalist is that if publication seems likely to bring a threat of a defamation action, he/she should take professional advice.

But the media's role in exposing wrongdoing is extremely important. As Lord Justice Lawton (then Mr Justice Lawton) said in a case in 1965:

“ It is one of the professional tasks of newspapers to unmask the fraudulent and the scandalous. It is in the public interest to do it. It is a job which newspapers have done time and time again in their long history. ”

20.2 What is defamation?

The law protects an individual's personal and professional reputation from unjustified attack. In civil law a statement making such an attack may be found to be a tort—a civil wrong for which a court may award monetary damages.

Defamatory statements are those published or spoken which affect the reputation of a person, company or organisation. A defamatory statement in written or in any other permanent form—including on the internet—is a libel, for which damages can be awarded. But a statement may be protected by a defence.

A defamatory statement which is spoken is the tort of slander, which may also incur damages unless a defence applies. But defamatory statements spoken in a radio, television, cable or web broadcast, or in the public performance of a play, are classed as libel by the Broadcasting Act 1990 and Theatres Act 1968 respectively. Libel and slander have different requirements in terms of what a claimant must prove, as chs. 21 and 25 explain.

The Defamation Act 2013 abolished the presumption of jury trial for defamation cases, so they are heard by a judge alone unless the court orders otherwise. This means the judge now decides the key issues of what the words mean and whether they have caused serious harm.

20.2.1 Definitions of a defamatory statement

A statement about a person is defamatory if it seriously affects his/her reputation by:

- exposing him/her to hatred, ridicule or contempt, or causing him/her to be shunned or avoided;
- lowering him/her in the estimation of right-thinking members of society generally; or
- disparaging the person in his/her business, trade, office or profession.

Section 1 of the Defamation Act 2013 says that a statement is not defamatory unless it has caused, or is likely to cause, serious harm to his/her reputation, which the Court of Appeal has held means 'connoting a tendency to cause' serious harm (*Lachaux v Independent Print Ltd* [2017] EWCA Civ 1334).

A company which wishes to sue must show that the statement has caused it, or is likely to cause it, serious financial loss.

Lawyers sometimes find it difficult to decide whether a statement is defamatory, and judges sometimes disagree.

Note the phrase 'right-thinking members of society generally' in the second definition—it is not enough for a claimant to show only that the words of which he/she complains have lowered him/her in the estimation of a limited class in the community which may not conform to that standard.

✱ Remember

It is almost always defamatory to say of a person that he/she is a liar, or a cheat, or is insolvent or in financial difficulties; whether the statement is a libel will depend on whether the publisher has a defence—for example, it can be proved true.

20.2.2 Meaning of words

The test in law of what words mean is what a 'reasonable person' would think they mean. In defamation law, a statement is held to have just one meaning—and this will not necessarily be the meaning intended by the author or publisher. Sir Anthony Clarke, Master of the Rolls, detailed the principles of deciding meaning in *Jeynes v News Magazines Ltd* [2008] EWCA Civ 130, saying (at paragraph 14):

> " They may be summarised in this way: (1) The governing principle is reasonableness. (2) The hypothetical reasonable reader is not naïve but he is not unduly suspicious. He can read between the lines. He can read in an implication more readily than a lawyer and may indulge in a certain amount of loose thinking but he must be treated as being a man who is not avid for scandal and someone who does not, and should not, select one bad meaning where other non-defamatory meanings are available. (3) Over-elaborate analysis is best avoided. (4) The intention of the publisher is irrelevant. (5) The article must be read as a whole, and any 'bane and antidote' taken together. (6) The hypothetical reader is taken to be representative of those who would read the publication in question. (7) In delimiting the range of permissible defamatory meanings, the court should rule out any meaning which, 'can only emerge as the produce of some strained, or forced, or utterly unreasonable interpretation . . . ' . . . (8) It follows that 'it is not enough to say that by some person or another the words might be understood in a defamatory sense'. . . . "

see 20.2.5, Bane and antidote

The words must be read in full and in their context, because a statement which is innocuous when standing alone can acquire defamatory meaning when juxtaposed with other material. Juxtaposition is a constant danger for journalists, particularly for sub-editors and those dealing with production. Those editing footage must take care how pictures interact with each other and with any commentary—what meanings are being created?

see also 21.2.2.5, Juxtaposition

20.2.3 Inferences

Many statements may carry more than one meaning.

- An inference is a statement with a secondary meaning which can be understood by someone without special knowledge who 'reads between the lines in the light of his general knowledge and experience of worldly affairs'.

For example, an inference is created if someone says: 'I saw the editor leave the pub, and he was swaying and his speech was slurred.' The inference is that the editor was drunk, though the term 'drunk' is not used. But for some statements there may be dispute about whether a defamatory inference was created.

20.2.4 Innuendoes

- An innuendo in the law of libel is a statement which may seem to be innocuous to some people but is defamatory to people with special knowledge.

For example, saying 'I saw our editor go into that house on the corner of Sleep Street' would not in itself be defamatory, unless the communication is to someone who knows that the house is a brothel.

The libel claimant who says he/she has been defamed by an innuendo must show not only that the special facts or circumstances giving rise to the innuendo exist, but also that they are known to the people to whom the statement was published.

👁 Case study

In 1986 Lord Gowrie, a former Cabinet Minister, received 'substantial' damages over a newspaper article which created the innuendo that he took drugs. He had recently resigned as Minister for the Arts and the *Daily Star* newspaper then asked: 'What expensive habits can he not support on an income of £33,000? I'm sure Gowrie himself would snort at suggestions that he was born with a silver spoon round his neck.' His **counsel** said the reference to expensive habits, the suggestion that he could not support those habits on his ministerial salary, the use of the word 'snort' and the reference to a 'silver spoon around his neck' all bore the plain implication to all those familiar with the relevant terminology that Lord Gowrie took illegal drugs, particularly cocaine, and resigned because his salary was not enough to finance the habit.

→ glossary

A journalist would clearly be mistaken to believe that using inference or innuendo is any safer in libel law than making a direct allegation.

20.2.5 Bane and antidote

Just as a defamatory meaning may be conveyed by a particular context, it might also be removed by the context. A judge said in 1835 that if in one part of a publication something disreputable to the claimant was stated that was removed by the conclusion, 'the bane and the antidote must be taken together'.

The House of Lords applied this rule in 1995 (*Charleston v News Group Newspapers Ltd* [1995] 2 AC 65), when it dismissed a case in which Ann Charleston and Ian Smith, two actors from the television serial *Neighbours*, sued the *News of the*

World over headlines and photographs in which their faces were superimposed on models in pornographic poses.

The main headline read: 'Strewth! What's Harold up to with our Madge?' The text said: 'What would the Neighbours say ... strait-laced Harold Bishop starring in a bondage session with screen wife Madge. The famous faces from the television soap are the unwitting stars of a sordid computer game that is available to their child fans. The game superimposes stars' heads on near-naked bodies of real porn models. The stars knew nothing about it.'

The actors' counsel conceded that anyone who read the whole of the text would realise the photographs were mock-ups, but said many readers were unlikely to go beyond the photographs and headlines.

Lord Bridge said it was often a debatable question whether the antidote was effective to neutralise the bane. The answer depended not only on the nature of the libel conveyed by a headline and the language of the text which was relied on to neutralise it, but also on the manner in which all the material was set out and balanced. In this case, no reader who read beyond the first paragraph could possibly have drawn a defamatory inference.

Lord Nicholls warned that words in the text would not always 'cure' a defamatory headline: 'It all depends on the context, one element in which is the layout of the article. Those who print defamatory headlines are playing with fire.' The ordinary reader might not notice words tucked away low down in an article.

20.2.6 Changing standards

Imputations which were defamatory 100 years ago may not be defamatory today, and vice versa. In the reign of Charles II it was actionable to say falsely of a man that he was a papist and went to mass. In the next reign similar statements were held not to be defamatory.

During the First World War a UK court held that it was a libel to write falsely of a man that he was a German.

It used to be defamatory to call someone homosexual, but now no 'right-thinking member of society' would think less of someone because he/she is gay. So wrongly stating that someone is gay would not in some circumstances be defamatory—although it would be if it were to imply that he/she lied about his/her sexual orientation.

👁 Case study

Singer-songwriter Robbie Williams won 'substantial' damages from publisher Northern and Shell in 2005 after the magazines *Star* and *Hot Star* ran stories alleging that he had omitted from a forthcoming authorised biography details of an alleged sexual encounter with a man in the lavatories of a club in Manchester and that, by disclosing details of his female conquests but not mentioning this episode, he was concealing his true sexuality. But the allegations were false—the publisher apologised, and paid damages and the singer's costs (*Robert Peter Williams v Northern and Shell Plc*, statement in High Court, 6 December 2005).

20.3 Why media organisations may be reluctant to fight defamation actions

Defamation law tries to strike a balance between the individual's right to a reputation and the right to freedom of speech, and so provides defences for those who make defamatory statements about others for acceptable reasons—see subsequent chapters. But media organisations can be reluctant to fight defamation actions, for a variety of reasons.

20.3.1 Uncertainty of how a judge will interpret meaning

- The first is the uncertainty about how a judge will decide the meaning of what was published—for example, a statement which seems innocuous to one person may equally clearly be defamatory to another.

20.3.2 Difficulty of proving the truth

Even if a journalist and his/her editor are convinced of a story's truth, they may be unable to prove it in court.

the truth defence is explained in 22.2

- People needed as witnesses to an event may not wish to become involved in a libel case; witnesses' memories may prove unreliable; they may forget detail by the time the trial begins; by the time the case gets to trial they may have moved and cannot be traced.

20.3.3 Huge damages could be awarded if trial lost

ch. 2 explains press regulation

- Media organisations considering contesting a libel action also find it difficult to assess what amount of damages might be awarded should they lose. Damages could now also be inflated by aggravated damages as a result of sections 34–42 of the Crime and Courts Act 2013, which allow a court to impose 'exemplary damages' on a publisher which has not signed up to a press regulator recognised under the Royal Charter system created in October 2013.

In the past juries have awarded huge sums. In 2000 the magazine *LM* (formerly *Living Marxism*) shut down after a jury awarded a total of £375,000 damages to two television reporters and ITN over a story accusing them of having sensationalised the image of an emaciated Muslim pictured through barbed wire at a Serb-run detention camp in Bosnia (*The Guardian*, 21 March 2000).

In 2002 libel judge Mr Justice Eady said that the ceiling for the most serious defamatory allegations was currently 'reckoned to be of the order of £200,000'—the figure he awarded that year, when trying a case without a jury, to each of two nursery nurses wrongly accused of sexual abuse (*Christopher Lillie and Dawn Reed v Newcastle City Council, Richard Barker, Judith Jones, Jacqui Saradjian and Roy Wardell* [2002] EWHC 1600 (QB)). In 2012 Mr Justice Tugendhat noted that the upper limit would now, taking into account factors including inflation, be around £275,000 (*Cairns v Modi* [2012] EWCA Civ 1382).

20.3.4 Huge costs

- Damages might be high, but they are usually much lower than legal costs in the case.

In one case Mirror Group Newspapers paid £15,000 in settlement of a defamation action but was then presented with a costs bill of £382,000—which was reduced on appeal.

In June 2010 martial arts expert Matthew Fiddes, a former bodyguard to entertainer Michael Jackson, dropped at a very late stage his defamation case against Channel 4 over a documentary about members of the Jackson family. By that time, Channel 4's costs exceeded £1.5 million. Mr Fiddes was operating on a no-win, no-fee conditional fee agreement (CFA).

→glossary

Section 40 of the Crime and Courts Act 2013—which had not been brought into force at the time of writing—will allow a court to refuse to award costs to a publisher which is not signed up with recognised press regulator even when it wins a defamation, privacy or harassment case.

20.3.5 It may be better to settle

It is not surprising that, faced with these kinds of figures and risks over costs and damages, even if the case is won at a trial, ardent campaigning editors may decide either not to carry a story or, having carried it, to avoid a trial by apologising and paying damages.

As most libel cases settle out of court, with the sums involved rarely disclosed, the ongoing cost of libel actions to media organisations is often underestimated. A settlement usually involves paying some or all of the other side's costs.

20.3.5.1 'No win, no fee' legal representation

The introduction of the CFA, known as 'no win, no fee', for libel cases in 1998 had a serious chilling effect on the media, significantly restricting what the public was able to read and hear, most obviously when articles, books or programmes were changed because of legal considerations.

((•))
see Useful Websites at the end of this chapter on 'no win, no fee'

→ glossary

Legal aid was never available for libel actions, so historically the libel courts were beyond the reach of people on modest incomes. But CFAs meant litigants without the means to sue could do so, represented by lawyers who received nothing if they lost a case but could claim a 'success fee' of up to a 100 per cent increase on fees if they won. In January 2010 the European Court of Human Rights held that a 100 per cent success fee claimed by Naomi Campbell's lawyers from Mirror Group Newspapers was a breach of the publisher's right to freedom of expression.

> 📖 *Campbell* was a privacy case—see 27.1, Development of the law.

In 2011 the Coalition Government announced that it would implement reforms recommended by Lord Justice Jackson in his report on costs, and stop success fees and premiums for insurance taken out by claimants to cover a winning defendant's costs from being reclaimed from a losing defendant. But that reform has been put on hold.

The media has argued that the CFA system allows an impecunious claimant to hold it to ransom. If the claimant loses, the media defendant is unlikely to recover its costs, while if he/she wins, the media defendant has to pay not only damages but also the lawyers' 'success fees' and associated insurance premiums. There is also no incentive for a claimant on a CFA to control what his/her solicitor spends, as the defendant will pay. The pressure to settle such cases rather than go to court is considerable.

20.4 Freedom of expression

Most journalists believe that defamation law, in attempting to 'strike a balance' between protecting reputation and allowing freedom of speech, has been tilted historically in favour of claimants.

ch. 1 explains the Convention generally

But developments in recent years, particularly the Defamation Act 2013, might help tilt the balance in favour of freedom of expression.

They are as follows.

ch. 23 explains the public interest defence

(1) The Human Rights Act 1998, which took effect on 2 October 2000, requires courts to pay regard to Article 10 of the European Convention on Human Rights, concerned with freedom of expression. The European Court of Human Rights has said that Article 10 does not involve a 'choice between two conflicting principles' but 'a freedom of expression that is subject to a number of exceptions which must be narrowly construed'.

→ glossary

(2) The decision of the House of Lords in *Reynolds v Times Newspapers* [2001] 2 AC 127, greatly extended the ambit of **privilege** defences and has now taken statutory form in section 4 of the Defamation Act 2013—the defence of 'publication on a matter of public interest'.

(3) The increased willingness of the courts to strike out cases in which a claimant could not show that a substantial tort had been committed has now been given

statutory expression in section 1 of the Defamation Act 2013, which says a statement is not defamatory unless it has caused, or is likely to cause, serious harm to the claimant's reputation. But the recent decision by the Court of Appeal in *Lachaux v Independent Print Ltd* [2017] EWCA Civ 1334 has undermined optimism about the beneficial effect of the reform for the media.

ch. 22 explains defences

Other reforms aiding freedom of expression include the introduction of qualified privilege for peer-reviewed publications in scientific and academic journals, the widening of qualified privilege in relation to courts and press conferences, and the liberalising of the honest opinion defence, formerly known as 'fair comment'.

20.5 Errors and apologies

Sometimes an innocent error leads to publication of a libel. The arrival of a solicitor's letter from a potential claimant which could start the journey to the High Court is the moment to take legal advice. Libel law is not a matter for an inexperienced person, because of the dangers of aggravating a problem by mishandling it. A reporter who receives a complaint about something which has been published should refer the issue to the relevant executive or editor.

ch. 22 explains the danger of ill-considered apologies

Publishing an apology or an inadequate correction can itself, in certain circumstances, create a further libel problem.

Taking the correct legal steps, including, if necessary, publishing a prompt apology or correction, can remove the heat from a libel threat and save thousands of pounds even if the claim is settled. A prompt apology can play a significant part in a court's consideration of whether a statement caused 'serious harm' to reputation, and could prevent a claim from being viable in the first place. Also, as ch. 25 explains, failure to correct an article which is known to be wrong, especially if it remains visible online, could leave the publisher liable to pay damages for malicious falsehood.

✳ Remember

The most common cause of libel actions against media organisations is a journalist's failure to apply professional standards of accuracy and fairness. The best protection against becoming involved in an expensive action is to make every effort to get the story right.

➡ Recap of major points

- A defamatory statement made in permanent form is generally libel, and if in transient form, it is generally slander—if it cannot be defended.
- In a defamation action, the test of what the words actually mean is what a reasonable person would take them to mean.

- Words may carry an innuendo, a 'hidden' meaning clear to people with special knowledge, or create an inference, obvious to everybody.

- The financial implications of losing a defamation action in terms of damages and costs are so punitive that journalists must always consider whether what they are writing or plan to broadcast will be defensible if a defamation action results.

((•)) Useful Websites

www.lawsociety.org.uk/for-the-public/faqs/conditional-fee-agreements/
Law Society explanation of 'no win, no fee' arrangements

http://inforrm.wordpress.com/
Inforrm blog site, which publishes analysis of defamation and other law

www.legislation.gov.uk/ukpga/2013/26/contents/enacted
Defamation Act 2013

www.legislation.gov.uk/ukpga/2013/26/notes/contents
Explanatory Notes to the 2013 Act

The claimant and
what must be proved

Chapter summary

This chapter details who can sue for libel. A **claimant** must prove that the material was published to a third party—a formality in a case against the media—that it is capable of bearing the defamatory meaning complained of, that he/she has been identified in it and that his/her reputation has suffered, or is likely to suffer, serious harm. But the claimant does not have the burden of proving the material is false. A claimant can sue anyone who 'publishes' the libel, including reporters and the publication's distributors. The practical effects of some of the reforms in the Defamation Act 2013 are not yet clear.

21.1 Who might sue?

All citizens as individuals have the right to sue for libel—that is, to be a claimant.

The availability of 'no win, no fee' arrangements, described in ch. 20, has opened the libel courts to greater numbers of people. This reinforces the need for journalists to be accurate and approach stories thus:

- Is what I am writing potentially defamatory?
- If so, do I have a defence?

21.1.1 Corporations, including companies

A corporation can sue for a publication injurious to its trading reputation. But, as this chapter explains, section 1 of the Defamation Act 2013 requires a claimant to show that the publication caused or was likely to cause 'serious harm' to reputation. To meet this requirement any body that 'trades for profit' must show that the publication 'has caused or is likely to cause the body serious financial loss'. Previously the threat of being sued by a company was significant. Although companies are likely to find it difficult to prove that they have suffered or are likely to suffer

see also
21.1.4,
Disparaging
goods

serious financial loss, for a smaller company even the loss of one prospective client may help to establish such loss. The mere fact that a company's share price has fallen is insufficient (*Collins Stewart Ltd & another v The Financial Times* [2004] EWHC 2337). But individual directors and managers may be able to sue, if 'identified'—see later.

21.1.2 Local and central government

ch. 25
explains
malicious
falsehood

→ glossary

The House of Lords ruled in *Derbyshire County Council v Times Newspapers* [1993] AC 534 that institutions of local or central government cannot sue for defamation in respect of their 'governmental and administrative functions' as this would place an undesirable fetter on freedom of speech. But they can sue as institutions for libels affecting their property, and for malicious falsehood if they can show **malice**.

Individual councillors or officials *can* sue if what is published is seen as referring to them personally. Lord Keith said in the *Derbyshire County Council* case:

> A publication attacking the activities of the authority will necessarily be an
> attack on the body of councillors which represents the controlling party, or on
> the executives who carry on the day-to-day management of its affairs. If the
> individual reputation of any of these is wrongly impaired by the publication any
> of these can himself bring proceedings for defamation.

An individual can sue for defamation if what is published 'identifies' him/her, which can happen even if he/she is not named. The legal test for identification is explained later in the chapter.

As a general rule, an association, such as a club, cannot sue unless it is an incorporated body, but words disparaging an association will almost invariably reflect upon the reputations of one or more of the officials who, as individuals, can sue if 'identified'.

21.1.3 Trade unions

The House of Lords seems to have accepted in the *Derbyshire County Council* case cited earlier that trade unions can sue, even though they are not corporate bodies. A union's officers can sue.

21.1.4 Disparaging goods

Can a publication defame a person or a firm by disparaging goods? This is an important question as product testing is commonplace on websites and in newspapers, magazines and other media.

The answer is yes. But it is not enough that the statement should simply affect the person adversely in his/her business—it must also impute to him/her discreditable conduct in that business, or tend to show that he/she is ill-suited or ill-qualified to do it (*Griffiths v Benn* [1911] 927 TLR 26, CA, applied in *James Morford and others v Nic Rigby and the East Anglian Daily Times Co Ltd* [1998] EWCA Civ 263).

For example, it will be defamatory to write falsely of a businessman that he has been condemned by his trade association, or of a bricklayer that she does not know how to lay bricks properly, if either can show that his/her reputation suffered, or was likely to suffer, serious harm as a result of the publication.

Not all words criticising a person's goods are defamatory—for example, a motoring correspondent could criticise a car's performance without reflecting on the character of the manufacturer or dealer. But the statement might prompt an action for malicious falsehood—see ch. 25.

The imputations which give most problems in this context are dishonesty, carelessness and incompetence.

In 1994 a jury awarded £1.485 million damages to the manufacturer of a yacht, Walker Wingsail Systems plc, over an article in *Yachting World* which contrasted the manufacturer's striking claims for the yacht's performance with its drastically poorer performance when tested by the journalist.

21.2 What the claimant must prove

A claimant suing for libel has to prove that:

- the publication is defamatory;
- it may be reasonably understood to refer to him/her—that is, 'identification'; and
- it has been published to a third person.

This can be remembered as 'defamation, identification, publication'.

21.2.1 Defamation and 'serious harm'

Legal definitions of defamatory statements are given in ch. 20. Broadly speaking, any allegation or smear which causes, or is likely to cause, or tends to cause, serious harm to a person's reputation among honest citizens will be defamatory.

see 20.2.1, Definitions of a defamatory statement

The claimant does *not* have to prove that the statement is false. If a statement is defamatory, the court assumes it is false. If the statement is true and the journalist can prove it is true, then there is a defence, as the next chapter explains.

The claimant does not have to prove intention: it is no use the journalist saying 'I didn't mean to damage this person's reputation'. However, as explained in ch. 22, intent is relevant in the 'offer of amends' defence. As ch. 23 explains, the **public interest** defence in section 4 of the Defamation Act 2013 provides protection in some circumstances for publication of untrue statements.

→ glossary

21.2.1.2 Serious harm

To win a defamation action the claimant must show that what was published has caused or is likely to cause 'serious harm' to his or her reputation.

But in 2017 the Court of Appeal ruled that this test in section 1 of the Defamation Act 2013 has not displaced the legal principle that publication of a defamatory statement can be presumed to damage reputation. 'Serious harm' it said, has to be proved—but this can be done by a process of inference from the seriousness of the defamatory meaning in what was published. This means that a court will not always require a claimant to produce direct evidence of harm because it can decide whether a statement has caused serious harm simply by looking at the seriousness of the defamatory meaning (*Lachaux v Independent Print Ltd* [2017] EWCA Civ 1334). The ruling has been seen as undermining the strength of the extra protection the serious harm test was expected to give defendants in defamation cases.

 See the Additional Material for this chapter on www.mcnaes.com for a case study on 'serious harm'. It concerns a defamation action which led in 2017 to a judge ordering controversial columnist Katie Hopkins to pay £24,000 damages because of what she said in two tweets.

21.2.2 Identification

The claimant must prove that the published material identifies him/her.

Some journalists believe they can play safe by not naming an individual—but omitting the name may prove no defence.

- The test in defamation law of whether the published statement identified the claimant is whether it would reasonably lead people acquainted with him/her to believe that he/she was the person referred to.

A judge said in 1826: 'It is not necessary that all the world should understand the libel; it is sufficient if those who know the claimant can make out that he is the person meant' (*Bourke v Warren* (1826) 2 C&P 307). That is still the law.

During the late 1980s and 1990s the Police Federation, representing junior police officers, sued many newspapers on behalf of its members. During the 33 months to March 1996 it launched 95 libel actions, winning them all and recovering £1,567,000 in damages. Many of the officers were not named in what was published, but it was claimed that acquaintances and/or colleagues would realise who they were.

Derogatory comments about an institution can reflect upon the person who heads it—newspapers have had to pay damages to head teachers, who were not named in the paper, for reports criticising schools.

21.2.2.1 Wrong photos or wrong caption

People are identified by what they look like, so using the wrong photo could identify someone in a defamatory context, even if he/she is not named.

Using file or 'stock' photographs or film to illustrate news stories or features is fraught with libel risks. A photo of a social function, with people holding drinks, is perfectly acceptable—but if it is later used as a stock shot to illustrate the perils of drinking, those pictured, particularly any teetotallers, may sue.

Confusion about who is shown in a photograph can be costly. In 2014 Thames Valley Police paid 'substantial' damages plus costs to a man whose photograph was wrongly released with a press release about a rapist (*Media Lawyer*, 23 April 2014).

21.2.2.2 Importance of ages, addresses and occupations

It can be dangerous to make a half-hearted effort at identification, particularly in reports of court cases.

👁 Case study

In *Newstead v London Express Newspapers Ltd* [1940] 1 KB 377, the *Daily Express* reported that 'Harold Newstead, a 30-year-old Camberwell man', was jailed for nine months for bigamy. Another Harold Newstead, who worked in Camberwell, sued, claiming the report was understood to refer to him—and won. He argued that if the words were true of another person, which they were, it was the paper's duty to give a precise and detailed description of that person, but the paper had 'recklessly struck out' the offender's occupation and address.

✳ Remember

A defendant's age, address and occupation, if mentioned in court, or provided by the court, should be given with his/her name in reports of the case unless the court directs otherwise. Ch. 15 explains that courts should give reporters such details.

21.2.2.3 Blurring identity increases risk

The problem with not fully identifying the subject of a story is not only that the person may argue in a libel case that he/she was the person referred to, but that someone else might claim that the words were also taken to refer to him/her. A newspaper quoted from a district auditor's report to a local council, criticising the authority's deputy housing manager. The paper did not name him. But a new deputy manager had taken over. He sued, saying he was thought to be the offending official.

21.2.2.4 Defaming a group

If a defamatory statement refers to someone as being a member of a group and includes no other identifying detail of that person, all members of the group, if it is sufficiently small, may be able to sue for defamation, even though the publisher intended to refer to only one of them.

For example, saying 'One of the detectives at Blanktown police station is corrupt' without naming that individual will allow all the detectives there to sue because the statement 'identifies' them to their acquaintances and colleagues.

Even if the publisher has evidence that one is corrupt, the rest will win damages. But if the group referred to is large, no one in it will be able reasonably to claim to have been identified merely by a reference to the group.

Case law does not set a clear figure for when a group is too large for those in it to claim that reference to the group identifies them as individuals. In one case, reference to a group of 35 police dog-handlers in one area of London was held to be enough to identify them as individuals (*Aiken and others v Police Review Publishing Ltd*, 12 April 1995, Unreported, [1995] CA Transcript 576 - T).

👁 Case study

A case in 1986 concerned a reference published by a newspaper to an allegation that detectives at Banbury CID had raped a woman. The newspaper did not name those allegedly involved. It was successfully sued by members of the group, which comprised only 12 detectives (*Riches and others v News Group Newspapers Ltd* [1985] 2 All ER 845).

Referring to a group may also identify those with particular responsibility for it. Saying 'The supermarket in Blanktown Road is run badly' refers to a small group of managers, each of whom could sue.

21.2.2.5 Juxtaposition

Placing a photograph incorrectly, or using the wrong picture, can cause expensive problems if it wrongly suggests by juxtaposition that someone shown is a person 'identified' in the accompanying story.

In 2002 motivational therapist and part-time nightclub doorman Shabazz Nelson won 'substantial' damages from *The Sun* after it used his picture with an article in which Oasis star Liam Gallagher alleged he and his girlfriend were assaulted by door attendants—referred to as 'monkeys'—at the Met Bar in London. The piece was illustrated by a picture of Mr Nelson, who was working there that night as a doorman. Mr Nelson had not assaulted Mr Gallagher or his girlfriend, had 'conducted himself in a perfectly proper and responsible manner', and was 'understandably concerned' that *Sun* readers who saw the article 'would have understood that he was the subject of Mr Gallagher's claims', Mr Justice Eady was told at the High Court.

Lack of care in the editing and 'voice-over' of footage can also cause trouble if the commentary is 'juxtaposed' with an unconnected image.

👁 Case study

In 1983 a Metropolitan Police detective constable won £20,000 damages from Granada TV after being shown walking out of West End Central police station during a *World in Action* programme on Operation Countryman, an anti-corruption investigation into the force. As he was shown emerging from the station the voice-over said: 'Since 1969 repeated investigations show that some CID officers take bribes.' The officer was not identified by name and there was no suggestion that he was guilty of such behaviour—he was merely a figure in a background shot. But this was enough to earn him healthy damages, because it wrongly 'identified' him as corrupt.

21.2.3 Publication

The claimant must prove that the statement was published. There is no defamation if the words complained of, however offensive or untrue, are addressed, in speech or writing, only to the person to whom they refer. To substantiate defamation, they must have been communicated to at least one other person. In the case of the news media, there is no difficulty in proving this—publication is widespread.

21.2.3.1 If very few readers see online material

There is an exception to this rule about publication for claimants suing over items published on the internet.

👁 Case study

In 2005 the Court of Appeal rejected a Saudi Arabian businessman's claim for defamation by ruling that it would be an abuse of process for any claimant to bring an action over material on the internet unless 'substantial publication' in England could be shown. In that case, the complained-of material was downloaded by only five people in England—three, including the claimant's lawyers, were in his 'camp' and the other two were unknown. There was no 'real or substantial' **tort** (*Dow Jones and Co Inc. v Yousef Abdul Latif Jameel* [2005] EWCA Civ 75).

But a tweet published to 65 people can justify a substantial five-figure award of damages (*Cairns v Modi* [2013] 1 WLR 1015, CA), as can internet publication to 550 people (*Times Newspapers Ltd v Flood* [2014] EWCA Civ 1574).

The court will not assume that internet publication is necessarily substantial publication (*Amoudi v Brisard* [2006] 3 All ER 294).

A court in Canada ruled that hyperlinks to articles containing defamatory material did not, in that case, amount to substantial publication of defamatory statements by the publisher of the article containing the hyperlinks (*Crookes v Wikimedia Foundation Inc.* (2008) BCSC 1424).

21.2.3.2 Who are the 'publishers'?

A person who has been defamed may sue the reporter, sub-editor, editor, publisher and broadcaster. All have participated in publishing the defamatory statement and are regarded as 'publishers' at common law. Others, such as the printer and distributor, may be protected from an action by section 1 of the Defamation Act 1996 or section 10 of the Defamation Act 2013—see 22.11, 'Live' broadcasts and readers' online comments.

21.2.3.3 Repeating statements of others

- Every repetition of a libel is a fresh publication and creates a fresh cause of action. This is called the 'repetition rule'. It is no defence to say that you, the publisher, are not liable because you only repeated the words of others.

The person who originated the statement may be liable, but anyone who repeats the allegation—for example, by publishing material from a defamatory press release—may also be sued. A common cause of libel actions is repeating statements made by interviewees without being able to prove the truth of the words. Also, a publisher who 'lifts' (copies and publishes) material published elsewhere is liable.

In 1993 and 1994 papers paid damages to defendants in the Birmingham Six case, who were jailed for terrorism but later cleared on appeal. Former West Midlands police officers were accused of fabricating evidence in the case, but prosecution of the officers was abandoned. The *Sunday Telegraph* subsequently reported one of the three officers as referring to the Birmingham Six and saying: 'In our eyes, their guilt is beyond doubt.' *The Sun* newspaper published an article based on the *Sunday Telegraph*'s interviews. It later carried an apology and reportedly paid £1 million in damages to the six.

Journalists on local newspapers must also be alert when handling the bygone days column. A doctor received damages for statements published afresh in 1981 in the 'Looking Back' column of the *Evening Star*, Ipswich. The statements, repeated from an article published 25 years previously, went unchallenged when first published—but see 21.2.3.5, The 'single publication rule' and online archives.

21.2.3.4 Online archives and repetition

The repetition rule is particularly relevant to websites containing archive material. It dates from the 1849 case of the Duke of Brunswick, who sued a newspaper for defamation after sending his butler to buy a back copy.

 See the Additional Material for this chapter on www.mcnaes.com for details of this case.

Nowadays the Duke would call up the archive version on the internet.

As ch. 22, explains, the limitation period for a defamation action is one year from the date of publication. But the limitation period for a defamation claim over material which has been placed directly on a website will begin from the date on which it is downloaded.

Under the repetition rule, each time an article or footage or sound recording in an internet archive was accessed by someone it was deemed to amount to a new publication, potentially giving rise to a new action.

It is especially important to remove from an archive any material which has been ruled to be libellous.

In 2006 a businessman, Jim Carr, won two libel damages payouts from the *Sunday Telegraph* over one story. In April that year he won £12,000 and an apology over an article published in November 2005. The newspaper later paid him a further £5,000 in damages over the same defamatory story, which, by an oversight, it had left on its website.

21.2.3.5 The 'single publication rule' and online archives

Section 8 of the Defamation Act 2013 introduces the 'single publication rule'. This means that in England and Wales the 12-month limitation period for bringing a defamation action runs from the date of the first publication of the complained-of statement 'to the public'. So if the allegation appears in a story in the print edition of a newspaper late on the evening of 1 January and the same story is then put on the newspaper's website at mid-morning on 2 January, the limitation period for both runs from January 1, as this was the first publication. Or, if the article is only online, the first publication is the first time any member of the public accessed it. Note that, in exceptional circumstances, courts can extend the 12-month limitation period.

Also, the 2013 Act says that the 'single publication rule' will not apply if the manner of the subsequent publication by the same publisher is 'materially different' from the manner of the first, and that when a court is deciding if there is a material difference, factors it can consider include 'the level of prominence that a statement is given' and 'the extent of the subsequent publication'. The Act's Explanatory Notes, referring to what may be 'materially different', say:

> " A possible example of this could be where a story has first appeared relatively obscurely in a section of a website where several clicks need to be gone through to access it, but has subsequently been promoted to a position where it can be directly accessed from the home page of the site, thereby increasing considerably the number of hits it receives. "

Publication by a *different* publisher of the same allegation will trigger a new limitation period for that specific publication, giving anyone who claims to have been defamed by the allegation the opportunity to sue that different publisher for defamation.

➡ Recap of major points

- A claimant suing for libel must prove three things:
- (1) a statement is defamatory; (2) it may be reasonably understood to refer to him/her; and (3) it has been published to a third person.

- The test of 'identification' is whether the words would reasonably lead people who know the claimant to believe he/she is the person referred to.

- Whether publication has caused serious harm may be proven, or the court may infer it from the seriousness of the defamatory meaning it carries.

- Publication is assumed in the case of traditional media. But this is not always the case with online publication.

- Every repetition is a fresh publication. The journalist is liable for repeating a defamatory statement made by an interviewee or source. But the single publication rule was introduced in the Defamation Act 2013.

22

Defences

Chapter summary

The law provides defences for media organisations sued for defamation—without them many of the stories published and broadcast each day would be suppressed for fear of a libel action. This chapter explains the main defences and gives practical advice on what a journalist must do when preparing a story to ensure it meets their requirements.

22.1 The main defences

Journalists need to know about how defamation defences work, as the steps they take in researching and writing a story will often determine whether a defence is available to avoid a costly defamation action. Some defences are now in the Defamation Act 2013.

The main defences are:

- **truth**—section 2 of the 2013 Act, replacing the common law defence of justification; → glossary
- **honest opinion**—section 3 of the 2013 Act, replacing the common law defence of honest comment or fair comment; → glossary
- absolute privilege;
- qualified privilege;
- accord and satisfaction;
- offer of amends.

The fact that new statutory defences in the 2013 Act repeal the common law defences of justification and honest comment means that courts must follow the words of the statute when making rulings. Cases decided before the statute came into force may be a guide to the correct approach, but only after the court has considered the statutory requirements.

22.2 Truth—its requirement

The defence requires that the published material complained of can be proved in court to be substantially true. Meeting this requirement gives complete protection against a libel action (the only limited exception arises under the Rehabilitation of Offenders Act 1974—see ch. 24).

The defence applies to statements of fact. If the words complained of are an expression of opinion, they may be defended as honest opinion.

Media organisations sued for defamation often rely on both truth and honest opinion as defences, applying each as appropriate to different elements of what was published.

- The standard of proof needed for a truth defence is that used in civil cases generally—the material must be proved true 'on the balance of probabilities'.

Although this is a lower requirement than 'beyond reasonable doubt', the standard of proof in criminal cases, a media organisation relying on a truth defence must have enough evidence to persuade a judge at trial that its version of the event(s) is correct.

22.2.1 The imputation of the libel must be proved

Section 2(3) of the 2013 Act says that, in a defamation case involving publication of two or more imputations involving the **claimant**, 'the defence under this section does not fail if, having regard to the imputations which are shown to be substantially true, the imputations which are not shown to be substantially true do not seriously harm the claimant's reputation'.

This means that a defendant does not have to prove the truth of every statement in what was published. But the most damaging imputation must be proved and the reputational damage it causes must outweigh any damage caused by unproved allegations. So if a newspaper runs a story saying that a politician is cruel to his children and swears at his neighbours, the former allegation is the most damaging. But a media organisation unable to prove the minor allegations might find it harder to persuade a jury of the truth of the major allegation.

22.2.2 Examples

The *Daily Telegraph* was sued by tennis player Robert Dee after reporting that he was 'ranked as the worst professional tennis player in the world after 54 defeats in a row ...'. The newspaper pleaded justification (now truth) and fair comment (now honest opinion). Mrs Justice Sharp held that the facts in the story were sufficient to justify any defamatory meaning the words were capable of bearing (*Robert Dee v Telegraph Media Group Ltd* [2010] EWHC 924 (QB), [2010] EMLR 20).

In July 2015 comedian Freddie Starr sued a woman who said he groped her when she was 15 years old and attending a Jimmy Savile TV show *Clunk Click*. Starr lost, which left him facing a costs bill unofficially estimated at about £1 million.

Starr had told Mr Justice Nicol at the High Court that he did not at first remember appearing on the show in March 1974—41 years ago—until footage showed him in the studio, with Karin Ward in the audience behind him. He rejected her allegation that he groped her and humiliated her in Savile's dressing room by calling her a 't**less wonder'.

Starr, 72, sued over interviews given to the BBC and ITV in October 2012, and statements on a website and in an e-book—and claimed he had lost £300,000 because of shows cancelled as a result of the allegations.

Ms Ward, 56, denied the slander and libel claims, and relied on the defences of justification and **public interest**.

→glossary

Mr Justice Nicol ruled that the claim in slander based on Ms Ward's interview with the BBC failed as it was brought outside the limitation period. The claim in libel was based on the broadcast of a clip from the BBC interview in *Panorama* and Ms Ward was not liable for the composite broadcast.

The judge said Starr's slander claim over an interview Ms Ward gave to ITV failed because she had proved that it was true that Starr groped her—an under-age schoolgirl—and humiliated her by calling her a 't**less wonder' (*Media Lawyer*, 10 July 2015).

Cases in which the media plead truth can be extremely complex.

👁 Case study

In 1997 *The Guardian* newspaper and Granada TV risked paying huge libel damages and costs when they defended a case brought by former Conservative Cabinet Minister Jonathan Aitken over reports in the newspaper and the *World in Action* programme that he was involved in arms dealings with Saudi businessmen and that he allowed an Arab business associate to pay his bill at the Ritz hotel in Paris, in breach of ministerial guidelines. Aitken resigned from the Cabinet in order, he said, to pursue *The Guardian* and 'cut out the cancer of bent and twisted journalism in our country with the simple sword of truth and the trusty shield of British fair play'. At a late stage in the trial *The Guardian* discovered vital evidence of credit card payments in the records of another hotel. Aitken, who had seemed to be winning, abandoned the case, facing a £2 million costs bill. He was later jailed for perjury (*The Guardian*, 8 June 1999).

22.2.3 Levels of meaning and reporting on police investigations

When considering reports linking a claimant with criminal or wrongful conduct, the courts recognise three levels of meaning:

- the person is guilty of the criminal offence or misconduct (a level 1 meaning)—if the court decides this meaning applies, then a publisher using the truth defence will have to prove that the offence or misconduct occurred; or

- he/she is reasonably suspected of the offence or misconduct (level 2); or
- there are grounds for an investigation—for example, by police (level 3).

These are known as *Chase* level 1, 2 and 3 meanings, having been detailed by Lord Justice Brooke in *Chase v News Group Newspapers* [2002] EWCA Civ 1772, [2003] EMLR 2180.

22.2.3.1 Proving reasonable suspicion or that there were grounds for an investigation

It may be defamatory to say someone is reasonably suspected of an offence or that there are grounds for investigating his/her conduct, because it implies there was conduct on the person's part which warrants the suspicion. So a successful plea of truth must prove conduct by the individual which gives rise to the suspicion or the grounds. It is no use saying other people told you about their suspicions (*Shah v Standard Chartered Bank* [1999] QB 241).

👁 **Case study**

In *Chase v News Group Newspapers Ltd* (cited earlier) *The Sun* newspaper paid £100,000 damages to children's nurse Elaine Chase for a story headlined 'Nurse is probed over 18 deaths'. Police were investigating the deaths of a number of terminally ill children she had treated but concluded—after the newspaper's story appeared—that there were no grounds to suspect her of an offence. *The Sun* tried to show there were reasonable grounds for suspicion, but the Court of Appeal said it was relying almost entirely on the fact that a number of allegations against Ms Chase had been made to the hospital trust and police. The only respect in which the newspaper focused upon the nurse's conduct concerned an allegation made after publication, which the Court said could not be taken into consideration.

22.2.4 Avoid implying habitual conduct

The statement that someone 'is a thief' may be true—but if the basis for the statement is just one minor conviction, for example, for stealing a packet of bacon from a shop, defence of truth would almost certainly fail, as the individual would argue that the words meant he/she was a persistent thief, whereas he/she was essentially an honest person who had had a single lapse.

22.2.5 Inferences and innuendoes must be proved

see also
ch. 20 on
meanings of
words

The truth defence will involve proving not only the truth of each defamatory statement, but also any reasonable interpretation of the words and any innuendoes lying behind them.

22.2.6 Persisting with a truth defence can be financially risky

Persisting in a defence of truth has financial risks. If it fails, the court may view critically a defendant's persistence in sticking to a story which it has decided was not true, and may award greater damages—see *Cairns v Modi* [2012] EWCA Civ 1382 in which Mr Justice Bean awarded cricketer Chris Cairns £75,000 in damages over match-fixing allegations, adding a further £15,000 in aggravated damages because of the defendant's 'sustained and aggressive assertion of the plea of justification'.

 See also 20.3, Why media organisations may be reluctant to fight defamation actions.

22.2.7 The investigative journalist—practical advice on procedure

The Additional Material for ch. 22 on www.mcnaes.com gives tips for journalists beginning to do investigations, to help them be able to prove the truth.

- For example, the journalist should persuade each witness to make a signed and dated statement before the story is published. In some circumstances it may be best to persuade him/her to sign an **affidavit**.

→glossary

A media organisation's case is often weakened because a journalist has failed to keep, in good order, notes or recordings and research which prove what someone said or what was published.

22.3 Honest opinion

The defence of honest opinion protects published opinion, not any statement put forward as factual. The defence is similar to the defence formerly known as 'fair comment', then as 'honest comment'. Section 3 of the Defamation Act 2013, which created the honest opinion defence, abolished that common law defence.

22.3.1 The requirements of honest opinion

The main requirements of the honest opinion defence, all of which must be met, are:

- the published comment must be the honestly held opinion of the person making it (though it may have been published by another party);
- it must be recognisable to the reader/viewer/listener as opinion rather than as a factual allegation;
- it must be based on a provably true fact or privileged material—so media organisations relying on the honest opinion defence should be prepared to run another defence, such as truth, absolute privilege or qualified privilege in tandem;
- it must explicitly or implicitly indicate, at least in general terms, the fact or information on which it is based.

see 22.4,
Privilege

22.3.1.1 Opinion must be 'honestly held', not 'fair'

The law does not require the 'truth' of the comment to be proved—comment may be responsible or irresponsible, informed or misinformed, but cannot be true or false. Defendants pleading honest opinion do not need to persuade the court to share their views. But they do need to satisfy it that the opinion on an established fact represents a view an honest person could hold. Mr Justice Diplock said in his summing up to the jury in *Silkin v Beaverbrook Newspapers* [1958] 1 WLR 743 (QB):

> The basis of our public life is that the crank and the enthusiast can say what he honestly believes just as much as a reasonable man or woman. It would be a sad day for freedom of speech in this country if a jury were to apply the test of whether it agrees with a comment, instead of applying the true test of whether this opinion, however exaggerated, obstinate, or prejudiced, was honestly held.

The defence will fail if a claimant can show that the person expressing the opinion did not in fact hold that opinion. It will also fail if, for example, the editor of a newspaper which published the comment—for example, in a column—did so when he or she knew, or should have known, that the author did not hold the opinion being expressed.

22.3.1.2 Only recognisable comment, not facts

A judge gave an example of an opinion protected by the fair comment defence, saying that if one accurately reports what some public man had done, then says 'such conduct is disgraceful', that is merely an expression of one's opinion—a comment on the person's conduct. But if one asserts that the man is guilty of disgraceful conduct without saying what that conduct was, one is making an allegation of fact for which the only defences are justification (now truth) or privilege.

👁 Case study

Sub-editors must take special care if they introduce comment into headlines. In 2003 the *Daily Telegraph* published articles making allegations about left-wing MP George Galloway based on documents said to refer to him which a reporter found in a ruined Government building in Baghdad soon after the invasion of Iraq. One story was headlined 'Telegraph reveals damning new evidence on Labour MP'. When sued, the paper did not claim the allegations were true but said the headline was an expression of opinion. But the judge said 'damning' had a plain meaning—'that is to say, that the evidence goes beyond a prima facie case and points to guilt'. The MP won the libel case (*George Galloway MP v Telegraph Group Ltd* [2004] EWHC 2786 (QB)).

 For more detail of this case, see the Additional Material for ch. 23, The public interest defence, on www.mcnaes.com.

22.3.1.3 The basis on fact or privileged material must be indicated

The requirements of section 3 of the 2013 Act reflect the decision of the **Supreme** →glossary
Court in *Spiller and another v Joseph and others* [2010] UKSC 53 that it was incorrect to require that the comment must identify the matters on which it was based with sufficient particularity to enable the reader to judge for himself/herself whether it was well founded. Instead, it said, the requirement was that the comment 'must explicitly or implicitly indicate, at least in general terms, the facts on which it was based'. The new statutory defence provides that an honest person must be able to hold the opinion on the basis of 'any fact' which existed when the statement complained of was published.

The exception to the rule that comment must be based on a true fact is when the comment is based on privileged material, such as a report of judicial proceedings or proceedings in Parliament. A media organisation can safely make scathing comments about a defendant convicted of a crime if based on privileged reports of the trial's evidence. The honest opinion defence will succeed in relation to what was published at the time of the conviction even if the defendant is later acquitted on appeal. The honest opinion defence should also protect publication of criticism of judges, magistrates and coroners, based on privileged reports of their actions in court.

22.3.2 Imputing improper motives

Because the Defamation Act 2013 repeals the common law defence of honest comment, earlier cases cannot be taken to be a definitive guide to how the courts will interpret its replacement, the honest opinion defence. But they might provide some indication.

The suggestion that someone has acted from improper motives has in the past been hard to defend as honest comment. But the Court of Appeal took a more helpful view when entrepreneur Richard Branson sued biographer Tom Bower for libel (*Branson v Bower* [2001] EWCA Civ 791, [2001] EMLR 800). Bower wrote of Branson's attempt to run the National Lottery: 'Sceptics will inevitably whisper that Branson's motive is self-glorification.' Bower said this was fair comment (which at that time was the name of the honest comment defence) but Branson said it was a factual allegation (that he had a questionable intention in bidding for the National Lottery) and was untrue.

Lord Justice Latham, giving the Court of Appeal's judgment, said comment was 'something which is or can reasonably be inferred to be a deduction, inference, conclusion, criticism, remark, observation', and that the judge in the lower court was fully entitled to conclude that Bower was expressing a series of opinions about Branson's motives.

22.3.3 Reviews

The honest opinion defence protects the expressions of opinion contained in reviews of, among other things, performances, books, holidays and restaurants.

22.3.4 Humour, satire and irony

In 2008 Sir Elton John sued *The Guardian* for libel over a spoof article written by Marina Hyde under the headline 'A peek at the diary of ... Sir Elton John'—a regular feature in the paper's Weekend section satirising the activities of celebrities and others. Sir Elton claimed the article meant his commitment to the Elton John Aids Foundation was insincere and that, once the costs of his White Tie and Tiara fund-raising ball were met, only a small proportion of the funds raised would go to good causes. *The Guardian's* defence was that the words were clearly comment and could not have the meaning claimed by the claimant.

Mr Justice Tugendhat struck out Sir Elton's claim, accepting *The Guardian's* argument that the words were a form of teasing, and that had it actually unearthed a story about a charity ball's costs leaving nothing for good causes, it would have treated it as a serious story and written it without any attempt at humour (*Sir Elton John v Guardian News and Media Ltd* [2008] EWHC 3066 (QB)).

22.4 **Privilege**

The public interest sometimes demands that there should be complete freedom of speech without any risk of proceedings for defamation, even if the statements are defamatory and even if they turn out to be untrue. These occasions are referred to as 'privileged'. Privilege exists under **common law** and **statute**.

22.5 **Absolute privilege**

The defence of absolute privilege, where it is applicable, is a complete answer and bar to an action for defamation. It does not matter if the words are true or false, or if they were spoken or written maliciously.

But while someone may speak on an occasion which is protected by absolute privilege, it does not follow that a journalist's report of those comments will also be protected by absolute privilege. Members of Parliament may say whatever they wish in the House of Commons without fear of being sued for defamation. The reports of parliamentary proceedings published on Parliament's behalf in *Hansard*, its official record, are protected by absolute privilege, as are reports published by order of Parliament, such as White Papers. But media reports of the contents of parliamentary publications enjoy only qualified privilege, a defence which, as this chapter explains, depends on there being a proper motive in publication.

22.5.1 The requirements of absolute privilege

ch. 18 explains tribunals

The only time journalists enjoy absolute privilege is when they are reporting court cases or the proceedings of certain types of tribunal.

In this context the requirements of absolute privilege are that what was published was:

- a fair and accurate report of judicial proceedings held in public within the UK, published contemporaneously.

The Defamation Act 2013 extended this protection to reports of proceedings in any court established under the law of a country or territory outside the UK, and any international court or tribunal established by the Security Council of the United Nations or by an international agreement, such as the European Court of Human Rights. A 'court' includes 'any tribunal or body exercising the judicial power of the State'.

Privilege for court reports is vital for the media because what is said in court is often highly defamatory, and reporting it would be impossible without this protection.

The law thus recognises that the media help sustain open justice, a principle examined in ch. 15. Privilege does not apply if the court (or tribunal) hearing is in private.

22.5.1.1 Reports must be fair

For absolute privilege to apply, a report of a court case must be 'fair and accurate'. This does not mean that the proceedings must be reported verbatim—a report will be 'fair and accurate' if:

- it presents a summary of the cases put by both sides;
- it contains no substantial inaccuracies;
- it avoids giving disproportionate weight to one side or the other.

In a case in 2006 (*Bennett v Newsquest* [2006] EWCA Civ 1149), Mr Justice Eady pointed out that a newspaper report of a criminal case, which was the subject of a defamation action, contained inaccuracies, then said:

> " The report must be fair overall and not give a misleading impression. Inaccuracies in themselves will not defeat privilege. Omissions will deprive a report of privilege if they create a false impression of what took place or if they result in the suppression of the case or part of the case of one side, while giving the other. "

A media organisation loses the protection of absolute privilege if its report is held to be unfair or inaccurate in any important respect.

- To be fair, a report of a trial must make clear that the defendant denies the charge(s) and, while it proceeds, that no verdict has been reached—for example, the report can conclude by stating: 'The case continues.'

22.5.1.2 How much of a court case must be reported to be fair?

In 1993 the *Daily Sport* paid substantial damages to a police officer acquitted of indecent assault. It reported the opening of the case by the prosecution and the alleged victim's main evidence, but did not include her cross-examination by the defence, which began on the same day and undermined her allegation. Later the paper briefly reported the officer's acquittal. He nevertheless sued. The settlement in the case means that the issue of how much of a day's proceedings in court must be covered for a report to be fair remains something of a grey area.

Trials may last for days, weeks or months, and the defence may later show that statements made by the prosecution were wrong. Reports of proceedings may be published each day, but the safest practice is that if the publication has reported allegations that are later rebutted, it should also carry the rebuttals.

22.5.1.3 Reports must be accurate with quotes attributed

All allegations in court reports must be attributed because a report that presents an allegation as if it were a proved fact is inaccurate. Do not write 'Brown had a gun in his hand' but 'Smith said Brown had a gun in his hand'.

A media organisation has no protection at all if it wrongly identifies as the defendant someone who is only a witness or unconnected with the case. A report which gets the charge or charges a defendant faces wrong could prove expensive in libel damages.

 See 21.2.2, Identification, explains the need for a report to fully identify a defendant.

Journalists must also avoid wrongly reporting that the defendant was convicted when he/she was in fact acquitted. One paper paid damages when it reported a man's acquittal on drug charges—but did so in terms which gave the impression that he was in fact guilty.

 See also the Additional Material for ch. 22 on www.mcnaes.com, 'Case study on accuracy'.

The courts do allow some leeway to publications compressing material in reports (*Elizabeth and Peter Crossley v Newsquest (Midlands South Ltd)* [2008] EWHC 3054 (QB)).

22.5.1.4 Reports must be contemporaneous

To have the protection of absolute privilege, court reports should be published contemporaneously with the proceedings.

chs. 12 and 19 explain postponement orders

- Contemporaneous means 'as soon as practicable'—for example, in the first issue of a newspaper following the day's hearing. For a broadcaster, it can be construed that the report should be aired on the same day of the hearing or early on the next day. For a weekly paper, contemporaneous publication may mean publishing the following week.

Sometimes reports of court proceedings have to be postponed because a court order compels this. Section 14(2) of the Defamation Act 1996 says that in these circumstances a story is treated as if it were published contemporaneously if it is published 'as soon as practicable after publication is permitted'.

Even if the report is not contemporaneous, it will still attract qualified privilege under statute and under common law, explained later in this chapter.

Reports of earlier sections of a hearing published to put later reports in context should still be treated as having absolute privilege (the *Crossley* case, cited earlier).

22.5.2 Privilege is only for reports of proceedings

Suppose a 'court report' in the media contains background matter or comment which did not originate from the court? In the *Bennett* case referred to earlier, the judge said this would not destroy the privilege of the report: 'Extraneous comments can be included or other factual material but it must be severable, in the sense that a reasonable reader could readily appreciate that the material did not purport to be a report of what was said in court.'

But the additional material is not covered by privilege.

22.5.3 Outbursts from the public gallery

Privilege may not protect defamatory matter shouted out in court—for example, from the public gallery by someone who is not part of the proceedings.

But if the comment is shouted by someone who has given evidence as a witness in the case, privilege would protect its inclusion in a court report, provided all the defence's requirements were met.

If the shouted comment is not defamatory, it can in defamation law be reported safely, no matter who made it.

22.6 Qualified privilege

Qualified privilege is available as a defence for the publication of certain types of information. This law, in effect, categorises this information as of importance to society. The defence allows these 'statements'—including media reports of certain documents and events—to be freely published in the public interest, with no requirement for the publisher to be able to prove them as true, though there are some preconditions.

22.7 Qualified privilege by statute

Schedule 1 of the Defamation Act 1996—now amended and expanded by the Defamation Act 2013—lists 'statements' to which the statutory form of qualified privilege applies, if the defence's requirements are met. For example, the defence applies to media reports of: press conferences; parliamentary debates held in public; public meetings; public meetings of councils, their committees and their sub-committees; and media reports of statements issued for the public by

see also ch. 23 on past convictions

Government departments, councils, police and other governmental agencies. It also protects non-contemporaneous reports of court cases held in public, including references to people's past convictions.

 The Schedule is set out in the Additional Material for this chapter on www.mcnaes.com.

22.7.1 The requirements of qualified privilege

The defence's requirements differ from those of absolute privilege. For absolute privilege, the publisher's motive is irrelevant. But a qualified privilege defence will fail if the claimant can show **malice** by the publisher or author.

22.7.1.1 Fair and accurate, without malice, and in the public interest

The basic requirements of the qualified privilege defence relating to those 'statements' listed by Schedule 1 are that:

- the published report must be fair and accurate, and published without malice.

There is also a general requirement for qualified privilege that:

- the matter published must be a matter of public interest, the publication of which is for the public benefit.

This can be summed up as 'published in the public interest'.

Malice in this context means ill-will or spite towards the claimant, or any indirect or improper motive in the defendant's mind. Lord Nicholls explained in *Tse Wai Chun Paul v Albert Cheng* [2001] EMLR 777, Court of Final Appeal, Hong Kong, that the purpose of the qualified privilege defence was to allow someone with a duty to perform, or an interest to protect, to provide information without the risk of being sued—and if a person's dominant motive was not to perform this duty or protect this interest, he/she could not use the defence.

So a journalist or editor might be denied the protection of qualified privilege if the court accepts that the motive for publication was not from a duty to inform the public but was spite—for example, the publisher aired a defamatory allegation merely to settle a private score.

The question of what is in the public interest is approached objectively and does not depend on the journalist or editor's views. If a reasonable person would be aware of facts contradicting those in a report, such as that a defendant to a claim which had been filed at court denied it and was contesting it, a court is unlikely to see publication of the report without including those facts as being in the public interest.

 See the Additional Material for ch. 15 on www.mcnaes.com for a case study of how in 2012 the *Mail on Sunday* lost a defamation action when a judge ruled that its report of a court case was not protected by qualified privilege because it was not sufficiently fair or accurate, and therefore publication was not in the public interest.

22.7.1.2 Is there a requirement to publish explanation or contradiction?

Schedule 1 to the 1996 Act sets out in Part 1 a list of statements having qualified privilege 'without explanation or contradiction' and in Part 2 a list of statements thus privileged but 'subject to explanation or contradiction'.

This difference is important.

- A publisher relying on qualified privilege under Part 2 to protect a report must, to retain the protection, publish a 'reasonable letter or statement by way of explanation or contradiction' if required to do so by anyone defamed in the report.

This will apply, for example, if a person wants the publisher to publish or broadcast a letter or statement from him/her responding to a report of a council meeting which defamed him/her. Failure to publish such a letter or statement would destroy the qualified privilege defence for what was published earlier. The Act says such a statement must be published 'in a suitable manner', meaning 'in the same manner as the publication complained of or in a manner that is adequate and reasonable in the circumstances'.

✱ Remember

Get legal advice if any statement that the complainant wants published gives rise—because he/she makes counter-allegations—to any risk of libelling another person. Publication of a statement of 'explanation or contradiction' is not protected by privilege under the 1996 Act, so the statement must be 'reasonable' in this respect, though common law privilege may apply.

see also 22.7.3, Privilege at common law, on replies to attack

A statement listed in Part 1 of Schedule 1—for example, a report of what is said in public in a legislature such as the UK Parliament, or a report of material published by a legislature, including *Hansard*, or by a Government department, or a report of what is said in a public register open to inspection, discussed later in this chapter—is not subject to the requirement to publish such a letter/statement by anyone defamed by the report (though an editor may decide it is newsworthy or ethical to do this).

Part I is the means by which the 1996 and 2013 Acts greatly widened the categories of statements protected, by including reports of proceedings held in public in foreign legislatures, foreign courts and of all public inquiries appointed by Governments.

22.7.2 Statute only protects a report of the occasion or material specified

The protection of statutory qualified privilege applies only to reports of the actual proceedings, events or material listed in Schedule 1 to the 1996 Act, as amended by the 2013 Act.

- For example, this qualified privilege in Part 2 of the Schedule protects a report of speeches by councillors in a council meeting held in public, but will not protect a report of defamatory allegations a councillor makes after the meeting when asked to expand on statements made during it.

What the councillor says in the meeting—such as that a builder is corrupt—can, if the meeting was held in public, be safely reported. But if the comment is made afterwards, the publisher who airs it would have no privilege and so would need to rely on the truth defence—that is, would have to prove the builder was corrupt, which might be impossible.

22.7.2.1 Reports of public meetings, press conferences, scientific and academic conferences

Reports of a public meeting on a matter of public interest held anywhere in the world are now protected by qualified privilege, by virtue of the 2013 Act, as are reports of press conferences held anywhere in the world for the discussion of a matter of public interest, and reports of scientific or academic conferences held anywhere in the world, or copies of, extracts from or summaries of material published by such conferences.

22.7.2.2 What is a public meeting?

Paragraph 12 of the Schedule, following amendment by the 2013 Act, defines a 'public meeting' as:

- a lawful meeting held anywhere in the world for the furtherance or discussion of a matter of public interest, whether admission to the meeting is general or restricted.

This definition is fairly wide, covering public meetings about a particular community or those held about national issues. The term 'restricted' means the definition can apply, for example, to a meeting called by residents of one village who exclude from it people from the neighbouring village. Again, the privilege is subject to the 'explanation and contradiction' requirement.

22.7.2.3 The nature of press conferences

The 2013 Act extended qualified privilege to coverage of press conferences held anywhere in the world on matters of public interest. This codified in statute a decision by the House of Lords in 2000 that a press conference, held after the issuing of a general invitation to the press, is a form of public meeting.

👁 Case study

Law firm McCartan Turkington Breen sued *The Times* over its report of a press conference, called by people campaigning for the release of a soldier convicted of murder, during which defamatory comments were made about the firm. It had represented the soldier. A jury awarded £145,000 damages to the firm, but on appeal Lord Bingham, the senior law lord, said: 'A meeting is public if those who organise it or arrange it open it to the public or, by issuing a general invitation to the press, manifest an intention or desire that the proceedings of the meeting should be communicated to a wider public.' Journalists could be regarded as 'the eyes and ears of the public' (*McCartan Turkington Breen v Times Newspapers Ltd* [2001] 2 AC 277).

In *McCartan*, The House of Lords also ruled that a written press release—handed out at the meeting, but not read aloud, and reported by the media—was in effect part of the press conference proceedings. This means that fair, accurate reports of documents handed out at a press conference also have qualified privilege in the context of coverage of the press conference.

22.7.2.4 Stories from documents open to public inspection

Paragraph 5 in Part 1 to the Schedule gives privilege for a fair and accurate copy of or extract from a document which the law requires to be open to public inspection.

! Remember your rights

Paragraph 5 means, for example, that the media have qualified privilege for material quoted fairly and accurately, etc, from publicly available records such as those at Companies House, the Land Registry or other public registries, even if the records themselves turn out to be inaccurate.

Paragraph 5 also gives qualified privilege to media reports of court documents which court rules say can be inspected—see ch. 15. But it does not apply to reports of documents released under the Freedom of Information Act 2000, though the public interest defence may apply to such reports. This defence is explained in ch. 23.

ch. 30 explains the FoI Act

22.7.2.5 Reports of statements issued for the public by Government agencies

Paragraph 9 in Part 2 of the Schedule gives qualified privilege, subject to explanation or contradiction, to 'a fair and accurate copy of or extract from' a notice or other matter issued for the public by Governments anywhere in the world and authorities anywhere in the world which have governmental functions. This includes Government departments, councils, and police forces and authorities, so would cover, for example, fair and accurate reports of official police statements, and statements made on behalf of local authorities—for example, press releases about consumer protection or environmental health matters.

- These statements could be defamatory—for example, a police press release might name a man and say officers want to question him about a murder. But the qualified privilege allows the media to report this without fear of being sued by the man, provided, if asked, that they publish his 'reasonable letter or statement of explanation or contradiction'.

There will be many occasions when a reporter will wish to report the misdeeds of a person but may be inhibited by the fear of a defamation action. The answer is often to obtain confirmation of the information in the form of an official statement by a police or local authority spokesperson.

✳ Remember

Statutory qualified privilege does not protect reports of information unofficially 'leaked' from such authorities, or of what was said by people who are not official spokespersons.

22.7.2.6 Not all authorities are covered

Paragraph 9 of the Schedule does not cover reports of all statements by people in authority—it does not cover, for example, reports of statements by spokespersons for British Telecom, a gas board, a water board, the rail companies, London Regional Transport, British Airport Authority or other bodies created by statute which are involved in providing day-to-day services to the public. But it seems likely that a fair and accurate account of the official statements of such a body would be held to be covered by privilege at common law, referred to later in this chapter.

22.7.2.7 Verbal comments by press officers

Suppose a reporter telephones a press officer at one of the bodies of the type specified under paragraph 9 of the Schedule. Is the report of the spokesperson's verbal comments protected by qualified privilege under the Act? The general position seems to be 'yes', unless the spokesperson was given no chance to make considered comments.

👁 Case study

In *Blackshaw v Lord* [1984] QB 1, Lord Justice Stephenson, referring to the protection paragraph 9 gives the media, said: 'It may be right to include ... the kind of answers to telephoned interrogatories which Mr Lord [a *Daily Telegraph* reporter], quite properly in the discharge of his duty to his newspaper, administered to Mr Smith [a Government press officer]. To exclude them in every case might unduly restrict the freedom of the press ... But information which is put out on the initiative of a Government department falls more easily within the paragraph than information pulled out of the mouth of an unwilling officer of the department.'

22.7.2.8 Disciplinary actions by private associations

Paragraph 14 in Part 2 of the Schedule gives qualified privilege to media reports of the findings or decisions of a wide variety of bodies—for example, in the field of sport, business or learning—anywhere in the world which have a constitution empowering them to make disciplinary decisions about members. So, for example, the media can safely report a decision by the British Horseracing Authority disciplinary panel to ban a jockey from racing, the Football Association Independent Regulatory Commission to discipline a player or a scientific association to censure an academic, if the association is of the type listed in paragraph 14. The protection does not apply to a report of the proceedings of such bodies, and is subject to the 'explanation and contradiction' requirement.

 For what privilege covers reports of the Court of Arbitration for Sport, see the Additional Material for this chapter on www.mcnaes.com.

22.7.2.9 Reports about companies

The 1996 and 2013 Acts also greatly extended qualified privilege with respect to reporting company affairs. Earlier, qualified privilege only covered reports relating to proceedings at public companies' general meetings. The Acts extended Part 2 privilege to documents circulated among shareholders of a listed company with the authority of the board or the auditors or by any shareholder 'in pursuance of a right conferred by any statutory provision', and to fair and accurate copies of, extracts from or summaries of any document circulated to members of the company about the appointment, resignation, retirement or dismissal of directors of the company or its auditors.

22.7.3 Privilege at common law

There are some circumstances in which the media can benefit from privilege in common law. This will apply, within certain bounds, to publication of a person's response to an attack on his/her character or conduct. Also, privilege in common law applies to reports of court cases and parliamentary proceedings, if held in public, in addition to statutory privilege. For more detail, see the Additional Material for ch. 22 on www.mcnaes.com.

22.8 'Accord and satisfaction', apologies and corrections

A media organisation can use the defence of 'accord and satisfaction' to halt a defamation case on the ground that the issue has already been disposed of—for example, by publication of a correction and apology which the claimant accepted at the time as settlement of his/her complaint. But negotiating an apology or correction is not a job for an inexperienced journalist.

22.8.1 'Without prejudice'

A solicitor acting for a client demanding a correction and apology will always avoid suggesting that this action by the media organisation will be enough in itself to settle the dispute, and will make it clear that the request is made 'without prejudice' to any other action that might be thought necessary.

What does this mean? The basic principle is that parties attempting to settle their differences before going to law should be encouraged to speak frankly—anything said or written in the course of negotiations to settle and described as 'without prejudice' (that is, off the record) cannot subsequently be used against a party in court if negotiations fail. The rule applies whether or not the phrase 'without prejudice' is expressly used, but it can be good practice for the media organisation to use it too.

Journalists speaking with someone complaining about a story need to distinguish between:

- discussions over an offer to publish a follow-up story or a correction; and
- discussions over settling a claim.

In the former case, which often involves the journalist and the subject themselves, the discussion need not necessarily be 'without prejudice'; the journalist may well want to refer to this discussion in court, to show fairness or lack of malice, or to mitigate damages.

In the latter case, often involving solicitors and mention of money, the discussion should be 'without prejudice'. As a general rule journalists should notify their insurers about potential claims immediately, and, if there are solicitors 'on the other side', the publisher should also involve its own lawyer.

22.8.2 Care needed in apologies and corrections

It is no defence for a media organisation to publish a correction and apology not agreed by the claimant.

Publishing such apology can make matters worse for the publisher, because:

- a court may find that it constitutes an admission that the material which prompted the complaint was defamatory;
- a badly drafted apology or correction might also repeat the original defamatory statement, further angering the person who complained about it, or even unwittingly libel someone else.

For example: 'In our article yesterday we said Mr Red hit Mr Green. But we wish to point out that Mr Red says Mr Green struck him first'. If this is published, Mr Green may sue over the wording of the apology.

 See the Additional Material for ch. 22 on www.mcnaes.com, 'Practical advice on waivers'.

On the other hand, if the claimant wins, the fact that the media organisation took prompt and adequate steps to correct the error, and to express regret, will reduce the damages if his/her reputation was seriously harmed despite the apology.

Complainants might also be prepared to sign waivers—statements saying they waive their right to legal redress in exchange for the publication of a correction and apology—which will provide a complete defence of 'accord and satisfaction'.

A practical danger for an editor who asks a complainant to sign a waiver is that the reader may not previously have realised that he/she has a claim for damages and, thus alerted, may consult a lawyer. The waiver is therefore most useful when the complainant has already threatened to consult a lawyer.

Inexperienced reporters sometimes try to avoid the consequences of errors without referring them to the editor, by trying to shrug them off or by incorporating a scarcely recognisable 'correction' (without apology) in a follow-up story—a highly dangerous course of action, which may further aggravate the damage and prompt the potential claimant to take more formal steps to secure satisfaction. Reporters should always tell the editor about a problem immediately so it can be dealt with properly.

22.9 Offer of amends

The media can defame a person unintentionally. The classic example was the case of Artemus Jones, in which a journalist introduced a fictitious character into a descriptive account of a factual event in order to provide atmosphere—referring to what he thought of as his fictional character as being at the Dieppe motor festival 'with a woman who is not his wife'. Unfortunately the name he chose was that of a real person, a barrister—and former journalist—from North Wales. Stung by the comments of his friends the real Artemus Jones sued and recovered substantial damages. Another example is when a story about one individual is understood to refer to another as in the case of Harold Newstead, explained in 21.2.2.2, Importance of ages, addresses and occupations.

The Defamation Act 1996 provides a defence known as 'offer to make amends'. To use it, a defendant who is alleged to have published a defamatory statement must make a written offer to publish a suitable correction and apology, in a reasonable manner, and to pay the claimant suitable damages and legal costs.

If the offer of amends is rejected, and is not withdrawn, it will be a complete defence unless the claimant can show that the defendant 'knew or had reason to believe' that the published statement was false and was also defamatory of the claimant.

Editors planning to make an offer of amends must not delay. If the resulting compensation is to be assessed by a judge, he/she will start by deciding what would be 'suitable damages' if the editor had made no offer of amends and will then award a 'discount' of perhaps 50 per cent as a 'reward' for making the offer. The *News of the World* received only a 40 per cent discount after it was slow to respond to a complaint and published an apology six months after the original story.

Once an offer is made it is binding.

22.10 **Leave and licence**

The 'leave and licence' defence is that the claimant suing for libel had previously agreed that the material could be published. If it is clear the material is defamatory, a publisher intending to rely on this defence needs to be sure he/she can prove there was such pre-publication agreement. The person who is going to be defamed by the material should be asked to sign a statement agreeing to its publication or be recorded agreeing. Otherwise it might be difficult to prove that consent was given if it was merely verbal.

Sometimes, even without an explicit agreement, the context will be that leave and licence was given—for example, by a pop star who chooses in an arranged interview to speak on the record about false allegations made against him/her, seeking to dispel them.

But in other circumstances, such as a media investigation into wrongdoing, the leave and licence defence will not be secured merely by the journalist giving the target the opportunity to comment.

22.11 **'Live' broadcasts and readers' online comments**

Newsagents and booksellers have a defence of innocent dissemination as they are merely the conduit for the passage of the words complained of and are not responsible for them. But the defence was not available to others, such as distributors and broadcasters.

The Defamation Act 1996, in section 1, and section 10 of the Defamation Act 2013 extended the defence, which now applies to anyone who was not the author, editor or publisher (as defined by the Act) of the statement complained of, who took reasonable care in relation to its publication, and who did not know and had no reason to believe that whatever part he/she had in the publication caused or contributed to the publication of a defamatory statement.

A court deciding whether a person took reasonable care, or had reason to believe that what he/she did caused or contributed to the publication of a defamatory statement, must have regard to:

- the extent of his/her responsibility for the content of the statement or the decision to publish it;
- the nature or circumstances of the publication; and
- the previous conduct or character of the author, editor or publisher.

Section 10 of the 2013 Act says a court does not have jurisdiction to hear and determine an action for defamation brought against a person who was not the author, editor or publisher of the statement complained of unless it is satisfied that it is not reasonably practicable for an action to be brought against the author, editor or publisher.

22.11.1 Live broadcasts protected by section 1

The list of categories of people who are not authors, editors or publishers for the purposes of the defence includes broadcasters of live programmes who have no effective control over the maker of the statement complained of.

In 1999 the research firm MORI and its head, Bob Worcester, sued the BBC over defamatory remarks made by controversial politician Sir James Goldsmith during a live radio interview. The BBC said it had a defence under section 1—but could it be said it had taken 'reasonable care'? It was argued it should have known Sir James was likely to say something defamatory and it should at least have used a 'delay button'. The case was settled before the jury reached a verdict.

Broadcasters in 'live' situations need to react quickly to halt or cut off defamatory utterances to be sure of benefitting from section 1.

22.11.2 Internet service providers and website operators

The section 1 defence is also available for internet service providers (ISPs) which provide a service as 'host' to enable people and companies to publish their own content on their websites. ISPs play a merely passive role in the process of transmission of any defamatory matter and are therefore not publishers under section 1. But an ISP may be successfully sued for libel if it fails quickly to take down defamatory material on a site it hosts after receiving a complaint about it. In *Godfrey v Demon Internet Ltd* [2001] QB 201 the ISP was successfully sued for material on a newsgroup it hosted which it left online for about 10 days after receiving a complaint. The claim was for damages for those 10 days.

22.11.3 Section 5 defence

Section 5 of the 2013 Act provides a new defence for website operators who follow the procedures detailed in the Defamation (Operators of Websites) Regulations 2013. The defence protects a website operator from a defamation action over postings from users if they follow the steps intended to allow a would-be claimant to act directly against the individual or individuals who posted the material and ensure that they keep within the specified timetable for doing so.

 see Useful Websites at the end of this chapter for the Regulations

 See the Additional Material for ch. 22 on www.mcnaes.com for a detailed explanation of this defence.

There is also an additional protection for those who 'host', 'cache' or are 'mere conduits' for internet publication—the Electronic Commerce (EC Directive) Regulations 2002. In outline, they are protected from liability to pay damages or any other financial remedy unless and until they have notice of the defamatory publication. This is why many ISPs operate 'notice and take down' procedures.

It is not yet known how these defences will operate in connection with each other.

22.11.4 The moderation of readers' comments posted on websites

Newspapers, magazines, TV channels and radio stations cannot use the section 1 defence in the 1996 Act in respect of content which staff place on their websites, as they are clearly publishers.

As regards comment posted there by readers, the section 1 defence and that in section 5 of the 2013 Act will, as long as the correct procedural steps are followed, offer some protection. Also, the media organisation might have a defence under regulation 19 of the Electronic Commerce (EC Directive) Regulations 2002 in relation to comments posted directly on to the sites by readers—discussed later.

Section 1 or Regulation 19 are unlikely to apply if the media organisation's staff moderate—check—material before it goes online, or subsequently check a comment which is clearly defamatory or attracts complaint, but let it remain online. But the section 5 defence in the 2013 Act may offer some protection, as it specifies that the defence 'is not defeated by reason only of the fact that the operator of the website moderates the statements posted on it by others'.

- The safest course is to remove a reader's comment from the website quickly if there is a complaint that it is defamatory. The material can be re-posted later if, after consideration, it is deemed safe.

👁 Case study

In 2009 Mr Justice Eady ruled that the *Croydon Guardian* was not liable as the publisher for comments posted on its website by others. A man had tried to sue for defamation about readers' comments posted about a report of a disciplinary tribunal case in which he was struck off as a solicitor. Mr Justice Eady said the newspaper was protected by the regulation 19 defence because it had not had actual knowledge of the alleged 'unlawful activity or information' until the man complained, and it had then removed the material including the comments, as soon as it became aware of the nature of his complaint (*Karim v Newsquest Media Group Ltd* [2009] EWHC 3205 (QB)).

22.12 General protection in regulation 19

Regulation 19 provides a general protection for website operators—including media organisations—in respect of comments posted directly onto the sites by readers. As explained earlier, it can protect against defamation actions, but it can also protect the operator if a reader posts a comment which breaches criminal law—for example, by threatening violence or identifying someone in a context in which by law he/she should have anonymity, such as a juvenile defendant or a rape victim—or breaches the Contempt of Court Act 1981 or is a contempt in some other way.

For the protection to apply, the operator must act 'expeditiously to remove or to disable access' to the comment as soon as it realises or is made aware that the comment is unlawful. The protection will not be available if such 'user-generated material' is moderated by the site's operator before it appears on the site.

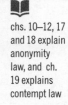
chs. 10–12, 17 and 18 explain anonymity law, and ch. 19 explains contempt law

22.13 **Other defences**

Defences which might be available are as follows.

The claimant has died A defamation action is a personal action. A dead person cannot be libelled. Similarly, an action begun by a claimant cannot be continued by his/her heirs and executors if he/she dies.

Proceedings were not started within the limitation period If the person suing did not begin the action within 12 months of the material being published, this should be a complete defence, unless there is a new publication of offending material. A court may extend the limitation period if it thinks it is in the interests of justice to do so. Reporters should date their notebooks, recordings and research material, and store them carefully, in case this proof is needed if someone sues towards the end of the limitation period or there is a possibility of using this material again after that. Journalists must remember that every repetition is a new publication.

 See 21.2.3.3, Repeating statements of others, for the case of the 'bygone days' column and 21.2.3.5, The 'single publication rule' and online archives, on this defence in the Defamation Act 2013.

➡ **Recap of major points**

- The main defences against an action for libel are truth, honest opinion, and absolute and qualified privilege.

- It is a complete defence (with one exception arising under the Rehabilitation of Offenders Act 1974) to prove that the words complained of are substantially true.

- A defendant can plead that an article expressing comment was an honestly held opinion on a matter of public interest.

- Absolute privilege applies to court reports, but reports must be fair, accurate and contemporaneous.

- Qualified privilege is available on many occasions under statute—for example, for a report of a public meeting. The defence is qualified because it is lost if the motive in publishing is malicious.

- Other defences include 'accord and satisfaction' and 'offer of amends'.

⊙ **More on www.mcnaes.com**

Test whether your story has a defence—see the Additional Material for ch. 22 on www.mcnaes.com.

((•)) **Useful Websites**

www.legislation.gov.uk/uksi/2013/3028/pdfs/uksi_20133028_en.pdf
   Defamation (Operators of Websites) Regulations 2013

23

The public interest defence

Chapter summary

This defence, introduced in the Defamation Act 2013, grew from the common law *Reynolds* defence, which was developed to allow journalists to fulfil their duty to report stories in the public interest, even if they included defamatory material they could not prove to be true, if the publication was the product of responsible journalism. Attempts to use the defence led to the courts closely examining whether a story was truly in the public interest, and the way in which it was researched and written. This chapter details the requirements of the new statutory defence and highlights the real difficulties journalists are likely to face in using it. Journalists should never consider using this defence without taking legal advice.

23.1 The birth of the defence

The 'public interest' defence created by the Defamation Act 2013 was intended to help liberalise libel law by protecting the publication of defamatory material concerning a matter of public interest, even if at the time the publisher cannot prove the material to be true. Editors hope it will increase the occasions on which responsible investigative journalism can safely be published. The defence originated from the '*Reynolds* defence', which evolved in **common law** and took its name from a 1998 case in which former Irish premier Albert Reynolds sued Times Newspapers, publisher of the *Sunday Times* (*Reynolds v Times Newspapers* [2001] 2 AC 127).

→glossary

The history of the public interest defence is explained in the Additional Material for ch. 23 on www.mcnaes.com.

 Ch. 1 explains the Convention's effect and see also 22.6, Qualified privilege.

23.2 The defence

The defence of publication on a matter of public interest is set out in section 4 of the Defamation Act 2013, which abolished and replaced the *Reynolds* defence. Parliament's intention was to clarify this area of law. The Explanatory Notes published when the Act was passed said the defence was intended to reflect the principles established in the *Reynolds* case and subsequent case law. The previous cases are therefore not binding authority for the statutory defence, but might be a 'helpful' guide to how it should be applied.

Section 4(1) says the defence is available if the defendant can show that the statement complained of was, or formed part of, a statement on a matter of public interest and that he/she reasonably believed that publishing it was in the public interest.

This provision, say the Explanatory Notes, is intended to reflect the common law *Reynolds* defence as it was detailed in *Flood v Times Newspapers* [2012] 2 AC 273.

The defence has two elements. Section 4(1)(a) requires that the words complained of were about a matter of public interest. If the publication passes this test, it then has to meet the requirements of section 4(1)(b), which has subjective and objective elements.

First comes the subjective element, which is the defendant's belief that publication was in the public interest; then comes the objective element, which is the question of whether it was reasonable, in all the circumstances, for the defendant to hold that belief.

23.3 The *Flood* case

In the *Flood* case, the *Sunday Times* ran a story saying that Detective Sergeant Gary Flood of the Metropolitan Police extradition unit was being investigated following an allegation of corruption. Det. Sgt Flood—who was later exonerated by an inquiry—sued for defamation. Mr Justice Tugendhat at first instance ruled that the newspaper report was protected by the *Reynolds* defence. But the Court of Appeal, taking an extremely narrow view of the defence, said it was not available because the journalists responsible for the article had failed to act responsibly, by failing adequately to verify the allegations in it.

The Supreme Court reversed that decision, saying that the newspaper was entitled to use the *Reynolds* defence. *Times Newspapers Ltd and others v Flood and others* [2017] UKSC 33; [2017] EMLR 19; [2017] 1 WLR 1415. Lord Brown said:

Lord Nicholls' list is given in 23.7, The responsible journalism test

> " In deciding whether *Reynolds* privilege attaches (whether the *Reynolds* public interest defence lies) the judge, on true analysis, is deciding but a single question: could whoever published the defamation, given whatever they knew (and did not know) and whatever they had done (and had not done) to guard so far as possible against the publication of untrue defamatory material, properly have considered the publication in question to be in the public interest? "

This, said Lord Brown, involved a host of different considerations, starting with the non-exhaustive list of 10 factors identified by Lord Nicholls in the original *Reynolds* case but also including other considerations.

23.4 The court must consider all the circumstances

Section 4(2) of the 2013 Act says that, in determining whether the public interest defence is made out, the court must have regard to all the circumstances of the case.

Courts will doubtless examine whether the journalism was conducted responsibly—and might be expected to have in mind, at least, the non-exhaustive list of 10 factors detailed by Lord Nicholls in the original *Reynolds* case. The Act itself places no requirement on a publisher to demonstrate that what was published was the result of 'responsible journalism', and the abolition of the common law defence means that the *Reynolds* case is no longer a binding authority. But the old cases showing the approach judges have taken to responsible journalism might give some indication of factors which might be taken into account in deciding whether the defendant's belief—that publishing it was in the public interest—was reasonable.

23.5 Audit trails to justify the public interest element and belief

Sir Brian Leveson suggested in his 2012 report into the press that any new regulator should require investigative journalists and their editors to produce an 'audit trail' of the development of a story, the investigation itself, and the issues considered and factors discussed when deciding whether to publish and whether the story was in the public interest.

 See 2.1.1, Fragmentation of press regulation, outlines the context of the report.

Whether the courts will require this as part of the public interest defence should become clearer when cases on the new defence have been decided. Some editors are already familiar with such 'audit trail' practices, because, for example, the BBC Editorial Guidelines require that use of undercover tactics must be approved by senior managers as being in the public interest and because in 2012 the Editors' Code was changed to require press editors, in the event of a relevant complaint about what was published and/or reporters' methods, to be able to demonstrate fully that they—the editors—held a reasonable belief that 'public interest' considerations applied. Chs. 2 and 3 explain these codes.

Section 4(4) of the 2013 Act states that, when deciding whether it was reasonable for a defendant to believe that publication was in the public interest, the court 'must make such allowance for editorial judgement as it considers appropriate'.

23.6 Defining the public interest

Both the Broadcasting Code and Editors' Code include some definitions of what journalism can be considered to be 'in the public interest'—for example, exposing crime, or showing that someone is misleading or endangering the public. The wording of those definitions was influenced by legal judgments in breach of confidence cases about the circumstances when the public interest justified publishing confidential or private material against someone's wishes. But the 2013 Act does not define the public interest. The Explanatory Notes say simply that 'this is a concept which is well-established in the English common law'.

The publication must be, or form part of, a statement on a matter of public interest, meaning that the court can either deal solely with the words complained of or take a holistic view of them in the wider context of the document or article in which they appear when deciding if overall this is a matter of public interest.

It was held that the *Reynolds* defence was available to anyone who publishes material in the public interest, including in a book. The same seems to apply to the new statutory defence.

In *Charman v Orion Publishing Group Ltd and others* [2007] EWCA Civ 972, [2008] 1 All ER 750 the Court of Appeal allowed the use of the defence to defeat a libel claim by a former police officer over Graeme McLagan's book, *Bent Coppers—The Inside Story of Scotland Yard's Battle against Police Corruption*.

In *Alexander Economou v David de Freitas* [2016] EWHC 1218 (QB), [2017] EMLR 4 Mr Justice Warby held that the father of a mentally vulnerable young woman who took her own life shortly before she was due to go on trial on a charge of making a false allegation of rape was entitled to rely on the public interest defence in relation to his contribution to media articles which were libellous of the man his daughter had accused. The case focused on the requirement in section 4 for 'reasonable belief' and how to establish whether the requirement was met.

 An analysis of this case is in the Additional Material for ch. 23 on www.mcnaes.com.

It seems from rulings so far that judges will consider material to be in the public interest if it is of 'real public concern'—but the test is not as strict as saying the public *needs* to know. The concept is also flexible—the degree of public interest required will vary according to the publication and market, as in the *GKR Karate* case (cited later in the chapter) in 2000, in which a judge found in favour of *Leeds Weekly News*, a free newspaper which was sued over a front-page article warning readers about the activities of doorstep salesmen selling karate club membership.

The judge said the fundamental question was one of public interest and the people of Leeds clearly had an interest in receiving this information (*GKR Karate Ltd v Yorkshire Post Newspapers Ltd* [2001] 1 WLR 2571).

23.7 The responsible journalism test

The question of whether an article was the product of responsible journalism will lie at the heart of any case in which the public interest defence is used. In the *Reynolds* case, cited earlier, in the House of Lords, Lord Nicholls, in the leading speech, set out a non-exhaustive list of factors a court should consider when examining whether a publication was the product of responsible journalism and therefore whether it could be protected by the new defence.

Lord Nicholls' list (with summarised explanation added in italics)

1. The seriousness of the allegation. The more serious the charge, the more the public is misinformed and the individual harmed, if the allegation is not true. *Therefore, the more serious the allegation, the greater should be the reporter's efforts to ensure that what is published is correct if the story is to be protected by the defence.*

2. The nature of the information, and the extent to which the subject matter is a matter of public concern. *The less the matter is of public concern, the weaker the defence. The defence will fail if a judge decides the matter is not of public concern—judges often say that what interests the public and what is in the public interest are two different things.*

3. The source of the information. Some informants have no direct knowledge of the events. Some have their own axes to grind, or are being paid for their stories. *It is important to note that courts are wary of unidentified informants, although a newspaper or broadcaster will not necessarily be penalised for refusing to identify a source.*

4. The steps taken to verify the information. *It is always important to check, whenever possible, to ensure that what you have been told is true or correct. Making no or insufficient checks before publication will be regarded as irresponsible journalism and the defence will fail.*

5. The status of the information. The allegation may have already been the subject of an investigation which commands respect. *For example, if a reputable agency—such as the police—has already decided the relevant allegations are not true, then the media must have sufficient reason to air them if the defence is to apply.*

6. The urgency of the matter. News is often a perishable commodity. *That is, the courts, when deciding if the defence applies, must take into consideration that journalists need to work and publish quickly.*

7. Whether comment was sought before publication from the claimant [*that is, the person who claims he/she was defamed*]. He may have information others do not possess or have not disclosed. An approach to the claimant will not always be necessary. *But generally the person who is the subject of an allegation should be approached. It is also important to make it clear in a story that, if the person about whom allegations have been made cannot be contacted, efforts have been made to reach him/her. Only rarely will an approach to the subject not be necessary.*

8. Whether the article contained the gist of the plaintiff's [*now claimant's*] side of the story. *That is, the journalism must be fair to benefit from the defence. Leaving out the claimant's side is a recipe for disaster.*

9. The tone of the article. A newspaper can raise queries or call for an investigation. It need not adopt allegations as statements of fact. *For example, the defence may not apply to material which brashly and unfairly suggests that*

unproven allegations are true. It is important to mind your phrasing. Make sure that what you write is what you mean—and that your meaning is clear to anyone who reads your copy, including the man on the Clapham omnibus. Sloppy writing will almost undoubtedly prove expensive.

10. The circumstances of the publication, including the timing. *That is, was it really so urgent that the story had to be published when it was? Could it have waited an hour or two, or a day or so?*

Reynolds Former Irish premier Albert Reynolds sued Times Newspapers, publisher of the *Sunday Times*, over an article he claimed meant he deliberately and dishonestly misled the Irish parliament by suppressing information about the appointment of Ireland's Attorney General as President of its High Court. Times Newspapers argued in its defence that, in keeping with Article 10 of the European Convention on Human Rights, the public interest in media coverage of political issues and in scrutinising the conduct of elected politicians should be protected by a common law form of qualified privilege.

Although the House of Lords established the *Reynolds* defence in its decision, it also held, by a majority, that the *Sunday Times* could not take advantage of it as it had conspicuously failed to 'give the gist of the subject's response' (point 8 on Lord Nicholls' list).

Asked at the trial why his account contained no reference to Mr Reynolds' explanation, the reporter said: 'There was not a word of Mr Reynolds' defence because I had decided that his defence ... there was no defence.' Mr Reynolds had addressed the Irish parliament on the issue, but the paper did not report his statement.

On the steps taken to verify the story (Lord Nicholls' point 4), the reporter, asked why he took no notes during his inquiries, said: 'I was not in note-taking mode.'

Loutchansky In 1999 *The Times* published articles alleging that international businessman Grigori Loutchansky controlled a major Russian criminal organisation involved in money-laundering and smuggling nuclear weapons.

The High Court judge rejected its claim to a *Reynolds* defence. The case went to the Court of Appeal, which agreed that the articles dealt with matters of public concern (Lord Nicholls' point 2), but made the following points.

- Implicating Mr Loutchansky in misconduct of the utmost gravity was manifestly likely to be highly damaging to his reputation, so a proportionate degree of responsibility was required of both journalist and editor (Lord Nicholls' point 1). *The Times* had failed to show this—the allegations were vague, the sources were unreliable, insufficient steps were taken to verify the information and no comment was obtained from Mr Loutchansky before publication.

- The High Court judge was entitled to find that 'such steps as were taken' by the reporter in his unsuccessful attempts to contact either Mr Loutchansky or his company, Nordex, or its lawyers were far less diligent than required by the standards of responsible journalism (Lord Nicholls' point 7).

- On the question whether the coverage contained the gist of Mr Loutchansky's side of the story (Lord Nicholls' point 8), it only contained the bare statement that he had 'repeatedly denied any wrongdoing or links to criminal activity', which was insufficient, given the seriousness of the unproven allegations published.

Both the *Reynolds* and *Loutchansky* cases show that journalists must have a good shorthand note to support what they write. Asked in court in the *Loutchansky* case to produce the note he made of a vital conversation he had had with his most important source, the reporter replied that he thought he must have made the note on a scrap of paper which he subsequently threw away (Lord Nicholls' point 4).

The Court of Appeal rejected the newspaper's appeal (*Loutchansky v Times Newspapers Ltd* [2001] EWCA Civ 1805).

The source of the information and the steps taken to verify it—Lord Nicholls' points 3 and 4—require more than a journalist making a number of calls which do not actually yield useful information or verification. In *Lord Ashcroft v Stephen Foley, Independent News and Media and Roger Alton* [2011] EWCA 292 (QB) Mr Justice Eady agreed with the claimant's argument that if sources provided no relevant information or none that was relied upon, the fact that they had been contacted was irrelevant. He added: 'Journalists, in other words, cannot collect 'brownie points' for having rung round a number of people who had no relevant information to give.'

23.7.1 Seeking comment from the claimant

A key point in many cases involving the *Reynolds* defence was whether the publisher sought comment from the claimant (Lord Nicholls' point 7).

Any damaging story should be put to the subject before publication. As Lord Nicholls said: 'He [the subject] may have information others do not possess or have not disclosed.' The courts regard observance of the practice as one indication of responsible journalism. But point 7 also states: 'An approach to the claimant will not always be necessary'—the view the court took in the *Jameel* case because of its special circumstances (*Jameel v Wall Street Journal Europe* [2006] UKHL 44. See www.mcnaes.com for details of this case).

Journalists should always try to put defamatory or damaging allegations to the subject if they intend to report them in the public interest.

23.8 Websites

The new defence is available to anyone who publishes material—so covers bloggers, Twitter users and everyone else with access to the internet.

But in *Flood*—discussed earlier—the Court held that the *Sunday Times* was protected by the *Reynolds* defence in relation to the copy of the story in its internet archive only until the date on which it learned that Det. Sgt Flood had been exonerated. Mr Justice Tugendhat said its failure to make clear that Det Sgt Flood was innocent—for example, by adding an indication to this effect to the online story—was not responsible journalism.

Journalists should keep the internet in mind when dealing with investigative stories—and ensure that archive material is updated to reflect changes in circumstances.

23.9 A delicate balance

The public interest defence in the 2013 Act is extremely important to the media, journalists and editors. It seeks to strike a balance between the right to reputation and a free press—but when it succeeds it means that a would-be claimant is deprived of any remedy for what might be a defamatory publication which severely damages his/her reputation. So the journalist's activities and professionalism will be closely scrutinised—in effect, the journalist's conduct will be on trial as much as, if not more than, that of the claimant.

Mr Justice Warby suggested in September 2017 that the time might have come to change the law so that claimants who found that defamatory statements were protected by the public interest defence would nevertheless be able to secure corrections.

Editors and journalists should consider publishing corrections in such cases, but take legal advice before doing so.

 Chs 2 and 3 detail the 'correction' requirements of the Editors' Code and the Broadcasting Code.

23.10 Neutral reportage

The section 4 'public interest' defence includes protection for neutral reportage—that is, when a dispute or issue is being reported even-handedly in instances in which the fact that allegations are being made by one person against another, or that something is a matter of controversy, is itself a matter of public interest, even though the publisher cannot prove which people in a dispute are telling the truth.

Section 4(3) says that if the complained-of statement (the reportage) was 'an accurate and impartial report of a dispute to which the claimant is a party', a court must, when determining whether it was reasonable for the publisher to believe that publishing it was in the public interest, disregard any omission by the publisher 'to take steps to verify the truth of the imputation conveyed by it'. But editors should be wary of reporting disagreements which have been generated artificially so as to give the impression of a 'dispute' which can reasonably be reported in the public interest.

Again, when considering if the defence applies, judges can be guided, but not bound, by case law, outlined below, on a variant of the *Reynolds* defence which became known as the 'neutral reportage' defence.

23.10.1 The *Al-Fagih* case

In *Al-Fagih v HH Saudi Research & Marketing (UK) Ltd* [2001] EWCA Civ 1634 the Court of Appeal held that a newspaper could rely on the *Reynolds* defence where it reported, in an objective manner, an allegation about someone made by an opponent during a political dispute. The defence was not lost merely because the newspaper had not verified the allegation. The newspaper had argued that, where two politicians made serious allegations against each other, it was a matter of public importance to report the dispute, provided that this was done fairly and accurately and that the parties were given the opportunity to explain or contradict.

23.10.2 The *BNP* case (*Roberts v Searchlight*)

Another case showed that a 'neutral reportage' defence could be used even when, by contrast with *Al-Fagih*, the journal and its staff were clearly not neutral. The test was whether the journalist has reported the matter neutrally. The anti-fascist magazine *Searchlight* reported a dispute between British National Party (BNP) factions, repeating defamatory allegations made in the BNP's own bulletin. The magazine, its editor and a journalist successfully argued that they had a defence of qualified privilege in common law as they were merely reporting the allegations, not adopting or endorsing them (*Christopher Roberts and Barry Roberts v Gerry Gable, Steve Silver and Searchlight Magazine Ltd* [2006] EWHC 1025 (QB)).

➡ Recap of major points

- The new statutory 'public interest' defence, which has its origins in the *Reynolds* defence, has two principal elements—the publication must be a statement on a matter of public interest, and the defendant's belief that publication was reasonable.

- Judges will be guided to an extent by case law on the *Reynolds* defence, and the new defence can protect 'neutral reportage'—accurate and impartial reports—of a dispute in which the claimant is involved.

((•)) Useful Websites

www.legislation.gov.uk/ukpga/2013/26/contents/enacted
  Defamation Act 2013

www.legislation.gov.uk/ukpga/2013/26/notes/contents
  Explanatory Notes to the Act

www.bailii.org/uk/cases/UKSC/2012/11.html
  Supreme Court's decision in *Flood v Times Newspapers Ltd*

www.bailii.org/uk/cases/UKHL/2006/44.html
  House of Lords' decision in *Jameel*

www.publications.parliament.uk/pa/ld199899/ldjudgmt/jd991028/rey01.htm
  House of Lords' decision in *Reynolds*

24

The Rehabilitation of Offenders Act 1974

Chapter summary

The Rehabilitation of Offenders Act 1974 allows people to live down previous criminal convictions after specified periods, which vary with the sentence they receive. It limits the defences journalists have against libel claims over a published reference to a 'spent' conviction if the **claimant** can prove it was published maliciously. The Act presents no problem for journalists if disclosing someone's criminal record is in the public interest.

24.1 Rehabilitation periods

The 1974 Act created the concept of **spent convictions**. Convictions become 'spent' after a 'rehabilitation period', which varies according to the sentence imposed, and includes a so-called Buffer period which runs from the end of the sentence. Some convictions, such as murder, which carries an automatic life sentence, are never spent.

for 'right to be forgotten' lawsuits against Google, see Late News

The aim was to allow people convicted of less serious offences to live down previous convictions and get a fresh start. There is no legal obligation to declare a 'spent' conviction when applying for most jobs, whatever the application form says, although there is for some occupations, such as working with children.

The Act also seeks to stop the media referring to someone's spent conviction without good reason.

Rehabilitation depends on the length of an offender's sentence. Serious crimes for which convictions never become spent are those for which an offender receives a jail sentence, or a term of detention in a young offender institution, of more than four years, whether the sentence is immediate or suspended, or an extended sentence for public protection, which is given for violent or sexual offences.

 Various types of sentence are explained in 7.6, Sentencing by magistrates, and 9.7, Sentencing at Crown court.

The rehabilitation periods determining when less serious convictions become spent vary from two years, for a prison sentence of six months or less, to seven years for a jail sentence of between 30 months and four years. But a further conviction during the rehabilitation period can extend it. Cautions and **absolute discharges** become spent immediately. Rehabilitation periods for many convictions are halved for those under 18, and in some cases are even shorter for those aged 12–14. Suspended sentences are treated as if they were put into effect. See Useful Websites at the end of this chapter for the rehabilitation periods.

→ glossary

24.2 The Act's effect on the media

The 1974 Act limits the defences available for a media organisation sued for libel for publishing reference to a person's spent conviction.

(1) A defence of **truth**—that the report of the previous conviction was true—will fail if the claimant can prove that the conviction was spent *and* the publication was malicious. This breaches the principle that truth is a complete defence to a defamation action, because the Act aims to deter the media from referring to a spent conviction without good reason.

see ch. 22 for explanations of all these defences

(2) The defences of absolute or qualified **privilege** are not available for reporting a spent conviction which is mentioned in court proceedings but is then ruled inadmissible by the court.

→ glossary

Example A man sues a newspaper for defamation after it publishes an accurate reference to his previous criminal conviction. Three defences are available.

- *Truth*—because there was a conviction, defamation law accepts that the conviction is proof that the person committed that crime. So a media organisation, once it proves the conviction—for example, from a court record—is not required to re-prove that the claimant committed the offence.

- *Qualified privilege* protects non-contemporaneous reports of court cases if the defence's requirements are met. Mention of a conviction is, in effect, a report of the court case in which the conviction occurred when the defendant pleaded guilty, or when magistrates or a jury announced the guilty verdict. The defence also protects quotations from the case, such as the judge calling the convicted defendant 'a scoundrel'.

- *Honest opinion* protects opinion expressed about the person based on the fact of the conviction, if the defence's requirements are met. If a council election candidate has a criminal conviction, an editorial comment column could safely publish the author's honestly held opinion that the conviction made the person unfit for public office. Similar comments from others could also be safely published if they were their honestly held opinions. Even if no such comment is made explicitly, a media organisation publishing the conviction in this context creates an inference that the person could be regarded as unfit for public office. The honest opinion defence should protect the media organisation over that inference.

see 20.2.3, Inferences, which explains this term

→glossary

Even if the conviction referred to is 'spent', the above defences apply unless the publication was malicious. There will be **malice** if a journalist or editor publishes a reference to a spent conviction merely to further some interest of his/her own or out of spite. In such a case the Act stops use of the truth defence, even though the conviction is a fact. Proof of malice also destroys the qualified privilege defence.

✳ Remember

In most news stories the media can refer to and comment on spent convictions—disclosing a council candidate's previous conviction or the criminal record of a dodgy businessperson—with no fear of libel consequences because the disclosures are in the public interest and no malice is involved.

24.2.1 Spent convictions revealed in court proceedings

A person giving evidence in any civil proceedings should not, generally, be asked about spent convictions.

But rehabilitated people who appear before criminal courts again, after their convictions have become spent, can still be asked about them.

Absolute or qualified privilege applies to media reports of a spent conviction mentioned in a court case unless the court ruled that the fact that the conviction exists was inadmissible.

Judges have been directed that spent convictions should never be referred to in criminal courts, unless this is unavoidable, and that no one should refer in open court to a spent conviction without the judge's authority.

24.2.2 Criminal penalties

There is no criminal penalty for journalists who mention a spent conviction. But it may be an offence for a public servant to disclose details of spent convictions other than in the course of official duties.

It is a criminal offence to get information of spent convictions from official records by fraud, dishonesty or bribery.

 Ch. 28 explains data protection, and ch. 35 explains 'misconduct' law and bribery law.

➡ Recap of major points

- Convictions become spent at the end of the rehabilitation period.
- A conviction leading to a jail term of more than four years is never spent.

- The rehabilitation period varies between seven years (in respect of a jail sentence of between 30 months and four years) and three months, although some offences become spent immediately.

- The Rehabilitation of Offenders Act 1974 restricts the libel defences available to journalists who maliciously refer to spent convictions.

((•)) Useful Websites

www.nacro.org.uk/wp-content/uploads/2017/05/Rehabilitation-of-Offenders-Act-1974-Guide-2017.pdf
Nacro guide to the Rehabilitation of Offenders Act 1974, with charts showing rehabilitation periods

25

Slander, malicious falsehood and obscenity

Chapter summary

Defamation in its spoken form is slander—and can present journalists with problems. This chapter examines those problems and looks at malicious falsehood, which occurs with the publication of a statement which is not defamatory but is false and can be shown to have caused financial loss. It also briefly examines law banning publication of obscene material.

25.1 Slander

The most obvious difference between the **torts** of libel and slander is, as ch. 20 explains, that libel is in permanent form (eg written words, a drawing or a photograph), while slander is spoken or in some other transient form.

But:

- defamatory statements broadcast on radio or television, or in a cable programme are treated as libel—Broadcasting Act 1990;
- as are defamatory statements in a public performance of a play—Theatres Act 1968.

For there to be slander, as with libel, the statement must be published to a third person, must refer to the **claimant**, and must cause his/her reputation serious harm.

A claimant in a slander case must prove the financial damage suffered, except in the case of:

ch. 21 explains what a libel claimant must prove

- an imputation that he/she has committed a crime punishable by imprisonment; or
- a statement calculated to disparage him/her in his office, profession, calling, trade or business.

Journalists are less likely to become involved personally in a slander action than a libel action, but must be aware of the dangers.

Suppose X says that Y, a borough councillor, used his position to secure building contracts—actionable because it disparages Y in his office of councillor. A reporter checking the story will have to interview people to reach the truth and must be wary of being sued for slander over questions asked during interviews in which the original slander might be repeated to a third party. There is also a risk that a message left on an answering machine could spark an action if it is heard or re-played by someone other than the claimant. There is also a risk if broadcasters shout allegations, in public, at people who have refused to be interviewed about them—the broadcast itself could spark a libel action, while the fact that the shouted question was heard by members of the public at the scene might tempt the subject to sue for slander as well.

The limitation period for bringing a slander action is one year.

25.2 Malicious falsehood

Publication of a false statement may cause a person financial damage even though it does not cast aspersions on his/her character or fitness to hold an office or follow a calling. For example, a false statement that a solicitor had retired from practice would cause loss as his/her clients would seek other solicitors to do their work. But it is clearly not defamatory to be considered retired.

The wronged person cannot sue for libel or slander if a published statement is not defamatory—but might be able to sue for malicious falsehood.

The claimant in a malicious falsehood action must prove the statement is untrue—in contrast with a libel action, where the court assumes that a defamatory statement is false unless the defendant can prove it to be true. He/she must also prove that the statement was published maliciously.

As with the defence of qualified **privilege** in libel law, **malice** means a statement made by someone who knows it is false, or is reckless as to its truth. However, a defendant who believes a statement is true but publishes it with the aim of injuring the claimant will also be viewed as motivated by malice (*Spring v Guardian Assurance plc* [1993] 2 All ER 273, CA). Negligence—that is, wrongly believing a statement to be true, and so failing to check it, when there is no aim to injure—is not malice.

→ glossary

The claimant in a malicious falsehood case does not have to prove that he/she has suffered actual damage if the words are in permanent form, such as printed words, and calculated—likely—to cause financial damage, or they are spoken or written and likely to cause him/her financial damage in his/her office, profession, calling, trade or business.

But once a claimant has proved financial damage, he/she can also claim damages for emotional distress, hurt feelings and so on—and these damages could be substantial because the defendant will be shown to have acted maliciously.

The limitation for bringing a malicious falsehood action is one year.

25.2.1 Meaning

Claims for malicious falsehood also differ from those for defamation because they are not based on the notion that a statement has only one meaning (*Ajinomoto*

Sweeteners Europe SAS v Asda Stores Ltd (No 2) [2010] EWCA Civ 609, [2011] 1 QB 497).

 See 20.2.2, Meaning of words, for this rule in defamation cases.

Journalists must be aware of the need for clear and concise writing, and the risk that, in a malicious falsehood claim, a court will take account of a range of meanings for a statement, one or more of which could leave them liable to pay damages.

👁 Case study

Former Conservative Party Co-Treasurer Peter Cruddas was initially awarded £180,000 in damages when he sued the *Sunday Times* for libel and malicious falsehood. The case arose from articles—published in 2012 after he met undercover journalists masquerading as potential donors to the Party—saying he asked for £250,000 in donations for them to meet David Cameron. But in 2015 the Court of Appeal cut the damages to £50,000, ruling that the trial judge was wrong in one of his findings that the meanings in the articles did not give a true account of what Mr Cruddas told the journalists. In the appeal judgment, Lord Justice Jackson said Mr Cruddas was effectively telling the journalists that if they were to donate large sums to the Conservative Party, they would have an opportunity to influence government policy and gain unfair commercial advantage through confidential meetings with the Prime Minister and senior Ministers. Lord Justice Jackson said it was 'unacceptable, inappropriate and wrong' for Mr Cruddas to do this, and therefore this meaning of the articles was 'substantially true'. But the Court of Appeal upheld findings of libel and malicious falsehood over two other pleaded meanings which it said the journalists knew were false—that Mr Cruddas made the offer even though he knew the money offered for meetings would come, in breach of the ban under UK electoral law, from Middle Eastern investors in a Liechtenstein fund, and that to evade that law he was happy that the foreign donors should use deceptive devices to conceal the true source of the donation. The *Sunday Times* said it did not think it had accused him of these meanings (*Cruddas v Calvert, Blake and Times Newspapers Ltd* [2015] EWCA Civ 171; Media Lawyer, 17 March 2015).

((•))
see Useful Websites at the end of this chapter for the full judgment

---

25.2.2 Corrections

see 20.5, Errors and apologies

An editor may realise that the facts of a story are wrong, but they were not defamatory and it was an honest mistake. If so, he/she should act quickly to publish an adequate correction. A failure to correct a story which is known to be wrong, especially if it remains visible online, could be held to be malicious.

25.2.3 Slander of goods and title

Two types of malicious falsehood are known as 'slander of goods' (false and malicious statements disparaging the claimant's goods) and 'slander of title' (false and malicious denial of the claimant's title to property). The word 'slander' is misleading in both cases. The damaging statement can be in permanent form or spoken.

25.3 Obscenity

It is an offence to publish obscene material—the test is whether the words or material published would tend to deprave and corrupt those likely to read them/it.

The Obscene Publications Act 1959 introduced a defence that the publication was 'for the public good . . . in the interests of science, literature, art, or learning, or of other objects of public concern'. The Obscene Publications Act 1964 made it an offence to possess an obscene article for publication for gain.

➡ Recap of major points

- Slander, a civil wrong (like libel), concerns defamatory words which (unlike libel) are spoken or in some other transient form.
- In slander (unlike libel), financial damage may need to be proved.
- Malicious falsehoods are false statements that, though not defamatory, may still be damaging. The claimant must prove that the statement is untrue and was published maliciously.

((•)) Useful Websites

www.bailii.org/cgi-bin/markup.cgi?doc=/ew/cases/EWCA/Civ/2015/171.html
Court of Appeal judgment in *Cruddas*

Part 4

Confidentiality, privacy and copyright

Breach of confidence

Chapter summary

The law of breach of confidence is based upon the principle that a person who is given information in confidence should not take unfair advantage of it. This chapter explains the kind of information and relationships considered confidential. A media organisation which publishes this type of information needs a legal defence to avoid having to pay damages. Governments, businesses and individuals use this law to protect information they regard as officially or commercially secret, or private. The main means of preventing a breach of confidence is an **injunction** banning publication of confidential information. This area of law was also the foundation of the law of privacy, the focus of the next chapter.

→ glossary

26.1 Development of the law

The law on breach of confidence is at its most straightforward in protecting commercial secrets. An employee has a duty to protect commercially sensitive information he/she creates or gains in the course of employment—such as market research data or plans for new products. That duty arises from the employment relationship. If an employee disloyally passes that information to the employer's commercial rival, that is a breach of confidence. In most instances the betrayed employer could, apart from sacking the employee, successfully sue him/her and the rival in the civil courts for damages to compensate for any financial loss suffered, because breach of confidence is a **tort**, a civil wrong. The duty to preserve confidentiality can automatically pass to anyone else who receives the material and realises its confidential nature. So, a media organisation to which a business's commercial secrets are leaked may also be successfully sued if it publishes these, unless it has a defence.

→ glossary

The law of breach of confidence can also protect material which is personally private. Queen Victoria's husband Prince Albert used it in 1848 to prevent commercial publication of private family etchings depicting their children and pets after copies were purloined from the printers to which they were sent by the Royal household to be printed merely as a personal collection (*Prince Albert v Strange* (1848) 1 Mac. & G. 25).

But what is now the wide scope of this law is a comparatively recent development.

26.1.1 Development of privacy law

Until 2000 UK law recognised no general right to privacy. So in previous decades people who believed their privacy was about to be infringed had to use the law of breach of confidence to prevent intrusions. Their main difficulty lay in the different nature of the two kinds of right. An obligation of confidence, by definition, arises, first, from the circumstances in which the information is given—a relationship which gives rise to one party owing a duty of confidence to another.

see 26.3, Breach of confidence and official secrets, explaining *Spycatcher*

In contrast, a right of privacy relating to information arises from the nature of the information itself and the principle that certain kinds of information are private and for that reason alone should not be disclosed. Many cases involving invasions of privacy did not result from breaches of confidence.

Privacy law evolved as judges began to abandon their strict view on the circumstances in which an obligation of confidence could occur. In the *Spycatcher* case in the House of Lords in 1988 (*A-G v Times Newspapers* (1992) 1 AC 191) Lord Goff of Chieveley said:

> A duty of confidence arises when confidential information comes to the knowledge of a person (the confidant) in circumstances where he has notice, or is ruled to have agreed, that the information is confidential, with the effect that it would be just in all the circumstances that he should be precluded from disclosing the information to others.

Lord Goff said he had expressed the duty in wide terms to include the situation where 'an obviously confidential document was wafted by an electric fan out of a window into a crowded street, or when an obviously confidential document such as a diary was dropped in a public place and then picked up by a passer-by'.

In this scenario the passer-by has no relationship with the person whose information he/she has picked up—but, because it is obviously confidential, in law the passer-by should not, for example, give or sell it to a media organisation for publication, unless there is a legal defence.

In 2000 the Human Rights Act 1998 came into force, incorporating into UK law the European Convention on Human Rights, Article 8 of which guarantees the right to respect for privacy and family life, as ch. 1 explains. In cases involving alleged breach of personal privacy, the courts started abandoning the legal contrivance of implying a confidential relationship where none existed, and so a separate type of tort—misuse of private information—developed. That is the focus of the next chapter.

26.2 Elements of a breach of confidence

There are three elements in a breach of confidence.

The information:

- must have 'the necessary quality of confidence';
- must have been imparted in circumstances imposing an obligation of confidence; and
- there must be an unauthorised use of that information to the detriment of the party communicating it (*Coco v AN Clark (Engineers) Ltd* [1969] RPC 41).

The phrase 'the party communicating it' means the person who originally communicates the information—that is, the person to whom the confidence is owed. For example, a company allows its employees to access commercially sensitive information about its products and finances—in effect, it communicates such information to them, and so they owe it a duty of confidence. A patient who tells a doctor about an ailment, or allows him/her to take blood tests or conduct a pregnancy test, is communicating information. The doctor and any other staff at the surgery or hospital owe the patient a duty of confidence in respect of that information.

Remember that a court enforcing the law of confidentiality does not require a direct relationship between the person who wishes to protect the information and the person who wishes to disclose it. This is because the law of equity operates on the consciences of the parties, so the legal criterion is whether a reasonable person would understand from the nature and circumstances of a disclosure that he/she was receiving information or material in confidence. Thus, a journalist who receives a leak of a company's commercially sensitive data or someone's medical records usually has a duty not to reveal it to others, just as an employee of that company or the patient's doctor has.

26.2.1 The quality of confidence

The law of breach of confidence safeguards ideas and information imparted or obtained in confidential circumstances. Generally, information is not confidential if it is trivial—for example, a company's canteen menu—or is already in the public domain.

26.2.2 Obligation of confidence

An obligation of confidence can arise in a variety of ways.

Contractual relationship Employees might have signed agreements not to disclose an employer's secrets. This applies as much to a celebrity's chauffeur who wants to sell to the media tales of what he saw and heard in his employment as it does to scientists employed in commercial research. Even if the written contract does not make this clear, there is an implied term in every employment relationship that an employee will not do anything detrimental to an employer's interests.

see 27.6.2, Relationships, which gives context

Personal relationship In 1967 the Duchess of Argyll prevented the *People* newspaper, and her former husband, from publishing marital secrets (*Argyll v Argyll* [1967] Ch 302). This was an early example of the courts accepting that a couple in a relationship owe a duty of confidence to each other about intimate matters, which still applies after they split up. By the 1980s the courts had extended the protection to prevent the publication of kiss-and-tell stories originating from less formal relationships. Disputes about whether such stories can be or should have been published are now generally dealt with in privacy law.

Unethical behaviour It now seems to be established by case law that journalists who obtain confidential information by unethical means such as trespass, theft, listening devices or long-range cameras are usually in breach of an obligation of confidence owed to the targets of this activity—an obligation created and breached by the tactics used.

If not, the case will probably be covered in privacy law. Electronic snooping is covered by criminal law.

> See too 27.9, Information obtained covertly, and explanation in ch. 35 of 'hacking' (snooping) offences.

26.2.3 Detriment

The confiding party must suffer, or be at risk of suffering, a detriment of some sort to be able to claim a breach of confidence, such as financial loss from exposure of commercially sensitive information. But in the *Spycatcher* case in the House of Lords, Lord Keith of Kinkel said it would be a sufficient detriment to an individual that information he/she gave in confidence was to be disclosed to people he/she would prefer not to know it. The detriment could be the adverse effect on someone's mental well-being or physical health, caused by unauthorised publication of his/her confidential, personal information.

26.3 Breach of confidence and official secrets

In 1985 the UK Government used the law of breach of confidence when attempting to stop publication of information acquired by Peter Wright during his former job as a senior officer of its internal security service, MI5. He planned to make money by selling his memoirs—a book called *Spycatcher*. The Attorney General, for the UK Government, sought an injunction to stop the book's publication, arguing that former members of the security services had an absolute and lifelong duty not to reveal any details of their employment.

In June 1986 the *Observer* and *The Guardian* newspapers carried stories giving brief details of some allegations Wright, who had retired to Australia, planned to publish. An English court then gave the Attorney General interim injunctions preventing both newspapers from disclosing any information Wright had obtained as a member of MI5. In 1988, after many legal actions involving the Government and newspapers, in the UK and abroad, the House of Lords ruled: that the original articles in the *Observer* and *The Guardian* in 1986 were not published in breach of confidence; that the Government was not entitled to a permanent injunction preventing the newspapers from making further comments on the book and using extracts from it; and that the Government was not entitled to a general injunction restraining the media from future publication of information derived from Wright.

The *Spycatcher* case showed that the Government was prepared to use the civil law of breach of confidence rather than rely on prosecutions under (controversial) official secrets law.

ch. 33 explains official secrets law

The case also established the principle that an injunction granted against one media organisation, to stop it publishing material, could cover all of them.

> For more details of *Spycatcher*, see the extended ch. 33 on www.mcnaes.com on official secrets law, and see Useful Websites at the end of this chapter for a BBC report of the House of Lords' judgment.

26.4 Injunctions

A person or an organisation who discovers that the media intends to publish confidential information without his/her/its consent can apply to the High Court for a temporary injunction to stop it.

Such an order is intended to 'hold the ring' until the case is fully heard. As a condition for obtaining an interim injunction the party applying for it must undertake to pay the other side damages if, at the trial, it is ruled that the order should not have been made.

But a media organisation, having been injuncted, may decide the cost of fighting the injunction or the case in a full trial is not worth it.

Disobeying an injunction can result in an action for contempt of court which could lead to an unlimited fine.

Section 12 of the Human Rights Act 1998 is intended to provide some protection against injunctions in matters involving freedom of expression. **Claimants** applying to the High Court for injunctions should only obtain them if they persuade the judge that they are 'likely' to establish at the trial that publication should not be allowed. Before the 1998 Act, the application might be without notice, which meant that only one party—the claimant—was represented and a defendant media organisation would only learn of the proceedings when it was served with the injunction. That can and still does happen—for example, injunctions have sometimes been granted when a newspaper has been printed and ready to go on sale. Section 12 says that if the defendant is not present when the application is made, the court must not grant an injunction unless satisfied either that the claimant has taken all practicable steps to notify the defendant or that there are compelling reasons for not giving notice.

→ glossary

26.4.1 The journalist's dilemma

The law of confidentiality regularly presents journalists with dilemmas. Suppose a reporter learns about some newsworthy misconduct from a source who received the information confidentially. The journalist should, as a matter of ethical conduct and because of the law of libel, approach the person alleged to have misbehaved to get his/her side of the story and to check facts.

For example, the BBC Editorial Guidelines tells broadcasters:

 When our output makes allegations of wrongdoing, iniquity or incompetence or lays out a strong and damaging critique of an individual or institution the presumption is that those criticised should be given a 'right of reply', that is, given a fair opportunity to respond to the allegations. 〞

A journalist who does make such an approach runs the risk that, as explained later, the subject will immediately obtain an injunction banning use of the information, killing the story before it can be published.

> ((•)) See Useful Websites at the end of this chapter for these Guidelines and see 3.4.13.2, Getting facts right and airing the other side of the story.

✳ Remember

You should certainly check a story which might be defamatory—but try do so without revealing that you have confidential material, to avoid laying yourself open to the risk of an injunction.

26.4.2 Injunction against one is against all

In 1987 the Court of Appeal ruled that when an interim injunction is in force preventing a media organisation from publishing confidential information, other media organisations in England and Wales which know of it can be guilty of contempt of court if they publish that information, even if they are not named in the injunction.

In 1989 two papers were each fined £50,000 for publishing extracts from *Spycatcher* because at the time of publication they knew that interim injunctions banned the *Observer* and *The Guardian* from publishing the material. The fines were later discharged, but the convictions were upheld and in 1991 the House of Lords confirmed the ruling on the law.

This legal device for silencing the media might be phrased in such a way that journalists are banned even from mentioning the existence of the proceedings—a so-called super-injunction. Super-injunctions are discussed in the next chapter.

An injunction issued by an English or Welsh court does not prevent publication in another country. In particular, it does not prevent publication in Scotland—though Scottish judges may be asked to impose their own injunction, known as an 'interdict'.

> See the www.mcnaes.com chapter on Scotland.

26.5 Remedies for breach of confidence

People or organisations claiming in a legal action that their confidential information has been unlawfully published can:

- ask a judge to issue an injunction to stop it being published again by that publisher or by others;
- seek an order for the confidential material, such as documents or pictures, to be 'delivered up'—that is, returned to the claimant or destroyed;
- sue the publisher for damages or 'an account of profits';
- ask a judge to order the publisher to reveal the source of the information, if this is not known, so that the source can be sued for damages and/or to stop disclosure of more confidential information.

26.5.1 Damages

These are likely to be higher in a case where the breach of confidence caused commercial loss—for example, the £1 million damages which *Hello!* magazine had to pay to *OK!* magazine in the *Douglas* case—rather than loss of personal privacy.

In the *Douglas* case it was ruled that the law of confidence protected what should have been the value of the exclusive, commercial deal which *OK!* had struck with Hollywood couple Michael Douglas and Catherine Zeta-Jones to take and publish photographs of their 'private' wedding reception, an arrangement which *Hello!* had undermined by publishing 'spoiler' photos of the occasion, secretly taken by an undercover paparazzo—see the Additional Material for ch. 26 on www.mcnaes. com for details of the case.

In 2008 Max Mosley, then president of the organisation which runs Formula 1 grand prix racing, was awarded £60,000 against the *News of the World* in an action alleging breach of confidence and unauthorised disclosure of personal information for its exposure of his participation in a sado-masochistic orgy with prostitutes. One of the prostitutes had breached the confidence of her arrangement with Mosley by telling the newspaper about and filming the orgy, and the newspaper was ruled to be liable for the damages.

26.5.2 Account of profits

A person misusing confidential information to make money may be asked to account for the profits to the person or organisation whose confidence was betrayed. A court may rule that the person who misused the information should pay some or all of these ill-gotten profits to the party betrayed. But for a media organisation, the order is more likely to be for damages, because of the difficulty a judge would face in deciding which story in its output at that time led to what profit.

26.5.3 **Order to reveal source**

ch. 34
explains the
ethics of
protecting
sources

A court can order a journalist to disclose the source of the confidential information. If the journalist promised the source anonymity, the ethical position is that he/she must keep that promise—and face the consequences of disobeying the court. The defiance could be deemed a contempt of court which could lead to a fine or, conceivably, to the journalist being jailed, though he/she may have some protection from Article 10 of the European Convention on Human Rights and the 'shield law' in section 10 of the Contempt of Court Act 1981.

👁 Case study

→ glossary

In 1989 an engineering company, Tetra Ltd, obtained injunctions against *The Engineer* magazine and its trainee reporter Bill Goodwin. The company, which was in financial difficulties, had prepared a business plan to help negotiate a substantial bank loan. A copy of the draft plan 'disappeared' from its offices, and the next day a source telephoned Mr Goodwin and gave him information about the company, including the amount of the projected loan and Tetra's forecast results. Mr Goodwin phoned the company and its bankers to check the information. Tetra obtained a **without notice** injunction banning publication of information derived from the draft plan, and later obtained an order that Mr Goodwin and *The Engineer* should hand over notes which would disclose the source. Mr Goodwin refused, and was fined £5,000. In 1996 the European Court of Human Rights ruled that the court order and the fine violated his right to freedom of expression under Article 10. Mr Goodwin was supported by the National Union of Journalists (*Goodwin v United Kingdom*, Application no. 17488/90 (1996) 22 EHRR 123).

26.6 **Defences**

Defences to an action for an alleged breach of confidence include:

- the information did not have 'the necessary quality of confidence' because:
  - of its nature—for example, it was trivial and/or disclosure was unlikely to cause much detriment; or
  - it was already in the public domain;
- it was in the public interest to publish the information—for example, to expose wrongdoing, negligence or hypocrisy.

The same arguments can be used against an application for an injunction.

26.6.1 **Information already in the public domain**

If a media organisation publishes commercially sensitive information leaked from a business, or information leaked from a public institution, a court is unlikely to grant an injunction or award damages for breach of confidence if the material was already widely in the public domain—for example, already published by other media outlets or by members of the public on internet sites and other social media.

Judges, as some have said, do not wish to make pointless orders like King Canute ordering the tide to recede.

But the scope for the public domain defence is more limited if personal privacy is infringed—for example, a judge might ban the media from publishing embarrassing private footage improperly copied from a celebrity's computer, to spare the celebrity further distress, and even if thousands of copies are already on the internet.

 The issue of what was already in the public domain was a feature of the *Watford Observer* case, which is outlined in the Additional Material for this chapter on www.mcnaes.com.

26.6.2 Publication in the public interest

Section 12 of the Human Rights Act 1998 says a court considering imposing an injunction in a matter affecting freedom of expression in which **journalistic material** is involved must have particular regard to the extent to which it is, or would be, in the **public interest** for the material to be published.

→glossary

→glossary

Even before the Act, journalists had successfully argued that disclosing confidential information would be in the public interest.

👁 Case study

The Court of Appeal ruled in 1984 that it was in the public interest for the *Daily Express* to publish information from an internal memo, leaked from a company making breathalyser equipment, which cast doubt on its accuracy at a time when police were using it to clamp down on drink-driving (*Lion Laboratories v Evans* [1985] QB 526).

But in 2017 international news agency Reuters was banned from publishing information apparently taken from documents sent in confidence to potential investors by a major hedge fund management company, Brevan Howard Asset Management. The Court of Appeal upheld the trial judge's decision that the public interest in maintaining the confidentiality of the information outweighed the public interest in reporting it.

 Details of the *Reuters v Brevan Howard* case are outlined in the Additional Material for this chapter on www.mcnaes.com.

26.6.3 Correcting 'a false public image'

In 2005 celebrities David Beckham and Victoria Beckham failed to get an injunction against the *News of the World* concerning information about the state of their marriage. The paper argued that the Beckhams had portrayed a false image about their private life, and so it was in the public interest for it to publish information from their former nanny that she had seen them having blazing rows (*Media Lawyer*, 25 April 2005).

26.7 Relevance of ethical codes

see 27.12, Relevance of ethical codes, and 4.1 The codes and intrusion

As the next chapter explains, in a case involving a claim of breach of privacy, which may include a claim of breach of confidence, the judge will—if the defendant is a media organisation—take into account what the relevant ethical code says and whether the organisation conformed to it. This could be the Editors' Code, the Broadcasting Code or the Impress Standards Code.

➡ Recap of major points

- The law says that a person who has obtained information in confidence must not take unfair advantage of it.
- The person who believes his/her confidence is to be breached can get an injunction preventing this.
- Disobeying an injunction is a contempt of court.
- If confidential matter is published, the person whose confidences were breached may be able to claim damages.

((•)) Useful Websites

http://news.bbc.co.uk/onthisday/hi/dates/stories/october/13/newsid_2532000/2532583.stm
BBC news archive story in the *Spycatcher* saga

www.bbc.co.uk/editorialguidelines/guidelines/fairness/right-of-reply
BBC Editorial Guidelines on fairness and right of reply

Privacy

Chapter summary

Celebrities and others use the law of privacy—misuse of private information—to prevent publication of information about their lives and activities. This chapter explains privacy law—and warns that journalists who electronically snoop on people or hack into their phone messages will probably be committing a crime as well as a **tort** which will leave them open to an expensive claim for damages.

27.1 Development of the law

As ch. 1 explains, in 2000 the Human Rights Act 1998 incorporated the European Convention on Human Rights—Article 8 of which guarantees the right to respect for privacy and family life—into UK law, giving it the specific law of privacy it had previously lacked.

Section 12 of the Act requires courts considering granting any order or **injunction** banning publication of information to have 'particular regard' to the importance of freedom of expression, guaranteed by Article 10 of the Convention. But in the *Douglas* case, Lord Justice Sedley rejected the view that section 12 gave greater weight to freedom of expression than to privacy, saying: 'Everything will ultimately depend on the proper balance between privacy and publicity in the situation facing the court.'

→ glossary

→ glossary

> ⬡ See the Additional Material for ch. 26 on www.mcnaes.com for more on *Douglas*.

ch. 28 explains the 1998 Act

In the House of Lords, in *In Re S (FC) (A Child) (Appellant)* [2004] UKHL 47, [2005] 1 AC 593 Lord Steyn made it clear that neither Article 8, guaranteeing the right to respect for privacy and family life, nor the Article 10 right to freedom of expression 'has as such precedence over the other'. This is also the view of the European Court of Human Rights (ECtHR).

👁 Case study

In 2004 supermodel Naomi Campbell won a privacy claim in the House of Lords after suing Mirror Group Newspapers for breach of her Article 8 privacy rights, breach of confidence and infringement of the Data Protection Act 1998.

The *Daily Mirror* had published detail about her receiving therapy from Narcotics Anonymous for drug addiction, including photos of her emerging into the street after leaving a session. Although she was only awarded a total of £3,500 damages for distress and injury to her feelings, her victory in law showed how Article 8 had changed the UK's legal landscape (*Campbell v Mirror Group Newspapers* [2004] UKHL 22).

Another landmark ruling, in 2004, was the European Court of Human Rights' judgment that Princess Caroline of Monaco's privacy was breached by the publication of photographs of scenes from her daily life, shopping or on holiday with her family, in public places. Important considerations in the decision was that she was not an elected politician, and had suffered years of being stalked and photographed by paparazzi, which had interfered with her human right, protected by Article 8, to enjoy social interaction with people (*Von Hannover v Germany*, Application no. 59320/00, 24 June 2004, ECtHR). But the Grand Chamber of the ECtHR has since stepped back from the position established in that case, as explained later in this chapter.

see 27.10, The public interest, for more on *Campbell*

27.2 The scope of Article 8

Article 8 of the European Convention on Human Rights says:

❝ 1.   Everyone has the right to respect for his private and family life, his home and his correspondence.

2.   There shall be no interference by a public authority with the exercise of this right except such as is in accordance with the law and is necessary in a democratic society in the interests of national security, public safety or the economic well-being of the country, for the prevention of disorder or crime, for the protection of health or morals, or for the protection of the rights and freedoms of others. ❞

Article 8 gives protection for privacy against a 'public authority', the media or anyone else, such as bloggers.

27.3 Remedies for breach of privacy

The remedies which courts will provide for a breach of privacy include damages and permanent injunctions to prevent material being published.

27.3.1 Damages

In May 2015 Mr Justice Mann awarded damages totalling more than £1.2 million to eight **claimants** whose phones were hacked by journalists at Mirror Group Newspapers (MGN), publisher of the *Daily Mirror, Sunday Mirror* and *Sunday People*. The highest sum—£260,250—went to actress and businesswoman Sadie Frost, while former footballer Paul Gascoigne was awarded £188,250. The case set a new high for damages for invasions of privacy. MGN lost its appeal against the level of damages.

→ glossary

ch. 35 outlines the hacking scandal

27.3.2 Injunctions and super-injunctions

A person who learns that a media organisation intends to publish material he/she considers private can seek an injunction to ban its publication. Initially, a judge may grant an interim (temporary) injunction to hold the position until the court can rule after a full trial hearing—which will be costly for the losing party—on whether the injunction should be permanent or lifted to allow publication.

The issue of injunctions and so-called super-injunctions—orders which include a clause banning the media or anyone from even publicising the fact that they have been made—attracted considerable media coverage in April and May 2011. Concern was expressed that freedom of expression, including that of the media, and the public's right to receive information was being irrevocably damaged by such bans. Footballers, actors and business people facing allegations—for example, of adultery—were granted orders giving them anonymity in these cases, to block publication of information about their private lives, while bloggers and Twitter users sought to undermine orders by naming those whom they claimed—sometimes incorrectly—had obtained them. The uproar led Lord Neuberger, then the Master of the Rolls, to issue useful Practice Guidance tightening up the rules on non-publication injunctions and requiring that, once an interim injunction was made, the case should normally proceed to a trial. The number of applications for privacy injunctions against the media subsequently dropped sharply.

section 26.4, Injunctions, gives more context

27.3.3 The permanent injunction *contra mundum*

An interim injunction is held, under the *Spycatcher* principle, to bind all those on whom it is served or who are aware of it. But an injunction made permanent after a full hearing (trial), binds only the particular parties—for example, media organisation(s)—against whom it was obtained. This means that another media organisation could then publish the information covered. The response of the courts in these circumstances has been to issue so-called *contra mundum* ('against the world') orders—orders of general effect which bind anyone who knows about them, including all media organisations made aware of them.

ch. 26 explains the *Spycatcher* case

→ glossary

This was the power used in 2000 by Dame Elizabeth Butler-Sloss, the then President of the Family Division of the High Court, in a ground-breaking injunction banning the media from revealing the new identities and whereabouts of Robert Thompson and Jon Venables, juveniles who murdered 2-year-old James Bulger. One reason that an injunction was granted was to protect their Article 8 privacy rights.

See 12.11, Indefinite anonymity for convicted defendants and others.

→glossary

In April 2011 Mr Justice Eady said the court's jurisdiction to grant an injunction *contra mundum* was available, wherever necessary and **proportionate**, for the protection of Convention rights whether of children or adults (*OPQ v BJM and CJM* [2011] EWHC 1059 (QB)).

In June 2015, Mr Justice Keehan, sitting in the Family Division of the High Court, issued a *contra mundum* injunction giving lifelong anonymity to a teenage girl who had been the victim of sexual exploitation by a group of Asian men in the Birmingham area, one of whom had fathered her child. There were, he said, 'compelling reasons' why the teenager, known only as AB, should be protected, and why her history as a victim of child sexual exploitation should remain confidential and private to her. The injunction was granted because the girl was not **automatically** entitled to lifelong anonymity under the Sexual Offences (Amendment) Act 1992 as no complaint was ever made that any sexual offence had been committed (*Birmingham City Council v Safraz Riaz and others* [2015] EWHC 1857 (Fam)).

→glossary

ch. 11 explains automatic anonymity for sexual offence victims

27.4 A shift in the law

At one point it seemed clear that, in a privacy case, unless there was a strong **public interest** justification—the material in question had to contribute to a debate of general public importance—the courts would issue injunctions to prevent publication of the sort of kiss-and-tell stories which were once the standard fare of tabloid journalism. But in February 2012 the ECtHR eased the position somewhat, saying that media coverage of celebrities' private lives was 'acceptable if in the general interest and if in reasonable balance with the right to respect for private life' (*Axel Springer AG v Germany*, Application no. 39954/08 (2012) 55 EHRR 66; *Von Hannover v Germany No. 2*, Applications nos 40660/08 and 60641/08).

→glossary

see also 27.10, The public interest

The factors a court will consider in deciding on injunctions include the degree to which the material makes a contribution to a debate of general interest—which does not just cover politics—how well-known the person concerned is, the subject of the report itself, the prior conduct of the person concerned, the method of obtaining the information and its truth, and the content, form and consequences of the publication.

27.5 Privacy versus freedom of expression

In a privacy case, what factors will persuade a judge that material which a media organisation seeks to publish *will* contribute to a 'debate of general interest to society'?

Decisions by the ECtHR indicate that it sees freedom of expression as having various levels of value to society, with political expression about the conduct of politicians in public office, at the top of the table. This means that an elected politician who conceals his/her improper behaviour from the electorate is unlikely to persuade a court that the media should be banned from exposing it. The higher up the hierarchy, the greater the protection the courts should give freedom of expression, and vice versa, although each case will, as the ECtHR and UK courts consistently stress, depend on its specific facts.

But, as outlined earlier, in the *Axel Springer* and *Von Hannover No. 2* cases the ECtHR acknowledged that society had a 'general interest' in debating matters other than politics. It quoted Resolution 1165 (1998) of the Parliamentary Assembly of the Council of Europe on the right to privacy, including paragraph 7, which said:

> " Public figures are persons holding public office and/or using public resources and, more broadly speaking, all those who play a role in public life, whether in politics, the economy, the arts, the social sphere, sport or in any other domain. "

In these cases the ECtHR adopted a wider approach to what could legitimately be published than it did in the first *Von Hannover* case (the *Princess Caroline* case, discussed earlier).

👁 Case study

In February 2012 Mr Justice Tugendhat declined to continue an interim injunction obtained by then Environment Secretary Caroline Spelman and her husband Mark which banned the *Daily Star Sunday* from reporting that their teenage son, Jonathan, an international rugby player, had, after being injured, taken drugs to aid his recovery which, while legal, were banned under anti-doping rules. Keeping the order in place was neither proportionate nor necessary, said the judge, who also quoted Resolution 1165. In effect, he held that, as Jonathan Spelman was an international rugby player, he was a public figure (*Spelman v Express Newspapers* [2012] EWHC 355 (QB)).

27.6 'Reasonable expectation of privacy'

A claimant seeking an injunction to stop the media publishing information about his/her private life and activities must first demonstrate that he/she has a 'reasonable expectation of privacy' in relation to the information. Only after that will the court go to the second stage, balancing the rights to privacy in Article 8 against the rights to freedom of expression in Article 10, and considering the proportionality of any interference with either right in a process called the 'parallel analysis', before conducting the 'ultimate balancing test' to reach a decision. This is the test set out in the *In Re S* judgment, referred to earlier in this chapter, and in 1.3.3, Weighing competing rights.

A court deciding if the expectation of privacy is reasonable may take into account the location of the event(s)—because the expectation may not be reasonable, for example, in respect of something done in a public place. But location may not be a key consideration. Someone who falls ill or suffers an accident in a public street has a reasonable expectation that this vulnerability gives them a right of privacy—for example, filming them in their distress would infringe it.

TV footage of eviction breached tenants' privacy, see Late News

Case study

In 2003 the ECtHR ruled that a British man's privacy was infringed when the media broadcast footage of his suicide attempt in the centre of Brentwood in 1994. The council released the footage to show that its installation of CCTV cameras helped save his life because police, alerted by the camera operators, took a knife from him. But the man, who was mentally ill at the time, was recognisable in images broadcast, despite the council's request that he should not be (*Peck v United Kingdom,* Application no. 44647/98 (2003) 36 EHRR 41). His complaints about this were upheld in 1996 by the broadcast regulators but he took a case to the ECtHR, because in 1996 the UK courts did not recognise a specific right of privacy.

> Ch. 4 gives examples of how the Independent Press Standards Organisation and Ofcom have interpreted 'reasonable expectation'.

27.6.1 Information concerning health

Information about health is normally treated as being of the highest confidentiality—people usually have 'a reasonable expectation' that information about their health is private.

In 2002 the Court of Appeal banned the *Mail on Sunday* from naming a local health authority where a healthcare worker, referred to as H, had quit his job after being diagnosed HIV positive. The High Court had earlier said it could name the authority, but not the healthcare worker.

Lord Phillips, then Master of the Rolls, said there was a public interest in preserving the confidentiality of healthcare workers who might otherwise be discouraged from reporting they were HIV positive. While the *Mail on Sunday* believed H's patients were entitled to know they had been treated by someone who was HIV positive, naming the authority would inevitably lead to the disclosure of H's identity, as only his patients would be offered HIV tests and counselling, the judge said. But the paper could say the healthcare worker was a dentist.

There are exceptions—in 2006 murderer Michael Stone failed to ban the press and public from seeing an independent inquiry report into the treatment he had received from mental health, probation and social workers before he killed. A judge said the report would assist public debate about treatment of the mentally ill and those with disturbed personalities (*Michael Stone v South East SH* [2006] EWHC 1668).

> Health—treatment for drug addiction—figured in the *Campbell* case—see 27.1, Development of the law, and 27.10, The public interest.

27.6.2 Relationships

The courts also recognise that people have a reasonable expectation that what they say and do intimately within a personal relationship is private—whether the relationship is a marriage, co-habitation, love affair or friendship. If, after the relationship ends, one person wants (often to earn money) the media to publish secrets from the relationship, the courts may injunct to protect the other person's Article 8 rights, or—if the information is already published—award damages for the infringement. It is now rare for a media organisation to be able to demonstrate that a claimant in such a case did not have a reasonable expectation of privacy, not only in relation to what happened within the relationship, but also over the fact that there was a relationship.

27.6.3 The privacy of sexual relationships

In the years immediately after the Human Rights Act 1998 came into force, courts took the view that not all sexual conduct was entitled to be viewed as confidential or, indeed, deserved legal protection. But the courts have become more willing to rule that adulterous or casual sexual affairs are matters in which one or both of the people involved have a reasonable expectation of privacy and will issue gagging orders—injunctions—unless the defendant (the party from the relationship who wishes to reveal the intimate matters) or the media can persuade the judge that there is a strong public interest in publishing the information.

If such material is published, damages could be awarded. For example, in 2008 Max Mosley, then president of the organisation which runs Formula 1 grand prix racing, won £60,000 from the *News of the World* for breach of privacy and—as ch. 26 explains—for breach of confidence over stories, photos and video footage it published about his participation in sado-masochistic activities with prostitutes (*Mosley v News Group Newspapers Ltd* [2008] EWHC 1777).

see also 26.5.1, Damages, for *Mosley*

In 2011 one footballer was known to have obtained two privacy injunctions banning the media from reporting on his sexual liaisons with two different prostitutes, with the court agreeing that the material was not in the public interest and that the player had a reasonable expectation that the information would remain private.

But another player, former England football captain John Terry obtained and then lost an interim injunction which had banned the media from reporting on his alleged relationship with a former team-mate's ex- partner. Mr Justice Tugendhat concluded that the injunction had been sought to protect Terry's reputation, and sponsorship and commercial deals relying on it, rather than his privacy. (*LNS v Persons Unknown* [2010] EWHC 119 (QB)).

👁 Case study

In March 2015, Mr Justice Warby discharged an interim injunction granted to Manchester United defender Marcos Rojo which had banned the media from running a kiss-and-tell story involving a fitness instructor with whom the player had cheated on his wife. The judge, who noted that Rojo had not given evidence to support his case, said it was claimed that the woman was blackmailing the player for £100,000—but in fact that was an offer made to her to buy her silence, with the blackmail claim being made only after she turned it down. What was left of the footballer's claim was 'relatively weak' (*YXB v TNO (No. 2)* [2015] EWHC 826 (QB)).

27.6.4 The claimant's family

The way in which the privacy or other rights of those linked to a claimant, such as family members or, in particular, children, will also influence the outcome of an application for an injunction was illustrated in a Supreme Court decision in 2016.

👁 Case study

The Supreme Court said both the High Court and Court of Appeal were wrong to decide to lift an interim injunction which stopped *The Sun on Sunday* publishing information about a married man in the entertainment industry referred to as PJS who had been involved in extra-marital sexual activity. 'Publication of the story would infringe privacy rights of PJS, his partner and their children', said Lord Mance.

" There is no public interest (however much it may be of interest to some members of the public) in publishing kiss-and-tell stories or criticisms of private sexual conduct, simply because the persons involved are well-known; and so there is no right to invade privacy by publishing them. It is different if the story has some bearing on the performance of a public office or the correction of a misleading public impression cultivated by the person involved . . . that does not apply here. "

He went on:

" As to public availability, it is true that the story has been accessible on the internet and social media, but, if the injunction were to be lifted, there would be intensive coverage of the story by *The Sun on Sunday* (and, there is little doubt, by other newspapers), as well as unrestricted internet and social media coverage, all of which would constitute additional and potentially more enduring invasions of the privacy of PJS, his partner and their children . . .

If publication were permitted now it would be likely to deprive a trial of any real purpose, since all privacy would by then have been destroyed. Damages after the event, whatever their measure, would be unlikely to give any real consolation or redress to any of those involved. "

Anyone with a spouse or partner and children will seek to put their rights into the balance when applying for a privacy injunction banning publication of stories of extra-marital affairs or other questionable behaviour.

27.7 Children's own privacy rights

The media must be careful about children, especially the children of celebrities and others in the public eye. Their age makes them more vulnerable than adults to the effects of media intrusion, and case law reflects this.

Using paparazzi pictures taken of youngsters in the street has led to privacy lawsuits.

👁 Case study

Rock star Paul Weller and his wife Hannah won £10,000 in damages for their children whose faces were 'plastered' over the MailOnline website in October 2012. Weller, 55, sued the newspaper's publisher, Associated Newspapers, on behalf of his daughter Dylan, who was 16 when the seven unpixelated pictures appeared, and twin sons John Paul and Bowie, who were 10 months old. A paparazzo had followed Weller and the children on a shopping trip in Santa Monica, California, taking photos despite being asked to stop. Associated Newspapers said the pictures were innocuous and inoffensive images taken in public places and that the Wellers had previously chosen to open up their private family life to public gaze to a significant degree. Mr Justice Dingemans said:

> In my judgment, the photographs were published in circumstances where Dylan, Bowie and John Paul had a reasonable expectation of privacy. This was because the photographs showed their faces, one of the chief attributes of their personalities, as they were on a family trip out with their father going shopping and to a cafe and they were identified by surname.

The Court of Appeal upheld the decision in November 2015, with Lord Dyson, Master of the Rolls, saying: 'The fact that a child's parent or parents are celebrities or public figures may not, without more, be relied on to argue that the child should have a lower reasonable expectation of privacy.' Mr Justice Dingemans was 'plainly entitled to find that the publication of the photographs did not contribute to a current debate of general interest', he went on, adding that the youngsters 'were only of interest to the MailOnline because they are children of a successful musician' (*Media Lawyer*, 16 April 2014; 20 November 2015).

But a majority of the Supreme Court held in 2015 that a 14-year-old whose photograph, taken during a riot in Northern Ireland and released by police in an attempt to identify offenders, did not have a 'reasonable expectation of privacy' or a 'legitimate expectation of protection' (*In re JR38* [2015] UKSC 42, [2015] 3 WLR 115 SC(NI)).

27.8 Can information be private if it is in the public domain?

A judge may refuse to ban publication of material if it is already widely published—for example, on many sites on the internet—or easily available to anyone. But each case is different.

In 2005 a judge granted an injunction restraining a newspaper from publishing the addresses of buildings acquired for housing vulnerable adolescents, although they would be known to neighbours and others living nearby, and the addresses might also be available from the Land Registry (*Green Corns Ltd v Claverley Group Ltd* [2005] EMLR 31).

What is the position with 'widely published' photographs? The Court of Appeal in the Douglas case (referred to elsewhere) said:

> Once intimate personal information about a celebrity's private life has been widely published it may serve no useful purpose to prohibit further publication. The same will not necessarily be true of photographs. Insofar as a photograph does more than convey information and intrudes on privacy by enabling the viewer to focus on intimate personal detail, there will be a fresh intrusion of privacy when each additional viewer sees the photograph and even when one who has seen a previous publication of the photograph is confronted by a fresh publication of it.

see also
26.6.1,
Information
already in
the public
domain

Any publisher wishing to show that information is in the public domain will have to establish that by evidence—and the court will scrutinise carefully what has been published.

27.9 Information obtained covertly

What if the information is obtained, for example, by bugging or long-lens photography?

One issue is that if a person is unaware of cameras or microphones, he/she may assume the situation is private and act or speak accordingly.

In 2006 the Court of Appeal referred to cases where a duty of confidentiality arose from information having been acquired by 'unlawful or surreptitious means'. The Court regarded the taking of long-distance photographs as being 'an exercise generally considered to raise privacy issues' (*Niema Ash and another v Loreena McKennitt and others* [2006] EWCA Civ 1714, [2007] 3 WLR 194).

In the Douglas case the wedding pictures were taken by an uninvited freelance photographer. The photographs of Naomi Campbell leaving a Narcotics Anonymous therapy session were also taken surreptitiously.

  For detail on *Douglas*, see the Additional Material for ch. 26 on www.mcnaes.com.

27.10 The public interest

Even before the Human Rights Act 1998, journalists could plead that disclosing confidential information was in the public interest—for example, to expose crime, other wrongdoing, hypocritical conduct or a threat to public safety. But judges are now much less likely to accept that a claimant's celebrity could generate a public interest in private conduct that would otherwise be protected.

In the *Naomi Campbell* case, publication of some detail was held to be in the public interest and some not. There were five distinct 'elements' of private information:

section 27.1, Development of the law, outlines *Campbell*

- the fact of Ms Campbell's drug addiction;
- the fact that she was receiving therapy for it;
- the fact that she was having therapy at Narcotics Anonymous (NA);
- details of the NA therapy and her reaction to it; and
- surreptitiously obtained photographs of her emerging from an NA session.

As the model had previously publicly denied using drugs, the first and second facts could be published in the public interest. But the rest could not, because of the intrusiveness of the disclosure and the likelihood that it would interfere with or disrupt her treatment.

Three of the judges—the majority—held that Article 10 considerations could not justify publishing the information. But two judges said the third, fourth and fifth categories added little of significance to the disclosure of the first and second, and that journalists should be given greater latitude. The difference of opinion between the judges illustrates the difficult decisions journalists might face when considering such stories.

27.10.1 The Data Protection Act 1998

The Naomi Campbell case also alerted the media to the implications for the law of privacy of the Data Protection Act 1998.

data protection law is explained in ch. 28

27.11 Electronic 'snooping', intercepting and hacking into communications

Journalists who use electronic equipment to spy on other people could be committing a crime as well as running the risk of being sued for infringing privacy.

 Ch. 35 explains the risks of being charged with hacking into computers, telephone message and email systems, or otherwise 'intercepting' communications—activity intrusive into privacy.

27.12 Relevance of ethical codes

Section 12 of the Human Rights Act 1998 also says a court considering a matter affecting freedom of expression must have particular regard to 'any relevant privacy code'. In cases involving the media, judges will consider, depending on the media sector involved, if the journalism has conformed to either the Editors' Code, overseen by Ipso, or any other code operated by any other regulator, or the Broadcasting Code.

 See chs. 2 and 3 for general detail on these codes, and ch. 4 for their privacy provisions.

If the journalism does conform, judges may be more likely to rule that any breach of confidence or privacy was justified by the public interest. The wording of the parts of each code relating to public interest justifications are, anyway, influenced by case law.

➡ Recap of major points

- The right to privacy is guaranteed by Article 8 of the European Convention on Human Rights.
- The law of privacy developed from the action for breach of confidence, but is now recognised as a separate tort of misuse of private information.
- The test in a privacy claim is whether the claimant has 'a reasonable expectation of privacy'.
- The right to privacy is not necessarily lost because the activity happened in public.
- There is a defence that publication was in the public interest.
- Other protections for privacy are in the Data Protection Act 1998, explained in ch. 28, and the Regulation of Investigatory Powers Act 2000, explained in ch. 35.

((•)) Useful Websites

www.judiciary.gov.uk/wp-content/uploads/JCO/Documents/Guidance/practice-guidance-civil-non-disclosure-orders-july2011.pdf
Master of the Rolls' Practice Guidance on privacy injunctions

28

Data protection

Chapter summary

The privacy of personal information kept on computers and in filing systems is safeguarded by data protection law. This covers data we give about ourselves to Government departments, councils, public institutions and commercial companies, and data they generate about us. The law affects journalists in three ways. First, a journalist may be prosecuted for using underhand methods to gain access glossary to people's personal data unless he/she has a **'public interest'** or other defence. Secondly, institutions—including police forces and schools—sometimes misunderstand data protection law when claiming that it stops them releasing information to the media. Thirdly, because journalists generate and store data about people—in research, news stories, recordings, pictures and footage—media organisations and freelance journalists must be lawful in how they process and publish data, to avoid paying damages for breaching privacy or being fined by the Information Commissioner.

Data protection law is complex, and is now turning into a new front in the constant battle between the media and those who would rather the public did not become aware of their activities, so proper legal advice is necessary if people claim that your news organisation is breaching their data protection rights.

28.1 Protection for stored data

The law recognises privacy rights relating to the vast amounts of information about each of us which is held in computer and manual records. It has been estimated that public and commercial institutions hold in total about 700 databases on each working adult. For personal data held on computer, these privacy rights were first provided in the Data Protection Act 1984. The Data Protection Act 1998 strengthened them and extended them to information about people contained in 'structured manual files'.

These rights are now being strengthened further with the European Union's adoption of the General Data Protection Regulation (GDPR), which was due to come into effect in the UK in May 2018. This will have effect after the UK's exit from the European Union through a new Data Protection Act, which was making its way through Parliament as the Data Protection Bill as this book was being prepared for publication. References to the law in this chapter are references to provisions in the Data Protection Bill. These might be changed before it becomes law, so look out for updates on www.mcnaes.com.

This law requires personal data to be kept securely. News stories have highlighted failures by public bodies or companies, such as when huge amounts of official or commercial data about individuals, including lists of clients or customers, their dates of birth, addresses and bank account details, have been found on unencrypted laptops or memory sticks left in pubs or taxis.

28.2 Data protection principles

A 'data controller' is the person who or organisation which determines why and how any personal data are processed. Data controllers include local authorities, health trusts, Government departments, commercial organisations, magistrates' courts and the police—in fact, any organisation or individual keeping personal data about people, including its own staff, in structured filing systems.

A 'data subject' is a person about whom the information is held.

Article 5 of the GDPR details six principles for legal handling of personal data. It must be:

   (a) processed lawfully, fairly and in a transparent manner;

   (b) collected for specified and legitimate purposes only, and not further processed in a manner incompatible with those purposes;

   (c) adequate, relevant and limited to what is necessary for those purposes;

   (d) accurate and, where necessary, kept up to date;

   (e) kept in a form which permits identification of data subjects for no longer than necessary for the purposes of the processing;

   (f) secure.

But personal data may be stored for longer periods if it is being processed solely for archiving purposes in the public interest, for scientific or historical research, or statistical purposes, as long as it is also covered by appropriate measures to safeguard individuals' rights and freedoms.

28.2.1 The rights of data subjects

The GDPR strengthens the rights of individuals to see the information held about them, and have it corrected, amended or even removed. Material processed and held for journalistic purposes is exempt from these rights. Journalists and news organisations holding information for journalistic purposes are not required to respond to questions about whether they hold data or what data they hold, and are not obliged to comply with requests to remove it. The best response to such questions is simply to refuse to respond to them.

28.2.2 Crimes of procuring, gaining or disclosing personal data

Clause 161 of the Data Protection Bill makes it an offence for anyone knowingly or recklessly, and without the consent of the data controller, to obtain or disclose personal data; procure the disclosure of personal data to another person; or retain unlawfully obtained personal data. A conviction is punishable by an unlimited fine. These provisions replicate those in section 55 the 1998 Act.

'Blagging' by a journalist to gain someone else's personal data—for example, phoning a bank and posing as someone else to get information about his or her account—would be an offence. A journalist and someone he or she pays to leak personal data from a data controller's records will be committing offences.

Clause 161 gives a defence if the person who obtained or disclosed the data can show that he or she acted in the reasonable belief that the data controller would have consented, or that they were acting legally.

It is also a defence to show that obtaining or disclosing the data was necessary for preventing or detecting crime—which might aid investigative journalists—or that in the particular circumstances it was justified as being in the public interest. The public interest is not defined.

Although data protection law has been in force for nearly three decades, most journalists know little about it, probably because threats of prosecution against journalists have been rare. But this is changing.

28.3 Increasing concern about data breaches

In 2006 the then Information Commissioner urged Parliament to make the offence of unlawfully obtaining personal data punishable by up to two years' imprisonment.

👁 **Case study**

The Information Commissioner reported in 2006 that a criminal investigation into one private detective's agency had revealed it had committed thousands of section 55 offences. The detective's records showed he had sold information to 305 named journalists working for a range of newspapers—supplying records of people's criminal convictions, car registration numbers, driving licence details, ex-directory phone numbers and mobile phone numbers, and more. The Commissioner said the targets included not only celebrities and public figures, but also people who had simply 'strayed by chance into the limelight'. He added that some disclosures of information might have been in the public interest, but noted that this defence was not raised by those working for the agency who were prosecuted (*What Price Privacy?* and *What Price Privacy now?*).

It should be remembered that no journalists were prosecuted in that investigation, and that journalists who dealt with this agency might in many cases have had a public interest justification for seeking such information, or accepting it when offered.

✳ Remember

The focus on how journalists gain information was intensified by the official inquiry into 'the culture, practices, and ethics of the press' by Lord Justice Leveson. Ch. 2 explains this, and that the Editors' Code bans accessing digitally held private information without consent unless there is a public interest justification.

28.4 When journalists' lawful inquiries are thwarted

When journalists ask for information organisations sometimes cite data protection to justify refusing to give it. But the Act covers personal data, not all data, and even personal data can be lawfully released in some circumstances—for example, if the 'data subject' agrees.

Data is only personal if it can lead to a living individual being identified.

28.4.1 Getting information from police

see Useful
Websites at
the end of
this chapter
for College
of Policing
guidelines

Police officers who claim the Act prevents them from releasing information may have misunderstood the law. People involved in road accidents and the victims of crime may ask police not to give the media their details. Guidelines issued by the College of Policing say these requests should be honoured unless police feel on a case-by-case basis that there is an exceptional reason why the details must be given, for example to help solve a crime.

The Act does not apply to dead people, so does not prevent police naming victims who have died once they are positively identified and immediate relatives notified.

28.4.2 Justifications for disclosure

Paragraphs 8 and 9 of Schedule 1 to the Data Protection Bill also allow the disclosure of personal data for the purposes of preventing or detecting unlawful acts, or protecting the public against dishonesty, malpractice, or other improper conduct, as well as incompetence, mismanagement and failures in services provided by a body or association. Official agencies may need to be reminded of this.

28.4.3 Getting information from courts

Journalists sometimes have difficulty obtaining information from courts.

Guidance for court staff from Her Majesty's Courts and Tribunals Service says: 'The Data Protection Act must not be used as a blanket excuse for withholding information.' It also makes clear that reporters may be given a defendant's address even if it has not been read out in court. See also 15.2, What information and help must criminal courts provide?

28.4.4 Getting information from schools

Department of Education guidance says schools and local authorities can set their own policies about when photos can be taken, and on releasing associated information for publicity, but that it will require the consent of pupils' parents or legal guardians.

Guidance from the Information Commissioner's Office (ICO) on photographs being taken by a local newspaper of a school awards ceremony says it will not breach data protection law 'As long as the school has agreed to this, and the children and/or their guardians are aware that photographs of those attending the ceremony may appear in the newspaper'.

((•)) See Useful Websites at the end of this chapter for the ICO guidance.

The ICO's guidance also says schools do not breach the Act by releasing exam results to the local media, and that in general, as a school has a legitimate interest in publishing results, pupils or parents or guardians do not need to consent.

28.5 Media and journalists as 'data controllers'

Media organisations and freelance journalists are data controllers, as they decide how they will use—for example, whether to publish—the personal data that they hold about individuals. The ICO keeps a public register of data controllers. The registration requirement mainly affects media managements, but freelances should also register. The Act puts virtually all responsibility for data protection on the data controller.

Because personal data must be kept securely, journalists should ensure that computerised contact lists—including those kept on memory sticks—are always encrypted.

28.5.1 Lawsuits

If someone sues a media organisation for an alleged intrusion into privacy, because of what was published or what else journalists did, the lawsuit may include an element claiming breach of data protection law. A media organisation which breaches someone's privacy is also likely, in the processing of information gained, to have breached their data protection rights. But cases show that the courts will examine the total effect on the **claimant**, and not differentiate between the wrong caused by the breach of privacy and the wrong caused by breach of data law.

 glossary

28.5.2 Special category personal data

for 'right to be forgotten' lawsuits, see Late News

Article 9 of the GDPR provides particular privacy protection for what it now calls 'special categories of personal data'—and bans processing of the information except in particular circumstances.

Special category personal data covers information about a person's:

- racial or ethnic origin;
- political opinions;
- religious or philosophical beliefs;
- trade union membership;
- physical and mental health;
- sexual orientation;
- sex life.

Article 10 of the GDPR requires that processing of personal data relating to criminal convictions must be carried out only under the control of official authority or when the proceedings are authorised by law which provides proper safeguards for data subjects.

The judge in the *Naomi Campbell* case (see 27.1, Development of the law) ruled that the information published by a newspaper about the nature and details of the therapy she was seeking was 'sensitive personal data' in respect of her physical or mental health.

The provisions of both Articles 9 and 10 are subject to exemptions, including the exemptions for journalistic purposes detailed in Schedule 2 to the Data Protection Bill, which are similar to the exemptions in earlier law.

 For detail of how exemptions in the law protect media activity which is in the public interest, and whether a 'subject access request' could threaten a journalist's protection of the identity of a confidential source, see the Additional Material for ch. 28 on www.mcnaes.com. The ICO has also published guidance for the media on data protection law—see Useful Websites at the end of this chapter, and the Additional Material for ch. 28 on www.mcnaes.com.

Journalists who comply with the relevant code of media ethics—see chs. 2, 3 and 4—have greater protection against being prosecuted or successfully sued for breach of this law.

➡ Recap of major points

- Journalists seeking information should realise that it is a criminal offence to procure the disclosure of personal data, unless there is a legal defence.

- Sometimes data law is mistakenly used as a reason to deny journalists information.

- The law has exemptions protecting journalism which is in the public interest.

((•)) Useful Websites

https://ico.gov.uk/
Information Commissioner's website

https://ico.org.uk/media/for-organisations/documents/1552/data-protection-and-journalism-media-guidance.pdf
The Information Commissioner's Office guide to data protection for the media

https://ico.org.uk/media/for-organisations/documents/1547/data-protection-and-journalism-quick-guide.pdf
The Information Commissioner's Office quick guide to data protection and journalism

www.app.college.police.uk/app-content/engagement-and-communication/media-relations/
College of Policing 2017 guidelines on relations with the media

https://ico.org.uk/media/for-organisations/documents/1136/taking_photos.pdf
Information Commissioner's guidance for schools about photos

https://ico.gov.uk/for_the_public/topic_specific_guides/schools/exam_results.aspx
Information Commissioner's guidance for schools about exam results

29

Copyright

Chapter summary

Copyright is a property right controlling who can copy work created by artistic and other intellectual endeavour. Copyright protects journalism articles, website content, books, photographs, films, sound recordings and music, TV and radio broadcasts. This chapter explains how copyright law, by deterring and punishing plagiarism, protects the ability of journalists and media employers to earn profit from their output. Copyright lasts for decades. Copyright also protects work created by others which journalists may wish to copy—for example, by quoting from or showing it.

29.1 What material does copyright protect?

The source of most UK law on copyright is the Copyright, Designs and Patents Act 1988, as amended by subsequent law.

Section 1 says copyright subsists in:

- 'original literary, dramatic, musical or artistic works'—which includes: all kinds of text whether handwritten, printed or online, such as journalistic and scientific articles, poems, lyrics, books, plays, scripts, shorthand or longhand records of speeches and interviews; musical manuscripts; photographs; design documents, templates; graphic works, maps, plans, sketches, paintings, sculptures; databases and computer programs;
- 'sound recordings, films or broadcasts', including journalism in these media, files and CDs of music, home and cinema movies, TV and radio output, and some types of internet transmissions;
- 'the typographical arrangement of published editions'—for example, how text and photos are 'laid out' in page design.

The copyright owner has the legal right to decide who can copy such works, and to what extent, and who can 'communicate' them to the public. Unauthorised copying of all or 'any substantial part' of any work in these categories is a criminal offence and a civil **tort** unless justified by a defence or exception. More than one type of copyright, with different owners, may co-exist in a product—for example, a documentary film will have copyrights in the script, footage and music, and in a website there will be copyrights in, for example, its text and any hosted videos. → glossary

29.2 Who owns copyright under the 1988 Act?

- The 'first owner' of copyright in a literary, dramatic, musical or artistic work is the author as creator. This definition includes the journalist as an article's writer, the photographer as creator of a photo, the artist who makes a painting or sculpture, etc. If authorship is joint, each author is a 'first owner' and permission is needed from each to copy the work.

The 'first owner' has the copyright unless he/she agrees—for example, for payment—to assign to another party the right to control who makes copies.

- The Act says an employer owns the copyright in a literary, dramatic, musical or artistic work—including a journalistic article or photo—created by an employee in the course of his/her employment. This is usually stated in the employment contract.
- A staff journalist only has the copyright in an article or photo if the employer specifically agrees to this, for example, in the contract of employment (1988 Act, section 11).
- Self-employed journalists, including freelance and commercial photographers, are the 'first owners' of copyright in their works.

see Assignment and Licensing, 29.8

The terms, including payment, under which freelances assign copyright or licence use of their work to media publishers, so they can legally publish it, may be specific to each deal, or governed by custom and practice.

- The 'first owner' of copyright in a sound recording is the producer, defined in the Act as the person/organisation who undertook 'the arrangements necessary' for creating the work.
- The 'first owners' of copyright in a film made on or after 1 July 1994, whether made for journalism or entertainment, are jointly the producer and principal director. The producer owns the copyright in films made earlier which are covered by the Act.
- The 'first owner' of copyright in a broadcast is the person or organisation 'making the broadcast'—that is, transmitting it, if responsible for content, or providing that content and arranging transmission. This is usually a broadcast company.
- The 'first owner' of copyright in 'the typographical arrangement of a published edition' is the publisher.

- The 'first owner' of copyright in 'computer-generated work', a category which the Act limits to circumstances of 'no human author', is the person or organisation undertaking 'the arrangements necessary' for the work's creation.

29.3 Copying from the internet, including social networking sites

The fact that material, including any photo, can be seen by all on the internet—for example, via Google Images—does not mean that anyone has the right to copy and re-publish it. Publishing material such as a photo or footage or an extract of 'original' text copied from the internet infringes any copyright in the work, unless the copyright owner consents, or a defence or exception applies. Downloading may itself be an infringement.

see also
29.18, 'Open content' licences

- Publishing photos copied from a social networking site—such as Facebook, Instagram, Flickr, Twitter or Tumblr—may infringe the copyright in the site and/or the copyright held by the person who created ('took') the photo, who might not even be aware that someone else has uploaded a copy onto the site.

◉ Case study

In 2016 Toby Granville, a senior editorial executive of the Newsquest/Gannett regional newspaper group, sent a memo to editors at its 215 UK titles warning that the copyright claims against the group had grown 'exponentially', causing 'real cost' in each region. The memo said photos found using Google or elsewhere on the internet should not be published without considering if this was lawful (Roy Greenslade, *The Guardian,* 27 July 2016).

> See also the case study, in the Additional Material for ch. 29 on www.mcnaes.com, about photographer Jason Sheldon suing a dance venue for breach of copyright after it used one of his photos of a popstar, which it found on the internet, in its posters.

If research discovers material—text, footage or photo—on someone's personal social media pages, a media organisation also may need to consider whether, apart from copyright law, ethical considerations mean it should not be used in news coverage—see 4.17, Material from social media sites.

29.4 Photos of TV images and photos shown on TV

Publishing a photo—for example, a 'screengrab'—of a television or film image without permission can infringe copyright under section 17 of the 1988 Act. Showing a photo on a TV programme without the copyright owner's permission is also an infringement, unless a defence applies.

29.5 Commissioner's copyright in older photos

Section 4 of the Copyright Act 1956 governs who owns copyright in literary, dramatic and artistic work, including photos, created before 1 August 1989—that is, before the 1988 Act came into force.

As explained earlier, the default position under the 1988 Act for work created by a freelance is that he/she owns the copyright. But the position for freelance work created before 1 August 1989—that is, under the terms of the 1956 Act—is different if it was a commissioned photo, or commissioned painted or drawn portrait, because the 1956 Act says that, in the absence of any other agreement, the copyright is owned by the commissioner—for example, a newspaper or magazine which hired a freelance to take that photo. A commission is an agreement that the work will be created in return for payment.

This difference between the two Acts decides who, as copyright owner, can successfully object to the use of an archived photo or demand payment for its use. In summary, the default positions in law are:

- Copyright in a commissioned photograph taken before 1 August 1989 is owned by the commissioner, even though the freelance or commercial photographer who took the photo may own the negatives or have digital copies. For example, a family wedding photo taken by a commercial photographer before 1 August 1989 will almost certainly have been commissioned by someone in the family, who will therefore probably own the copyright.
- The photographer or his/her employer owns the copyright in a photo taken before 1 August 1989 which was not commissioned. Copyright in a photograph taken on or after 1 August 1989 is owned by the photographer's employer, or by the photographer if he/she is self-employed. This position is not changed by the mere fact that there was a commission for it to be taken, but can be changed if the commissioner insists as part of the deal that the copyright is assigned to him/her.

A celebrity who commissions a photographer to take pictures of a family occasion may well insist on the copyright being assigned to him/her, to control their use.

29.6 'Private and domestic' photographs and films

Section 85 of the 1988 Act gives a 'moral right', in essence a privacy right, to people who commission photographs or films for 'private and domestic purposes'.

- The right is that no copies of a photo or film commissioned for private and domestic purposes should be published, issued to or exhibited to the public without the commissioner's agreement.
- Commissioners have this right even if they do not own the copyright of that work, and the moral right means they can sue and recover damages from

see 29.13, Defences to alleged infringement of copyright

ch. 27 explains general privacy rights

see 29.12,
Legal
remedies for
infringe-
ment of
copyright

anyone who publishes such a photo or film—for example, one that records a
family occasion—without their permission.

- A publisher who uses the photo or film in breach of copyright could also be
  sued by whoever owns the copyright—for example, by the photographer.

Consider this hypothetical case: a woman is hurt in a train crash. A journalist
traces a relative, who emails the journalist a copy of a picture of the woman, taken
some years previously at her wedding. If the relative took the picture himself/
herself and agrees to its publication, there is no infringement of copyright. If the
wedding picture was taken by a commercial photographer commissioned by the
bridegroom (that is, the injured woman's husband), the photographer will probably own the copyright and may be glad to accept a fee for media publication of
the picture. But the husband may not want it published. He may sue for breach of
his moral right and win, even if he is not in the photo.

This 'moral right' can be waived. But otherwise it lasts as long as the copyright—see later in this chapter.

 For detail of other 'moral rights', held by authors/creators, see the Additional Material for ch. 29 on
www.mcnaes.com.

When a big story breaks about someone, the media tend to rush to get copies of
photos of the person from relatives or friends, or family-held footage, or may copy
photos from social media, and adopt a 'publish first, worry later' approach. Many
people do not know about copyright, or the moral right arising from the commis-
sioning of a photo or film for private and domestic purposes. But some do, and if
they own either right, and did not consent to the publication, they may demand
payment or damages and/or that the photo or footage is no longer published.

👁 Case study

A judge ruled in 2012 that photos created by a photographer as a present
for his friend Carina Trimingham, who appeared in them, were not 'commissioned' because he was not obliged by any financial deal to create them and
so she had no moral right to control their use. The *Daily Mail* and *The Mail on
Sunday* published copies of them. She was in the news because of her affair
with a married Cabinet Minister. See the Additional Material for ch. 29 on www.
mcnaes.com for more detail on this case.

29.7 The scope of copyright protection

Copyright is automatically in force as soon as a work is created in any permanent
form. In the UK, copyright does not have to be registered. Copyright protects
an 'original literary, dramatic, musical or artistic work', as described earlier.

'Literary' in this context includes any work, written or spoken, which exists in some permanent form—it has no reference to a work's literary or artistic merits.

29.7.1 What is 'original'?

The legal definition of 'original' has for some decades in UK law simply required that the work was originated by the creator(s) using some element of 'skill, labour and judgment' (see, for example, *Express Newspapers plc v News (UK) Ltd* [1990] 3 All ER 376).

The elements of skill, labour, judgement, time or expense have not needed to be great. So the 'originality' threshold is low. Judges cite the rough guideline that 'anything worth copying is usually worth protecting'.

- Skill, labour and judgement spent in creating a bus or rail timetable, or tide table or a database, mean that such works have been protected by copyright, vested in the 'first owner' as creator or, if employed, his/her employer.
- Copyright could also subsist in even a fairly basic form of map, diagram, drawing or sketch, so journalists should also beware of reproducing these without permission.

But a commonplace expression such as 'love is blind'—for example, if used in a book title—will not be protected by copyright because of lack of originality.

29.7.2 Signal rights

Copyrights in what the Act terms 'films' (which is the 'first fixation of films') and in broadcasts are 'signal rights' which a judge has described as 'entrepreneurial rights which protect the investment' of the producer and broadcaster respectively (*England and Wales Cricket Board Ltd and Sky UK Ltd v Tixdaq Ltd and Fanatix Ltd* [2016] EWHC 575 (Ch)). Copyright in a sound recording is also a 'signal right'. The 'signal right' means such works—which include raw footage, unedited audio and 'live transmissions'—are not required to be 'original', in the sense of being intellectual creations, to be protected by copyright. This meant in the case cited there was no need for the judge to rule on whether the creative input of the director and others in that broadcast, sports coverage—for example, selection of camera angles, use of 'close ups' and slow motion—should be categorised under the 1988 Act as 'original, dramatic work', although it could be (and such input into TV dramas and cinema films would be). The word content of a script or 'live' commentary in broadcasts and films is protected by its own copyright as 'literary work', if it passes the low 'originality' threshold.

 See 29.13.1.2 and the Additional Material for ch. 29 on www.mcnaes.com for more details of the *England and Wales Cricket Board* case. See the Additional Material for copyright which exists in TV and radio programme listings; and for the 2012 ruling by the European Court of Justice that copyright did not exist in lists of Premier League football fixtures.

29.7.3 No copyright in news or in unrecorded ideas

Copyright does not protect ideas—it controls the right to copy the form or manner in which ideas are expressed or executed. The law of breach of confidence, explained in ch. 26, would apply in some circumstances if a considered 'idea' with commercial value were exploited in breach of 'confidential' discussions about it.

* There is also no copyright in facts, news or information. Copyright exists in the form—for example, sentences, a photo, footage—in which these things are expressed, and in the selection and arrangement of the material for publication.

29.7.4 'Lifting' stories

the defamation danger in lifting stories is explained in 21.2.3.3

News organisations often include in their stories facts—such as political initiatives or a famous person's death—which are 'broken' by rivals. This is known as 'lifting' a story. There is no copyright infringement in reporting in a *re-written* version the facts uncovered or published by others (*Springfield v Thame* (1903) 89 LT 242). But there may be infringements in 'lifting' verbatim phrases and quotes from the original report, depending on the extent—see 29.13.1, What is 'substantial'?, and 29.9, Copyright in speeches and interviews.

👁 Case study

High Court judge Sir Nicolas Browne-Wilkinson said in 1990: 'For myself, I would hesitate a long time before deciding that there is copyright in a news story which would be infringed by another newspaper picking up that story and reproducing the same story in different words.' He said that ruling against such 'picking up', when the re-writing was not verbatim, would not be in the public interest. He also observed that, as the practice among UK national newspapers of copying quotes from each other was so widespread and rarely led to copyright disputes, it could be argued that the newspapers gave each other implied licence for the practice by 'acquiescence' (*Express Newspapers plc v News (UK) Ltd* [1990] 3 All ER 376).

see 29.16, Acquiescence

Changing the odd word or two when writing a news report by 'lifting' facts from a rival report will not be enough to avoid copyright infringement. But the 1988 Act's defence of **'fair dealing'** for reporting current events can allow a media organisation to copy some quotes and other sentences from a rival's report, and to broadcast short extracts of footage or audio already broadcast by a rival—see later in this chapter.

→ glossary

29.8 Assignment and licensing

Copyright owners can 'assign' copyright, wholly or in part, to another person or organisation, either temporarily or for the copyright's duration. This transfers, to that other party, control over who can copy the work and to what extent. Or the owner can 'licence' another party to exploit the work in a particular deal or territory. An owner who licences retains the copyright and so the overall control of copying.

Section 90 of the 1988 Act says an assignment of copyright is not effective unless it is in writing and is signed by or on behalf of the person assigning it—for example, the 'first owner'.

A licence need not be in writing. In journalism, licences are often agreed verbally, or implied by what has become custom and practice. For example, freelance journalists who regularly send articles or photos to newspapers know their fee rates, and whether they also want the right to use the work in magazine supplements and on websites, or possibly in overseas editions and for syndication.

((•))
see Useful
Websites at
the end of
this chapter
for NUJ
freelance
guide

The licence could be for the work to be published on only one occasion. Any doubts on either side about licence terms should be discussed then agreed in writing before the work is published.

29.8.1 Readers' letters for publication

- A reader sending a letter for publication has by implication licensed the media organisation to publish it once, but retains the copyright.

If the organisation subsequently wants to publish a compilation of readers' letters as a book, it will need to contact each letter-writer to seek a licence to re-publish the letters.

29.9 Copyright in speeches and interviews, and in notes or recordings of them

Copyright exists in spoken words such as public speech as soon as the speaker's words are recorded in some form, with or without permission. The copyright arises even if the speech is not delivered from a script, but is, for example, uttered in an improvised comedy show or in an interview with a journalist. The speaker, as the author of a 'literary work'—that is, his/her words as recorded—owns the copyright in that work, unless he/she is speaking in the course of his/her employment, in which case the employer owns the copyright, or is reciting words in which someone else holds copyright (for example, from a play script).

As copyright protects the 'original' product of 'skill, labour and judgment', there is no copyright in casual conversational or trite remarks, in short jokes already in circulation, or in commonplace or ill-judged sayings.

Section 58 of the 1988 Act—a specific defence for journalism—says it is not infringement of copyright to use a record of all or part of a speaker's words for reporting current events, as long as:

(1) the record of the words—that is, as recorded on tape or digitally, or in shorthand or longhand—is a direct record of their utterance and is not

taken from a previous record or broadcast (as taking the record from such sources could infringe the copyright in those sources);

(2) the speaker did not forbid any note or recording being made of his/her words and making the record of them did not infringe any pre-existing copyright (it might, if the speaker were quoting someone else's words);

(3) the use made of the record of the words, or extracts from it, is not of a kind prohibited by the speaker (or anyone else who owns copyright in words used by the speaker) before the record was made;

(4) the record is used with the authority of the person who is lawfully in possession of it—who would usually be the journalist who took notes or made a recording of the speaker's words, or his/her employer.

A journalist should not be overly concerned about infringing a speaker's copyright when reporting verbatim a speech from a note or recording made of a speech or an interview, as usually a speaker who knows he/she is a journalist has consented to publication, expressly or by implication. Even if a speaker withholds consent, one or more of the fair dealing defences can apply as regards some quotation—see later in this chapter.

The first and fourth conditions listed earlier reflect the fact that, apart from the speaker's copyright in the recorded words, a separate copyright exists in the actual record—the audio-recording, shorthand or longhand note—because of the skill, labour and judgement involved in making it (*Walter v Lane* [1900] AC 539). The journalist who made the record will, if a freelance, be 'first owner' of that copyright. If the record was made in the course of his/her employment, the employer owns it.

29.10 Copying to report Parliament and the courts

Section 45 of the 1988 Act says copyright is not infringed by anything done for the purposes of reporting parliamentary and judicial proceedings. Section 45 means there is no copyright infringement in reporting proceedings of the UK and Scottish Parliaments, the Northern Ireland and Welsh Assemblies, or in reporting the proceedings of courts or—see ch. 18—of tribunals (and a broad definition in the 1988 Act means section 45 covers reports of proceedings of any official tribunal not classed as a court).

! Remember your rights

Section 45 means that the media does not infringe copyright if, when it covers court cases, it publishes copies of documents, photographs or footage supplied by the prosecution under the 2005 protocol—see 15.13.3, The 'Publicity and Criminal Justice System' protocol, or with the court's permission for publication, see 15.13.2 on a relevant 'practice direction'. See the Additional Material for ch. 29 on www.mcnaes.com for a section 45 case study.

29.11 How long does copyright last?

Durations of copyright, set out in sections 12–15 of the 1988 Act, can be summarised as follows.

- Copyright in a literary, dramatic, musical or artistic work—including a journalism article or a photo—lasts for the author's (that is, creator's) lifetime, then a further 70 years from the end of the calendar year in which he/she dies. The copyright can be bequeathed to the creator's heirs. The duration is the same even if the copyright is owned by an employer or has been assigned to a company.
- Copyright in a work of computer-generated music or graphics lasts for 50 years from the end of the year in which it was made.
- Copyright in a sound recording published or communicated to the public lasts 70 years from the end of the year in which that first happened.
- Copyright in a broadcast lasts 50 years from the end of the year in which it was made.

There are different (but still lengthy) periods of copyright for various other works, such as films, works of unknown authorship and for some particular circumstances.

 See the Additional Material for ch. 29 on www.mcnaes.com about copyright in 'orphan works'—that is, copied when the owner of the copyright could not be traced to gain permission.

29.11.1 Crown copyright

Work produced by civil servants in the course of their employment is protected by Crown copyright, which can last up to 125 years.

29.12 Legal remedies for infringement of copyright

29.12.1 Civil law

- A copyright holder who discovers that someone plans to infringe that right can get a High Court or county court **injunction** to stop it.   →glossary
- If the infringement has happened, an injunction can ban any repetition. The copyright owner can also sue the infringer for damages or for 'an account of profits', to claim any profit made from the infringement.
- The court can also order all infringing copies of the work to be handed to the copyright owner or destroyed.

The damages awarded by a court may reflect its view that there has been a flagrant breach of copyright.

29.12.2 Criminal law

Infringing copyright is also a criminal offence. Prosecutions tend to be confined to cases of large-scale piracy. In 2014 a Walsall man who helped make more than 700,000 pirate copies of the Hollywood film *The Fast and the Furious* was jailed for 33 months (Press Association, 3 September 2014).

29.13 Defences to alleged infringement of copyright

A question regularly asked by journalists is: 'How much can we copy or quote without infringing copyright?' One consideration is whether the copyright owner, in the case of copied text or quotes, will think it worth the effort to sue—but copyright can reside in a single sentence.

29.13.1 What is 'substantial'?

Section 16 of the 1988 Act says it is an infringement of copyright to copy the whole or 'any substantial part' of a work. In a copyright lawsuit concerning 'original literary, dramatic, musical or artistic works', the issue of what is a 'substantial' part may be decided on 'the quality of the originality' in what was copied, including the importance of the copied material in relation to the rest of the original work, rather than merely to how much was copied (*Newspaper Licensing Agency Ltd v Meltwater Holding BV* [2010] EWHC 3009 (Ch)).

For example, a face may be a small part of a photograph but is probably more important, as regards its commercial value, than the rest of the picture. A court dealing with disputed copying of a 'literary work' would consider, when deciding if the copying was of a 'substantial' part, to what degree unauthorised verbatim publication—which might be of the most interesting or sensational part, but only of a few sentences—might devalue the commercial value in the whole work's copyright.

29.13.1.1 'Literary' works

In the *Meltwater* case High Court judge Mrs Justice Proudman drew on the 2009 judgment in which the European Court of Justice (ECJ) ruled that a single extract of 11 consecutive words from a newspaper article could be protected by copyright as being a 'substantial' part if that work had sufficient originality (Case C-5/08 *Infopaq International A/S v Danske Dagblades Forening* [2010] FSR 495). Mrs Justice Proudman said: 'The ECJ makes it clear that originality rather than substantiality is the test to be applied to the part extracted. As a matter of principle this is the only real test.'

 See the Additional Material for ch. 29 on www.mcnaes.com for the *Meltwater* judgment. It upheld copyright protection for headlines and short text extracts electronically 'scraped' from newspapers' websites by a company monitoring various news subjects for its subscribers.

29.13.1.2 Broadcasts, sound recordings, films—and paraphrasing text

As explained earlier, the 1988 Act does not require films, broadcasts or sound recordings to be 'original' to be protected by copyright. In 2016 a judge ruled that an eight-second 'clip' of footage of a key moment in a cricket match was a 'substantial part' of TV coverage of the match that day (*England and Wales Cricket Board*, cited earlier).

The issue of what is a 'substantial part' is not always relevant for the news media when it wants to report factual revelations from a literary work (e.g. a document), as its contents can be paraphrased or summarised in news coverage to avoid quoting verbatim, which means it will not have been copied. And if the copying of any work by a news media organisation, for its news output, might be ruled to be of a 'substantial' part, its editor can—unless the work is a still photo, see later—aim to rely on a fair dealing defence, because then the issue of how much can legally be copied must be assessed in terms of 'fairness', which gives more leeway for copying to be legal than the substantiality criterion does.

29.14 Fair dealing defences

The four 'fair dealing' defences in section 30 of the 1988 Act recognise the public interest in news coverage and some other types of publication being free of some copyright restraints.

29.14.1 Defence of fair dealing for the purpose of reporting current events

- Section 30 of the Act allows publication of work protected by copyright 'for the purpose of reporting current events', even if there is no consent from the copyright owner.
- But there must be 'fair dealing' by those publishing it for this purpose and an accompanying 'sufficient acknowledgement' of the work copied.
- 'Fair dealing' means fair practice—for example, the publisher should not take unfair commercial advantage of the copyright owner by excessive publication of the copied work.
- 'Sufficient acknowledgement' means that a report, in a newspaper, magazine, website or other textual medium, must:
  - cite the work's title, or include some identifying description of it; and
  - name its author/creator, unless it was published anonymously (section 178).
- Photographs are specifically excluded from the fair dealing defence of 'reporting current events', because otherwise no news photographers could earn their living by selling their pictures.

Case law suggests that a court will be less likely to uphold the fair dealing defence if the work copied has been 'leaked' to the media organisation. But the defence will probably not be undermined if the leak—for example, of an internal company memo—reveals wrongdoing or a threat to public safety. In such a case, the defence may protect verbatim publication of an entire document. But if the copyright in a text or document has a legitimate commercial value, judges will expect the media to make only limited use of verbatim extracts, so that the copyright owner's ability to exploit that value is not compromised unfairly. See, for example, the *Ashdown* case discussed in the Additional Material for ch. 29 on www.mcnaes. com in which the Court of Appeal ruled that *Sunday Telegraph*, by quoting verbatim or nearly verbatim some 20 per cent of a nine-page document, was unfair in that case's circumstances and that 'one or two short extracts from it would have sufficed' to satisfy readers than the reporting was authoritative.

In *Ashdown* the judgment suggested that the term 'current events' could cover events which occurred two years before the disputed copying—or possibly, in some circumstances, events from 30 years ago—if the copied work helped them be re-examined in new revelations in media coverage.

Although the fair dealing defence does not cover still photographs, it does cover media use—that is, if 'fair'—of copied film footage and sound recordings, including in digital forms.

👁 Case study

In 1991 the High Court dismissed a copyright action by the BBC against British Satellite Broadcasting (BSB) over the use in the satellite company's sports news programming of highlights from BBC coverage of the World Cup football finals, to which the Corporation had bought exclusive rights. The court said BSB's use of short clips showing goals scored, 14–37 seconds in length and up to four times in 24 hours, with a BBC credit line included as acknowledgement, was protected by the defence of fair dealing for reporting current events (*BBC v British Satellite Broadcasting* [1991] 3 All ER 833 (Ch D)).

After this 1991 case, major UK broadcast organisations reached a formal agreement permitting limited copying in news content of each other's sports footage.

The Act says sound recording, film or broadcast reports of current events do not need to acknowledge the copied work's title, or other description of it, or the identity of its author/creator 'where this would be impossible for reasons of practicality or otherwise'. This reflects the difficulty of including all such detail in a broadcast of a short piece of copied footage or audio. But acknowledgements—for example, by announcement or by showing in copied footage the logo of the channel from which it was copied—help prove fairness, and such use of a logo is 'sufficient acknowledgement'.

29.14.2 Defence of fair dealing for the purpose of criticism or review

Section 30 of the Act allows publication of copies of a work, even without the copyright owner's consent, 'for the purpose of criticism or review'.

- But the work must already have been 'made available to the public' *with* the copyright owner's consent—for example, published or exhibited. The defence does not protect use of leaked or stolen material.

- There must also be 'fair dealing' by those publishing it for criticism or review and an accompanying 'sufficient acknowledgement' of the work.

The 'fair dealing' and 'sufficient acknowledgement' requirements are in essence the same as those required for the defence of fair dealing in reporting current events.

Authors or creators who have released works to the public may well be happy for extracts from them to appear in criticisms or reviews, as they will receive wider publicity. But the defence applies irrespective of whether they object. Case law is that the defence can protect the showing in a TV programme of several photos for the purpose of a critique or review of the 'ideas or philosophy' manifest in the copied work, not just assessment of the work's quality as literature or art.

The requirement of fairness means that in a dispute about the extent of the use of copied material a court would consider if the media organisation genuinely sought to critique the copied work(s) or had the baser motive of taking commercial advantage.

 Case studies of media organisations relying on these fair dealing defences are in the Additional Material for ch. 29 on www.mcnaes.com. It outlines too the *English and Welsh Cricket Board* case, in which the judge made clear that the fair dealing defence for reporting current events can cover the work of 'citizen journalists'.

29.14.3 Defence of fair dealing for use of quotation

In 2014 section 30 of the 1988 Act was amended to create a general defence for use of quotation. The requirements, all of which must be met, are that the work being quoted has been made available for the public (it is not—for example—a leaked or stolen document/recording), that the use is 'fair dealing' (see earlier), that the extent of the quotation is no more than is required 'by the specific purpose for which it is used' and that the quotation is accompanied by 'sufficient acknowledge-ment' (see earlier), 'unless this would be impossible for reasons of practicality or otherwise'. The 'quotation' could be by use of part of a recording otherwise pro-tected by copyright (see Schedule 2 to the Act).

This new defence can protect quotation in journalism of short extracts when this is not covered by the other fair dealing defences—because it is not to report 'cur-rent events' or to review. It also protects, for example, theatres and record com-panies when they use in promotional material quotes from newspaper reviews.

The Intellectual Property Office (IPO) guidance is that the quotation defence can cover copying of a photograph but only in 'exceptional' circumstances.

((•))
see Useful Websites at the end of this chapter for IPO guidance

29.14.4 Defence of fair dealing for the purpose of caricature, parody or pastiche

The amendment in 2014 to section 30 also created a defence of copying for the purposes of caricature, parody and pastiche. Again, the copying must be limited so that it does not take 'unfair' commercial advantage of the copyright owner by excessive publication of the copied work.

29.15 **Public interest defence**

The public interest defence in copyright **case law** is narrow, reflecting the fact that the 'fair dealing' defences have an inherent, public interest element and permit some copying, and that more extensive copying of verbatim text, a sound recording or footage may not be needed to report what its content is. But whereas the defence of fair dealing for the purpose of reporting current events cannot protect the unauthorised copying (publication) of a still photo, the 'public interest' defence can protect publication of any copyrighted work, including a still photo, if the purpose is to expose it as an immoral work, or one damaging to public life, health, safety or the administration of justice, or as a work which incites immoral behaviour, and in some other circumstances—for example, if police ask the media to publish a photo (for which the police do not own the copyright) of a person whom they wish to trace.

👁 Case study

In 2010 the *Reading Post* succeeded with the public interest defence in the small claims court after being sued by the owner of copyright in several photos which it had copied from a website. Police had directed the *Post* to the site, which showed the apparent exploits of 'urban explorers' inside abandoned buildings. The *Post* said it published the pictures to highlight police concerns that these activities involved criminal damage, including graffiti, and to help identify those involved. The judge said he felt the pictures were posted on the website to encourage the activities, which could cause an accident, and the public to suffer, and were a serious social problem (*Newspaper Society website*, 28 January 2010).

 For other examples of journalistic use of the 'public interest' defence, and for detail of the 'incidental infringement' and 'innocent infringement' defences, see the Additional Material for ch. 29 on www.mcnaes.com.

29.16 **Acquiescence**

A copyright owner who does not complain for an extended period of time after becoming aware that a person or organisation has copied the work may be deemed by a judge to have implicitly agreed—acquiesced—to the copying.

29.17 **Do hyperlinks breach the copyright in the material linked to?**

European Court of Justice rulings are that a website which uses a hyperlink, including by 'framing', to direct a reader or viewer to another website does not infringe copyright in the material displayed there if it can be seen there by any internet user and has been displayed there by or with the consent of the owner of the copyright in that material or otherwise lawfully. But in other circumstances hyperlinking can be ruled to breach copyright. For more detail on this complex law, see the Additional Material for ch. 29 on www.mcnaes.com.

29.18 'Open content' licences

Some creators—including some who post photographs on social media sites such as Flickr—give a general, 'open content' licence for people to copy and distribute their work free of charge, provided that attribution to the creator is included and specified conditions are honoured. The licence may be in the Creative Commons format. One condition may be that the use of the work is not commercial, which would exclude use in journalism for which consumers pay. A different licence would have to be agreed with the copyright owner to permit such journalistic use, unless a defence applied.

see Useful Websites at the end of this chapter for Creative Commons site

 For detail on 'moral rights' held by authors/creators, including to be identified as such when their work is published, and for an outline of the law on 'passing off' and trademarks, see the Additional Material for ch. 29 on www.mcnaes.com.

➡ Recap of major points

- Copyright law controls who can commercially exploit literary, musical, dramatic and artistic works, including journalism articles and photos, as well as the exploitation of sound recordings, film, broadcasts and typographical arrangements.

- There is no copyright in news in itself, only in the form in which it is expressed.

- Defences of fair dealing are available for publication of copyrighted work if the copying is not excessive and if the publisher honours requirement for attribution to the creator(s).

- But photographs are excluded from the fair dealing defence which covers reporting news and current events.

- A copyright owner whose rights are infringed can seek an injunction and/or damages.

((•)) Useful Websites

www.gov.uk/government/organisations/intellectual-property-office
Intellectual Property Office, a Government agency—see its guides to copyright and trade marks

www.gov.uk/government/uploads/system/uploads/attachment_data/file/448269/Exceptions_ to_copyright_-_An_Overview.pdf
Intellectual Property Office guide, *Exceptions to Copyright*

www.londonfreelance.org/advice.html
London freelance branch of the National Union of Journalists—advice on copyright

www.gov.uk/courts-tribunals/intellectual-property-enterprise-court
Intellectual Property Enterprise Court

www.epuk.org/resources/faq
Copyright advice provided by Editorial Photographers group.

http://creativecommons.org/licenses/
Guide to Creative Commons copyright licences

www.gov.uk/topic/intellectual-property/copyright

Part 5

Information and expression

The Freedom of Information Act 2000

Chapter summary

The Freedom of Information (FoI) Act 2000, which came into effect in 2005, created the UK's first general right of access to information held by Government departments and public authorities. Use of this right has produced many exclusive stories, some about the highest reaches of Government. But FoI is bedevilled by bureaucratic delay and wide-ranging exemptions. This chapter deals with FoI law as it applies in England, Wales and Northern Ireland, and information access rights in the Environmental Information Regulations 2004. There is a more detailed version of this chapter onwww.mcnaes.com.

30.1 Introduction to the Act

The Act gives people the right to require 'public authorities' to disclose information they might not otherwise publish, without charging for finding and collating it, subject to cost limits.

The parliamentary expenses scandal in spring 2009 highlighted the Act's shortcomings. FoI requests by campaigner and journalist Heather Brooke forced House of Commons officials to disclose some details of what some MPs were claiming in expenses for their second homes.

see 30.4.2,
Cost limits

But the official disclosures were anodyne in comparison with the truth, which emerged when full details were leaked to the Telegraph Media Group—and showed that MPs 'flipped' their main and second homes to maximise expenses, claimed for items such as moat-clearing and duck houses, did not have to produce receipts and had claimed for things ranging from dog biscuits to bath plugs.

30.1.1 Difficulties with FoI obligations

The Act has brought many newsworthy disclosures by national, regional and local journalists.

Many public bodies are helpful when responding to FoI requests, but others delay answering requests or are extremely slow when considering the 'public interest test' (discussed later in the chapter). Research published on the Institute for Government website in April 2017 showed that the Government was becoming more secretive, with the number of FoI requests Whitehall departments were refusing to answer growing from 25 per cent in 2010 to 41 per cent by the end of 2016.

Government departments and other public bodies often seek to use the Act's exemptions to thwart requests for information, and numerous requestors win appeals to the Information Commissioner and the First-tier Tribunal (Information Rights). Journalists using the Act need to be systematic and persistent—it is still a worthwhile tool for investigative journalism.

30.2 What is a 'public authority' under the Act?

The Act covers about 100,000 major and minor bodies in the public sector, including:

- national Government departments and ministries such as the Home Office, Foreign Office and Prime Minister's Office;
- the House of Commons, the House of Lords, and the National Assemblies of Northern Ireland and Wales;
- the armed forces;
- local government—metropolitan, city, county, district and parish councils, transport executives, waste disposal agencies, police forces, fire services;
- national park authorities;
- universities, colleges and schools in the state sector;
- the National Health Service, including primary care trusts, hospital trusts, health authorities, and doctors' and dentists' practices;
- various advisory councils and regulatory bodies with statutory powers, such as Ofcom and the General Medical Council;
- the Universities and Colleges Admissions Service (UCAS), National Police Chiefs' Council, Financial Ombudsman Service (FOS) and companies entirely owned by local authorities are also now subject to the Act.

It does not define 'public authority', but lists, in Schedule 1, the bodies and organisations it covers. More have been added by statutory instruments.

30.3 Institutions and agencies not covered by the Act

The security and intelligence agencies—MI5, MI6 and GCHQ—are exempt, and so not required to respond to FoI requests. Courts and tribunals are not covered, though some information gathered or created in their functions will be available if a request is made to the Government department holding it, such as the Ministry of Justice.

The following are not public authorities under the Act: housing associations; charities; private prisons; harbour authorities; and MPs and Peers, as individuals.

The Royal Family never came under the Act. But an amendment which came into force in January 2011 gave the Queen, Prince of Wales and Prince William absolute exemption from any request for information. Other members of the Royal Family, such as the Duke of Edinburgh and Prince Harry, remain subject to a qualified exemption—public bodies holding information about them should release it if there is a public interest in disclosure.

 Check www.mcnaes.com for updates on the FoI Act covering more bodies.

30.4 How the Act works

A public authority should respond to a request for information within 20 working days by supplying the information or explaining that it cannot do so because:

- it does not hold it—in most circumstances this must be made clear;
- providing it would exceed the cost limits for free provision—see later in the chapter;
- it is exempt from disclosure.

For some exempt categories—for example, information held in confidence or concerning national security—an authority does not have to say what it holds if denying or confirming its existence would undermine the purpose of the exemption.

see 30.5,
Exemptions

Journalists should check an authority's website for information before making an FoI request, as it might already publish the material—the Act says each authority must have a 'publication scheme'. If the information is not listed, journalists should ask the official who coordinates the authority's FoI matters about what information it holds. Section 16 of the Act says authorities must offer 'advice and assistance', including on how to frame requests to stay within the cost limits for free responses.

A requestor's reason for wanting information should play no part in an authority's decision on providing it.

An authority which has to apply the 'public interest test' (see later) to see if an exemption applies may take more than 20 working days to respond. It must consider, even if some information sought is deemed exempt from disclosure, if the request can be met in part by releasing non-exempt information.

30.4.1 What is information?

Section 84 of the Act defines information as 'information recorded in any form'. The right under the Act is for *information* to be communicated to the requestor, not necessarily in the form of particular documents, though requests often refer to particular documents, which are supplied. 'Document' includes electronic documents (*Dominic Kennedy v Information Commissioner and Charity Commission* [2010] EWHC 475 (Admin), [2010] 1 WLR 1489).

An authority does not have to gather information it does not already hold.

((•))
see Useful
Websites at
the end of
this chapter
for dataset
guidance

The Protection of Freedoms Act 2012, by amending the 2000 Act, gave requestors greater rights to have datasets held by public authorities sent to them in electronic, re-usable form.

30.4.2 Cost limits

A Government department required to disclose requested information must do so free if it costs no more than £600. All other public authorities covered by the Act must provide such information free if doing so costs no more than £450. Cost is estimated by assessing—at £25 an hour—the staff time reasonably needed to determine whether a body holds the information, to find and retrieve it, and if necessary to extract it from a document. If the cost limit is exceeded, the authority does not have to supply any information requested, but may *choose* to do so, without charge or at a price reflecting the cost of providing it. An authority which can comply with part, but not all, of a request within the cost limits has a duty under section 16 to offer a requestor advice to see if he/she wishes to re-define or limit the request. If the information is to be provided on paper, the requestor can be charged a reasonable price for photocopying. Information can often be sent by email.

Journalists should make requests as specific as possible. A requestor may get round a cost limit by breaking a 'large' request into several smaller ones, sent serially. But authorities may 'aggregate' the cost of two or more requests made within 60 days by the same person for the same or similar types of information—that is, treat them as being part of a single request—and refuse them if in total they breach the cost limit for one request. Authorities should not use aggregation powers to frustrate a sequence of requests each of which, on the basis of information sent previously, digs further into a topic by asking for further different information.

30.4.3 Advice and assistance

Section 16 requires a public body to give prospective or actual requestors 'advice and assistance, so far as it would be reasonable to expect the authority to do so'.

- It should, if asked, tell a requestor *before* he/she makes a request what information of the type sought might be available, and help frame a request.
- It should give guidance to avoid a request breaching the cost limit for providing information free.

Section 1(3) allows a body which 'reasonably requires' further detail to identify and locate information to clarify this with the requestor, and, if such further detail is not provided, not to comply with the request. The Information Commissioner has made clear that a public authority which tells a requestor that the information is already in the public domain should also indicate where it can be found.

30.5 Exemptions

Bodies may refuse to supply information on various grounds—exemptions. The Information Commissioner's Office website has guidance on these.

see Useful Websites at the end of this chapter for ICO guidance

30.5.1 Absolute exemptions

Some exemptions are 'absolute'—the authority does not have to give a reason for refusing disclosure beyond stating that the exemption applies because of the nature of the information. Absolute exemptions include:

Section 21—information reasonably accessible by other means

Section 23—information supplied to the public authority by or relating to bodies dealing with security matters

Section 32—court records

Section 40—personal information

Section 41—information provided to the authority in confidence by another party

Section 44—information the disclosure of which is forbidden by other law

ch. 28 explains data protection law

 See the extended version of this chapter on www.mcnaes.com for more detail on these exemptions.

30.5.2 Qualified exemptions

The other exemptions are 'qualified'—the Act says information may be withheld only if the public interest in withholding it is greater than the public interest in disclosure. A public body which declines to supply information in these categories must show how it applied the public interest test.

see Useful Websites at the end of this chapter for this ICO guidance

The Act does not define 'public interest'. But in guidance in 2013 the Information Commissioner said that public interest factors which should encourage public authorities to disclose information included:

- general arguments in favour of promoting transparency, accountability and participation;
- that disclosure might enhance the quality of discussions and decision making generally;
- that the balance might be tipped in favour of disclosure by financial issues— such as if the information requested involves a large amount of public money;
- the specific circumstances of the case and the content of the information requested in relation to those circumstances;
- the age of the information;

- the timing of a request which, in respect of information relating to an investigation, may be relevant;
- the impact of disclosure upon individuals and/or the wider public.

The Campaign for Freedom of Information has stressed the importance of applicants pursuing requests to the First-tier Tribunal (Information Rights) if necessary and not accepting a public authority's initial refusal. Requestors should not assume that the Information Commissioner will automatically recognise the public interest case for disclosing information and should raise it in appeal correspondence.

Qualified exemptions include:

Section 24—information which if disclosed is likely to prejudice national security

Section 27—information which if disclosed is likely to prejudice international relations

Section 31—information held by an authority for law enforcement functions

Section 35—information relating to formulation or development of Government policy

Section 36—information the disclosure of which is likely to prejudice effective conduct of public affairs

Section 43—commercial interests

 See the extended version of this chapter on www.mcnaes.com for more detail on these exemptions.

30.5.2.1 Delays in the public interest test

The Act does not set a deadline for completing the 'public interest test' over an FoI request—considering it may mean the 20-day period for responding to requests instead becomes months. But a public body must tell a requestor within the 20-day limit that a qualified exemption might apply.

30.6 If the information is not supplied

If an authority takes no decision on supplying the information within the 20-day limit, or refuses to supply it because of the cost limit or an exemption, a requestor can request an 'internal review' of the decision, which should be conducted by an official other than the one involved in the refusal. There is no timescale for completing this review. The Information Commissioner's Office has said that 20 working days (from the time a request for a review is received) is a reasonable time for a review and that in no case should the time exceed 40 working days. A requestor dissatisfied with the result of a review can appeal to the Information Commissioner.

30.7 The Information Commissioner and the First-tier Tribunal (Information Rights)

The Freedom of Information Act 2000 is enforced by the Information Commissioner, who also oversees the Data Protection Act 1998.

The Commissioner can: order a body to release information if he/she disagrees with a refusal to disclose it; question an authority's claim not to hold requested information; and question its estimate that disclosure would exceed the cost limit.

If a requestor claims an authority has not responded within the 20-day limit, the Commissioner can, under section 52, serve it with an enforcement notice requiring compliance with the Act. As an ultimate sanction, he/she can ask the High Court to punish an authority's failure to comply with the notice as contempt of court. Section 48 gives him/her the power to issue a 'good practice recommendation' specifying the steps an authority should take to improve compliance.

Requestors and public authorities dissatisfied with the Information Commissioner's decision can appeal to the First-tier Tribunal (Information Rights) within 28 days of receipt of the decision. The Tribunal, part of the First-tier Tribunal in the administrative justice system—see ch. 18—publishes its decisions online.

((•))
see Useful
Websites at
the end of
this chapter
for the Tribunal's site

30.8 Ministers' power of veto

Cabinet Ministers can veto notices issued by the Commissioner requiring Government departments to disclose requested information. A veto can be challenged in law.

30.9 The FoI Act's coverage of media organisations

The BBC, Channel 4 and S4C—public service broadcasters—were made subject to the Act, but in a limited way as disclosure provisions only apply to information they hold 'for purposes other than those of journalism, art or literature'. It does not require these broadcasters to comply with:

(1) requests attempting to reveal journalists' confidential sources;

(2) requests by rival news organisations, or by the subjects of journalistic investigations (that is, 'data subjects'), aimed at securing, before or after broadcast, material gathered in a journalistic investigation, including any footage/audio not broadcast.

The Supreme Court has ruled that if information is held for journalistic purposes, it is exempt from disclosure even if it is also held for other purposes (*Sugar (Deceased) (Represented by Fiona Paveley) v BBC and another* [2012] UKSC 4, [2012] 1 WLR 439, [2012] 2 All ER 509).

30.10 Environmental information

The Environmental Information Regulations 2004 (EIR) require public authorities to provide information about environmental matters. They give, in the environmental field, the public—and journalists—more powerful rights of access to information than those in the FoI Act. A public authority receiving a request for information within the scope of the EIR should automatically deal with it under the EIR rather than under the Act (ideally the request should refer to the EIR). For guidance on using the EIR, see Useful Websites at the end of this chapter.

Environmental information covers air, water, land, natural sites and living organisms—including genetically modified (GM) crops—and discharges, as well as noise and radiation. The EIR cover more bodies than the FoI Act, with fewer exemptions—for example, information about emissions cannot be withheld because of commercial confidentiality.

All bodies subject to the FoI Act are also subject to the EIR and the same 20-day deadline applies to requests for information. Privatised water and sewerage companies in England and Wales are not subject to either the Act or the EIR, although they are in Scotland.

The EIR require that public authorities must assist those requesting information.

EIR requests can be turned down on grounds of national security. But all refusals are subject to a public interest test and requests can be refused only if the public interest in non-disclosure far outweighs the public interest in disclosure. A 'reasonable' fee can be charged for EIR requests.

30.11 Legal issues in using FoI disclosures in stories

ch. 29
explains
copyright
law

Publication of material disclosed under the FoI Act or the EIR brings no special protection against an action for defamation. The FoI Act and EIR do not confer statutory qualified privilege on such reports.

 Chs. 22 and 23 explain defamation defences.

 →glossary

→glossary

Material disclosed under either the Act or the EIR will be protected by **copyright**. But a **fair dealing** defence applies to citing some text verbatim for the purposes of reporting current events.

➡ Recap of major points

- The Freedom of Information Act 2000 gives a general right of access to information held by public authorities including Government departments and local authorities.
- But there are wide-ranging exemptions and plenty of potential for delays in responding.
- The Act obliges public authorities to offer requestors advice to enable them to word their requests in such a way that they are more likely to succeed.
- The Information Commissioner hears appeals against a body's refusal to supply information. The First-tier Tribunal (Information Rights) can hear appeals against the Commissioner's decisions.

■ The Environmental Information Regulations 2004 provide powerful rights of access to information in fields they cover.

((•)) Useful Websites

www.opsi.gov.uk/Acts/acts2000/ukpga_20000036_en_1/
Freedom of Information Act

https://ico.org.uk
Information Commissioner's Office (ICO)

http://ico.org.uk/for_the_public/official_information
ICO guidance on advice and assistance for requestors

www.ico.org.uk/~/media/documents/library/Freedom_of_Information/Detailed_specialist_
guides/the_public_interest_test.ashx
ICO guidance on the public interest test

http://foia.blogspot.com/
Campaign for Freedom of Information's UK FoI Blog

http://heatherbrooke.org/category/freedom-of-information/
FoI articles by specialist Heather Brooke

www.gov.uk/government/uploads/system/uploads/attachment_data/file/235286/0033.pdf
Code of Practice for public authorities on FoI requests

https://ico.org.uk/media/for-organisations/documents/1151/datasets-foi-guidance.pdf
ICO guidance on release of datasets

https://ico.org.uk/for-organisations/guide-to-the-environmental-information-regulations/
what-are-the-eir/
ICO guidance to public authorities on EIR

www.Folman.com
Blog written by an FoI practitioner, including a useful guide on making FoI requests

https://foi.directory/
FoI Directory site run by Matt Burgess

31

Other information rights and access to meetings

Chapter summary

The public and journalists have rights to information under various laws, most notably about the workings of local government. These rights can be used to get policy documents from public bodies and ensure journalists can report important meetings. For some types of material the laws are better than the Freedom of Information Act 2000 (see previous chapter), as they offer quicker rights to obtain copies of or inspect documents. Because there is much detail in these laws, a longer version of this chapter is provided on www.mcnaes.com.

31.1 Local government

Local government is a major source of stories and should be subjected to rigorous scrutiny by journalists. But devolution means that at present journalists' and citizens' rights to access to information from principal authorities differs in England and Wales.

Authorities fall into two categories. Principal authorities include county councils, district councils, London boroughs, the London Assembly and fire authorities.

Parish councils and community councils are not principal authorities.

31.2 Principal authorities

The Local Government Act 2000, amended by the Localism Act 2011, introduced new models of 'cabinet style' local government, of which two survive—a leader (elected by council members) and cabinet, and a directly elected mayor and cabinet. Access to information from principal authorities which have not adopted these models remains governed by the Local Government Act 1972, as amended by the Local Government (Access to Information) Act 1985. Law in these Acts is explained later in this chapter.

Some details of the rights of journalists and the public to attend and report on meetings of local authorities and some other public bodies are available in the guidance *Open and Accountable Local Government* published by the Department for Communities and Local Government—see Useful Websites at the end of this chapter.

 See too the extended version of this chapter on www.mcnaes.com for fuller details of these rights, and about the laws which require parish councils and community councils to hold public meetings and provide information. Such laws as regards Police and Crime Commissioners, health authorities and NHS trusts are discussed later in the chapter.

31.3 The Local Government Act 2000

Regulations covering access to information under the 2000 Act are contained in **statutory instruments** and apply to unitary authorities, London borough councils, county councils and district councils in England operating executive arrangements under the Act.   → glossary

The Local Authorities (Executive Arrangements) (Meetings and Access to Information) (England) Regulations 2012 and Openness of Local Government Bodies Regulations 2014 allow journalists and anyone else reporting on authorities in England do so by filming or recording meetings, and live blogging and tweeting from them. In Wales, the Assembly has published a Code of Recommended Practice on Local Authority Publicity for Wales which encourages councils to permit filming.

((•)) See Useful websites at the end of this chapter for the Code of Recommended Practice.

References in this chapter are to the 2012 Regulations, unless otherwise stated.

31.3.1 When bodies must meet in public

Meetings of decision-making bodies—local authority executives and their committees—must be open to the public (regulation 3).

But the public may be excluded if it is likely that:

- confidential information would be disclosed in breach of the obligation of confidence;
- the decision-making body concerned passes a resolution to exclude the public during an item in which disclosure of exempt information is likely— the resolution must describe the exempt information; or
- it is necessary to maintain orderly conduct or prevent misbehaviour at a meeting.

The public may only be excluded under the first two for the part or parts of the meeting during which confidential or exempt information is likely to be disclosed.

👁 Case study

In June 2017 the leader of the Royal Borough of Kensington and Chelsea announced that the public and press would be barred from a Cabinet meeting to discuss the disastrous fire at the authority-owned Grenfell Tower, in which 71 people died, because of fears of disruption, and because concerns that reporting could prejudice the public inquiry set up to investigate the tragedy. A group of media organisations persuaded Mrs Justice O'Farrell to make a High Court order that the council must allow journalists to attend, on the grounds that there was no legal basis on which they could be excluded as they would not cause disruption. But when the reporters entered the meeting council leader Nicholas Paget-Brown, in the chair, immediately abandoned it. The decision attracted widespread criticism, including a rebuke from Downing Street, and Mr Paget-Brown stepped down as leader the following day (*Press Gazette,* 29 June 2017; *The Guardian,* 29 and 30 June 2017; *Media Lawyer,* 4 July 2017).

31.3.1.1 Confidential information

'Confidential information' is information provided to the local authority by a government department upon terms (however expressed) forbidding its disclosure to the public, or information the disclosure of which to the public is prohibited by or under any enactment or a court order.

31.3.1.2 Exempt information

Exempt information in England is information relating to a variety of subjects, including, for example: an employee or office holder of the authority, or of the magistrates' courts or probationary committee; a particular council tenant or applicant for council services or grants; care of children; an individual's financial or business affairs; and labour relations matters between the council and its employees. Any part of an agenda, report or other document which contains exempt information does not have to be made available for inspection. Exempt information in Wales is similar, but less wide-ranging.

The fact that exempt information is to be discussed at a meeting does not impose an obligation on the authority to discuss it in private.

ch. 30 explains the FoI Act

The categories of exempt information are wider than the categories of information which an authority is not obliged to disclose under the Freedom of Information Act 2000—so exempt material might be obtained through an FoI request.

31.3.2 Notice of public meetings

A decision-making body must display a notice giving the time and place of a public meeting at its offices, and on its website, at least five clear days before the meeting or, if it is convened at shorter notice, when it is convened (regulation 6).

31.3.3 Access to agendas and reports

A copy of the agenda and every report for a meeting must be available for public inspection at the authority's office and on its website (regulation 7). Copies of reports do not have to include material relating only to matters to be dealt with in private.

Any document which has to be available for inspection by the public must be available for at least five clear days before the meeting or, if the meeting is convened at shorter notice, when it is convened. If all or part of a report for a public meeting is not available for public inspection, it must be marked 'not for publication' and say that it contains confidential information, or exempt information, which must be described.

Regulation 20 says this does not authorise the disclosure of confidential information in breach of the obligation of confidence, or of anything likely to contain exempt information or the advice of a political adviser or assistant.

31.3.4 Notification of private meetings

A decision-making body planning to meet in private must give at least 28 days' notice of its intention by publishing a notification explaining the reasons at its offices and on its website (regulation 5).

It must publish a further notice at least five days before the meeting takes place, with a statement of the reasons for holding it in private, details of any representations made about why it should be in public and a statement of its response.

A decision-making body which wishes to hold a meeting so quickly that it cannot comply with these requirements must obtain consent to do so from the chair or deputy chair of a relevant scrutiny committee or, in their absence, the authority's chair or deputy chair.

31.3.5 Key decisions

Special rules apply when a 'key decision' is to be made—this is covered by regulations 9 and 10. A key decision is one which is likely:

- to result in the authority incurring spending or making savings which are significant having regard to its budget for the relevant service or function; or
- to be significant in terms of its effects on communities living or working in an area comprising two or more wards or electoral divisions.

31.3.5.1 Publicity in connection with key decisions

At least 28 days before a key decision is made, a local authority must publish a document giving details about it. Regulation 10 says this must specify, among other things, the issue to be decided and a list of the documents submitted to the decision maker for consideration in relation to it.

If the public might be excluded from the meeting at which the issue is to be discussed, or documents relating to the decision do not have to be disclosed to the public, the notification must contain particulars of the matter, but cannot contain any confidential exempt information or details of advice from a political adviser or assistant.

If the required notification period for a meeting to make a key decision is impractical, the decision may only be made five clear days after various authority members have been notified of the fact in writing, and a copy of that notification has been made available for public inspection and published on the authority's website.

 For more detail of regulations 9 and 10, see the extended version of this chapter on www.mcnaes.com.

31.3.6 Documents that must be made available after a meeting

A written statement must be produced 'as soon as reasonably practicable' after a public or private meeting at which an executive decision is made (regulation 12). The statement must include a record of the decision and the reasons for it. An executive decision made by an individual or a key decision made by an officer must be recorded similarly.

A media organisation which requests copies of any of the documents available for public inspection must be supplied with them on payment of postage, copying 'or other necessary charge for transmission' (regulation 14).

31.4 Register of interests

The Localism Act 2011 places a duty on councillors to enter certain personal interests on a publicly available register. Failure to disclose interests is a criminal offence punishable by an unlimited fine and possible disqualification from membership of the authority for up to five years.

! Remember your rights

If you encounter someone who has custody of a document which must be available for public inspection but who intentionally obstructs you exercising a right to inspect or make a copy of it, or refuses to supply a copy of it, you can warn them that they are committing an offence punishable by a fine of up to £200 under section 100H(4) of the Local Government Act 1972 and under regulation 22 of the Local Authorities (Executive Arrangements) (Meetings and Access to Information) (England) Regulations 2012.

31.5 Copyright and defamation

Regulation 21(3) and (4) of the 2012 Regulations say any member of the public may reproduce any document supplied to him/her or made available for public inspection under the Regulations, or provide commentary on it, in any publicly available medium. This will not infringe **copyright** in the document as long as the local authority is the copyright holder. This regulation does not authorise infringement of anyone else's copyright.

ch. 29 explains copyright law

→ glossary

On defamation, it extends the protection of qualified **privilege** to the publication of any defamatory matter contained in any document required by the Regulations to be open to inspection by the public and supplied to, or available for inspection by, members of the public or supplied for a newspaper's benefit.

→ glossary

 Remember

If a local authority holds a meeting in private under any of the legislation referred to, a defamatory media report of the discussion in such meetings and of documents considered in them, if leaked unofficially to the media, will not be protected by qualified privilege under Schedule 1 to the Defamation Act 1996.

Media coverage of an official statement issued to journalists about a meeting held in private will be privileged under the 1996 Act if the defence's requirements are met.

Media coverage of the public proceedings of local authorities, whether in full council, committees or sub-committees, and of minutes, agendas, reports or other documents officially made available to journalists or the public, will also be privileged.

 Section 22.6, Qualified privilege, explains the requirements of this defence.

31.6 The Local Government (Access to Information) Act 1985

The Local Government (Access to Information) Act 1985 predates the introduction of cabinet-style councils. It inserted new parts—Part VA and Schedule 12A—into the Local Government Act 1972, containing the requirements set out in the following passages (which include later amendments).

31.6.1 When meetings must be in public

All meetings of principal authorities, their committees and their sub-committees must be open to the public unless dealing with confidential or exempt information (although the position about working parties and advisory or study groups, which may in effect act as sub-committees without the name, is unclear).

Principal authorities, their committees and their sub-committees must exclude the public when confidential information is likely to be disclosed.

A local authority may exclude the public when disclosure of exempt information is likely by passing a resolution, which must state the part of the meeting to which the exclusion applies and describe the category of exempt information (the categories are in Schedule 12A to the 1972 Act).

While the meeting is open to the public, 'duly accredited representatives' of newspapers or news agencies must, under section 100(6)(c) of the 1972 Act, be afforded reasonable facilities for taking their report.

31.6.2 Documents that must be made available

A newspaper or news agency must on request (and on payment of postage or other transmission charge) be supplied with (a) agendas, (b) further particulars necessary to indicate the nature of the items on the agenda and (c) if the 'proper officer' thinks fit, copies of any other documents supplied to council members, although he/she may exclude from what he/she sends out any report, or part of a report, relating to items not likely to be discussed in public.

Late items, reports and supplementary information can be admitted at the meeting only if the chair regards the matter as urgent and specifies the reason for the urgency.

Copies of agendas and of any report for a meeting of a council must be open to public inspection at least five working days before the meeting (except for items not likely to be discussed in public). Where a meeting is called at shorter notice they must be open to inspection when the meeting is convened.

31.6.3 Fire authorities and joint bodies

The 1972 Act also applies to fire authorities, meetings of joint consultative committees of health and local authorities, and to some joint boards.

! Remember your rights

There are other rights to inspect council records—for example, planning applications. For details, see the longer version of this chapter on www.mcnaes.com.

31.7 Parish and town councils, and Water Act bodies

The Public Bodies (Admission to Meetings) Act 1960 sets out information and access rights relating to parish, town and community councils, parish meetings and meetings of bodies set up under the Water Act 1989—regional and local flood defence committees, regional rivers advisory committees, salmon and freshwater fisheries advisory committees, and customer service committees. The longer version of this chapter on www.mcnaes.com explains these rights.

31.8 Access to financial accounts

Journalists often miss golden opportunities to find local authority stories by using rights in section 26 of the Local Audit and Accountability Act 2014 and the Accounts and Audit (England) Regulations 2011. 'Local authorities' includes fire and civil defence authorities.

Section 26 of the Act says 'any persons interested' may—in a period of 20 full working days before a date appointed by the local authority's auditor—inspect its accounts and 'all books, deeds, contracts, bills, vouchers and receipts and other documents relating to those records', and make copies.

! Remember your rights

The 2014 Act makes it a criminal offence for any officer or councillor to obstruct local taxpayers or electors exercising their rights to view and copy the (non-exempt) material. Authority press officers who try to involve themselves in the actual inspection should be warned off. For detail of these and other inspection rights to probe an authority's financial matters, including expenses paid to councillors, see the longer version of this chapter on www.mcnaes.com.

31.9 Health authorities and NHS trusts

Admission to meetings of local health authorities and NHS trusts, and rights to their agendas, are subject to the Public Bodies (Admission to Meetings) Act 1960.

Department of Health guidance to these bodies in 1998 (Health Service Circular no. 1998/207) said the government was 'committed to ending what it sees as excessive secrecy in decision making in public bodies', and that although authorities and trusts could exclude press and public in the public interest under the terms of the 1960 Act, they were expected to conduct their business in public in as open a manner as possible.

The 1960 Act gives the same rights of admission to any committee of a health authority consisting of all members of the authority.

The Health and Social Care Act 2001 gave new powers to overview and scrutinise committees of those local authorities with social services responsibilities (county councils, London borough councils, unitary authorities), and these are subject to similar access to information provisions as other committees covered by Local Government (Access to Information) Act 1985, explained earlier. But extended exemptions apply, which go further than the exemptions in the 1985 Act by exempting also information on (1) a person providing or applying to provide NHS services, (2) an employee of such a person, or (3) information relating to a person's health. Minutes, agendas and reports are open to public inspection for only three years, and background papers for only two years.

31.10 Police and Crime Commissioners

Police and Crime Commissioners must, under provision in sections 5 and 12 of the Police Reform and Social Responsibility Act 2011, publish a Police and Crime Plan and annual reports. Financial and other information, including a register of interests, must be published, as specified in the Elected Local Policing Bodies (Specified Information) Order 2011.

31.10.1 Police and crime panels

((•))
see Useful
Websites at
the end of this
chapter for
the Order and
Regulations

Much of the law on access to information referred to in this chapter also applies to the police and crime panels in each police area—see the Police and Crime Panels (Application of Local Authority Enactments) Regulations 2012.

31.11 Quangos

Many day-to-day services to the public which were administered by bodies on which representatives of the public served have become semi-independent agencies with managing bodies staffed by appointees rather than representatives.

The term 'quango' (quasi-autonomous non-governmental organisation) describes taxpayer-funded non-elected public bodies operating outside the Civil Service. Generally, there is no right of access to meetings of quangos, although there is a right to information to most of them under the FoI Act, explained in ch. 30.

✳ Remember

The public must be admitted to meetings of local magistrates advisory committees at least once a year. For detail, see the longer version this chapter on www.mcnaes.com.

➡ Recap of major points

- People have rights to other information from local authorities, such as annual budget figures and agendas, as well as rights to attend meetings.

- In certain circumstances authorities have the right to withhold documents or to deny public access to meetings.

- Laws giving rights to examine accounts can be very good sources of stories, provided the journalist knows where to look.

- There are rights to attend the meetings of health authorities and these bodies are required to publish each year their performance in key areas of health provision.

((•)) Useful Websites

www.gov.uk/government/uploads/system/uploads/attachment_data/file/343182/140812_Openness_Guide.pdf

Department for Communities and Local Government guidance, *Open and Accountable Local Government*

http://gov.wales/docs/dpsp/publications/140814-local-authority-publicity-en.pdf

Welsh Assembly Code of Recommended Practice on Local Authority Publicity

www.legislation.gov.uk/uksi/2012/2089/contents/made

Local Authorities (Executive Arrangements) (Meetings and Access to Information) (England) Regulations 2012

www.bleadon.org.uk/media/other/24400/SN06046.pdf

House of Commons Briefing Paper No 06046, 10 November 2015, on local government transparency in England

www.legislation.gov.uk/uksi/2012/2479/article/1/made

Elected Local Policing Bodies (Specified Information) Order 2011 and amendments

www.gov.uk/government/uploads/system/uploads/attachment_data/file/143836/publishing-information.pdf

Government guidance to Police and Crime Commissioners on publishing information

www.legislation.gov.uk/uksi/2012/2734/made

Police and Crime Panels (Application of Local Authority Enactments) Regulations 2012 and their Explanatory Notes

32

Reporting elections

Chapter summary

The Representation of the People Act 1983 makes it a criminal offence to make or publish false statements about election candidates. There are restrictions on publishing 'exit polls'. Broadcast journalists must be impartial when covering elections and referendums.

32.1 False statements about candidates

Section 106 of the Representation of the People Act 1983 makes it an offence to:

- make or publish a false statement of fact about the personal character or conduct of an election candidate in order to affect how many votes he/she gets.

To constitute the offence, the falsity must be expressed as a fact, as distinct from a statement which is clearly merely comment or an opinion about the candidate. It is a defence for someone accused of publishing such a false statement to show that he/she had reasonable grounds for believing when it was published that it was true, and did at that time believe it was true (even if it turns out to be untrue).

Section 106 (5) makes it an offence:

- to publish a false claim that a candidate has withdrawn from the election, if the publisher knows it to be false and published it to promote or procure the election of another candidate.

Breach of section 106 is punishable by an unlimited fine. If the publisher is a company, its directors can be convicted. The law is not aimed specifically at the media, but is meant to deter 'dirty tricks' by those campaigning in elections and their supporters. In 2010 Labour MP Phil Woolas lost his seat when he was convicted of illegal practices under section 106 by publishing election addresses containing statements about Liberal Democrat candidate Robert Elwyn Watkins—involving where he lived, his attitude to Muslim extremists and his election expenses—which he had no reasonable grounds for believing were true and did not believe were true (*Robert Elwyn James Watkins v Philip James Woolas* [2010] EWHC 2702 (QB)).

The ban on false statements applies from when formal notice is given that an election is to take place until the election ends. For local government elections, this period is about five weeks. For national Parliamentary elections, the period begins with the date of the dissolution of Parliament or any earlier time at which Her Majesty's intention to dissolve Parliament is announced.

If the false statement is defamatory, the publisher could also face a libel action. But the criminal sanction in the 1983 Act gives a quicker remedy, as a candidate who can prove a **prima facie** case that he/she has been traduced by such a false statement can obtain an **injunction** preventing its repetition, whereas the legal rule against **prior restraint** means it is harder to get an injunction in a libel action, which could take months to be settled or resolved at trial. The 1983 Act prohibits all such false statements, including those which are defamatory. A journalist who in 1997 published false allegations on the internet that an election candidate was a homosexual was fined £250 under the Act. An inaccurate statement that someone is homosexual is not, in itself, defamatory. But in the context of an election, it could cost a candidate votes, for example by persuading voters with anti-gay religious beliefs not to support him/her.

→ glossary
→ glossary
→ glossary

see 20.2.6, Changing standards

32.2 Defamation dangers during elections

Election candidates and their supporters might make defamatory allegations about rivals, using terms such as 'racist', 'fascist' and 'liar' and a media organisation which publishes them could be successfully sued for libel if it has no defence.

There is no statutory privilege for media publications of candidates' election material or of what they say. But qualified privilege protects fair and accurate reports of public meetings and press conferences, if the requirements of that defence are met.

> Ch. 20 has definitions of defamatory statements and ch. 22 explains qualified privilege.

✳ Remember

Journalists reporting speeches by extremist candidates should remember that speakers, and reports of their speeches, are subject to the laws against stirring up hatred, including on racial and religious grounds. The www.mcnaes.com chapter, 'The incitement of hate', explains that law.

32.3 Election advertisements

The law says only an election candidate or his/her agent may incur any expenses relating to his/her campaign, including for publishing an advertisement. It

is an offence for anyone else to pay for such an advertisement unless authorised to do so, in writing, by the election agent. This stops well-wishers putting
advertisements in newspapers on behalf of candidates without their express
authority.

32.4 Broadcasters' duty to be impartial

Section 6 of the Broadcasting Code has detailed rules on how broadcast output
must be impartial in election and referendum periods. Ofcom has fined several
radio stations after presenters or others made partial declarations of support for
political candidates or parties.

👁 **Case study**

In 2008 Ofcom fined Talksport radio £20,000 for breach of the impartiality requirement, after presenter James Whale directly encouraged listeners to vote
for Conservative candidate Boris Johnson in the London mayoral elections
and criticised Labour candidate Ken Livingstone (*Ofcom Broadcast Bulletin*, No.
123, 8 December 2008).

Among the rules in section 6 of the Broadcasting Code are that:

- due weight must be given to the coverage of major parties during the election period, and broadcasters must also consider giving appropriate coverage to other parties and independent candidates with significant views and
  perspectives (rule 6.2);
- if a candidate takes part in an item about his/her particular constituency, or electoral area, then opportunity to take part must be offered
  to all candidates within the constituency or electoral area representing parties with previous significant electoral support or where there
  is evidence of significant current support, including any independent
  candidate (rule 6.9);
- any constituency or electoral area report or discussion after the close of
  nominations must include a list of all candidates standing, giving first
  names, surnames and the name of the party they represent or, if they
  are standing independently, the fact that they are an independent candidate. This must be conveyed in sound and/or vision. Where a constituency report on a radio service is repeated on several occasions in the
  same day, the full list need only be broadcast once, but the audience
  should be directed to where the list can be seen—for example, a website
  (rule 6.10).

See Useful Websites at the end of this chapter for section 6. Ch. 3 covers impartiality and includes a case study of an Ofcom adjudication in 2016 against Fox News
for breach of rule 6.2—see 3.4.1, Due impartiality and due accuracy.

32.5 **Exit polls**

The term 'exit poll' describes any survey in which people who have voted are asked which candidate and/or party they voted for. Such surveys can often produce data which accurately predict an election result, hours before it is officially declared. Many democratic nations, including the UK, restrict when such data/predictions can be published on the grounds that publishing the information, or predictions based on it, before polls close could skew the election result. The concern is that telling people who have yet to vote which candidate/party appears likely to win, with information apparently soundly based on votes already cast, could make people change their original voting intentions.

These possible effects are seen as potentially contaminating the democratic process, in that: (a) the later group of voters will have made choices on data not available to those who voted earlier; and (b) those data, and any prediction apparently based on them, might be inaccurate—or even falsified to influence voting.

Section 66A of the Representation of the People Act 1983, as inserted by the 2000 Act of the same title, makes it a criminal offence to:

- publish, before a poll is closed, any statement about the way in which voters have voted in that election which is, or might reasonably be taken to be, based on information given by voters after they have voted; and to
- publish, before a poll is closed, any forecast—including any estimate—of that election result, if the forecast is based on exit poll information from voters, or might reasonably be taken to be based on it.

So, for example, it would be illegal to broadcast, or put on a website, before polling stations closed, the statement: 'Fifty-five per cent of the people we have questioned say they have voted Labour today'.

This law applies to Parliamentary elections and by-elections, council elections, Welsh Assembly and Scottish Parliamentary elections. It applies in respect of exit polls conducted to focus on an individual constituency or ward, or on voting nationally. Publication of material in breach of section 66A leaves the publisher liable to an unlimited fine or a jail term of up to six months. Publication of exit polls during polling for European Parliamentary elections is also prohibited (SI 2004/293).

It is legal to publish, at any time, opinion poll data on voting intentions which was gathered before voting began, as the information was not based on how people say they actually voted. It is also legal to report the results of exit polls, and any forecast based on them, as soon as polling has finally closed, as TV programmes frequently do. But it is not always accurate now to talk of 'an election day'. For example, experiments to encourage more people to vote may mean that in some places voting takes place over several days. It will be an offence to publish an exit poll, or forecast apparently based on it, during any of the polling days, until the polls close on the final day.

👁 Case study

During elections for the European Parliament in June 2004, *The Times* published an opinion poll which had asked people how they voted in areas using all-postal ballots. The Electoral Commission, the independent elections watchdog, said this amounted to an exit poll and referred the matter to the Crown Prosecution Service, but later reported that the CPS had concluded that it would not be appropriate to take any further action (Electoral Commission report on European Parliamentary elections, 21 December 2004).

Rule 6.5 of the Broadcasting Code has a similar control on publishing exit polls and indeed goes further. It says: 'Broadcasters may not publish the results of any opinion poll on polling day itself until the election or referendum poll closes. (For European Parliamentary elections, this applies until all polls throughout the European Union have closed.)' Rule 6.4 bans discussion and analysis of election and referendum issues during polling, a period which begins when polling stations open. This rule does not apply to any poll conducted entirely by post.

BBC Editorial Guidelines take the same approach.

32.6 Election counts

Journalists, including photographers and TV crews, attend election counts so declarations of the result can be quickly aired. There is no statutory right to attend a count—admission is at the discretion of the Returning Officer, who has legal responsibility for security and procedures at the count. The Electoral Commission's media handbook for the 2017 General Election said members of the media wishing to attend a count had to apply to the Returning Officer.

👁 Case study

In the 2010 General Election, journalists were initially banned from the count at Staffordshire Moorlands, and told by council officials running it that they had to stay in a separate room, apparently because of fears that their presence in the counting hall would be disruptive. The ban was lifted after lawyers for the *Staffordshire Sentinel*, *Leek Post and Times* and the BBC wrote to the acting Returning Officer protesting that it was undemocratic and breached the right to freedom of expression under Article 10 of the European Convention on Human Rights. The *Sentinel* also planned to get round the ban by having three staff members accredited as 'observers' at the count (*Media Lawyer*, 6 May 2010).

((•)) Registering as an observer takes 10 days, and accredited observers must be allowed into the count—see Useful Websites at the end of this chapter.

The Returning Officer at the high-profile by-election at Oldham East and Saddleworth in January 2011, which followed Phil Woolas's removal as MP, referred to earlier, refused to allow journalists into the count, despite protests from the BBC and Press Association, saying there would be too many to accommodate comfortably. Journalists had to stay on a balcony overlooking the hall, with communication with candidates, agents and others being 'facilitated' by Oldham Council press officers.

➡ Recap of major points

- Once an election is called it is a criminal offence to publish a false statement about the personal character or conduct of a candidate with the intention of affecting the number of votes he/she gets.

- It is an offence to publish before the end of polling any data obtained in exit polls on how people have voted, or any prediction of the election result based on such data.

- The Broadcasting Code requires broadcasters to follow certain practices to ensure impartiality in coverage of elections and referendums, and restrict use of opinion (including exit) polls.

((•)) Useful Websites

www.ofcom.org.uk/tv-radio-and-on-demand/broadcast-codes/broadcast-code/section-six-elections-referendums
Section 6 of the Broadcasting Code, on elections and referendums

http://stakeholders.ofcom.org.uk/binaries/broadcast/guidance/831193/section6.pdf
Ofcom's guidance on section 6 of the Code

www.bbc.co.uk/editorialguidelines/guidelines/politics/elections
Section 10 of BBC Editorial Guidelines on 'Politics, Public Policy and Polls'

www.bbc.co.uk/editorialguidelines/guidance/surveys
BBC Editorial Guidance on opinion polls, surveys, questionnaires, votes and straw polls

www.electoralcommission.org.uk/
Electoral Commission

www.electoralcommission.org.uk/elections/electoral_observers
Electoral Commission guidance on observers

http://library.college.police.uk/docs/APPREF/Schedule-of-election-and-referendum-related-crimes-and-penalties.pdf
College of Policing Schedule of election and referendum-related crimes and penalties

33

Official secrets

Chapter summary

Official secrets legislation protects national security. It has not been used in recent years to prosecute journalists, but has been used to jail civil servants and others who have given journalists sensitive information. Police could search the home and newsroom of a journalist who is thought to have breached this law, seize their records and try to identify the source. There is no public interest defence for anyone facing prosecution.

33.1 Introduction

The Official Secrets Acts of 1911 and 1989 protect national security, and can be used to enforce the duty of confidentiality owed to the UK state by Crown servants or employees of companies doing military and other sensitive work. Crown servants include civil servants, members of the armed services, the police and civilians working for them. The Acts impose a similar duty on members of the security and intelligence services.

Part of the legislation was designed to punish those who spy or plan to spy on the UK for foreign powers. In 2012 Royal Navy Petty Officer Edward Devenney, 30, was jailed for eight years when he admitted breaching the Official Secrets Act 1911. Aggrieved by failure to gain promotion, he rang the Russian embassy, intending to pass nuclear submarine secrets. But he was caught by MI5.

Official secrets legislation can also punish those who leak sensitive information to journalists or members of the public. Publishing such material makes it available to hostile powers, terrorists and criminals, and can embarrass the UK's allies—for example, by disclosing diplomatic correspondence.

Using the law to punish leaks is controversial. Attorney Generals have approved prosecutions of Crown servants and others who, on grounds of conscience, leaked information to the media to throw light on controversial Government policies. In such cases the media and others have questioned whether the prosecution was intended to protect vital state secrets or to stifle debate about matters embarrassing to the Government. A journalist seen as being an accomplice to a leak could be prosecuted. Journalists and their editors could also be prosecuted for circulating or publishing such information. As the law is complex, there is a longer version of this chapter on www.mcnaes.com, which includes a summary of the Law Commission's 2017 proposals to reform this law, and reaction to them.

the Attorney General's role is explained in 1.6

33.2 The law's consequences for journalists

As this book went to press no journalist had been successfully prosecuted, let alone jailed, under official secrets legislation for many years.

👁 Case study

In 2013 Edward Snowden leaked to journalists material he copied when he was a contractor with the US National Security Agency. After travelling to Hong Kong, Snowden publicly revealed he was the leaker, saying he wanted to expose the extent of the USA's and UK's secret surveillance of the world's communications systems. *The Guardian*, drawing on this material, revealed some detail of the UK's secret cooperation with the USA in this surveillance, including emails. *The Times* quoted a former head of the UK's surveillance base GCHQ as saying that it had to be assumed that Snowden's travels meant UK intelligence files had been hacked from his computer by China and Russia, which was 'the most catastrophic loss to British intelligence ever'. But by late 2013 *The Guardian* had not been charged with breaching official secrets law for receiving or publishing some of Snowden's material, although a threat of legal action meant that the newspaper complied with a demand by Government officials that they should destroy computer hard drives containing copies of files he leaked (*The Guardian*, 10 June, 19 and 20 August 2013; *The Times*, 11 October 2013).

 See the chapter, 'Terrorism and the effect of counter-terrorism law', on www.mcnaes.com for David Miranda's detention in the Snowden saga.

Although officialdom is reluctant to use official secrets law to prosecute journalists, journalists must know about the law to be ready to protect confidential sources of information, because this—as ch. 34 emphasises—is a moral obligation. The journalist might not be jailed for a story—but the source might. Police seeking to identify the source of leaked information could raid a journalist's newsroom, office or home. The journalist might be arrested and threatened with prosecution.

Sources are generally dealt with more severely than journalists. In 2007 former civil servant David Keogh and Leo O'Connor, who had worked as an MP's researcher, were jailed for six months and three months respectively for leaking a memo to the *Daily Mirror* about a conversation US President George Bush and UK Prime Minister Tony Blair had about the Iraq war.

> The longer version of this chapter on www.mcnaes.com provides detail of the above case, others in which sources were jailed and how a journalist's home was raided by police. Ch. 34 in this book explains police powers to search.

👁 Case study

The Official Secrets Acts continue to be cited when officialdom wants to stop police 'whistleblowers' speaking to the media. In 2015 the *Grimsby Telegraph* reported from an unnamed police source that, after a 'restructure' in staffing, some 3am–7am shifts had only four officers working in the whole of North East Lincolnshire. Humberside Police and Crime Commissioner Matthew Grove denied the claim, telling the paper: 'If any police officers are telling you the number of officers on duty, they are breaking the Official Secrets Act and becoming criminals.' *The Times* described his comment as 'ridiculous'. Mr Grove later said: 'I signed the Official Secrets Act on taking office as Commissioner, and felt that to provide sensitive information such as that disclosed would breach the principles of the Act.' He added: 'I would never try to 'gag' police officers from giving their views as has been implied, but ask them to consider the wider impact on the public and their colleagues before they do' (*Grimsby Telegraph*, 15 May and 5 June 2015; *Press Gazette*, 4 June 2015).

33.2.1 Reluctance to prosecute journalists

The reluctance of officialdom to use official secrets law against UK journalists is partly an effect of the legislation. The 1989 Act contains defences which journalists can use, but sources cannot—for example, a journalist has a defence that disclosure of the information was not 'damaging' to state interests.

John Wadham, a lawyer who was formerly director of the civil rights organisation Liberty, has said of the lack of prosecutions of journalists:

> ❝ It is partly because governments don't like to be seen to be trying to put journalists in prison and partly because juries are less sympathetic to civil servants—who are employed to keep their mouths shut, who are aware of the rules but break them, and who breach the trust with employers and colleagues—compared with journalists, who are paid to find things out and publish them. ❞

See the longer version of this chapter on www.mcnaes.com about how UK governments have used injunctions to stop publication of leaked 'official secrets'. See too 26.3, Breach of confidence and official secrets, about the *Spycatcher* case.

33.3 The 1911 Act

Section 1 of the Official Secrets Act 1911 is concerned with spying, but journalists need to know about it. Section 1 makes it an arrestable offence, carrying a penalty of up to 14 years' imprisonment, to do any of the following 'for any purpose prejudicial to the safety or interests of the state':

  (a) approach, inspect, pass over, be in the neighbourhood of or enter any prohibited place (see below);

  (b) make any sketch, plan, model or note that might be or is intended to be useful to an enemy;

  (c) obtain, collect, record or communicate to any person any information that might be or is intended to be useful to an enemy.

Offences under (c) are most relevant for journalists. Section 3 of the 1911 Act gives a lengthy and wide-ranging definition of a 'prohibited place' as including 'any work or defence, arsenal, naval or air force establishment or station, factory, dockyard, mine, minefield, camp, ship, or aircraft', as well as 'any telegraph, telephone, wireless or signal station, or office' when any such property is used by the state. Statutory instruments added British Nuclear Fuels plc and Atomic Energy Authority sites to the list of prohibited places.

The media must remember that taking photos or gathering information outside or near prohibited places, even for routine news coverage of events such as peace protests, could be held to be a breach of the Act if, for example, material gathered and published jeopardises security at a defence base.

33.4 The 1989 Act—the journalist's position

The 1989 Act defines offences of disclosure by reference to various classes of information. These include information about: security and intelligence; defence; international relations; official investigations into crime—for example, by police or other agencies; official interception of communications, including 'phone-tapping', and of emails and letters; prison and custody facilities; and matters entrusted in confidence to other states or international organisations.

Section 5 of the 1989 Act says a person—for our purposes, a journalist—commits an offence by disclosing without lawful authority information protected by the Act, knowing or having reasonable cause to believe that it is protected against disclosure, if he/she receives it from a Crown servant or Government contractor either without lawful authority or in confidence, or receives it from someone else who received it in confidence from such a person.

See the version of this chapter on www.mcnaes.com for more detail of what must be proved.

33.4.1 Damage test but no public interest defence

Though the 1989 Act can catch journalists and members of the public, it is directed particularly at security service members, other Crown servants and Government contractors. The degree of damage (by disclosure) to state interests necessary for conviction under the Act varies according to the class of information and the category of person accused. The damage alleged to have occurred could be, for example, to the capacity of the armed forces to carry out certain duties or to British relations with another state.

There is no public interest defence in official secrets cases—and information can be classed as secret even if it has been published previously.

Breaching the 1989 Act is punishable by a jail term of up to two years and/or a fine.

33.5 The public and media may be excluded from secrets trials

Section 8 of the Official Secrets Act 1920 allows the public and media to be excluded from secrets trials when publishing evidence would be 'prejudicial to the national safety'.

33.6 Defence and Security Media Advisory Notice system

The Defence and Security Media Advisory (DSMA) Committee is the head of a joint government/media system through which the media can get specific guidance on how to avoid inadvertent disclosure of information damaging to the UK's national security and defence. It has published five standing 'notices' giving general guidance. These are widely known as 'D-Notices' (defence notices) but are now officially known as 'DSMA-Notices'.

((•))
see Useful
Websites at
the end of
this chapter
to read the
DSMA-Notice

These five standing DSMA-Notices cover:

(1) military operations, plans and capabilities;

(2) nuclear and non-nuclear weapons, defence equipment and counter-terrorism equipment;

(3) ciphers and secure communications;

(4) identification of sensitive installations and home addresses;

(5) UK security and intelligence services, and special forces.

The system is based on voluntary self-censorship by the media. Editors who consult the DSMA-Notice secretary sometimes decide to limit what is published and sometimes publish information that they might otherwise have left out. The DSMA Committee has no statutory enforcement powers.

 See the longer version of this chapter on www.mcnaes.com for further details about the DSMA-Notice system, including its evolution as a reform after *The Guardian* decided not to contact the former committee before publishing the first tranche of material leaked by Edward Snowden.

➡ Recap of major points

- Official secrets law is complex and frequently controversial. There is a longer version of this chapter on www.mcnaes.com.

- This law protects national security and the safety of citizens, and can be used against foreign spies, terrorists or other criminals.

- But journalists say it is sometimes used to punish those who leak information which is politically embarrassing for the Government and to deter the media from revealing such information.

((•)) Useful Websites

www.dsma.uk/
Defence and Security Media Advisory Notice system

www.parliament.uk/briefing-papers/SN02023
House of Commons Library, *Note on Official Secrecy*

34

The journalist's sources and neutrality

Chapter summary

It is an ethical principle that journalists protect sources of confidential information. Journalists often have to rely on information from people whose safety or careers would be at risk if they were known as the sources. If naming them became commonplace, journalists' jobs would be much harder—fewer people would be willing to speak to them, and many important stories would never emerge. Various bodies have powers to demand that journalists reveal where they got a story, or to obtain journalists' phone, internet and email records. This chapter explains those powers and how journalists can protect confidential sources, and warns that investigative journalists suspected of receiving leaks of sensitive official information should expect to be placed under secret surveillance. Sometimes the reason why journalists refuse to hand over material or give evidence is to maintain a reputation for neutrality.

34.1 Protecting your source: the ethical imperative

→ glossary

Clause 14 of the Editors' Code states: 'Journalists have a moral obligation to protect confidential sources of information.' This clause is not subject to the **public interest** exceptions in the Code, which does not give any circumstance which justifies breaching it.

The National Union of Journalists' code of conduct has a similar clause. It too has no exception to the principle.

The Impress Standards Code says the anonymity offered to a source must be protected 'except where the source has been manifestly dishonest'. The Broadcasting Code, explained in ch. 3, says in practice 7.7: 'Guarantees given to contributors, for example relating to the content of a programme, confidentiality or anonymity, should normally be honoured.'

Ch. 2 introduces the Editors' Code and Impress's Code. See Useful Websites at end of this chapter for the National Union of Journalists' code.

Journalists' codes in nations all round the world state the essence of this principle. If confidential sources were not sure that journalists would protect their identities, many stories of great public interest would never be published. Remember that, whether the story is local or national, if a confidential source's employer or anyone hostile to him or her discovers the source's identity this could have life-changing consequences for him/her.

👁 Case study

In 2007 the Press Complaints Commission ruled that a newspaper breached clause 14 of the Editors' Code in an article about the possible closure of Burnley mortuary. A man who spoke to the paper on condition he was not identified was referred to in the article as 'a worker at Burnley's mortuary'. As he was one of only two people who worked there—the other was his boss—his employers identified him as the paper's source, and he was sacked for gross misconduct. The paper said the reporter had not known, and had no reason to know, that the man was one of only two employees. But the PCC said it should have established with the man how he should be described (*A man v Lancashire Telegraph*, adjudication issued 31 October 2007).

34.2 **Article 10 rights**

Journalists need to protect the identities of 'whistleblowers' who leak information about incompetence, negligence or wrongdoing by or within organisations such as police forces, Government Ministries, other state agencies, councils and companies, or about other matters which the media argue it is in the public interest to disclose.

A public servant or anyone who leaks sensitive information from an organisation could—if their identity is discovered—be sacked, and be prosecuted and jailed if the leaking is punishable as a criminal offence.

The 'whistleblower' could be prosecuted, for example, for breaching the Data Protection Act, or under official secrets law, or for alleged misconduct in public office. Chapters 28, 33, 35 respectively explain these laws and how under some circumstances the journalist who gets information from such a source could also be prosecuted.

UK law recognises to some extent that journalists need confidential sources to reveal important matters to society. Journalists facing legal consequences for refusing to identify a source can assert rights under Article 10 of the European Convention on Human Rights, which protects the right to receive and impart information, and freedom of expression.

 Article 10 is explained in 1.3

34.2.1 **European jurisprudence**

The European Court of Human Rights (ECtHR) has held—for example, in the 2013 ruling in *Telegraaf Media Nederland Landelijke Media B.V. and others v The Netherlands* (Application no. 39315/06)—that:

- Article 10 protects a journalist's right—and duty—to impart information on matters of public interest provided he/she is acting in good faith to provide accurate and reliable information in accordance with the ethics of journalism.

This jurisprudence, to which UK judges pay heed, is that the law should only require a journalist to reveal the identity of a confidential source, or surrender any material which could do that;

- if this is necessary in a democratic society because of an 'overriding requirement in the public interest'.

It could be argued in court, against the journalist, that it is in the public interest for the source to be identified because the leaked information gives good reason to suspect the source has committed a crime (whether that is the leaking itself or some other offence) or because the leaking is of sensitive information and so could infringe other people's right to privacy to such an extent that this factor is the override.

But the ECtHR has stated, in the *Telegraaf* ruling and others, that the conduct of the source—that he or she has committed a crime or may have some selfish motivation or has caused false information to be published—does not in itself override the journalist's Article 10 rights to refuse to reveal his/her identity. The crime suspected will have to be of sufficient gravity, not a minor one. The ECtHR has also ruled that using the law to try to discover a journalist's source's identity should, if that use is justifiable, be proportionate to a specific, legitimate aim in the particular case, and should not allow, for example, a wider trawl of records or material to discover what else the journalist has been doing. Also, to comply with the **proportionality** principle, the investigating state agency should have exhausted other means of identifying the source before using its powers and the law against the journalist.

But it cannot be guaranteed, at the outset of a journalist's contact with a source who wants his or her identity to be kept confidential, that an investigating agency trying to identify the source, or a judge, will agree that Article 10 rights should prevail.

> Other Convention rights may apply for the journalist—see 34.5, Article 8 rights to privacy and family life, and 34.6.1.3, Article 2 'right to life' may also be engaged.

34.2.2 **Court orders to name or produce material which could identify a source**

Police or another state agency can in some circumstances apply to a judge for a court order requiring a journalist or media organisation to name a source or produce material which might identify him/her. A company attempting to discover who leaked confidential information might ask a judge for an order requiring identification of the source, to stop further leaks damaging its business. A journalist or editor who decides on an ethical basis to defy either type of order must be prepared to face the legal consequences—a substantial fine, or possibly a jail sentence for contempt of court, although in the past four decades no UK journalist has been jailed for such a contempt.

A list of practical steps journalists can take to protect sources' identities is given later in this chapter, which also outlines the law on such orders.

34.3 Be prepared for communications and records to be probed

Arguably the biggest threat to journalists' ability to protect confidential sources comes from powers police and other state agencies have to investigate suspected crime by intercepting the content of phone and electronic communications or analysing data these generate. Some such powers are necessary so police can, for example, monitor suspected criminals and thwart terrorism. But the extent to which these powers can be used is controversial.

34.3.1 Interception of communications

If serious crime is suspected, and for other specified reasons, the police and the UK's state security and intelligence agencies can apply to the Home Secretary for a warrant to intercept people's communications during their transmission in phone or internet networks or when stored as data in such systems. The warrant requires phone and internet companies to cooperate with the interception, which could include recording—tapping—what is said in phone calls, harvesting for analysis what is said in texts, voicemail and emails, and copying the contents of posted letters. It can show who supplied what information to a journalist. In UK law material gathered from such interceptions cannot be used as evidence in legal proceedings, because the policy of successive UK Governments has been to maintain operational secrecy about interceptions to preserve their effectiveness. A person whose communications are intercepted will almost certainly not be told it has happened (it will not be denied or confirmed unless a complaint to the Investigatory Powers Tribunal—a type of court—leads it to rule the interception was unlawful, and even then details may not be disclosed).

((•)) See Useful Websites at the end of this chapter for more information about the Tribunal.

If the interception identifies the journalist's source, the source could then be prosecuted with admissible evidence such as records extracted by the police from a journalist's mobile phone or laptop, or documents seized by police searching a journalist's home or office, using powers described later in this chapter.

The Investigatory Powers Act 2016 was created to be the legal framework for 'interception' and replace earlier legislation. It has some safeguards to protect civil liberties including that investigating agencies must alert the Home Secretary

such searches occurred in Operation Elveden, see ch. 35

if the purpose of the proposed interception is to discover the identity of a journalist's source, so there can be particular consideration of the necessity for the warrant and that its scope is proportional. These safeguards include (secret) co-approval of warrants by a 'Judicial Commissioner', who is a current or former High Court judge, and subsequent reviews by an Investigatory Powers Commissioner, a senior judge. These safeguards, which were improved to some extent as a result of lobbying by media and other organisations when Parliament created the Act, are explained in detail in the Additional Material for this chapter on www.mcnaes.com.

But official secrecy about interception means a journalist is unlikely ever to discover if his or her communications were intercepted, or if the safeguards protected them and therefore protected the identity of the confidential source.

 Operational information about interception by state agencies is covered by the Official Secrets Act, see 33.4.

The best protection for such a source is for the journalist to assume interception could happen—see Practical Steps to Protect Sources.

When this chapter went to press, parts of the 2016 Act were not in force, including because a ruling by the European Court of Justice meant that some parts of the Act were inconsistent with EU law, and so earlier legislation remained in effect. Check www.mcnaes.com for updates, and the Additional Material for this chapter on that site.

34.3.2 Probing of communications data

In law 'communications data' is not the content of a communication but records kept in phone or internet systems, including the name of the account holder, phone numbers used in calls and texting, dates/times a call began and ended, or when a text was sent, email addresses used by sender and recipient, date and time of sending, and a person's internet browsing history. The data will generally give the locations of those involved in a communication when it occurred—for example, from the geolocation facility of smart phones or from the landline or wi-fi connection. Communications data can be used in evidence to confront and prosecute, or justify sacking someone who has leaked information to the media. A journalist whose communications data has been used to trace a confidential source may only find out about that from a source who has been confronted with the data.

A part of the Regulation of Investigatory Powers Act (RIPA) 2000, which the 2016 Act is due to replace, gives the UK's security and intelligence services, police and a wide range of other public authorities—including, for example, local authorities—legal powers to access communications data for a wide range of purposes, including investigating suspected crime, if authorised by the designated senior official within that body. Originally the only authorisation needed to access a journalist's communications data was from a senior officer within the agency, with no specific requirement for him/her to consider whether the journalist's Article 10 rights meant it should not be given. The ease and secrecy with which police could use RIPA to obtain such data made a mockery of journalists' rights to protect confidential sources. Controversy about this led to the *Press Gazette*'s campaign 'Save Our Sources' and other protests.

In 2015 the Interception of Communications Commissioner's Office responded to these concerns by publishing a report which disclosed that in the three years to early October 2014, 19 police forces had accessed communications data in a total of 34 investigations into suspected illicit relationships between 233 public officials (sources) and 82 national, regional and local journalists. Some of these authorisations to access journalists' communications data were triggered by media publication of material leaked or suspected to have been leaked, or by journalists indicating to police press offices that they had such material. The report did not identify the journalists or sources. The Office said there was no random trawling of communications data but that in general the senior police officers who gave authorisations did not give due consideration to journalists' Article 10 rights or sufficiently consider 'the question of necessity, proportionality and collateral intrusion'.

 For a case study on how the Investigatory Powers Tribunal ruled in 2017 that Cleveland police's accessing of three journalists communications data was unlawful, see the Additional Material for ch. 34 on www.mcnaes.com.

34.3.3 The code

The Government responded to journalists' concerns about RIPA powers by introducing a legal requirement for police to apply to a Crown court judge for a 'production order' if they want to obtain journalists' communications data. This requirement, in the Acquisition and Disclosure of Communications Data Code of Practice, means that applications must be made under procedure detailed in the Police and Criminal Evidence Act 1985 (PACE), explained later in this chapter, and that journalists or media organisations whose data is being sought must be given the opportunity to oppose the application in court.

But provisions in the 2016 Act which have yet to come into force provoked further controversy because they would remove the right of journalists or media organisations to be given notice of an investigating agency's intention to seek authorisation to access their communication data.

The Government insisted the 2016 Act had adequate safeguards, in that its section 77—reflecting ECtHR jurisprudence—says that:

European Jurisprudence, outlines that law

- if the authorisation is to get the data for the purpose of identifying or confirming a source of journalistic information, and the authorisation is not to help avert an imminent threat to life, it must be approved by a Judicial Commissioner;
- the Commissioner, when deciding whether to approve, must 'in particular' have regard to the public interest in protecting a source of journalistic

information and the need for there to be another 'overriding public interest' before a relevant public authority seeks to identify or confirm such a source.

34.3.4 Information stored in networks or equipment

Police, security and intelligences agencies have powers of 'equipment interference' to extract material from computer networks, computers and mobile phones. The 2016 Act contains some safeguards about using these powers to identify a journalist's source or to gain **journalistic material**, explained in the Additional Material for ch. 34 on www.mcnaes.com. If the relevant device has been seized, the owner may be told extraction will follow and be required to provide an encryption key, and could be jailed for a refusal—for up to two years, or up to five years if the issue is national security. A journalist should not bank on a password or encryption being unbreakable. Also, if the extraction can be done remotely, he/ she may not know of it.

→ glossary

34.4 Be prepared to be watched or bugged

→ glossary

Various **statutes** give the police and other high-level state investigation agencies powers, subject to approval procedures, to carry out surveillance to investigate serious crime. Surveillance can include following people to see who they meet, or placing secret cameras and listening bugs in cars, homes or other property. Such tactics could be deployed to attempt to identify a journalist's source.

👁 Case study

for what such 'misconduct' is, see 35.2.1

In 2008 *Milton Keynes Citizen* reporter Sally Murrer and Mark Kearney, a former detective accused of leaking information to her, walked free after a judge ruled that prosecution evidence gathered by police bugging Mr Kearney's car was inadmissible. Mr Kearney faced charges of misconduct in public office (the alleged leaking) and Ms Murrer was charged with aiding and abetting the misconduct. Judge Richard Southwell said at Kingston Crown court that gathering evidence by using the listening device was an unjustifiable violation of the Article 10 freedom of expression rights of both, and of Ms Murrer's Article 10 rights to protect her sources. The judge said the information allegedly leaked was not sensitive, let alone 'highly sensitive' and the police action could not be justified (*R v Kearney and Murrer, Media Lawyer,* 28 November 2008).

Anyone who discovers he or she has been subject to surveillance can ask the Investigatory Powers Tribunal to rule on whether the infringement of privacy rights and—in the case of a journalist—of Article 10 rights was justified by another overriding requirement in the public interest and whether, if it was, the surveillance was proportionate. If the surveillance does not meet these criteria, it will be unlawful. If it leads to the journalist being prosecuted over information leaked from an organisation, the journalist should ask the court to rule on whether it was legal.

 Laws which enable such surveillance are outlined in the Additional Material for ch. 34 on www. mcnaes.com.

34.5 Article 8 rights to privacy and family life

If an investigating agency wants to intercept anyone's communications or access their communications data, or police—using powers outlined in this chapter—propose to search their home, their Article 8 rights—to respect for privacy and family life—must be considered. In 2013 the ECtHR ruled that a warrant for a police search of a newspaper's office issued by a Luxembourg court infringed Article 8 rights as well as Article 10 rights.

 For more detail of this case, see the Additional Material for this chapter on www.mcnaes.com.

34.6 Expect a 'production' order or a search for material

Various statutes empower police and other official investigators, when investigating crime, to obtain court orders requiring a person to surrender material, or in some circumstances enabling them to search premises without warning to seize material. If the investigation is to discover the identity of a journalist's confidential source, the order could be for surrender of documents or notes of interview, and in a police search such material or objects suspected of containing it—computers, phones, and memory sticks—could be seized.

 for extraction from seized devices, see 34.3.4

34.6.1 The Police and Criminal Evidence Act 1984 (PACE)

Police who want someone to be compelled to surrender documents or other material need a court order in most circumstances. PACE is the legislation they use most when applying for these orders.

34.6.1.1 Special procedure material

PACE gives special protection to 'journalistic material', defined as 'material acquired or created for the purposes of journalism'. Police seeking to compel journalists or media organisations to surrender such material must use PACE's 'special procedure', which means they must apply to a High Court judge, a recorder or a circuit judge. If the application succeeds the judge makes a 'production order'— an order requiring the person or organisation holding the material to produce it to police. Disobeying an order is a contempt of court, punishable by a jail term of up to two years or an unlimited fine.

→ glossary

→ glossary

The application is normally 'on notice', so the holder of the material has the chance to attend the hearing to argue against granting the order.

PACE says that before making the order a judge must be satisfied that:

- there are reasonable grounds for believing that a serious offence has been committed;
- that the material the police want would be admissible evidence at a trial for that offence and of substantial value to the investigation;
- that other methods of obtaining it have been tried without success, or have not been tried because they seem bound to fail;
- and producing the material to the police would be in the public interest, having regard to
  - the benefit likely to accrue to the investigation if the material is obtained; and
  - the circumstances under which the person in possession of the material holds it.

 The Act's 'special procedure' appears to give journalistic material useful protection. But some judges have interpreted it in a way which makes the protection less valuable than was hoped—see 'Photos and footage of disorder', later in this chapter.

34.6.1.2 Excluded material

 Under PACE, **excluded material** is exempt from compulsory surrender. It includes journalistic material which a person holds in confidence—for example, from a source promised confidentiality by a journalist.

But material which was already liable to search and seizure under the previous law is not protected. For example, a stolen document acquired by a journalist, even from a confidential source, would not be 'excluded material' because it would already be liable to seizure under a warrant issued under the Theft Act 1968.

34.6.1.3 Article 2 'right to life' may also be engaged

In some circumstances a journalist resisting a police application for a production order may need to cite his or her rights in Article 2 of the European Convention on Human Rights, as well as citing Article 10 rights. Article 2 protects the right to life.

👁 Case study

In 2009 a judge accepted that the Article 2 rights of Suzanne Breen, the then Northern Editor of Ireland's *Sunday Tribune* newspaper, meant that she should not be compelled to produce to police notes and records of a phone call she received from a spokesperson for the Real IRA terrorist group claiming responsibility for two murders. She had refused a police request to do this. The judge ruled that her life would be at 'real and immediate' risk from the Real IRA were she to be forced to produce the information. She has condemned terrorist violence (*In the matter of an application by D/Inspector Justyn Galloway, PSNI, under paragraph 5 Schedule 5 of the Terrorism Act 2000 and Suzanne Breen* [2009 NICty 4]).

34.6.2 Expect your premises to be searched

A journalist protecting the identity of a source should be alert to the possibility of his or her home or office being searched by police arriving with a search warrant.

34.6.2.1 Search warrants under PACE

Instead of asking for an order for a journalist or media organisation to produce (surrender) material, police can apply to a circuit judge for a search warrant under PACE to obtain either non-confidential or confidential material. The person or media organisation does not have to be told of the application, and has no right to be heard by the judge.

Before granting a warrant, a judge must be satisfied that the criteria for ordering the production of the material are satisfied, and that one of the following circumstances applies:

- it is not practicable to communicate with anyone entitled to grant entry to the premises;
- it is not practicable to communicate with anyone entitled to grant access to the material;
- the material contains information which is subject to an obligation of secrecy or a restriction on disclosure imposed by statute (for example, material subject to the Official Secrets Act) and is likely to be disclosed in breach of that obligation if a warrant is not issued; or
- giving notice of an application for an order may seriously prejudice the investigation.

 See the Additional Material for this chapter on www.mcnaes.com for further detail of search powers.

34.6.3 Counter-terrorism legislation

The Terrorism Act 2000 enables a court to issue a warrant for police investigating a terrorist offence to search premises, or a court to issue an order for a journalist to 'produce' research material to police, for a journalist's source to be identified. This was the law police sought to use against Suzanne Breen, whose case was cited earlier. The requirements for police seeking such an order are much easier to meet than those under PACE.

✳ Remember

Journalists and news organisations facing the possibility of an application for a production order should make clear that they intend to take a stand on the issue of public interest journalism—for example, that handing over the material would chill investigative journalism about terrorism—and cite case law on Article 10 protections for confidential sources.

> See www.mcnaes.com for the online chapter, 'Terrorism and the effect of counter-terrorism law', including how such law might affect journalists who interview sources from terrorist organisations.

34.6.4 Official Secrets Acts

Section 9 of the Official Secrets Act 1911 gives police powers to make searches, subject to PACE as regards journalistic material. For more detail of police powers under official secrets law, see the extended version of ch. 33 on www. mcnaes.com.

34.7 Article 10 in breach of confidence cases

ch. 25 explains breach of confidence

In common law judges have the power to order disclosure of the identities of wrongdoers (*Norwich Pharmacal Co v Customs and Excise Comrs* [1974] AC 133). In law the term 'wrongdoer' may include a person who breaches a duty of confidence—for example, owed by an employee to a Government department or company—by leaking to the media sensitive information gained in that employment.

👁 Case study

In 1989 a High Court judge ordered Bill Goodwin, a trainee reporter on *The Engineer* magazine, to disclose his source of information for a story about an engineering company's financial difficulties. He refused, and was fined £5,000 for contempt of court (*X Ltd v Morgan-Grampian (Publishers) Ltd* [1991] 1 AC 1). The Court of Appeal and House of Lords upheld the decision, saying disclosure was 'necessary in the interests of justice' because the company had a right to know who was leaking information about it. Mr Goodwin went to the ECtHR which in 1996 agreed that the UK courts had breached his Article 10 rights (*Goodwin v United Kingdom* (1996) EHRR 123). It said protection of journalistic sources was a basic condition for press freedom, and a court order to disclose a source could not be compatible with Article 10 unless it was justified by an overriding requirement in the public interest, which did not exist in this case.

see, for more detail on the *Goodwin* case

34.8 Practical steps to protect sources

When a source who wants to remain confidential supplies material for publication, the journalist should consider the following points:

((•))
see Useful Websites at the end of this chapter for other steps

- Journalists should only promise confidentiality if the nature of the offered information means publishing the story will be defensible ethically as being in the public interest, which may protect in law against police investigation or against a court order to reveal the source's identity, and against the journalist being prosecuted for an offence related to the leaking—for definitions in ethics codes of 'public interest' stories, see chs. 2 and 3, and see, Guidance for prosecutors on whether a journalist should be prosecuted. Staff journalists should generally obtain authority from their editor to promise confidentiality, because of the legal consequences which may follow for the media organisation.
- Journalists should alert the source to steps he/she should take to avoid being identified and warn of the risk of that happening which might already exist, particularly if the method of initial contact—such as a phone call to a newspaper—has created such a risk.
- Journalists should double-check how the source wants to be described in what is published, so that description does not betray his or her identity—see the mortuary case study in 34.1, Protecting your source: the ethical imperative.
- Ensure, by checking with the source before publication, that none of the material, if published, will in itself identify him/her as the source.

If the story being pursued is likely to be sensitive for police, other state agencies or other public bodies whose investigatory powers are described in this chapter, or may provoke a claim for breach of confidence, of data law or of privacy, these steps should be among the security measures adopted:

- The journalist and source should not email each other.
- If phones have to be used for contact, each should have a pay-as-you-go mobile bought anonymously with no GPS facility.
- These phones should not be used to go online or for anything else apart from calls related to the story, as they might otherwise come to the attention of potential investigators.
- Journalists and sources should not carry or take any phone with them when they meet, because all phones produce some geolocation in communications data.
- Do not meet sources where there are CCTV cameras.
- The journalist and the source should each keep their pay-as-you-go phone physically apart from the devices they routinely use, as communications data tracking the movement of the usual devices might match that of the pay-as-you-go phone, linking them.

- Journalists should avoid keeping any material which might help identify the source, including any material the source has supplied, on any device or in any place where it may be found.
- If such information has to be stored, it should be kept secure.
- A document or computer file supplied as a leak from within an organisation should be copied by being typed out to create a fresh document or file, and the original then destroyed—some markings in the original document (see *Tisdall* case—the next case study) or metadata in the original file could help disclose the source.
- If the material has to be kept digitally, it should be in an encrypted device— such as a memory stick or external hard drive—which should only be opened using a computer which is not linked to any physical or wi-fi network.
- Payments to sources should be untraceable.

34.9 The 'shield law' has not always shielded

In section 10 of the Contempt of Court Act 1981 Parliament created what is sometimes referred to as a 'shield law' to protect journalistic activity.

Section 10 says: 'No court may require a person to disclose, nor is any person guilty of contempt of court for refusing to disclose, the source of information contained in a publication for which he is responsible, unless it is established to the satisfaction of the court that disclosure is necessary in the interests of justice or national security, or for the prevention of disorder or crime.'

As indicated earlier, section 10 did not shield Bill Goodwin in the UK courts. Since the European Convention of Human Rights began directly influencing UK law in 2000, consideration of the effect of section 10 has been subsumed, in legal disputes over whether a journalist should be required to identity a source, in the focus on whether the journalist's Convention rights—referred to in this chapter— should prevail or if there is any 'overriding requirement in the public interest'. But it is worth noting that history shows that UK judges tend to accept the Government's interpretation of what is needed to protect 'national security'.

◉ Case study

In 1983 *The Guardian* was ordered to return to the Government a leaked photocopy of a Ministry of Defence document revealing the strategy for handling the controversial arrival of US Cruise nuclear missiles, due to be based in the UK. *The Guardian* did not know the informant's identity, but, realising that it might be revealed by examination of the document, argued that section 10 meant it did not have to hand it over. The House of Lords ruled that the interests of national security required disclosure of the informant's identity, because—it said —publishing this document posed no threat to national security, but the person who leaked it might leak another. *The Guardian* handed over the document after being threatened with heavy punishment for contempt of court for any further refusal to surrender it. It had markings showing that it had been created by a photocopier in the Foreign Office, and consequently the informant—Foreign Office clerk Sarah Tisdall—was convicted under the Official Secrets Act of leaking it, and jailed for six months (*Secretary of State for Defence v Guardian Newspapers Ltd* [1985] AC 339).

ch. 33 deals with official secrets law

✳ Remember

Had *The Guardian* destroyed the document after using it to prepare the article but before being ordered to hand it over, Ms Tisdall's identity would probably have remained secret.

34.10 Tribunals of inquiry

A journalist who, by refusing to name a source, refuses to cooperate with an inquiry held under the Inquiries Act 2005 could be punished by the High Court for contempt. For more detail, see the Additional Material for ch. 18 on www.mcnaes.com.

34.11 Other statutes

Various other statutes could affect journalists by placing them under a legal obligation to disclose information, for example to an official investigation into fraud or share-dealings. See the Additional Material for ch. 34 on www.mcnaes.com for further detail.

34.12 Maintaining a reputation for neutrality

Reporters who cover events which lead to prosecutions of those involved or civil lawsuits may be asked—for example, by the prosecution or defence—to give evidence of what they themselves have seen. Most journalists in this situation will wish to retain their reputation for neutrality and will agree to be a witness only after receiving a **subpoena** (in civil cases) or witness summons (in criminal cases).

→ glossary

34.12.1 Photos and footage of disorder

In several cases, police applications to judges for production orders under PACE have been to obtain all photographs taken and footage shot by the media in coverage of riots or other disorder. Although such material does not reveal the identity of any sources promised anonymity, there is the principle of the media maintaining neutrality. Most editors and journalists take the view that they should hand

see, The Police and Criminal Evidence Act 1985 (PACE)

over such material only after careful consideration, and generally only after a court order, arguing that if it becomes routine for police to obtain such unpublished photographs or footage not broadcast, journalists, photographers and camera operators will be seen as an arm of state surveillance, which could increase the danger that they will be attacked when covering such events. But judges tend to grant such police applications.

 For a case study of when a judge did not grant a police request to supply such images, see the Additional Material for ch. 34 on www.mcnaes.com.

➡ Recap of major points

- It is an ethical imperative that a journalist does not reveal the identity of a source who has been promised confidentiality.

- The European Court of Human Rights has ruled that a court order compelling a journalist to disclose a source's identity cannot be compatible with Article 10 of the Convention unless the order is justified by an overriding requirement in the public interest.

- This safeguard for journalism in European jurisprudence also applies to use of powers held by state agencies trying to discover a source.

- But various laws can allow these to conduct such investigations including by putting journalists and others under surveillance, so journalists should presume that might happen and act accordingly.

((•)) Useful Websites

www.ipso.co.uk/editors-code-of-practice/
  Editors' Code

www.nuj.org.uk/about/nuj-code/
  National Union of Journalists Code of conduct

https://impress.press/standards/impress-standards-code.html
  Impress Standards Code

www.ofcom.org.uk/tv-radio-and-on-demand/broadcast-codes/broadcast-code/
  section-seven-fairness
  Broadcasting Code section 7

https://ipco.org.uk/default.aspx
  Investigatory Powers Commissioner

http://www.ipt-uk.com/
Investigatory Powers Tribunal

www.cps.gov.uk/legal/p_to_r/prosecuting_cases_where_public_servants_have_disclosed_
confidential_information_to_journalists/
Crown Prosecution Service guidance on journalists' confidential sources

http://journalism.cmpf.eui.eu/discussions/best-practices-for-journalists-using-
confidential-sources/
'Best Practices and Tips for Using Confidential Sources' by Gill Phillips

www.journalism.co.uk/news/protecting-journalist-sources-lessons-in-communicating-securely/
s2/a553653/
'Protecting journalist sources: Lessons in communicating securely' by Sarah
Marshall from interview with James Ball

https://ijnet.org/en/blog/digital-security-tips-and-resources-journalists
'Digital Security Tips and Resources for Journalists' by Sherry Ricchiardi

35

The risks of being charged with bribery, misconduct, hacking or intercepting

Chapter summary

The way journalists gain information may leave them and their sources at risk of prosecution. Journalists offering or paying money to sources may be accused of conspiring with the source to commit 'misconduct in public office', or of bribery. Hacking into a computer, a phone voicemail or email system, or intercepting communications, may also be prosecuted as an offence. Few of the relevant statutes contain a public interest defence. But the Director of Public Prosecutions has said in guidance to prosecutors that the public interest should always be considered when decisions are taken on whether to prosecute journalists in cases arising from their work. Journalists who realise they may be suspected of such offences should consider whether there is a sufficient public interest to justify what they plan to do—and remember that some offences may also leave them open to being sued in the civil courts for damages. This chapter details the main risks.

35.1 More than 60 journalists arrested or charged

In 2011 the Metropolitan police reopened inquiries into the hacking scandal at the *News of the World* after media revelations suggested that the police's original investigation, which led to a reporter and a private detective being jailed in 2007, had failed to result in all those responsible being prosecuted.

 See 35.6, Regulation of Investigatory Powers Act (RIPA) 2000.

Police also investigated other alleged offences. In December 2015, *Press Gazette* reported that at least 67 journalists who had worked or were working for London-based national newspapers had been arrested or charged in connection with alleged offences including hacking into mobile phone messages, hacking into emails, and making corrupt payments to police officers and other public servants.

The scale of these police inquiries into alleged criminality in or associated with journalism is unprecedented in the UK, and possibly in any democracy. Yet it should be noted that the journalists who were arrested and/or charged were almost all from only two national newspaper groups—News International and Mirror Group Newspapers, and mainly from the former.

The police investigation into corrupt payments was called Operation Elveden, and it led to 34 journalists being arrested or charged, according to *Press Gazette*. A total of three journalists were convicted, with all three convictions being overturned on appeal. But 34 people, including public servants—police officers, prison officers and civil servants—who sold information to newspapers were convicted of selling information to journalists. Some were prosecuted after News International, owner of *The Sun* and the *News of the World*, gave police information about payments to them.

The Crown Prosecution Service has issued a list of offences 'most likely to be committed' in cases involving journalists. The consent of the Director of Public Prosecutions or Attorney General is needed before proceedings can be launched for some of these offences. Some are outlined below.

35.2 Guidance for prosecutors on whether a journalist should be prosecuted

The Director of Public Prosecutions published guidance for prosecutors on the factors they should consider when deciding whether journalists—or their sources—should be charged with criminal offences which might have been committed in the course of the journalists' work. The guidance acknowledges that prosecuting journalists might have an impact on the Article 10 rights of the media and public to freedom of expression and to receive and impart information, both at common law and under the European Convention on Human Rights.

((•)) See Useful Websites at the end of this chapter for this guidance, which includes the list of possible offences.

It points out that it is important at the outset to distinguish between the public interest served by these rights and the separate question of whether a prosecution is in the public interest—for example, the public interest in punishing criminality. In general terms, it says, once prosecutors have decided that there is sufficient evidence to continue with a case, they must consider whether it is in the public interest to go ahead and prosecute.

The guidance says this decision involves considering a variety of factors. The nature of the information gained or sought by the journalist would be one factor—for example, is the information that a crime has been, is being or is likely to be committed by someone? Or does it show that someone has failed or is likely to fail to comply with any legal obligation? Or that conduct capable of disclosing a miscarriage of justice has occurred, is occurring or is likely to occur? Or is the conduct capable of raising or contributing to an important matter of public debate?

The guidance indicates that if the journalist gained or sought information in these categories, the public interest in such information coming to light weighs against the public interest in prosecuting the journalist for alleged criminality in his/her news-gathering methods.

ch. 1 explains the Article 10 rights

On the other side, prosecutors also have to consider the overall criminality of that activity—including its effects, the vulnerability of any of its victims and whether the journalist's or source's behaviour was repeated or involved corruption.

35.2.1 Misconduct in public office

This is a common law offence dating from the thirteenth century with which public officials will be charged when accused of disclosing to the media (or others) information which is not specifically protected by legislation such as the Data Protection Act 1998 or Official Secrets Acts.

 Ch. 28 deals with data protection law affecting journalism and ch. 33 with official secrets law.

The 'misconduct' may be by an act, or an omission, but must be wilful, and the offender must be a public officer acting as such. Public officials include police and prison officers, civil servants, magistrates, judges, registrars, and council and court officials. The offence can be committed even if no money changes hands. Lord Justice Pill, in the Court of Appeal in *Attorney General's Reference No. 3 of 2003* [2004] EWCA Crim 868, [2005] QB 73, [2004] 3 WLR 451, [2005] 4 All ER 303 said there must be 'a serious departure from proper standards before the criminal offence is committed; and a departure not merely negligent but amounting to an affront to the standing of the public office held. The threshold is a high one requiring conduct so far below acceptable standards as to amount to an abuse of the public's trust in the office holder. A mistake, even a serious one, will not suffice.'

👁 Case study

In June 2015, Robert Norman, aged 54, a prison officer at top-security Belmarsh jail, was jailed for 20 months for misconduct in public office after being convicted of having been the paid mole of the *Daily Mirror* and *News of the World* for five years. The jury heard he was paid more than £10,000 for 40 tips to a reporter between 30 April 2006 and 1 May 2011 (*Media Lawyer*, 2 June 2015).

In January 2015, a senior Ministry of Defence official who pocketed £100,000 from the sale of scoops to *The Sun* was jailed for 12 months. Bettina Jordan-Barber, aged 42, was cultivated by a reporter as his 'number one military contact', providing him with exclusive details of Army disciplinary investigations, sex scandals and casualties in Afghanistan. The mother-of-two, the wife of an Army officer, admitted conspiring to commit misconduct in public office between January 2004 and January 2012. The Old Bailey heard she came across confidential information in her senior Andover-based job compiling briefing notes to pass on to Ministers and the Ministry of Defence press office (*Media Lawyer*, 20 March 2015).

In March 2013, prison officer Richard Trunkfield was jailed at the Old Bailey for 16 months after admitting misconduct in public office by selling *The Sun* information about Jon Venables, one of the killers of James Bulger, who was being held at

Woodhill Prison, where he worked. That same day former Surrey policeman Alan Tierney was jailed for 10 months for selling *The Sun* details of the separate arrests of footballer John Terry's mother and Rolling Stone Ronnie Wood. Another officer who sold information was jailed for two years (*Media Lawyer*, 27 March 2013).

35.2.2 Conspiracy to commit the misconduct

The associated charge for a journalist would be conspiring to commit the misconduct—for example, an alleged plot involving the public official and/or another person for information to be supplied in breach of this law—or aiding and abetting the offence. The recent use of the offence against journalists has prompted calls for legislation to introduce a proper public interest defence for media organisations and those working for them. The offence was the basis for the controversial and discredited prosecution of journalist Sally Murrer in 2008—see 34.4, Be prepared to be watched or bugged.

The convictions of former *News of the World* crime editor Lucy Panton and former *News of the World* and *The Sun* journalist Ryan Sabey on charges of conspiring to commit misconduct in public office were overturned by the Court of Appeal in 2015, on the grounds that the judges at their trials should have told the juries that, in order to convict, they had to be satisfied that the alleged misconduct had positively harmed the public interest.

A third journalist, *The Sun* crime reporter Anthony France, was convicted in May 2015 of conspiring to commit misconduct in public office by paying a police officer for stories, and given a suspended sentence by a judge who described him as being of 'hitherto unblemished character'. The conviction was overturned by the Court of Appeal, which said that the trial judge, who had faced 'an unenviable task', should have given the jury more detailed instruction about the factors relevant to the question of the public interest, so that it could weigh carefully the seriousness of the breach.

35.3 The Bribery Act 2010

A journalist who pays a source for information could in some circumstances be charged under the Bribery Act 2010. A source could also be charged under the Act if he/she could be accused by another party—for example, the employer—of acting improperly by giving the journalist information. Offences under the Act can be committed by anyone, not just public officials.

When the Act first came into force it was described as the toughest bribery legislation in the world, and there were fears that it could mean that journalists, particularly those working on investigations, would be breaking the law by paying confidential sources.

By late 2017 no journalist had been charged under the Act. But this legislation, and the 'misconduct' cases, have caused media organisations to review procedures about paying or otherwise rewarding sources of information, to avoid breaching these laws.

35.3.1 The bribery offences

The 2010 Act creates four main offences—bribing someone, accepting bribes, bribing foreign officials and failing, as a commercial organisation, to prevent bribery. All four can only be prosecuted with the consent of the Director of Public Prosecutions. The Act does not include a public interest defence.

It is an offence to offer, promise or give a financial or other advantage to get someone 'improperly to perform a relevant function or activity', or to reward someone for such improper performance, or to do so knowing or believing that accepting the inducement would itself be improper performance.

It is irrelevant whether the person to whom the advantage is offered, promised or given is the same person who performs the function or activity concerned, and it does not matter whether the offer is made directly or through a third party.

The offence of being bribed is covered by four sets of circumstances, where someone:

- requests, agrees to receive or accepts a financial or other advantage—a bribe—intending that as a result he/she or someone else will improperly perform a relevant function or activity;
- seeks or accepts a bribe when doing so constitutes improper performance of a relevant function or activity;
- seeks or accepts a bribe as a reward for his/her own or someone else's improper performance of an activity;
- improperly performs an activity in anticipation of or as a consequence of him/herself or someone else having sought or accepted a bribe.

The Act says that in all four of cases it does not matter whether the bribe is accepted directly or through a third party, or whether it is, or is to be, for the benefit of that person or another person.

In the second, third and fourth cases it is irrelevant whether the person receiving the bribe knows or believes that the performance of the function or activity is improper. In the final case, if the function or activity is being performed by someone other than the person receiving the bribe, it does not matter whether that other person knows or believes that the performance is improper.

Section 3 says the Act covers

- any function of a public nature,
- activities connected with a business, trade or profession,
- things done in the course of employment,
- activities performed by or on behalf of a body, whether corporate or unincorporated,

as long as a person performing it is expected to do so in good faith, or impartially, or is in a position of trust by virtue of what he/she is doing. He/she is covered by the Act even if he/she has no connection with the UK and acts are performed outside the UK.

35.3.1.1 Penalties

The penalties on summary conviction are up to six months in prison and/or an unlimited fine, and on conviction on indictment, up to 10 years in jail and/or an unlimited fine. → glossary

Section 6 creates the offence of bribing a foreign public official if the person paying intends to influence the official in his/her capacity as a public official and also intends to obtain or retain business or an advantage in the conduct of business.

35.3.1.2 Companies

A company is guilty of the section 7 offence of failing to prevent bribery if someone associated with it bribes someone with the intention of obtaining or keeping business for the company, or getting or keeping an advantage in the conduct of the company's business.

This is a **strict liability** offence—meaning the prosecution does not have to prove any intention to commit it—but it is a defence for a company to prove that it had adequate procedures in place intended to stop people associated with it from bribing others. The offence is punishable by an unlimited fine. → glossary

35.4 Cases in which the public interest was clear

There are clear examples of when a possible breach by journalists of the law of 'misconduct in public office' or of the Bribery Act 2010 might be considered to be justified as being in the public interest.

One was the exposure by the *Daily Telegraph* of the scandal of MPs' unjustifiable and inflated expenses claims, in that the newspaper had paid a considerable amount of money for the information on which its exposés were based.

see also 30.1, Introduction to the Act, on the expenses story

This was before the Bribery Act came into force, but it was later made clear that prosecutors would not have brought a case.

The first criminal conviction under the Bribery Act came after *The Sun*, in the public interest, risked being prosecuted itself under the Act by paying Redbridge magistrates' court office worker Munir Yakub Patel a £500 bribe—which it secretly filmed him accepting—to stand up a story that he was taking bribes to keep details of a traffic offence summons off a court database. This led to him being jailed. So far no journalists have been charged with or convicted of bribery.

> See the Additonal Material for ch. 35 on www.mcnaes.com for hypothetical case studies on whether a journalist paying for information could be deemed to breach the Bribery Act 2010.

35.5 The Computer Misuse Act 1990

The Computer Misuse Act 1990 creates computer hacking offences of unauthorised access to a computer with the intention of:

- getting to any program or information it holds; or
- committing or facilitating the commission of an offence; or

- impairing a computer so as to stop or hinder access to any program or data held in any computer; or
- impairing or intending to impair the operation of any such program or the reliability of any such data.

It is also an offence to make, adapt, supply or offer to supply any article intending or believing that it will be used to commit or help the commission of one of these offences.

Penalties range from six months in prison and/or an unlimited fine on summary conviction, and up to 10 years in prison and/or an unlimited fine if convicted on indictment.

These offences clearly cover computer hacking activities, such as hacking into someone's emails. The unauthorised access offences require that the defendant must have known that the intended access was unauthorised—which will generally not be an issue if a journalist has accessed someone else's computer.

The Act itself does not contain a public interest defence, but acting in the public interest will help protect journalists.

Case study

ch. 3 explains
Ofcom's
role, and ch.
4 explains
the Code's
privacy
section

The Crown Prosecution Service announced in March 2013 that Sky News reporter Gerald Tubb would not be prosecuted for hacking into the emails of back-from-the-dead canoeist John Darwin and his wife Anne, who were jailed in 2008 after staging his 'death' to make a fraudulent life insurance claim.

Malcolm McHaffie, CPS deputy head of special crime, said a prosecution would not be in the public interest. In July 2013 Ofcom cleared Sky News of having breached the Broadcasting Code, saying that it had concluded that the 'exceptional circumstances of this case outweighed Mr and Mrs Darwin's expectation of privacy', and that Sky's conduct was 'warranted in the particular circumstances of this case' (*Media Lawyer*, 29 March and 1 July 2013).

35.6 The Regulation of Investigatory Powers Act 2000 (RIPA)

This Act contains a series of offences which could affect journalists, all of which can be prosecuted only with the consent of the Director of Public Prosecutions. There is no public interest defence in the Act itself.

Section 1 contains the offences of unlawfully intercepting any communication being transmitted through a public postal service, or through a public or private telecommunication system. When this chapter went to press, this section was due to be replaced by similar law in the Investigatory Powers Act 2016.

Private investigator Glenn Mulcaire, who hacked (intercepted) phone messages for *News of the World* royal correspondent Clive Goodman, admitted five offences under the 2000 Act when the two men were jailed in January 2007. Mulcaire was given a six-month sentence and Goodman received four months.

The two men had also admitted the Criminal Law Act 1977 offence of conspiring to intercept communications without lawful authority.

In July 2014 former *News of the World* editor Andy Coulson was given an 18-month jail term after being convicted of conspiring to intercept voicemail messages. Six other former *News of the World* journalists have also been convicted of phone-hacking. In law, messages stored for later retrieval are classified as still being 'in the course of transmission', thus putting voicemail within the scope of 'interception'.

The scandal erupted again in 2011 when *The Guardian* revealed the huge scale of phone-hacking at the *News of the World* and that it had hacked into the voicemails on a murdered schoolgirl's phone. This led to the *News of the World*'s closure in June 2011.

 Ch. 27 refers to privacy lawsuits arising from hacking by Mirror Group journalists—see 27.3.1, Damages.

✳ Remember

As ch. 2 explains, the Editors' Code specifically protects the privacy of 'digital communications' and bans the interception of private or mobile telephone calls, messages or emails.

35.6.1 Recording phone calls

Journalists frequently record the calls they themselves make or receive. In law interception occurs in the course of transmission, so recording telephone conversations by a device at either end of the communication is not interception and is lawful. For ethical considerations on recording phone calls, see 2.4.4.2 Recording interviews and phone calls, and 3.4.16 Secret filming and recording—deception and privacy.

35.7 The Wireless Telegraphy Act 2006

The Wireless Telegraphy Act 2006 prohibits the use without authority of wireless apparatus with intent to obtain information about the contents, sender or addressee of any message, and prohibits the disclosure of any such information.

35.8 Perverting the course of justice

Perverting the course of justice is a common law offence. It includes falsifying, concealing or destroying evidence or potential evidence, such as emails, records or files, and so on. Criminal proceedings do not have to be in progress when the act is done for an offence to be committed. Police who reopened inquiries into allegations of widespread phone-hacking by the *News of the World* arrested a number of people in connection with allegations of perverting the course of justice in relation to the inquiry.

35.9 The Serious Crime Act 2007

Sections 44–46 of the Serious Crime Act 2007 make it an offence intentionally to encourage or assist an offence, or to do so believing the offence will be committed, or to do so believing that that offence or another will be committed.

The penalty for each offence is any penalty the offender would be liable to face if he/she were convicted of the anticipated offence.

These offences would cover, for example, the position of a journalist or editor who commissions a private investigator or someone else to hack into someone's emails.

 For defences in the Digital Economy Act for journalists who receive leaked information from Government departments, see the Additional Material for this chapter on www.mcnaes.com. Ch. 4 deals with the risk of journalists being charged with harassment. The risk of journalists being charged under counter-terrorism law is discussed in the www.mcnaes.com chapter, 'Terrorism and the effect of counter-terrorism law'.

➡ Recap of major points

- News-gathering activities may leave journalists at risk of being charged with criminal offences such as conspiracy to commit misconduct in public office or with bribery.

- Public officials—police, prison officers and others—who sell information to the media may also face criminal prosecution for misconduct in public office.

- Hacking into computers, emails and voicemail messages is a criminal offence.

- The Director of Public Prosecutions has issued guidance saying that the issue of public interest must be considered before journalists are prosecuted in connection with news-gathering activities.

((•)) Useful Websites

www.cps.gov.uk/legal-guidance/guidance-prosecutors-assessing-public-interest-cases-affecting-media
Crown Prosecution Service guidelines for prosecutors assessing whether journalists should be charged—the list of offences most likely to be concerned in such cases appears in Annex A to the document

www.sfo.gov.uk/publications/guidance-policy-and-protocols/bribery-act-guidance/
Serious Fraud Office and Director of Public Prosecutions guidance on the Bribery Act 2010 is available via this website

36

The right to take photographs, film and record

Chapter summary

Journalists should know their rights when gathering visual images or making recordings in the streets or countryside. There is no criminal law restricting photography or filming or recording in public places. Concern has grown in the media that over-zealous police officers, security guards and members of the public raise invalid objections to journalists using cameras. Photographers have been wrongly arrested. This chapter covers laws which are sometimes officiously cited or used against journalists and the civil law of trespass.

36.1 Introduction

Many police officers, police community support officers and members of the public help the media. But some do not and become officious or hostile to journalists going about their lawful business. In tense situations, journalists may find laws being invalidly used or cited against them. Official guidance issued to police reflects the law—that officers have no power to prohibit the taking of photographs, film or digital images in a public place, whether the shots are of crowds, bystanders or buildings.

Controversially, urban development has meant some apparently 'public' spaces—for example, thoroughfares in shopping malls—are now private property, not public highways, and security staff may intervene unless journalists get permission to take pictures, film, or record there.

36.2 Trouble with the police in public places

A photographer, radio reporter, video-journalist or film crew must get in close for their pictures and/or sound. They may be attacked by disorderly people and—even during a small-scale event—be improperly arrested by police as tension rises.

👁 **Case study:**

In 2010 the Metropolitan Police paid photo-journalists Marc Vallée and Jason Parkinson £3,500 each in damages after armed officers stopped them from taking video footage and photos at a protest outside the Greek Embassy. Diplomatic Protection Group officers, claiming the pair were not allowed to film them, pulled Vallée's camera away from his face and covered the lens of Parkinson's camera (*Media Lawyer*, 28 June 2010).

36.2.1 Police guidelines on media photography and filming

((•))

see Useful Websites at the end of this chapter for this guidance

Journalists having problems at an incident or crime scenes will need to refer police to 'authorised professional practice' guidance issued to them by the College of Policing. The guidance section on 'Engagement and communication—media relations' includes this passage:

- Reporting or filming from the scene of an incident is part of the media's role and they should not be prevented from doing so from a public place.
- Police have no power or moral responsibility to stop the filming or photographing of incidents or police personnel. It is for the media to determine what is published or broadcast, not the police.
- Once an image has been recorded, the police have no power to seize equipment, or delete or confiscate images or footage without a court order.
- Where police have designated a cordoned area, the media must respect it in the same way as the public, unless a media facility within a cordoned area has been authorised by police.
- The best possible vantage point for media should be considered, providing it does not compromise operational needs.

The College's guidance to police on 'Public order—communication' includes these points:

- Production of a UK Press Card should allow the holder release from any area subject to containment, unless the behaviour of the holder is cause for concern.
- Police cannot give or deny permission to the media to enter private premises whether the premises are directly involved in the police operation or not—the person who owns or controls the property makes that decision.
- If someone who is distressed or bereaved asks for the police to intervene to prevent members of the media filming or photographing them, the police may pass on their request, but there is no power to prevent or restrict media activity.

! **Remember your rights**

Police who want to view or seize journalistic material must first get a court order under the Police and Criminal Evidence Act 1984, explained in ch. 34. If a person is searched by police because of a reasonable suspicion of a terrorism offence, they can seize a camera for its images to be inspected—see 36.2.4, 'Stop and search' under the Terrorism Act 2000.

36.2.2 False imprisonment

A journalist who is subject to unlawful physical restraint—such as being locked in the cells or physically restrained by a police officer—might be able to sue for false imprisonment, see 5.3.2 and 13.11.2. Movement must be completely restricted; barring a photographer from going in one particular direction—for example, towards the scene of a crash—is not false imprisonment.

◉ Case study

Wiltshire police paid compensation to photo-journalist Robert Naylor after an incident in 2009 when he went to a canal to report on a death in a boat fire. A police sergeant told him he could not take photos because of 'respect for deceased'. Soon afterwards, as he started back to this car, he was dragged to the ground, arrested and handcuffed for allegedly 'breaching the peace'. Wiltshire police later accepted he was unlawfully detained and apologised (*Media Lawyer*, 30 March 2011).

36.2.3 Public order and 'obstruction' offences

Police officers sometimes warn media photographers or video-journalists that they may be arrested.

The arrest might be for a **common law** breach of the peace or under section 5 of the Public Order Act 1986. Arrest for breach of the peace is only justified if harm has been done or is likely to be done to a person or his/her property in his/her presence, or when a person is in fear of being harmed. Section 5 allows arrest if anyone uses threatening or abusive words or behaviour, or disorderly behaviour, likely to cause 'harassment, alarm or distress' to another person. Though the journalist is not intending to cause distress, etc., in some situations the mere fact that he/she is taking pictures or shooting footage, perhaps of someone or a group who object to this, may prompt an arrest.

Section 137 of the Highways Act 1980 make it an offence for someone 'without lawful authority or excuse' to obstruct free passage along a highway in any way. This power allows police to arrest journalists in a public place who fail to move on when asked to do so.

Section 89 of the Police Act 1996 says that a person commits an offence if he/she 'resists or wilfully obstructs a constable in the execution of his duty, or a person

→ glossary

((•))

see Useful Websites at the end of this chapter for further guidance on public order offences assisting a constable in the execution of his duty'. The obstruction does not have to be a physical act—it may occur, for example, if someone makes it more difficult for the constable to perform his/her duty. A journalist who persists in taking photographs or shooting footage, and engages in argument with a police officer, therefore runs the risk of arrest.

 For two case studies of photographers being paid compensation or acquitted after arrest, see the Additional Material for ch. 36 on www.mcnaes.com. For an outline of the police's general powers of arrest, see 5.2, Arrests.

36.2.4 'Stop and search' under the Terrorism Act 2000

Complaints by photographers of excessive use by police of 'stop and search' powers under the Terrorism Act 2000—for example, if a photographer were taking pictures of buildings—have decreased since the Government amended the law to produce a more tightly defined 'stop and search' power in the Act's section 47A. This change is primarily concerned with the criteria police can use to designate areas as being at risk of terrorist attack. Police in such areas are still permitted to stop and search an individual without 'reasonable suspicion'. A revised code of practice issued to police makes clear that they have no power under the 2000 Act to stop filming or photography of incidents or of police officers and that it is not an offence to film/photograph a public building or in public places. Police retain power under section 43 of the Act to stop and search, and to seize equipment, if they 'reasonably suspect' someone is a terrorist.

👁 Case study

In 2017 freelance photographer Eddie Mitchell was arrested and held for an hour after a civilian employee of Sussex police challenged him about why he was taking photos of the outside of Hove Town Hall council offices. He was on a public street and—as he was not doing anything unlawful, and having told her he was a photographer photographing the building—declined to give his name. She asked him to go inside the Town Hall where two police officers, based in a 'pop up' police station, arrested him and searched him including by inspecting images in his camera, telling him they were using powers in section 43 of the Terrorism Act 2000. He was allowed to leave after they accepted he was not doing anything illegal. Mr Mitchell said the police had abused their power. A Sussex police force spokesperson said the action was appropriate in that the 'threat level' of terrorist attacks was high *(Mail Online* and *The Guardian*, 4 May 2017).

 See Useful Websites at the end of this chapter for the code of practice in full. See the www.mcnaes. com chapter, 'Terrorism and the effect of counter-terrorism law', for other counter-terrorism laws which could affect journalists.

36.3 Trespass and bye-laws

Property owners who object to photography or filming or recording on their sites may decide to enforce objections by using the civil law of trespass, which forbids unlawful entry to land or buildings. Because trespass is a **tort**, the remedy is an action in the civil courts which could result in an injunction to prevent further trespass and/or damages. Also, the occupier of property or land may use reasonable force to eject the trespasser. Police may lawfully assist, though they have no duty to do so.

There is no trespass if a journalist photographs, films or records an event on private land from an adjoining site where he/she has permission or a right to be—for example, a public highway. But such media activity might lead to a subject suing for intrusion into privacy, or complaining to Ipso, Impress or Ofcom.

Trespass can also include 'trespass to the person'—for example, compelling a person to be filmed by stopping him/her from entering his/her home or a workplace. Trespass to goods means, for instance, picking up a document without permission and photographing it.

Trespass is not usually a criminal offence, so a police officer threatening an arrest for civil trespass is wrong in law. However, there are trespass offences for certain sites—for example, Ministry of Defence (MoD) land and railway property—and there is a specific offence of aggravated trespass. Also, bye-laws ban photography in and of MoD establishments.

see ch. 4 on news-gathering avoiding intrusion and ch. 27 on privacy

> For details of the criminal offence of aggravated trespass, which has been used to prosecute protesters in 'occupations' and could be used against photographers at the scene, see the Additional Material for ch. 36 on www.mcnaes.com.

ch. 33 explains official secrets law on 'prohibited places'

36.4 Intrusion and harassment

Chapter 4 covers what ethics codes say about intrusive photography, filming and recording, including when a child is the subject. That chapter also covers intrusion into grief and explains that paparazzi who stalk people could be sued or prosecuted for harassment.

➡ Recap of major points

- There is no law against photography, filming or recording in public places.
- But journalists need to be familiar with the law on trespass and the general powers police have to arrest those 'obstructing' them or the highway.
- Police have been issued with guidelines that they should help the media take photos and gain footage, but individual officers may need reminding of these

((•)) Useful Websites

www.app.college.police.uk/app-content/engagement-and-communication/media-relations/
  College of Policing guidance: 'Engagement and communication—media relations'

www.app.college.police.uk/app-content/public-order/planning-and-deployment/communication
/?s=public+order+communication
  College of Policing guidance; 'Public order—communication'

www.met.police.uk/advice-and-information/photography-advice/
  Metropolitan Police 'Photography advice'

www.gov.uk/government/publications/
code-of-practice-for-the-exercise-of-stop-and-search-powers
  Code of Practice for police 'stop and search' powers under the Terrorism Act 2000

www.cps.gov.uk/legal/s_to_u/trespass_and_nuisance_on_land/
  Crown Prosecution Service guidance on trespass offences

http://media.gn.apc.org/photo/index.html
  National Union of Journalists London Freelance branch advice for photographers

http://media.gn.apc.org/fl/streets.html
  National Union of Journalists London Freelance branch; 'Advice for photographers
  covering demonstrations'

www.epuk.org/resources/faq
  Editorial Photographers site: resource section

Northern Ireland

Chapter summary

Media law in Northern Ireland is, with some exceptions, particularly in defamation law, the same as that in England and Wales. In the few important cases involving the media which have gone to the High Court, cases in England have been cited. The Supreme Court in London is the final court of appeal for criminal and civil cases on major points of law. Restrictions on reports of **preliminary hearings** → glossary before magistrates, prior to committal to Crown court, follow Northern Ireland law but restrictions on reports of criminal proceedings involving juveniles are along the lines of those in England. Victims or alleged victims of sexual offences must remain anonymous. It is an offence to disclose the identity of a juror who is serving or has served on a trial in Northern Ireland.

37.1 The law is broadly the same as in England and Wales

The law in Northern Ireland, including the courts structure, is broadly the same as that in England and Wales. Scotland has its own system.

 See the www.mcnaes.com chapter on Scotland.

Many of the laws applicable in England and Wales extend to Northern Ireland by means of Orders made by the Secretary of State.

The Lord Chief Justice of Northern Ireland is assisted by High Court judges and circuit judges who try cases in the Crown court. Civil cases are heard by High Court judges sitting in the Northern Ireland High Court which deals with cases of unlimited financial value, or circuit judges sitting in the county court, which deals with cases valued at up to £30,000.

→glossary   Most cases in magistrates' courts are heard by a **district judge** and decisions in this court can be appealed to the County Court or occasionally, the Court of Appeal. Two lay magistrates and a district judge sit for youth and family law cases. The media has restricted reporting rights on these.

✳ Remember

In 2016 the Lord Chief Justice in Practice Note 1 gave a general permission for reporters to use live-text communication devices in court—see 12.3, Tweeting, emailing and texting 'live' reports from court, for similar permission in England and Wales.

37.2 **Defamation**

Defamation law in Northern Ireland and England diverged when the Westminster Parliament passed the Defamation Act 2013 to reform the law. Northern Ireland's Government, the Executive, decided against adopting the legislation automatically. A consultation process took place and was completed in early 2015 but it is expected to be some time before the law is changed.

> ⊙ Check www.mcnaes.com for updates.

The result is that reforms in the 2013 Act have no effect in Northern Ireland, which continues to operate under the Defamation Act (Northern Ireland) 1955 and the relevant parts of the Defamation Act 1996. Thus, there is no statutory requirement in Northern Ireland for **claimants** to prove that they have suffered 'serious harm' to their reputation from what was published, while website operators have fewer defences in relation to user-generated content. Even if a website publisher has procedures to enable complaints to be remedied, it can be sued in Northern Ireland much more easily than in England or Wales. Also the new statutory defences in England and Wales of **truth, honest opinion** and of responsible publication on matters of public interest do not apply. Instead defendants in Northern Ireland have to rely on the **common law** defences of justification, honest comment and qualified **privilege** (under the *Reynolds* principles, see ch. 23) respectively. Furthermore, the 2013 Act's absence from Northern Ireland means there is no 'single publication rule' there. This means that each day a defamatory publication remains online there, this represents a new starting point for the 12-month period within which the publisher can be sued.

> 📖 For the England and Wales position, see 21.2.3.4 and 21.2.3.5 about the, 'single publication rule' and online publication.

Another notable difference is that awards for defamation can potentially be higher in Northern Ireland than England and Wales. This was alluded to in the 2016 case in which Sinn Fein politician Philip Flanagan was ordered to pay £48,000 damages to Ulster Unionist politician Thomas Elliott because of a defamatory tweet.

> The 'justification' and 'honest' comment defences are explained on www.mcnaes.com in the Additional Material for this chapter. For general principles of defamation law, see chs. 20 to 25 where some explanation is given solely in the context of the law in England and Wales.

37.3 Contempt of court

The Contempt of Court Act 1981 applies in Northern Ireland, and rulings in contempt law by the High Court in London are equally applicable there. The only significant difference is that there is a higher frequency of trials in Northern Ireland held without juries. Such trials are for serious charges, usually those allegedly connected with terrorism or sectarianism. Crown courts in England and Wales too can sit without juries but such exceptional cases are much rarer. It has been argued that the absence of a jury means there is a much-reduced likelihood of media publication creating a substantial risk of serious prejudice to those proceedings, which would be a contempt. But the risk remains that the evidence of witnesses might be affected by what is published pre-trial when the case is 'active'.

ch. 19 explains contempt law

37.4 Reporting restrictions

Guidelines on reporting restrictions issued in 2008 by the Judicial Studies Board for Northern Ireland say courts are encouraged to exercise their discretion to hear media representations when considering optional reporting restrictions.

see Useful Websites at the end of this chapter for this guidance

37.4.1 Preliminary hearings

Committal proceedings must be in open court except where it appears to the court that justice would not be served by reporting of the whole or part of the hearing. The Magistrates' Courts (Northern Ireland) Order 1981 (SI 1981/1675) prohibits publication of a report of any opening statement made by the prosecution. There is no automatic ban on reporting evidence, but the Act allows a court to prohibit publication of any evidence if it is satisfied that publication would prejudice the defendant's trial. The court may impose additional restrictions where objection is taken to the admissibility of evidence. The court may, if satisfied that the objection is made in good faith, order that such evidence and any discussion on it shall not be published.

37.4.2 Crown courts

Restrictions under the Criminal Justice Act 2003 on reporting prosecution appeals against the termination of a trial by a judge, or against an acquittal, were

see 9.4.9 for this law in 2003 Act

extended to Northern Ireland under the Criminal Justice (Northern Ireland) Order 2004 (SI 2004/1500).

37.4.3 Juveniles in court

A child under 10 cannot be charged with a criminal offence in Northern Ireland. Youth courts deal with offences committed or allegedly committed by those below the age of 18. The Criminal Justice (Children) (Northern Ireland) Order 1998 (SI 1998/1504), as amended, makes it an offence in reporting the proceedings to publish the name, address or school, or any particulars likely to lead to the identification of anyone under 18 involved in youth court proceedings. This includes a defendant, witness or alleged victim/victim. It is also an offence to publish a picture of/or including anyone under 18 so involved. A youth court may lift the restrictions in the public interest as regards a convicted young offender, but must first give parties to the proceedings an opportunity to make representations.

Under Article 22 of the 1998 Order, an adult, criminal court may order that nothing should be published which would identify those under 18 involved in the proceedings as a defendant, witness or victim/alleged victim. An order is not effective if the person has reached 18.

 Law applying to media reports of youth court cases in England and Wales, explained in ch. 10, is similar to that in Northern Ireland. That chapter explains too the 'section 39' orders used in England and Wales which are comparable to Article 22 orders.

The 1998 Order empowers a court in any criminal proceedings to exclude everyone not concerned in the case, when it considers that a child's evidence is likely to involve matter of an indecent or immoral nature. There is no specific provision for the press to remain, unlike the position in England and Wales under section 37 of the Children and Young Persons Act 1933.

 See 15.9, Statute law on open and private hearings, for detail on section 37.

As in England and Wales, there is no automatic anonymity in Northern Ireland for persons under 18 being investigated by police, until and unless youth court proceedings begin. This meant that a boy, then aged 15, arrested in Northern Ireland for the 2015 hacking of TalkTalk's customer details was named by some newspapers before a court order was put in place to protect his identity. A change in January 2018 to clause 9 of the Editors' Code means that the Independent Press Standards Organisation will rule the clause to have been breached by a member organisation whose reporting identifies a juvenile under the age of 16 who is under police investigation, unless his or her identity is already in the public domain in that regard, or there is parental consent to the identification, or a public interest exception applies—see 5.15, Juveniles under investigation.

37.4.4 Domestic proceedings

Reporters may attend domestic proceedings but reports must be confined to four categories of information and there is automatic anonymity for children involved in family cases. For more detail, see the Additional Material for this chapter on www.mcnaes.com. A court may, under the Children (Northern Ireland) Order 1995, direct that no person shall publish any material which is intended, or likely, to identify any child under 18 as being involved in non-criminal proceedings (that is, for which there is not automatic anonymity under the Order) except to the extent which the court may allow. The court has power to sit **in private** when exercising any power under the 1995 Order.

 →glossary

 See also ch. 14 on family cases.

37.4.5 Sexual, human trafficking and female genital mutilation offences

Victims and alleged victims of rape and other sexual offences are given lifelong anonymity by the Sexual Offences (Amendment) Act 1992 and the Criminal Justice (Northern Ireland) Order 1994 (SI 2004/2795). This law is essentially the same as in England and Wales, as is the law providing anonymity for victims/alleged victims of female genital mutilation—see ch. 11. Although the law against 'human trafficking' in section 2 of the Modern Slavery Act 2015, referred to in that chapter, does not apply in Northern Ireland, a victim/alleged victim of an offence of trafficking for the purposes of sexual exploitation—for example, prostitution—which arises there has anonymity under the 1992 Act because of the sexual nature of the offence, and there is anonymity under a Northern Ireland statute for victims of other categories of trafficking.

For more detail on this trafficking law, see the Additional Material for this chapter on www.mcnaes.com.

37.4.5.1 Identifying defendants in sexual offence cases

Neither the 1992 Act nor the 1994 Order gives a court discretionary powers to impose restrictions such as a ban on identifying a defendant in a sexual offence case in order to protect the victim.

see also 16.10, Sexual offence law does not give anonymity for defendants

Yet courts in Northern Ireland have made orders banning the identification of a defendant, citing the 1992 Act or the 1994 Order, on the grounds that publishing his/her name would either lead to the identification of the complainant or be detrimental to the complainant's well-being. These purported orders should be challenged by the media.

See the Additional Material for ch. 37 on www.mcnaes.com 'Bans on identifying defendants', for instances in which defendants in various types of criminal case in Northern Ireland have been given anonymity, leading journalists and others to protest that the open justice principle has been eroded.

37.4.5.2 Identifying jurors

The Juries (Northern Ireland) Order 1996 (SI 1996/1141), as amended, makes it an offence to identify someone as being or having been a juror in Northern Ireland, or as being listed as a juror or selected for inclusion on the jury list. But there is a defence that the publisher had a reasonable belief that disclosing the juror's identity was lawful.

 See also 12.5, Contempt risk in identifying or approaching jurors.

37.4.5.3 Photography, filming and recording at court

ch. 12 explains the 1925 Act and also covers the ban on audio-recording in courts

The Criminal Justice (Northern Ireland) Act 1945, like the Criminal Justice Act 1925 in England and Wales, bans photography, filming or sketching in a court or its precincts. Guidelines from the Judicial Studies Board say the court can issue guidance, by way of a map, on the extent of the precincts.

✱ Remember

www.mcnaes.com has a chapter outlining Scottish media law.

➡ Recap of major points

- The law in Northern Ireland, including the courts structure, is broadly the same as in England and Wales, with minor variations.

- It is easier to sue for defamation in Northern Ireland than in England and Wales. The claimant does not have to prove serious harm, the defences are weaker and each day a defamatory statement is online is a considered a fresh publication.

- Reporting restrictions in Northern Ireland broadly follow those in England and Wales but many of them are contained in Orders made by the Secretary of State rather than in Acts of the UK Parliament.

((•)) Useful Websites

www.jsbni.com/Publications/reporting-restrictions/Pages/default.aspx
    Judicial Studies Board for Northern Ireland guide to reporting restrictions

www.justice-ni.gov.uk/
    Northern Ireland courts and tribunals services

Part 6

Online chapters

38

The incitement of hate

Chapter summary

Freedom of expression has boundaries. One boundary is that making or publishing some kinds of threatening statement is a crime. As this chapter explains, it is illegal to stir up hatred against people because of their race or religious beliefs or their sexual orientation. Such offences can be committed in speech, or in printed, broadcast or online material.

Chapter available online at www.mcnaes.com.

39

Scotland

Chapter summary

The law of Scotland affects journalism in different ways from that in England and Wales. This chapter briefly outlines the Scottish legal system and its judiciary, and shows how reporting restrictions affect coverage of criminal proceedings, especially cases involving children. Media organisations based in other parts of the UK may need to pay special consideration to what they publish in Scotland, because contempt laws are interpreted differently.

Chapter available online at www.mcnaes.com.

Terrorism and the effect of counter-terrorism law

Chapter summary

The heightened threat of terrorism in recent years has led to more counter-terrorism laws in the UK, some controversial because of their actual or potential interference with journalists' work. These laws ban the gathering of certain information, and restrict what can be published. As this chapter shows, the wide scope of counter-terrorism law has the potential to deter journalistic investigation of the causes and control of terrorism. Journalists who interview people who have joined terrorist groups—for example, the so-called Islamic State—should be aware that a court may order that the interview records and these sources' identities must be disclosed to the police.

Chapter available online at www.mcnaes.com.

Appendix
The Editors' Code of Practice

The Independent Press Standards Organisation (IPSO), as regulator, is charged with enforcing the following Code of Practice, which was framed by the Editors' Code of Practice Committee and is enshrined in the contractual agreement between IPSO and newspaper, magazine and electronic news publishers.

Preamble

The Code—including this preamble and the public interest exceptions below—sets the framework for the highest professional standards that members of the press subscribing to the Independent Press Standards Organisation have undertaken to maintain. It is the cornerstone of the system of voluntary self-regulation to which they have made a binding contractual commitment. It balances both the rights of the individual and the public's right to know.

To achieve that balance, it is essential that an agreed Code be honoured not only to the letter, but in the full spirit. It should be interpreted neither so narrowly as to compromise its commitment to respect the rights of the individual, nor so broadly that it infringes the fundamental right to freedom of expression—such as to inform, to be partisan, to challenge, shock, be satirical and to entertain—or prevents publication in the public interest.

It is the responsibility of editors and publishers to apply the Code to editorial material in both printed and online versions of their publications. They should take care to ensure it is observed rigorously by all editorial staff and external contributors, including non-journalists.

Editors must maintain in-house procedures to resolve complaints swiftly and, where required to do so, cooperate with IPSO. A publication subject to an adverse adjudication must publish it in full and with due prominence, as required by IPSO.

1. Accuracy

i)   The Press must take care not to publish inaccurate, misleading or distorted information or images, including headlines not supported by the text.

ii)   A significant inaccuracy, misleading statement or distortion must be corrected, promptly and with due prominence, and—where appropriate—an apology published. In cases involving IPSO, due prominence should be as required by the regulator.

iii) A fair opportunity to reply to significant inaccuracies should be given, when reasonably called for.

iv) The Press, while free to editorialise and campaign, must distinguish clearly between comment, conjecture and fact.

v) A publication must report fairly and accurately the outcome of an action for defamation to which it has been a party, unless an agreed settlement states otherwise, or an agreed statement is published.

2. *Privacy

i) Everyone is entitled to respect for his or her private and family life, home, health and correspondence, including digital communications.

ii) Editors will be expected to justify intrusions into any individual's private life without consent. In considering an individual's reasonable expectation of privacy, account will be taken of the complainant's own public disclosures of information and the extent to which the material complained about is already in the public domain or will become so.

iii) It is unacceptable to photograph individuals, without their consent, in public or private places where there is a reasonable expectation of privacy.

3. *Harassment

i) Journalists must not engage in intimidation, harassment or persistent pursuit.

ii) They must not persist in questioning, telephoning, pursuing or photographing individuals once asked to desist; nor remain on property when asked to leave and must not follow them. If requested, they must identify themselves and whom they represent.

iii) Editors must ensure these principles are observed by those working for them and take care not to use non-compliant material from other sources.

4. Intrusion into grief or shock

In cases involving personal grief or shock, enquiries and approaches must be made with sympathy and discretion and publication handled sensitively. These provisions should not restrict the right to report legal proceedings.

5. *Reporting suicide

When reporting suicide, to prevent simulative acts care should be taken to avoid excessive detail of the method used, while taking into account the media's right to report legal proceedings.

6. *Children

i) All pupils should be free to complete their time at school without unnecessary intrusion.

ii) They must not be approached or photographed at school without permission
of the school authorities.

iii) Children under 16 must not be interviewed or photographed on issues involving their own or another child's welfare unless a custodial parent or similarly
responsible adult consents.

iv) Children under 16 must not be paid for material involving their welfare, nor
parents or guardians for material about their children or wards, unless it is
clearly in the child's interest.

v) Editors must not use the fame, notoriety or position of a parent or guardian
as sole justification for publishing details of a child's private life.

7. *Children in sex cases

1. The press must not, even if legally free to do so, identify children under 16
who are victims or witnesses in cases involving sex offences.

2. In any press report of a case involving a sexual offence against a child—

i) The child must not be identified.

ii) The adult may be identified.

iii) The word 'incest' must not be used where a child victim might be identified.

iv) Care must be taken that nothing in the report implies the relationship
between the accused and the child.

8. *Hospitals

i) Journalists must identify themselves and obtain permission from a responsible executive before entering non-public areas of hospitals or similar institutions to pursue enquiries.

ii) The restrictions on intruding into privacy are particularly relevant to enquiries about individuals in hospitals or similar institutions.

9. *Reporting of Crime

i) Relatives or friends of persons convicted or accused of crime should not
generally be identified without their consent, unless they are genuinely relevant to the story.

ii) Particular regard should be paid to the potentially vulnerable position of children under the age of 18 who witness, or are victims of, crime. This should
not restrict the right to report legal proceedings.

iii) Editors should generally avoid naming children under the age of 18 after arrest for a criminal offence but before they appear in a youth court unless they can show that the individual's name is already in the public domain, or that the individual (or, if they are under 16, a custodial parent or similarly responsible adult) has given their consent. This does not restrict the right to name juveniles who appear in a crown court, or whose anonymity is lifted.

10. *Clandestine devices and subterfuge

i) The press must not seek to obtain or publish material acquired by using hidden cameras or clandestine listening devices; or by intercepting private or mobile telephone calls, messages or emails; or by the unauthorised removal of documents or photographs; or by accessing digitally-held information without consent.

ii) Engaging in misrepresentation or subterfuge, including by agents or intermediaries, can generally be justified only in the public interest and then only when the material cannot be obtained by other means.

11. Victims of sexual assault

The press must not identify victims of sexual assault or publish material likely to contribute to such identification unless there is adequate justification and they are legally free to do so.

12. Discrimination

i) The press must avoid prejudicial or pejorative reference to an individual's race, colour, religion, sex, gender identity, sexual orientation or to any physical or mental illness or disability.

ii) Details of an individual's race, colour, religion, gender identity, sexual orientation, physical or mental illness or disability must be avoided unless genuinely relevant to the story.

13. Financial journalism

i) Even where the law does not prohibit it, journalists must not use for their own profit financial information they receive in advance of its general publication, nor should they pass such information to others.

ii) They must not write about shares or securities in whose performance they know that they or their close families have a significant financial interest without disclosing the interest to the editor or financial editor.

iii) They must not buy or sell, either directly or through nominees or agents, shares or securities about which they have written recently or about which they intend to write in the near future.

14. Confidential sources

Journalists have a moral obligation to protect confidential sources of information.

15. Witness payments in criminal trials

i)   No payment or offer of payment to a witness—or any person who may rea-sonably be expected to be called as a witness—should be made in any case once proceedings are active as defined by the Contempt of Court Act 1981. This prohibition lasts until the suspect has been freed unconditionally by police without charge or bail or the proceedings are otherwise discontinued; or has entered a guilty plea to the court; or, in the event of a not guilty plea, the court has announced its verdict.

*ii) Where proceedings are not yet active but are likely and foreseeable, edi-tors must not make or offer payment to any person who may reasonably be expected to be called as a witness, unless the information concerned ought demonstrably to be published in the public interest and there is an over-rid-ing need to make or promise payment for this to be done; and all reasonable steps have been taken to ensure no financial dealings influence the evidence those witnesses give. In no circumstances should such payment be condi-tional on the outcome of a trial.

*iii) Any payment or offer of payment made to a person later cited to give evi-dence in proceedings must be disclosed to the prosecution and defence. The witness must be advised of this requirement.

16. *Payment to criminals

i)   Payment or offers of payment for stories, pictures or information, which seek to exploit a particular crime or to glorify or glamorise crime in general, must not be made directly or via agents to convicted or confessed criminals or to their associates—who may include family, friends and colleagues.

ii) Editors invoking the public interest to justify payment or offers would need to demonstrate that there was good reason to believe the public interest would be served. If, despite payment, no public interest emerged, then the material should not be published.

The public interest

There may be exceptions to the clauses marked * where they can be demon-strated to be in the public interest.

1.   The public interest includes, but is not confined to:

i)   Detecting or exposing crime, or the threat of crime, or serious impropriety.

ii) Protecting public health or safety.

iii) Protecting the public from being misled by an action or statement of an individual or organisation.

iv) Disclosing a person or organisation's failure or likely failure to comply with any obligation to which they are subject.

v) Disclosing a miscarriage of justice.

vi) Raising or contributing to a matter of public debate, including serious cases of impropriety, unethical conduct or incompetence concerning the public.

vii) Disclosing concealment, or likely concealment, of any of the above.

2. There is a public interest in freedom of expression itself.

3. The regulator will consider the extent to which material is already in the public domain or will become so.

4. Editors invoking the public interest will need to demonstrate that they reasonably believed publication—or journalistic activity taken with a view to publication—would both serve, and be proportionate to, the public interest and explain how they reached that decision at the time.

5. An exceptional public interest would need to be demonstrated to over-ride the normally paramount interests of children under 16.

The Editors' Code is reproduced above by permission of the Regulatory Funding Company

© *Regulatory Funding Company 2018.*

Book list

Chapter 1, Introduction

Free Speech, Eric Barendt (Oxford University Press, 2nd edition, 2007)

Media Law and Human Rights, Andrew Nicol, Gavin Millar and Andrew Sharland (Oxford University Press, 2nd edition, 2009)

Chapter 2, Press regulation

An Inquiry into the Culture, Practices and Ethics of the Press: Executive Summary and Recommendations, Lord Justice Leveson (The Stationery Office, 2012 and at http://webarchive.nationalarchives.gov.uk/20140122145147/http://www.official-documents.gov.uk/document/hc1213/hc07/0779/0779.asp)

Privacy and Media Freedom, Raymond Wacks (Oxford University Press, 2013)

Journalism Ethics and Regulation, Chris Frost (Routledge, 4th edition, 2015)

Chapter 3, Broadcast regulation

Understanding Broadcast Journalism, Stephen Jukes, Katy McDonald and Guy Starkey (Routledge, 2017)

Journalism Ethics and Regulation, Chris Frost (Routledge, 4th edition, 2015)

Media Regulation: Governance and the Interests of Citizens and Consumers, Peter Lunt and Sonia Livingstone (Sage, 2012)

Chapter 4, News-gathering avoiding unjustified intrusion

Newsgathering: Law, Regulation and the Public Interest, Gavin Millar and Andrew Scott (Oxford University Press, 2016)

Chapters 5–9 (which cover crime and the criminal courts system)

Blackstone's Criminal Practice 2018, David Ormerod QC and David Perry QC (general editors) (Oxford University Press, 2018)

Chapter 13, Civil courts

Civil Litigation 2017–2018, Susan Cunningham-Hill and Karen Elder (Oxford University Press, 2017)

Civil Litigation 2015/2016, Kevin Browne and Margaret Catlow (College of Law Publishing, 2017)

The Online Court: Will IT Work?, Joshua Rozenberg (Kindle edition, on Amazon, 2017)

Chapter 14, Family courts

The Family Court Practice, Lord Wilson of Culworth, Anthony Cleary, Lady Justice Black (eds.) (Jordan Publishing, 2017)

The Family Court without a Lawyer: A Handbook for Litigants in Person, Lucy Reed (Bath Publishing Ltd, 3rd edition, 2017)

Court of Protection Handbook, a user's guide, Alex Ruck-Keene, Kate Edwards, Anselm Eldergill and Sophy Miles (Legal Action Group, 2nd edition, 2016)

Transparency in the Family Courts: Publicity and Privacy in Practice, Julie Doughty, Lucy Reed and Paul Magrath (Bloomsbury Family Law, 2018)

Chapter 15, Open justice and access to court information

Newsgathering: Law, Regulation and the Public Interest, Gavin Millar and Andrew Scott (Oxford University Press, 2016)

Open Justice: A Critique of the Public Trial, Joseph Jaconelli (Oxford University Press, 2002)

Chapter 17, Coroners' courts

Coroners' Courts: A Guide to Law and Practice, Christopher Dorries (Oxford University Press, 3rd edition, 2014)

Chapter 19, Contempt of court

Arlidge, Eady and Smith on Contempt, Patricia Londono, A T H Smith and Sir David Eady (Sweet and Maxwell, 5th edition, 2017)

Chapters 20–25 on defamation and related law

Duncan and Neill on Defamation, Sir Brian Neill, Richard Rampton, Heather Rogers, Timothy Atkinson and Aiden Eardley (LexisNexis, 4th edition, 2015)

Blackstone's Guide to the Defamation Act, James Price and Felicity McMahon (Oxford University Press, 2013)

Gatley on Libel and Slander, Richard Parkes QC, Professor Alastair Mullis, Godwin Busuttil, Adam Speker, Andrew Scott and Chloe Strong (Sweet and Maxwell, 12th edition, mainwork and 2nd supplement, 2017)

Carter-Ruck on Libel and Privacy, Cameron Doley and Alastair Mullis (general eds.) (LexisNexis, 6th edition, 2010)

Chapter 26, Breach of confidence

Confidentiality, Charles Phipps and Roger Toulson (Sweet and Maxwell, 3rd edition, 2012)

Chapter 27, Privacy

Privacy and Media Freedom, Raymond Wacks (Oxford University Press, 2013)

Celebrity and Royal Privacy, the Media and the Law, Robin Callender Smith (Sweet and Maxwell, 2015)

Tugendhat and Christie: The Law of Privacy and the Media, Mark Warby and Nicole Moreham (eds.) (Oxford University Press, 3rd edition, 2016)

Privacy and Freedom of Expression, Richard Clayton and Hugh Tomlinson (Oxford University Press, 2nd edition, 2010)

Carter-Ruck on Libel and Privacy, Alastair Mullis and Cameron Doley (general eds.) (LexisNexis, 6th edition, 2010)

Privacy Injunctions and the Media, A Practice Manual, Iain Goldrein (Hart Publishing, 2012)

Media and Public Shaming: Drawing the Boundaries of Disclosure, Julian Petley (ed.) (Reuters Institute for the Study of Journalism, 2013)

Chapter 28, Data protection

Data Protection Law and Practice, Rosemary Jay (Sweet and Maxwell, 4th edition main-work and supplement, 2014)

Data Protection: A Guide to UK and EU Law, Peter Carey (Oxford University Press, 5th edition, due 2018)

Chapter 29, Copyright

Copinger and Skone James on Copyright, Nicholas Caddick, Gillian Davies and Gwilym Harbottle (Sweet and Maxwell, 17th edition, 2016, 1st supplement 2017)

Chapter 30, The Freedom of Information Act 2000

Freedom of Information: A Practical Guide for UK Journalists, Matthew Burgess (Routledge, 2015)

Blackstone's Guide to the Freedom of Information Act 2000, John Wadham, Kelly Harris and Eric Metcalfe (Oxford University Press, 5th edition, 2013)

The Law of Freedom of Information, John Macdonald and Ross Crail (eds.) (Oxford University Press, 3rd edition, 2016)

Chapter 33, Official secrets

The Snowden Files: The Inside Story of the World's Most Wanted Man, Luke Harding, (Guardian Faber Publishing, 2014)

Media Law, Geoffrey Robertson and Andrew Nicol (Penguin, 5th edition, 2008)

National Security and the D-Notice System, Pauline Sadler (Dartmouth Publishing Co Ltd, 2001)

Official Secrets: The Use and Abuse of the Act, David Hooper (Coronet Books, 1988)

Secrecy and the Media: The Official History of the D-notice System, Nicholas John Wilkinson (Routledge, 2009)

Chapter 34, The journalist's sources and neutrality

Newsgathering: Law, Regulation and the Public Interest, Gavin Millar and Andrew Scott (Oxford University Press, 2016)

Chapter 35, The risks of being charged with bribery, misconduct, hacking or intercepting

Hack Attack: How the truth caught up with Rupert Murdoch, Nick Davies (Vintage, 2015)

Beyond Contempt: The Inside Story of the Phone Hacking Trial, Peter Jukes (Cadbury Press, 2015)

mcnaes.com online chapter: Terrorism and the effect of counter-terrorism law

Terrorism and the Law, Clive Walker (Oxford University Press, 2011)

Blackstone's Guide to the Anti-Terrorism Legislation, Clive Walker (Oxford University Press, 3rd edition, 2014)

Glossary

Absolute discharge A decision by a court after conviction that the offender should not be punished for the crime.

Affidavit A statement given on oath to be used in court proceedings.

Alibi A claim by an accused that he/she can show he/she was not at the scene when a crime was committed and is therefore innocent.

Allocation The procedure at magistrates' courts to determine whether an **either-way** criminal case is dealt with by magistrates or by a Crown court. Also known as the **mode of trial hearing**.

Arraignment The procedure at Crown courts when charges are put to defendants for them to plead guilty or not guilty.

Automatic, automatically Terms used for reporting restrictions which ban publication of certain information if no court order is needed to put them into effect in respect of a particular case or individual. Statutes specify the circumstances in which they operate.

Bail The system by which a person awaiting trial, or appeal, may be freed by a court pending the next hearing. *See also* **Police bail**

Bailiff A court official who enforces its orders.

Case law The system by which reports of previous cases and the judges' interpretations of the common law are used as precedents where the legally material facts are similar.

Circuit judge A judge appointed to sit at a Crown court or county court within a circuit—one of the regions of England and Wales into which court administration is divided. Unlike High Court judges, circuit judges do not go on circuit—that is,

travel to various large centres dispensing justice.

Claim form The document which begins many forms of civil action.

Claimant The person who brings an action in the civil court.

Committal for sentence, committed for sentence When a defendant at a magistrates' court who has admitted an offence or been convicted at trial is sent to Crown court to be sentenced because the magistrates decide their powers of punishment are insufficient. (There are no reporting restrictions on committals for sentence.)

Common law Law based on the custom of the realm and the decisions of judges through the centuries rather than on Acts of Parliament.

Community punishment An order that an offender must carry out unpaid work in the community under a probation officer's supervision.

Concurrent sentences Two or more sentences of imprisonment imposed for different offences; the longest one is the sentence actually served.

Conditional discharge A decision by a court that a convicted defendant should not be punished unless he/she re-offends—the condition of the discharge being that if he/she commits another crime within a specified period, for example a year, he/she can be punished for both the new and the original offences.

Conditional fee agreements (CFAs) 'No win, no fee' agreements—their use was extended to defamation cases in 1998 under the Conditional Fee Agreements Order 1998.

Contra mundum An injunction or order which binds all those who are aware that it has been made. Although the Latin means 'against the world', such orders only have effect within the jurisdiction in which they are made.

Copyright The law which protects the rights of the creators of original literary, dramatic, musical and artistic works, including photographs.

Counsel Barrister (singular or plural), not solicitor.

Disclosure and inspection The process whereby each side in a court action serves relevant documents on the other, which has the right to inspect them.

District judge A county court judge who also decides smaller cases, family law cases, presides at public examinations in bankruptcy and deals with cases under the informal arbitration procedure.

District judge (magistrates' courts) A full-time legally qualified magistrate.

Editors' Code of Practice Code of ethics enforced by the Independent Press Standards Organisation (Ipso) as regulator for newspapers, magazines and their websites.

Either-way offence One triable either summarily at magistrates' court or by a jury at Crown court. In an either-way case a defendant who has indicated a plea of not guilty has the right to opt for jury trial at Crown court. But if he/she opts for summary trial, the magistrates may decide that the case is too serious for them to handle and must be dealt with at Crown court. *See also* allocation; mode of trial hearing

Evidence-in-chief The main evidence a witness gives before being cross-examined.

Ex parte See **Without notice**

Excluded material Material which is exempt from compulsory disclosure under the Police and Criminal Evidence Act 1984 (PACE). It includes journalistic material that a person holds in confi-dence and which consists of documents or records.

Fair dealing The limited use of **copyright** material for reporting news or current affairs, or for criticism or review or quotation, under which the work is properly identified and attributed to its author.

Honest opinion A defence to a libel action, formerly known as 'honest comment' or 'fair comment'; the defendant does not have to show the words were fair, but must show they were an honestly held opinion.

Impress Standards Code The code of ethics overseen by Impress, the regulator recognised by the Press Recognition Panel.

In camera Proceedings in a courtroom which are heard in secret, with the media and public excluded (for example in Official Secrets Acts or terrorism cases).

In chambers Used to describe the hearing of an application which takes place in the judge's room. If there is no legal reason for such a hearing to be held **in private**, journalists who want to report it should be admitted if 'practicable'.

In private A term used of a court hearing **in camera** or one **in chambers** which the press and public are not entitled to attend.

Indictable offence A charge which may be tried by a jury at Crown court, which will therefore be either an **indictable-only offence** or an **either-way offence**.

Indictable-only offence One which can only be tried by a jury at Crown court.

Indictment A written statement of the charge(s) put to the defendant at the **arraignment** at Crown court.

Inherent jurisdiction The powers of a court deriving from common law rather than statute. The inherent jurisdiction of lower courts, for example magistrates' courts, is more limited than that of the higher courts, for example the High Court.

Injunction A court order requiring some-one, or an organisation, to do something specified by the court, or forbidding a specific activity or act.

Interdict The Scottish term for an **injunction.**

Journalistic material Material acquired and created for the purposes of journal-ism. Special protection is given to jour-nalistic material in the sections of the Police and Criminal Evidence Act 1984 that lay down the procedure whereby the police may search premises for evidence of serious arrestable offences.

Judicial review A review by the Queen's Bench Divisional Court, part of the High Court, of decisions taken by a lower court, tribunal, public body or public official.

Legal aid Public money provided to pay for legal advice and legal representa-tion in court for a party in a civil case or a defendant in a criminal case, if his/her income is low enough to qualify for such aid.

Malice In law not only spite or ill-will but also a dishonest or improper motive. Proof of malice can be used by a **claim-ant** in a libel action to defeat a defence of qualified privilege.

Mitigation A plea for leniency in the sentence due to be imposed, citing exten-uating circumstances, which is made in court by or on behalf of a convicted offender.

Mode of trial hearing The hearing at a magistrates' court to decide whether an **either-way** case is dealt with by that court or proceeds to a Crown court. Also known as the **allocation** procedure.

Narrative verdict/narrative conclusion A short statement by a coroner or inquest jury detailing the circumstances and manner of a person's death which takes the place of the traditional 'short-form' verdicts.

Newton hearing A hearing involving a defendant who has pleaded guilty but offers a substantially different version of events to that alleged by the prosecution, at which the court hears evidence so it can decide which version it accepts as forming the basis for the sentence. Newton was the defendant's name in the relevant precedent case.

Ofcom Broadcasting Code Code of ethics used by Ofcom to adjudicate on com-plaints against broadcasters.

Police bail The system whereby police can release a person under on-going investigation on conditions, including that they return to a police station on a later date, when they may be ques-tioned again, charged, or told there will be no charge. They can be arrested if they breach the conditions. After being charged, they can be bailed by police to attend court or may be taken there in custody.

Preliminary hearing A hearing, before any trial, at a magistrates' or Crown court.

Prima facie Literally, 'at first sight'. In criminal law a 'prima facie case' is one in which a preliminary examination by a court has established that there is sufficient prosecution evidence for it to proceed to trial. In journalism ethics the term 'prima facie grounds' means that preliminary inquiries have established there is sufficient evidence or sufficient ground of suspicion to justify use of deception or undercover tactics in an investigation.

Prior restraint The power which courts have to stop material being published. In defamation law there is a general rule against prior restraint. Judges are extremely reluctant to ban publica-tion of material which the media argue can be successfully defended in any future trial.

Privilege A defence, absolute or qualified, against an action for libel which attaches to reports produced from certain events, documents or statements.

Proportionate/Proportionality The principles that an action must not exceed what is reasonable or necessary to achieve the desired objective; and that competing interests must wherever possible be kept in balance. So, for example, damages for a **tort** such as defamation should be proportionate to the reputational damage the **claimant** has suffered, or, to be more colloquial, the punishment should fit the crime. Another example: A newspaper's undercover investigation into wrongdoing is proportionate if it does not intrude into people's privacy to an extent more than necessary for the investigation's aim.

Public interest The phrase 'in the public interest' is used by judges to define when an individual's rights, for example to privacy, can legally be infringed if this produces a sufficiently major benefit to society, for example from investigative journalism. But judges may also decide that a general 'public interest', for example in the confidentiality of medical records, needs to be upheld against media activity. Codes of ethics use the phrase too, to indicate when journalists may be justified in infringing people's rights.

Recorder An assistant judge at Crown court who is usually appointed to sit part time (for example for spells of a fortnight). Barristers and solicitors are eligible for appointment as recorders.

Remand An individual awaiting trial can be remanded on **bail** or in custody.

Robbery by force or threat of force theft. The word 'robbery' is often wrongly used to describe simple theft.

Skeleton arguments The documents in which each side in court proceedings sets out the bases of their cases. Journalists should normally be allowed to see them to help them report the proceedings.

Spent conviction A conviction that is no longer recognised after the time (varying according to sentence) specified in the Rehabilitation of Offenders Act 1974. After this time, a media organisation referring to the conviction might not have available some of the normal defences in the law of libel.

Statements of case Documents including the **claim form**, particulars of claim, defence, counterclaims, reply to the defence and 'further information documents' in a civil action—reports of which are now protected by **privilege**.

Statute An Act of Parliament—that is, primary legislation created by Parliament.

Statutory instrument Secondary legislation which can be enacted without parliamentary debate by a Minister to make detailed law (for example rules and regulations) or amendment to the law, under powers given earlier by a statute. Statutory instruments are also used to phase in gradually, for administrative convenience, legal changes brought about by Acts.

Strict liability A strict liability offence does not require the prosecution to show intent on the part of the accused. Statutory contempt of court is a strict liability offence.

Sub judice Literally 'under law'. Often applied to the risk which may arise in reporting forthcoming legal proceedings. Frequently used by authority as a reason for not disclosing information. But this is not the test for strict liability under the Contempt of Court Act 1981.

Subpoena A court order compelling a person to attend court to give evidence.

Summary offence A comparatively minor offence which can usually only be dealt with by magistrates.

Summary trial Trial at a magistrates' court.

Supreme Court The name originally given to the Court of Appeal, the High Court and the Crown courts as a combined system. From October 2009 the House of Lords appellate committee (the court commonly referred to as 'the House of

Lords' or 'Law Lords') became the UK Supreme Court.

Surety A person, usually a friend or relative of the defendant, to whom a court entrusts the responsibility to ensure that the individual, having been released on bail, returns to court on the due date. The surety may pledge a sum of money as the guarantee that the defendant will answer bail and risks losing it if the defendant fails to do so.

Taken into consideration The system under which a defendant admits having committed offences with which he/she has not been charged, thus clearing the slate and avoiding risk of subsequent prosecution for those offences.

Theft Appropriation of another's property with the intention of permanently depriving the other of it.

Tort A civil wrong, such as defamation or medical negligence, for which monetary damages may be awarded.

Truth The defence in defamation actions that the words complained of are substantially true.

Warranted Term used in the Ofcom Broadcasting Code to indicate that an ethical norm can be breached if there is a public interest justification or some other exceptional justification.

Without notice Previously known as *ex parte*, meaning 'of the one part'. An injunction without notice is one granted after a court has heard only one side of the case. An order granted *inter partes* is one made after a hearing at which all sides involved were represented.

Table of Cases

Table of Statutes

The European Convention on Human Rights (ECHR) is tabled under Schedule 1 to the Human Rights Act 1998

Table of Statutory Instruments

Table of European Materials

Index

A